CW00924925

The Unromantic Castle

JOHN SUMMERSON

The Unromantic Castle

AND OTHER ESSAYS

With 238 illustrations

THAMES AND HUDSON

Filmset in Great Britain by Servis Filmsetting, Ltd.
Printed and bound in Singapore

Contents

To the memory of my father
SAMUEL JAMES SUMMERSON
manufacturer of railway lines and man of letters
Born West Auckland, Durham, 3 April 1851
Died Haughton-le-Skerne, Durham, 7 November 1907

Preface

I HAVE called the pieces which make up this book 'essays', but the reader will soon perceive that they lack the casual artistry of the true essay and that nearly all of them are either contributions to specialist periodicals or pieces intended to be read aloud in a sixty-minute period and in an academic setting – in a word, lectures. I have called the whole lot essays, partly for the sake of consistency with a similar collection published forty years ago called *Heavenly Mansions and other Essays on Architecture*, and partly to avoid the word 'lecture' which, in English usage, tends to convey a combination of physical malaise and mental anguish which I deplore.

The order in which the essays are placed is chronological by subject, except in the case of the first essay which gives its title to the whole and contains an autobiographical twist which would make it go lamely with the Victorian numbers at the further end of the book (perhaps it is the only piece which is a proper essay).

So the collection really starts with the account of the Elizabethan John Thorpe. This derives partly from the article in the *Architectural Review* for November 1949 in which I recorded my discovery of Thorpe's identity and background, and partly from further studies connected with my editing of Thorpe's book of architecture for the *Walpole Society* (Vol. XL, 1966).

The essays on Inigo Jones and Wren appeared in the sixties, and are followed by an analysis of the English classical country house which helped to solve some of the problems of that complex subject, and by two essays on special aspects of Sir John Soane's work, his obsession with sarcophagi and mausolea and the evolution of his Bank Stock Office.

Of the Victorian articles, the first three are less concerned with architectural style than with builders and building. They turn the subject of Victorian architecture inside out. Architects and patrons fall into the background and we are confronted with a combination of social and technological history which has never been seriously handled. In the torrent of writing about Victorian things in the last forty years these aspects have been almost totally ignored (the only description I have seen of the building technology in Victorian England is a thesis by a Japanese scholar who has never been in England). In the last two Victorian essays, however, we are back with the styles – City and Suburban. The Suburban essay, written in 1948, was I think the first attempt to take the subject seriously. Up-to-date students may find it quaint.

With the last three essays we come to our own century. One of them goes some way to clarifying the complex stylistic tissue of Mackintosh's Glasgow School of Art; the second analyses Lutyens' great design for the Roman Catholic Liverpool Cathedral.

Finally there is the paper which proposes a 'theory' of Modern architecture. As this was written in 1957 it will seem to many readers as archaic as John Thorpe. I have included it, after much hesitation, for its 'curiosity value'. It marks, for me, the moment when the thought of my generation (the MARS Group generation) lost touch with the real world. There is not, I think (though others may differ), much wrong with the general argument and there is a measure of truth in the conclusion. But it was not the conclusion which history required. The nature of the Modern Movement and the irreversible changes which it brought about are, seen from 1990, a different matter altogether and one which I happily leave to another generation of essayists.

I offer my thanks to the editors and publishers who have permitted the reproduction of the essays from the printed pages of their publications. A detailed list of these is given on page 281. For the illustrations I am indebted first and foremost to John Piper for allowing me to reproduce his 1939 photographs of Riber Castle. Other sources are indicated at the end of the book.

JOHN SUMMERSON

I · The Unromantic Castle

1. Riber Castle, Matlock, Derbyshire, a distant view across the fields

2. Cast-iron and wood at play in the 'saloon' at Riber Castle

At the end of each day at Riber Castle the headmaster came round the dormitories and turned out the gas. We could hear him coming, padding along the lower corridors, climbing the private stairs, then traversing two sides of the gallery. Our dormitory was called 'the bay' because it had no doors, only thick red curtains in a wide opening with the gallery beyond. Through this the headmaster would appear, bidding us 'good-night, gentlemen,' and extinguishing the solitary jet of the chandelier. The mantle glowed and faded. Silence was the order of the night, but it was then that we used to talk in hushed voices, dreaming aloud about the building to which our parents had committed us. The four of us in 'the bay' – three boys from midland towns and myself, a refugee from a school in the conventional and boring South – were nearly half the school, for in 1915 the complement was but eleven. Eleven boys in this castellar hulk, planned with ludicrous optimism to fulfil a function which it never served and could not serve; decorated with the naive barbarity of a methodist turned Caliph. No wonder we wove fantasy within and round it, flushing our minds with delicious horrors and shocking impossibilities.

Of our nocturnal inventions I remember nothing – only the thrill of invention, of adding one more enormity to the ghosts and monsters, secret rooms and walled-up victims, underground passages and concealed machines. Sometimes we half believed our own romances and there was one room where, for no reason except our own consent, we were reluctant to go alone or in the dark; while the rooms in the four towers, used for nothing, continually empty and continually out of bounds were the fount and origin of grotesque imagery.

Riber Castle awed us. We felt something of the oppression which Beckford confessed to having experienced in his father's monumental house, the original Fonthill. Everything at Riber was big and comfortless. There was scarcely a small room in the building. Even the water closets were enormously high, their thrones massive. The rooms which served as dormitories and class rooms were over-windowed, flooded with light and bitterly cold so that we had to be heated not only by iron pipes behind the skirting but by the biggest cast iron stoves I have ever seen, black rococo furnaces, which projected into the rooms and roared furiously behind sliding shutters. But the castle was not only gaunt and bare. No building, surely, was ever so lacking in elegance or grace. Our elders and betters called it 'ugly' (without caring much either way) and we believed them.

But it was a fiercely stirring place, and I find it more exciting to remember than the suave converted Georgian mansion which was the background of my earlier school days. It was, moreover, an admirable school. Kept by a rosy-cheeked, bearded clergyman of modest stature, great teaching ability, Spartan habits, but humane views as to the essential comforts of a boarding school, it flourished under his methodical rule for over forty years (1888–1929). His name was John William Chippett and I have never heard an old pupil speak of the man but with respect or of his castle but with affection. I could write at length and with nostalgic prolixity about the school; about the chapel, with its perfectly square altar, whose reredos was a plate glass window looking across to Matlock Bank; about the cricket team which, as it comprised the entire school, put up a rather comical display when boys from neighbouring schools came to play and incidentally to goggle at the strange building which they knew only as a landmark; about the stout, stern but kindly trio who comprised the domestic staff and dwelt, like satellites, in little square castellated boxes round the main building.

But all this is only an episode in the Castle's history. The school took root in what had been intended for a private residence, with accommodation for paying guests of a class somewhat above that of the average 'hydropathic' patron. To us school-boys, the precise origin of our Castle did not much matter. We knew, however, the name of Smedley. We could see Smedley's Hydro across the valley; we knew Smedley's Wood across the fields; and in our idle romancing we made the most of a perfectly unwarrantable 'Smedley's Ghost,' believed to have been seen in the jam store. But it is only for the purpose of this essay that I have had the curiosity to find out who this Smedley was.

John Smedley, it appears, was born in 1803 and came of an old lead-mining family of yeoman status.[1] His father, however, had turned from mining to the more speculative and ambitious trade of worsted-spinning, in which, after a short run of success he met with pronounced and persistent failure. He sailed close to bankruptcy. Then his younger son died and that crushed the poor man, so he left the business in John Smedley's hands, John being then about twenty. For nearly fifteen years the new master of Lea Mills was properly up against it. To save himself he had to break through the competition of the big Yorkshire wholesalers, and he did break through, largely by striking out new shapes in underclothes and by adapting the cotton manufacturer's technique to wool production. By 1838 'Smedley's hosiery' stood for something and there was a fair balance at the bank. He married; and took his bride, the daughter of a local vicar, to Switzerland.

It was an unlucky honeymoon, because John Smedley caught cold in a damp Swiss church, came home unwell and developed typhus fever. He was very ill indeed. After the fever, nervous debility and hypochondria got hold of him. Doctors did him no good, and he was drifting to a torpid retirement at Cheltenham, when somebody suggested a cure which he had never thought of – *water*. He went to Ben Rhydding Spa, in Yorkshire, and got well. That was the beginning. For the Smedley who returned cured from Ben Rhydding was wholly different from the Smedley who had dawdled in a Swiss church with such unfortunate results. With renewed health came a new interest in life, an awakening to religion, a sense of power and, as his acquaintances soon learnt, a dauntless capacity for interference. John Smedley was changed, and by the grace of God – and of water – he was going to change the world. He gave up the idea of retirement and descended on Lea Mills like a giant refreshed, not indeed with wine, but with the more permanently stimulating specifics of Hydropathy and Free Methodism.

He lost no time in bestowing these blessings on his work-people. A free hospital was extemporized at the Mills and the whole of the personnel, whether ailing or not, was required to go through the therapeutic ritual. The production of underclothes was disorganized while experiments with dripping sheets, wet packs and douches occupied the time and attention of master and men. And there was no doubt about it; those who *were* ill were very often cured, and the others were none the worse. The water treatment was amplified by homely remedies such as Fearn's Family Pills and the provision of minor comforts like the loan of goloshes on wet nights. But the other obligatory course of improvement which no employee of Smedley's could safely evade was, of course, Religion, and here, as in the water cure, the plan of procedure was laid down with great exactitude by the boss. Formerly, he had held orthodox Church views. But in the access of truculence which attended his cure he had broken the last bonds of superstition and become Free. He inclined to Methodism, but found, at the same time, that no sect of religion was perfect and that a man's best hope of salvation was to stand outside them all. This freedom, however, was not a thing to be universally allowed. The workers at Lea Mills were required to conform strictly to the method of worship evolved by their employer, not only when they met under his leadership, in the morning prayer interval, but when they worshipped in their several independent chapels, most of which Smedley himself had, indeed, built. There was an embarrassing occasion when a special form of prayer, compiled by Smedley for 'his' congregations, and printed in quantities ready for use, was humbly but firmly declined by the worshippers, who felt bound to confess a preference for the procedure laid down by John Wesley.

Smedley's moderate success as a religious leader bears no comparison to his achievement as the founder of Hydropathy on Matlock Bank. This was prodigious. He began by taking a few guests into his house for treatment. Then he took over the small establishment of a local pioneer and ran it on his own lines. That was in 1853. Ten years later he was already planning the first part of the great hotel which bore his name and was for many years the aristocrat of Matlock Hydropathics. He bullied his guests just as he bullied his work-people – and with the same excellent object, their own good. Smoking and alcohol were banned and a schedule of petty fines was enforced ranging from 1d. for lateness or mentioning the word 'crisis' at meals, to 10s. 6d. for walking into the ladies' bathroom. The atmosphere of school-room discipline probably had its attraction for the stuffy, creaking neurotics who flocked to Smedley's from the board rooms and counting houses of the industrial areas. Anyway, the Hydro was a success from the beginning and Smedley became the uncrowned King of Matlock Bank.

John Smedley might fairly be described as a fortunate and very able quack – fortunate, because he hit on a line which was, at worst, harmless and, at best, of a sort that scientific medicine was able to endorse with enthusiasm. As a man, he was a self-help product of a type which, in the last century, was neither uncommon, nor likeable. Sorely up against it for the first half of his life, he acted the part of a local demi-god for the other half; and if his tyranny was not unmixed with kindliness and generosity it certainly showed those qualities in an unattractive setting – though more unattractive to us, perhaps, than to the harsh world of industrial non-conformity in which it originated. In manner and appearance, Smedley reflected his inner self. An acquaintance has described him as 'straight as a dart, quick in his movements, determined in expression and extremely particular about the precise observance of his rules.' In other words, a flint-faced martinet. 'He was nothing if not original and independent; nothing if not intense and extreme. Whether in matters of dress, in business, in religion or in medicine, the impress of his individuality could always be recognized.'

It could be recognized, too, in his architecture. For this versatile egoist, who despised doctors and clergymen, despised also professional architects. All the buildings which he paid for were built from his own designs. They were inefficient, ugly and sometimes unsafe; but they were his. Among them were six Free Methodist Chapels, the new Hydro on Matlock Bank – and Riber Castle. It was in 1862 that Smedley, feeling the time had come to live in greater state and ease, bought property in the hill village of Riber. After a preliminary sojourn at Riber Hall, he built what is now the Upper Lodge, a castellated block, adumbrating the character of the greater building which was to follow and which is the main subject of this essay. The crown of Riber Hill was a direct incitement to John Smedley's mania for interference. There it was, conspicuously vacant, right opposite the Hydro on Matlock Bank. He considered building a tower, 225 feet high, to be presented to the nation as an observatory. For some reason this was found impracticable and it immediately gave way before the project for a great Riber Castle to serve the double function of a residence for the Smedleys and a guest house for the more distinguished and ungregarious individuals who came to Matlock to follow the water cure. Soon after 1862 the plans were made and a quarry opened. The Castle rose rapidly on its rock foundation and was finished, inside and out, at a cost of about £60,000. John and Caroline Smedley moved in, and there they passed the remainder of their lives, John dying in 1874 and Caroline in 1892. I have never heard that they entertained very much or that the Castle ever fulfilled its function as a guest house. In the district it was always spoken of as a failure and a folly.

Now, if you look at John Piper's pictures of Riber Castle, you will see that it is not only very ugly, but has the rare characteristic of being stylistically unclassifiable. There is all the difference between the ugliness produced by an incompetent *architect* and that produced by a man wholly ignorant of architecture and possessing a less than rudimentary experience of architectural forms. It is this kind of ugliness which was so striking at Riber. One can hardly call it 'primitive', but primitive, in a way, it is. Not the sort issuing from the innocence of folk-art but with a savagery of its own century bred in the haunted, cluttered mind of a man who has seen the Alps, visited the cathedrals, the castles, the châteaux and absorbed some of the vanity of their builders, with an appetite to convert his wealth into 'galleries', 'saloons', 'canopies', 'clerestories', 'spiral staircases' and the rest. Had Smedley employed a professional he would have got a house unmistakenly, however crudely, stamped with a style – Italian, Norman, Gothic or Baronial. As it was he produced an object of indecipherable bastardy – a true monster.

How did the concept of this castle-monster form in Smedley's mind? The rectangle with a tower at each corner, which is the basis of it, is a deep-rooted formula which has travelled through English taste from the Middle Ages without being for long lost to view. It is not characteristic of feudal castles, but it is *supposed* to have been. The Elizabethans, who were quite as taken with 'sham castle' fantasies as the Georgians, developed it in their great houses – such as Hardwick Hall, which Smedley must have known. Vanbrugh recognized the theme as a basic idea and used it in the ornamental castle at Claremont and, less literally, for Blenheim, while the later 18th century used it for many a hill-top folly – Ralph Allen's Castle at Bath is an example. The formula sank very deep into popular consciousness and emerges in the wooden toy castle of the old-fashioned nursery. It may be relevant to compare Riber with another amateur's castle –

3. A typical Riber doorway, framed with exotic mural ornament *4.* One of the two spiral staircases, leading to the minstrels' galleries and the four towers

'Jezreel's Tower' at Gillingham. Jezreel, who began his career as a private soldier and ended as a religious crank with an enormous following, was as innocent of architectural sophistication as Smedley, and his citadel at Gillingham has just the same basic plan – a rectangle with corner towers, and smaller excrescences to mark the centres of each side.

Apart from battlements, external detail at Riber is almost non-existent, nothing but a few 'eye-brow' cornices to the windows. The walls are built of large grit-stone blocks, matching most of the houses and all the field walls for miles. It is a hard unchanging substance, gratifying to that lust for permanence characteristic of the Smedley mind and the Smedley epoch.

Inside, however, there were outbursts of the sheerest nonsense, especially in the 'saloon', the space contained in the centre of the mass. This rose through two storeys to a clerestory and a waggon roof and was interrupted at first-floor level by a sort of bulkhead on the saloon side to which was fixed a continuity of giant zig-zags, each zig *2*
and each zag not less than ten feet long and impanelled with transparent undulations. Where zig met zag were originally (unless my memory deceives me) either dragons' heads or some floral flourish. Above the gallery, set back a few feet, was what we used to call 'the canopy', a set of pointed arches depending from the ceiling and terminating in pendants of menacing acuity. At either end of the saloon, at the high level of the clerestory were 'minstrels' galleries', approached by spiral stairs not built into the walls *4*
but spiralling up on their own, cork-screw style. To complete the picture, two frail iron

arches, richly floriated, crossed the saloon, their sole purpose being the suspension of two very heavy and impressive chandeliers. There was ornament everywhere, painted on the walls or scroll-work cast in iron to form balustrades or brackets projecting from the iron pillars which served to support the fabric and hold it together. The whole thing was mad, unclassifiable, out on an art-historical limb. How did it happen?

Some of it seems to have been ready made. Macfarlane's Catalogue of 1862 is highly suggestive but I have found no direct quotations. The iron columns are of a Macfarlane type however, and must surely have been supplied from stock, perhaps by some Sheffield iron-founder. The same goes for the ceiling ornaments which were of a kind found on any large ceiling of the 1860s – mostly cast in *papier-mâché*.

Riber Castle is now 120 years old and nothing but a grit-stone shell, a dead monument of no account, roofless, windowless, unlisted by the local planning authority and now an organized home for wild life.[2] Its deadness is its wonder. How could such a building possibly have happened? It still rivets the attention in that big-boned Derbyshire landscape; to have lived in it is to have experienced raw, uncouth, sub-architectural qualities not often met with and, once encountered, not easily forgotten. And there is one memory of Riber which, for me, will always justify its enormities. It belongs, as I remember, to early mornings of late summer or early autumn, when the valley below becomes a giant bowl of mist, of the density and whiteness of cotton wool. The sun comes up behind the castle and projects its shadow on the surface of the mist. Fantastically elongated, the shadow reaches all the way to Matlock Bank, an image of incredible majesty and elegance. As the mist dissolves so does the image and the shelving hydros of Matlock Bank take its place. The spell withdraws into the carcase on Riber Hill.

What, the reader may well ask, happened to the school? After my time (1915–1918) it flourished for about a decade, its numbers increasing to a score or more, chiefly because an exceptionally able housekeeper undertook to fulfil the duties which had been too much for the headmaster's invalid wife. But the headmaster himself grew old and in 1924 sold the school as a going concern and took himself off to live in one of Matlock's comfortable hydros. The new owner brought the telephone, motor-cars and other alien machines to the Castle and, predictably, was soon heading for bankruptcy. In 1929 the school was closed and the Castle sold 'for a song' to the local authority. In 1939, John Piper, the painter, and J.M. Richards of the *Architectural Review*, rambling through Derbyshire, 'discovered' Riber. Piper, fascinated by the horror of it, photographed it inside and out. Through Richards the photographs came into my hands, with an invitation to write about them. They brought back to me the four years during which I was a Riber boy, years which were among the most luminous and liberating of my life and in which architecture first intruded itself into my adolescent brain.

II · John Thorpe and the Thorpes of Kingscliffe

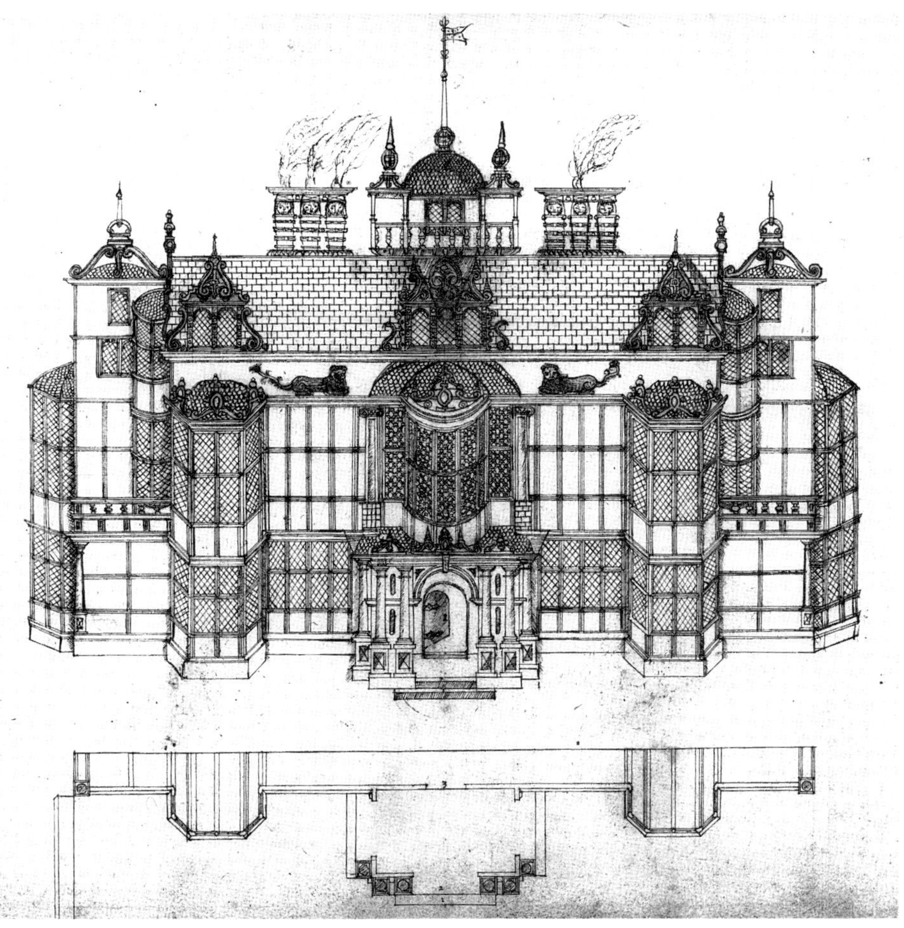

5. Design for a timber-frame house, probably Campden House, Kensington, built by Sir Walter Cope who entertained Elizabeth I here in 1597

6. The Griffin monument at Braybrooke, c.1568, here attributed to John Thorpe's father, Thomas, the builder of Kirby Hall. See also the porch at Dingley (Ill. 14). The cockle shell appears in several works by the Thorpe family (see ills. 14, 15, 17)

ON THE PRINCIPAL FACADE of the Victoria and Albert Museum, lodged between the upper windows, is a set of statues. They represent the great men of English art and architecture, the architects ranging from William of Wykeham, who stands for the Middle Ages, to Sir Charles Barry who stands for the century which was just closing when the museum was built. Among the intermediate figures is one in Elizabethan dress – a wholly imaginary portrait of John Thorpe. Who was he? His presence here is an unspoken tribute to Horace Walpole who discovered and promoted Thorpe on the strength of a book of architectural drawings bearing his name which he came across in the Earl of Warwick's library. He announced his discovery in a supplement of the 1782 edition of his *Anecdotes of Painting in England*[1] where he acclaimed John Thorpe as 'a very capital artist of the reigns of Elizabeth and James I', a verdict which nobody cared to dispute. Later, the book came into the hands of the earl's second son, the Hon. Charles Greville, and was sold, after his death in 1810, to John Soane, the architect, who greatly esteemed it and in whose Museum it has remained ever since. The book received scholarly attention from time to time, but it was only in 1949 that Thorpe's identity was established, the dates of his birth and death approximately settled and his contribution to Elizabethan and early Stuart architecture given some sort of definition. We cannot now go all the way with Walpole's acclaim of 'a very capital artist', especially because many of the designs in his book are not by Thorpe at all. Nevertheless, there is firm documentary evidence of his distinction as a man of intellectual attainment, dedicated to architecture, a recognized and respected figure in the building world of his time. We need not grudge him his niche.

Soane, in his melancholy last years, pored over Thorpe's plans, fascinated by their whimsical oddity. His curiosity was shared by his pupil and assistant, C. J. Richardson, who had the free run of the Museum before and after its founder's death. He re-drew many of the plans and published them, with others, as *The Architectural Remains of the Reigns of Elizabeth and James I* in 1840. He believed, as Walpole had done, that Thorpe had designed nearly everything in the book, and that 'there were very few celebrated houses then existing in which Thorpe was not engaged.'[2] Although nothing was known of him except his name, Thorpe became the hero of Elizabethan and early Stuart architecture. One ingenious amateur even decided that John Thorpe must be an *alias* for John of Padua, thus solving, at one terrific blow, all major problems of attribution in the reigns of four Tudors and one Stuart.[3]

The first scholar to approach the problem of John Thorpe with a proper degree of caution was, I think, Wyatt Papworth, the editor of the *Dictionary of Architecture* and Soane Curator from 1892 to 1894. Papworth's article in the *Dictionary* gives, without superfluous comment, most of the references to Thorpe to be found in the Calendars of State Papers and other printed sources, including the invaluable personal reference, noticed by Peter Cunningham in 1867,[4] in Peacham's *Gentleman's Exercise*. Unfortunately, Papworth misread a sentence in that passage, construing it as an indication that reference was intended to *two* Thorpes, father and son, living in 1612, thus confusing the biographical issue for himself and his successors. Harry Sirr,[5] for instance, writing in 1911, fell into the same trap, which was a pity because some other clues to which he drew attention in that year were (as it turns out) the right ones.

The architectural historians of the last generation, being themselves architects, wrote broadly and discursively about Thorpe's plans, but troubled little about his biographical identity. J.A. Gotch[6] (1894) wrote of him as 'a practical man' and of work 'actually carried out', expressions which brought Wyatt Papworth down on him with a challenging review in the *RIBA Journal.*[7] Sir Reginald Blomfield[8] (1897) was, on the other hand, a little contemptuous of him and guessed that he should be classed with Norden, as a measurer rather than an architect – a guess which does contain an element of truth. In the following year, Campbell Dodgson balanced the *pros* and *cons* very cautiously in his *Dictionary of National Biography* article, giving Thorpe the benefit of some half a dozen buildings, including Kirby Hall, Northants, Holland House, Kensington, and, of course, the famous plan based on his own initials. Dodgson's assessment has been followed by most recent writers, but a new champion of Thorpe as a designer appeared, rather surprisingly, in the shrewd and experienced H. Avray Tipping,[9] who followed Gotch in believing that he was concerned with Wollaton Hall as well as Kirby and saw him as a potent influence in early Jacobean planning.

Kirby is the only house with whose beginnings Thorpe can be said confidently to have been associated, for the excellent reason that it bears the inscription, in Thorpe's hand:

Kerby whereof I layd ye first stone A^o 1570.

This statement frustrated for over a century all attempts to ascertain the span of John Thorpe's career or its place in the history of Elizabeth's reign. It was only when evidence accumulated that John Thorpe must have been about seven when the stone was laid and that there was nothing very extraordinary about children performing this act, that the truth dawned. If it does not immediately solve all the problems represented by his book it places them in a light which if not brilliant is at least steady.

The main facts now established concerning John Thorpe are these. He was born about 1563, the second son of Thomas Thorpe of Kingscliffe, Northants, a mason, and probably the builder of Kirby Hall. In 1570, at the behest of his father, he applied a trowel to the foundation stone of the house. He went to London in or before 1584, and was one of the Clerks in the Queen's Works till 1601; later, he practised as a surveyor and held various offices as such under the Crown. He died, very old and possessed of considerable property, in 1655.

Round these main facts lies a great deal of interesting material and it will be advisable to deal with it in sections. First, the history of the Thorpe family. Second, the circumstances of the building of Kirby Hall. Third, the story of John Thorpe himself. And, fourth, a reconsideration of his famous book in the light admitted by this new biographical perspective.

The Thorpes of Kingscliffe

Kingscliffe is a large village, full of old stone houses, about nine miles from Stamford. There is a handsome cruciform church, with a central tower and spire. In the north transept, against the east wall and more or less hidden by the organ, is a stone
17 monument with a Roman Doric frame, a broken pediment above and a shaped 'apron'

below. This is the monument of the Thorpe family, erected in 1623 by two cousins to honour their ancestors and record their generations. Some scraping vandal has done away with nearly all the inscription, but it is preserved for us by Bridges.[10] It begins by telling us of three generations of Thomas Thorpes – Thomas *proavus*, Thomas *avus* and Thomas *pater* – all buried in one tomb. It then mentions three sons of Thomas *pater*, their names being Henry, John and Thomas, and six daughters, giving under each name the number of sons and daughters begotten by them. The total adds up to the impressive figure of 80 – all grandchildren of Thomas *pater*. Then come three Old Testament quotations in praise of fecundity, a statement that the family originally sprang from the Thorpes of Ashwellthorp, near Wymondham, Norfolk, and, finally, a sentence in which the first-born of Henry and Thomas beseech the blessing of God, on their descendants. The first-born of John is, rather curiously, omitted, and it must be supposed that he did not participate in the erection of the monument.

Unluckily, the inscription gives not a single date other than that of its erection in 1623, so we have to turn to documents. The earliest and most vital is the will[11] of Thomas *avus*, who died in 1558. It is simple and typical. Thomas leaves 2d. to the mother church of Peterborough, the same to the high altar and 4d. to the bells. To his wife, Rose, he leaves his house and appurtenances for her life. Afterwards they are to go to his son Thomas, who is to pay another son, Henry, five shillings a year for twelve years. If Thomas dies without heir male, the house goes to Henry. But the most important bequest (for us) is this: 'I gyve to Thomas my sonne all my toles.' These must have been the tools of a craftsman and, in the circumstances I am about to describe, we can hardly be wrong in assuming that they were those of a mason. The will, therefore, gives us the fundamentally important information that at least two generations behind that of John Thorpe were masons and that John Thorpe's father (Thomas *pater*) had begotten no son by 1558.

Thomas *pater* becomes a highly interesting person as soon as we realize that, if any of the Thorpe family had anything to do with the building of Kirby, it must have been he. He inherited the tools in 1558 and died (the Kingscliffe registers tell us) in 1596.[12] His will I cannot find, which is disappointing because one would hope to discover there some indication of the position he achieved and the wealth he acquired as perhaps the most eminent free-mason in one of the most aristocratic counties in England.

The next documents of importance are three copies of a Visitation of Northamptonshire, made in 1618 and now in the British Library.[13] From these we learn about Thomas *pater's* marriages and offspring. He married twice. By his first wife, Elizabeth Frisby of Kingscliffe, he had one son, Henry, and several daughters. By his second wife, whose maiden name we are not given, he had two more sons, John and Thomas, as well as more daughters. Of the three sons, John, the second, was to become the distinguished London surveyor. The eldest son, Henry, who remained in Kingscliffe, will, no doubt, have inherited most of the family property on his father's death in 1596 as well as all the 'roles'. He married twice and had fourteen sons and three daughters. He was certainly something of a builder, for it appears from the Works Accounts that he served as a clerk-of-the-works when alterations were made for the King at Collyweston in 1606. He paid a subsidy in 1609,[14] was in trouble with the Privy Council for hunting and killing deer in Rockingham Forest in 1620,[15] and died in 1624.

His will[16] is an interesting document but provides no further hint that he had anything to do with building; so we can only speculate whether he was the man who continued the building of Kirby in the early years of the 17th century.

The third brother, Thomas, became a free-mason of real distinction, not only in Northamptonshire, but in London and elsewhere. He worked at Eltham Palace in 1604, using Northamptonshire stone. In 1605, he was working at Whitehall. Then, in 1607, three warrants[17] were issued for assisting one Thomas Thorpe with transport to bring stone from the counties of Rutland, Lincoln and Northampton for the building of London's Aldgate. Kingscliffe lies near the border of all three counties and the probability that we can recognize Thomas Thorpe of Kingscliffe in this transaction is great. A further reference is in a list[18] of Commissioners for Surveying the Duchess of Suffolk's lands in 1609. Here Thomas Thorpe's name appeared next to that of John, but was erased in favour of Simon Dee. Finally, and most impressively, we find Thomas Thorpe's name associated with those of Robert Lyminge and Thomas Style in the accounts for Blickling, Norfolk, between the years 1619 and 1623. Of this great building, Lyminge was certainly the designer; Thorpe will have been the principal master-mason. For the rest, we know that he married Wyburgh Hunt of Collyweston and had eleven children, but his will I cannot find, nor can I be sure of the date of his death.[19]

The history of the Thorpe generations follows closely the pattern of its period. Thomas *avus* is the simple artificer with only his house and furniture and the tools of his trade to leave behind him. His son rises to a status equivalent to the yeoman and almost certainly acquired land.[20] His sons aspire to gentility: Henry Thorpe styled himself gentleman by 1610,[21] while John Thorpe was probably gentle by virtue of his office in the Queen's Works as early as 1584.[22] By 1612 John had adopted the coat of arms which I shall have occasion to mention later on. On the monument of 1623, where this coat of arms is blazoned, there is no mention whatever that any of the Thorpes pursued a craft or profession. Gentility had been achieved.

The building of Kirby Hall

And now let us return to Thomas Thorpe *pater*, the only member of the family who can reasonably be supposed to have laid, or superintended the laying of, the first stone of Kirby Hall. The date of that event, given in the Thorpe book as 1570, corresponds accurately to the dates 1572 and 1575 which appear on the upper parts of the fabric. The owner of Kirby[23] was Sir Humphrey Stafford, whose family had held the manor of Kirby since 1542 and whose grandfather, another Sir Humphrey, had been 'one of the esquires for the body' to Henry VIII.[24] The Staffords were also 'of Blatherwick', a parish very close to Kirby and next door to Kingscliffe.

Sir Humphrey Stafford was not a man of any particular importance, and his name rarely occurs in the vast quantity of Elizabethan correspondence which has been calendared; and we have no means of knowing why he should have started to build a house of such great size and startling character as Kirby. It is fair to assume that he knew his great neighbour, Lord Burghley, whose house near Stamford, twelve miles away was, in 1570, one of the main outposts of the new architecture, inferior only to

7. Kirby Hall, north side of the court, showing the giant order of pilasters, 1570–72. The attic storey and window surrounds are 17th.-century additions

Longleat (then in progress) in its loyalty to the antique taste. Many things about the design of Kirby suggest that it originated in the Burghley circle, which means that not only Burghley but Sir John Thynne of Longleat and Sir Thomas Heneage of Copped Hall may have been among its god-parents. The original plan of Kirby (in Thorpe's book) particularly resembles Burghley House in its north (entrance) front, where the central opening is flanked by two projections, intended, no doubt, to be read as a single, broad gate-tower of the Burghley type. The Kirby plan differs from Burghley chiefly in the development of large, projecting blocks at each corner (embryonic at Burghley) and in the formation of an open courtyard on the south, which novelty, however, I suspect was for convenience rather than beauty and is not quite so important as has sometimes been suggested.

The most novel and exciting thing about Kirby was and is the employment and distribution of the classical orders in the courtyard and, more especially, the deployment of a *giant* pilaster order. This order occurs on the long east and west sides, and the south end, widely spaced, but, on the north, is concentrated into a truly 7
spectacular pilastrade. So far as we know this was the first occasion in England in which the giant order, extending through two storeys, was used. The orders had, up to that date, been introduced only as small-scale decorative adjuncts, never extending beyond the height of a single storey. Here at Kirby they are given their proper authority, as they are in Michelangelo's Capitoline palaces which must, ultimately, be the source from which the Kirby specimens issue.

Whether this grand idea was Thomas Thorpe's we shall never know. The probability is that somebody who had been to Rome or studied Modern Rome from the few books available, had dictated the idea. We may, I think, assume that Thomas Thorpe executed it, perhaps even to the extent of devising and cutting the carved ornaments.

These ornaments are an entertaining study, lending themselves readily to analysis. Some come directly out of familiar books. Thorpe evidently had a copy of Serlio at his
8, 10 disposal.[25] From this he took, among other things, the 'Vitruvian scroll' which runs along the coping of the parapet;[26] the ornament on the soffits of the arch of the porch and of the central arch of the loggia;[27] the caps of the two giant pilasters flanking the latter opening;[28] and the enrichment of the dies which support the finials on the bay-
12 windows.[29] He also, it seems, had a copy of John Shute's *Chief Groundes of Architecture*, published in 1563. The plates in this, however, did not appeal to him so much as the title-page,[30] from which he stole the arabesques, with candelabra and *putti*, which
13 adorn the panels of the two central pilasters of the loggia. Thirdly, he used Hans Blum's *Quinque Columnarum etc.*[31] for the Ionic capitals on the long sides of the quadrangle. There are other palpable 'quotations'; such, for instance, as the rich paterae in the friezes of the small doorways. These come either from a Flemish engraving or (very likely, I think) from a tapestry border of the period.

When one has subtracted all the borrowings at Kirby Hall there is still quite a lot to be accounted for. Thus, the three ornamental gables on the hall block, including the especially rich frontispiece over the porch, derive from no engraved source (except in an almost invisible sequence of Serlian enrichments) but are, more or less, inventions, deriving their character from a current school of design rather than specific sources or authorities. This brings us to the question: what sort of masons were the Thorpes and what type of design were they practising before the great task of Kirby was put into their hands?

This question has to be resolved without the aid of documents and the answer must be speculative. If we look round Northamptonshire for houses and funeral monuments of the 1560s having affinities with Kirby Hall (a task facilitated by the splendid photographic survey by G. Bernard Mason in the National Monuments Record), we shall soon come across a dozen or more cases worth close examination. At
14 Dingley Hall[32] is a two-storey porch dated 1558, the unmistakable prototype of the
15 porch at Kirby. It is similar in silhouette and proportion, but less refined in detail, the entrance arch being pure native Tudor. This could be a late work of Thomas Thorpe *avus*, who died in the year it was dated. Then, at Apethorpe[33] is a chimney-piece of 1562, closely related to a (possibly much earlier) chimney-piece at Boughton;[34] and both these are loosely related to the porch and chimney-piece at Deene Park,[35] a mere half-hour's walk from Kirby. All this work is in a style which seems to have come to this country from France and the earliest examples of which (e.g. the tomb and gatehouse at Layer Marney, Essex) date from 1525–30.[36] How this type of design spread about the country we have no exact means of knowing, but it probably spread as the result of contacts between masons rather than through the medium of engravings. Masons who could do work in the new style were in request at the end of Henry VIII's reign and used to pass from house to house, recommended by one building enthusiast to another.

8, 9. Motifs at Kirby taken from printed sources. Left: ornament from Serlio, Book III. Right: soffit of the arch in the porch at Kirby *10, 11.*Left: capital from Serlio, Book IV. Right: capital of one of the giant pilasters flanking the north entrance inside the court

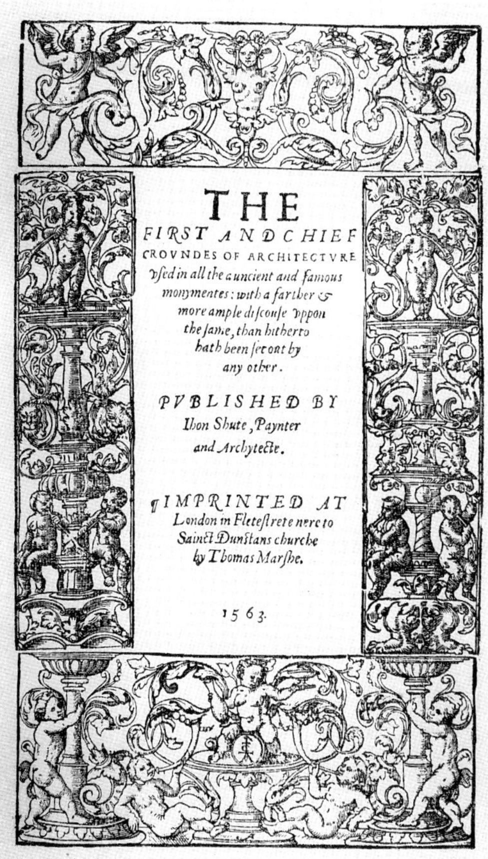

THE
FIRST AND CHIEF
GROVNDES OF ARCHITECTVRE
vsed in all the auncient and famous
monymentes: with a farther &
more ample discouse uppon
the same, than hitherto
hath been set out by
any other.

PVBLISHED BY
Ihon Shute, Paynter
and Archytecte.

¶ IMPRINTED AT
London in Fletestrete nere to
Sainct Dunstans churche
by Thomas Marshe.

1563.

12, 13. Left: titlepage of John Shute's *The First and Chief Groundes of Architecture*, 1563. Right: detail of one of the pilasters on the north side of the courtyard at Kirby

John Chapman, who worked for Sharington at Lacock, for Thynne at old Longleat and for the Duke of Northumberland at Dudley is a well-known example.[37] The Thorpes seem to have acquired this Anglo-French style of ornament and practised it in Northamptonshire. I am pretty sure that we are safe in attributing the Dingley porch to them and the fireplaces are certainly of the same school. But by far the most impressive example of mason's work, from the point of view of its relationship to what we find at
6 Kirby, is the Griffin monument at Braybrooke.

This monument is a massive affair, filling the whole width of a transept window. It commemorates three members of the Griffin family, the builders of Dingley, and was probably erected soon after 1568.[38] That it is from the same hand as the non-bookish detail at Kirby is almost certain. The vases surmounted by heraldic beasts reappear (rather simplified) on the Kirby gables; so does the scallop-shell in its moulded hood; while the clumsily fluted frieze of the monument is found on the Kirby chimneys. The panelled dies of the pedestal recall the mantelpieces at Apethorpe and Deene and the baluster-shaped Ionic columns are versions, in the round, of pilasters on the Apethorpe mantelpiece, whose date is 1562.

The value of this monument is that, in conjunction with the related works I have mentioned, it shows us what kind of ornament Thomas Thorpe was doing before Sir Humphrey Stafford employed him to build Kirby and before somebody put Serlio, Shute and Blum into his hands. For Kirby is the work of a Tudor mason with a considerable knowledge of the Anglo-French fashion in ornament who has suddenly, and probably on somebody's instructions, taken to books. I doubt very much if he *read* the books; he simply used them as a quarry, borrowing a Serlio fireplace-jamb to enrich a die, an antique mosaic design for an incised soffit ornament and Shute's publisher's title-page for the filling of a pilaster panel! This untutored larceny is amusing. But the wonderful thing about Kirby is the way that Thorpe's feeling for his art produced a really lovely house and one which enchants the eye long before the mind has been aroused to ask the why, the how and the whence.

Sir Humphrey Stafford died in 1575 and his representatives almost immediately sold the incomplete Kirby to Sir Christopher Hatton. The purchase money was paid in 1578. Now Sir Christopher was already far advanced with his own house, Holdenby, a house very much larger than Kirby and based (as he himself confessed) on Burghley's new house at Theobalds.[39] Little remains of Holdenby, but there are still, incorporated into the small existing house on the site, a porch and some chimney-stacks, precisely in the style of Kirby.[40] So it looks very much as if Hatton had procured the services of Stafford's principal free-mason. For a year or two, Thomas Thorpe may well have been looking after both houses at once. At Kirby, Hatton is supposed to have built the prominent southward extension, terminating in twin bay-windows; and it was he, perhaps, who ordered the completion of the gallery block with its range of Flemish strap-work gables. In this work, we lose sight of Thomas Thorpe and his style. I do not believe that he could have turned so readily to the strap-work technique as to build those gables at Kirby. Were they his, I feel that they would either have been patently copied from de Vries or strongly tinged with the Anglo-French ornamentalism which was his early and persistent predilection. I suggest that one of two things happened. Either Sir Christopher Hatton turned another mason on to Kirby when the place

14. Porch of Dingley Hall, Northamptonshire, 1558, possibly by Thomas Thorpe, senior. It was built for the Griffin family, whose monument is illustrated on p. 18. *15.* Porch of Kirby Hall, which has many features in common with that of Dingley. The central window is a 17th.-century insertion

became his, or the gables and the south-west wing are later than his time and later than Thomas Thorpe *pater*. If the latter is the correct answer, it is, of course, possible that the strap-work represents the style either of Henry or of the youngest Thomas Thorpe,[41] brothers of John. As we have seen, Henry acted, on one occasion at least, as clerk-of-works to the Crown; while there is every indication that Thomas was a mason of a very high order indeed. Either may have been in charge of Kirby for a considerable time. It is rather significant that certain designs in the Thorpe book do strongly reflect the style of the Kirby gables. They are, I feel sure, in the hand of John Thorpe; but, as we shall see in a moment, John Thorpe did not sever himself entirely from Northamptonshire and it would not be extraordinary if some of his drawings reflected, or indeed influenced, the style of the other brothers.

So much for the association of the Thorpe family with Kirby.

Henry Thorpe died in 1624[42] and Thomas, most probably in 1626,[43] after which date we need not look for further connections between the family and the house. There was, to be sure, yet another Thomas (grandson of Thomas *pater*) in the parish but of him we know nothing except that he died intestate in 1642,[44] at the age of 48. Four years before that, the work proceeding at Kirby had changed to the pure Italian style of the Carolean court; and the name of Thorpe had been extinguished by that of Nicholas Stone, and, perhaps, the even more illustrious name of Inigo Jones.

The life of John Thorpe

We return now to our central character, John Thorpe, the surveyor. The combined pattern of the Thorpe genealogy and of dated events in John's career suggests that he was born in, or very near, the year 1563.[45] Thus he was, as I have said, about seven when the first stone of Kirby was laid. This gives rise to the important question: did he or did he not lay that stone? I find it difficult to believe that the famous text already quoted is not in John Thorpe's hand. Of his father's hand we have no specimens (his drawing of the first floor of Kirby is void of texts) and, in any case, the ground-floor plan drawn by John to accompany his father's drawing of the first floor, is stylistically later in date than 1596, the year of Thomas's death, and it is on this drawing that the inscription occurs. It is probable that the text is a record of the first significant date in John Thorpe's memory, a record made when he was an old man; the record of an occasion when his father, following an ancient tradition, placed his hands on the first stone of the great new house.[46]

Whatever the truth, it does not radically affect our story, since it is obvious that John Thorpe cannot have borne any responsibility for Kirby. He will probably have learnt the rudiments of drawing from his father. He may have got to know something more about draughtsmanship and surveying as a result of the periodical presence in the district of Ralph Treswell, an agent of Sir Christopher Hatton's, and whose Northamptonshire surveys of 1580 onwards still exist.[47] But the first firm date in his career is supplied by the presence of his name in the Declaration of Accounts of the Queen's Works for the year ending March 31, 1584.[48]

John Thorpe's removal, at the age of about twenty, from Kingscliffe to London is not surprising; many younger sons of yeoman families were leaving their villages at a much earlier age to be apprenticed in the capital. What is, at first sight, rather astonishing is that he should walk straight into a Clerkship in the Queen's Works at the decent salary of 12d. per day. Only influence in a pretty high quarter could have effected that; but such influence was not remote in the case of a lad whose father was almost certainly known to Sir Christopher Hatton; and whose home was within walking distance of the palace of the great Burghley himself.

Anyway, Thorpe was installed in London by 1584 or, just possibly, a year earlier. Of the nature of his employment, the accounts[49] give us an accurate idea. Four or five or sometimes more clerks were employed in the Queen's Works, all at the same daily wage. They were allocated to the various undertakings for which the Surveyor of H.M. Works was responsible, these consisting principally of the Tower of London, Whitehall Palace, Somerset House, Greenwich and Hampton Court and any other Royal palaces which required repair or alteration. The functions of the clerks differed.

Some were clerks of the works; others were clerks in a more strictly clerical sense and engrossed the accounts. Wherever John Thorpe's function is specified, it is usually as one of the latter class, but he also appears occasionally as 'the Surveyor's Clerk' as distinct not only from the 'Clerk of the Works' but also from the 'Comptroller's Clerk'. Probably the functions were, to an extent, interchangeable but it is worth noting that John Thorpe does not appear on any occasion as a practical superintendent of building works. On the other hand, he made an elaborate survey of Eltham Palace,[50] probably in 1590, and was making drawings in his book at least as early as 1596.[51]

From 1584 to 1585, Thorpe was engaged on Whitehall, Hampton Court and Oatlands. In subsequent years he put in long stretches at Whitehall but occasionally worked at the Tower, at Greenwich, at Richmond and, for a period of one year, from 1596 to 1597, at two Surrey houses which were being prepared for a Royal Progress. None of the work carried out during his time was of any great importance; it consisted largely of maintenance work, minor alterations like the insertion of new doors and windows, and the occasional construction of fountains or ornamental seats in the several Privy Gardens. His fellow-clerks included several interesting people who, with their senior officers, constituted perhaps the most competent circle of architectural expertise in the country. Thorpe served under four Surveyors – Thomas Graves,[52] the designer of the first Banqueting House; Thomas Blagrave; Robert Adams,[53] expert on fortifications; and William Spicer.[54] Among the Clerks, the most persistent name is that of John Marshall; other clerks were Matthew Switzer (of whom more presently), Simon Basil[55] (1595 to 1598, in which year he became Comptroller) and Robert Stickles[56] (from 1598). A certain John Symonds[57] had been one of the Clerks shortly before Thorpe's arrival (Thorpe may have had his place); he died in 1597, leaving small legacies for mourning rings to many of the officers of H.M. Works including Thorpe. These people were all of some account, mostly rather older than Thorpe and reasonably well off. There were, no doubt, perquisites attached to the clerkships and we know that Stickles and Symonds certainly, and the others almost certainly, took fees for supplying 'platts' to gentlemen about to build.[58] Switzer owned land, Stickles is one of the few Jacobeans to be referred to in print by a contemporary[59] as an 'architect,' and Symonds, whom we know as a clever designer, whom Burghley sometimes employed, was able to divide among his friends, when he died, a wardrobe of the most princely character.

Thorpe remained at Her Majesty's Works for seventeen or eighteen years, his employment ending, apparently, in September 1601. He was then about thirty-eight, with a family. He had married, nine years previously, the daughter of a well-to-do woodmonger of St Martin-in-the-Fields, Simon Greene.[60] Greene, in his youth, had come up to London from the country,[61] his native parish being Brampton in Huntingdonshire, which is but 20 miles, as the crow flies, from Kingscliffe. So the Greenes may have been known to the Thorpes before John Thorpe's arrival in London. Rebecca Greene was seventeen-and-a-half when she married John Thorpe,[62] at St Martin's, in 1592. He was about twenty-nine. She bore him a large family of children – five sons and seven daughters, according to the Kingscliffe monument; the first son (b. 1598) was, of course, christened Thomas in loyalty to the three original generations. The Thorpes lived in St Martin's parish, and John Thorpe continued to live there till the end of his life. The precise location is not apparent until 1640, when the rate-books[63] disclose that he was in Little Church Lane, a narrow street (destroyed in 1830) near the east end of St Martin's church; but it is clear from the similar ordering of the earlier rate-books that he had been there at least since 1607.

After his departure from the Queen's Works, Thorpe's activities are at first obscure. He had evidently hoped to get one of the higher places in the Works, probably that of Comptroller, for there is a letter at Hatfield[64] from Sir Henry Neville to Sir Robert Cecil recommending his suit for a reversion. Neville wrote from Paris, being Ambassador there at the time, and this has given rise to the idea that Thorpe may have been in his *entourage* there; but there is no doubt that he was fully engaged in the Works up to the autumn of 1601. At the same time, one cannot help connecting the presence, in Thorpe's book, of a plan of a house in Paris, dated 1600,[65] with Neville's embassy of that and the previous year.

Neville's recommendation may have been of rather doubtful value, for by the end of the year the Ambassador was locked up in the Tower for complicity in the Essex plot. Nevertheless, it is in Government employment that we meet Thorpe next. In August, 1604, he was paid £40 for 'survayinge certaine of his mat^ies lands for suche purpose as his mat^ie hath appointed.'[66] Towards the end of the same year he was paid £53 3s. 4d. for something more explicit, having been sent, 'by commandment of the Lord Treasurer of England' (i.e. the Earl of Dorset) to the Isle of Sheppey to survey certain (unspecified) lands.[67] His fee was £40; the rest of the sum was for travel and attendance and for the accidental laming of his horse in the course of the survey.

So, by 1604, Thorpe had become an independent, and highly paid, surveyor of land for the Government. Thereafter, entries in the order books[68] are frequent. There was another expedition in that year to Sheppey, accompanied by John Gawber, a fellow surveyor. Then, in 1605, Thorpe was first in Kent and Sussex, surveying 'lands and tenements' and later in Northamptonshire, his home county, to survey Holdenby House, which had passed to the Government on Hatton's death. In 1606, he was paid for work in Lincolnshire and Hampshire and a large additional sum for his work at Holdenby. The Holdenby job was apparently very thorough, since Thorpe and three assistants were 'a longe time emploied in drawing doun and wrighting faire the plotts,' with 'the severall rates and valewes' of both house and land. About the same time, he surveyed Ampthill House, Beds., and Theobalds, Robert Cecil's own home, then being exchanged, at the King's desire, for Hatfield. There are several other references, between 1606 and 1611, to these two great estates, where Thorpe was evidently the surveyor principally involved in the exchange; and in the British Library is a fine coloured map[69] of Theobalds bearing his name and the date 1611. From February 1606 to August 1609 he was acting as a Commissioner for the sale of Royal woods in Northamptonshire, Huntingdon and Rutland, the rate of pay (including expenses) being the high one of 15s. per day. Further amounts are entered to him for the portage of large sums of cash from Northamptonshire to the Exchequer. He was again nominated[70] a Commissioner in 1609, this time in connection with the sale of the Duchess of Suffolk's lands, and it is in a draft list of this Commission, bearing the Earl of Salisbury's signature, that his brother's name (as we suppose) was inserted and then removed.

Thorpe's duties in Northamptonshire at this period took him back to Kingscliffe (a Royal manor, as its name implies) more than once, so it is not fanciful to see the later Kirby work (perhaps by one of his brothers) reflected in drawings in this book. He was at Kingscliffe in 1609, inspecting a house he must have known all his life – Westhay Lodge,[71] occupied by the Ashley[72] family, one of whom married John Thorpe's youngest sister, Jane.[73] Thorpe signed a report[74] recommending that the Lord Treasurer be moved to have repairs to this house put in hand, seeing that other Royal lodges in the country had been similarly favoured.

Constantly, during this period, we find Thorpe acting with the famous John Norden,[75] a man fifteen years or so his senior, who had already projected and partly written his series of county histories and had held surveyorships under the Crown since 1600. Ralph Treswell, whom we met earlier on as Sir Christopher Hatton's agent, also reappears as one of the Crown surveyors, now associated with his son, Robert, who, from 1597, combined the family profession with the office of Somerset Herald. The association of the younger Treswell, Norden and Thorpe crystallized permanently when in 1610 Treswell was appointed Surveyor-General of Woods South of Trent and when, a few months later, Norden and Thorpe were nominated his assistants.

The three men were to divide Southern England between them. John Thorpe's patent,[76] which issued on April 21, 1611, charged him with the survey, personally or by deputy, of 'all our Castells, Parks, fforts and Lodges' in nine counties: Middlesex, Surrey, Essex, Hertfordshire, Kent, Berkshire, Buckinghamshire, Northamptonshire and Rutland. 'Survey' in this context did not necessarily involve making drawings. The appointment was an inspectorate and Thorpe was merely to 'testify' to the Lord Treasurer concerning work required to be done on Royal buildings in these counties. For this work he was to receive an annuity of £20 for life, with 10s. a day travelling expenses.

This appointment meant that during the following years, Thorpe was constantly travelling about the country, either inspecting and reporting on buildngs or else completing special survey assignments. Thus, in 1616, he joined Norden in surveying Kirton in Lincolnshire, a county outside the terms of his patent.[77] In the Cambridge Library is a list, of about this date, of 'Bookes of Survaies delyvered in by Mr. Norden and Mr. Thorpe.'[78] During the summer months of each year he must have been always on the move and there is no doubt that, during his travels he collected information about houses and copied the more up-to-date plans into his book. Systematic research on all the manors known to have been visited by Thorpe would probably enable us to identify many more of the plans than has hitherto been possible.

It is now perfectly clear what Thorpe's life-work really was. From 1604 onwards, he was one of the busiest and most eminent land-surveyors in England. By 1610, his position was such that he was able himself to become the owner of a quite considerable property. He bought from his old colleague in the Works, Matthew Switzer, two estates, on which he laid out no less than £960. It is as surprising to find Switzer, of whom we know next to nothing, in possession of so much land, as to find Thorpe able to buy it at such a price. 104 acres of it was at Winkfield, in the Forest of Windsor; the remainder (19 acres) was at Egham and consisted of a close of meadows called Thames Meads and a grove of woods.[79] There were dwelling-houses on both properties and, judging by the price, the rents accruing from them must have been considerable. One can only regard the transaction as a large capital investment on Thorpe's part, calculated to keep him in decent circumstances for the rest of his life, while leaving something substantial to his family at his death.

At Egham, Thorpe paid a quit rent of 6d. for his land; his name appears in a Rental of 1622[80] and, from time to time, in the Manor Court Rolls until 1654, the year previous to his death.[81] It is unlikely that he resided either at Egham or Winkfield.

It was in 1612, two years after the purchase of land and one after the issue of the patent, that the book appeared which contains a Latin epigram by Thorpe and, in the text, that unique personal reference to him which I mentioned earlier. The book is *The Gentleman's Exercise*, by Henry Peacham. It had appeared previously in 1607 under a different title.[82] But the 1612 edition, which also appeared with the title *Graphice or the Most Auncien and Excellent Art of Drawing and Limning disposed into three Bookes*, by Henrie Peachum, London, printed by W.S. for Johne Browne, is the first in which the Thorpe reference occurs (on page 172). The book is largely a primer in heraldry, and Peacham adopts a lively form of dialogue between teacher and pupil. He shows his
16 pupil a coat of arms (engraved in the text) and asks him to describe it. The pupil does so, correctly. Peacham then proceeds:

> It did belong to the Abbot of Tame, whose name was *Thorpe*, and now borne of Master *John Thorpe* of the parish of Saint *Martins* in the Field, my especiall friend, and excellent Geometrician and Surveiour, whom the rather I remember, because he is not onely learned and ingenuous himselfe, but a furtherer and favorer of all excellency whatsoever, of whom our age findeth too few.

Having bestowed this tribute, Peacham is reminded that he has two other friends in the same parish, 'lovers of learning, and all vertue'. One is a Master Christopher Collard, who does not otherwise come into our story. The other is Thorpe's father-in-law, Simon Greene, the woodmonger, whom we now find dignified with the office of 'Purveyor of his Majesties Stable.' Finally, Peacham throws another bouquet to 'the aforenamed Master *John Thorpe* his sonne, to whom I can in words never be sufficiently thankefull'. It is the 'his' in this passage which Papworth and others read as an expanded genitive, instead of a pronoun referring to Greene, the proper interpretation.

Peacham, seen through his writings, was a quaint, vivacious character with that romantic love of pedantry so characteristic of his time and some skill as a draughtsman.[83] He was about thirteen years younger than Thorpe. Why he had reason to be so grateful to him we are not told, but we are in Peacham's debt for handing down to us the only glimpse of John Thorpe as a person which we possess.

The coat of arms,[84] which Peacham takes the opportunity of displaying to flatter his friend, had perhaps been adopted by Thorpe not very long before. There is no grant to John Thorpe or any of his family in the College of Arms[85] and it looks as if he merely assumed the arms on the grounds of some putative relationship to an Abbot of Thame. The bearings were assumed not only by John but by the Thorpes of Kingscliffe, for in a sketch in one of the 1618 Visitations the arms of 'John Thorpe of London' have a crescent for difference (he being a second son). The coat of arms without difference

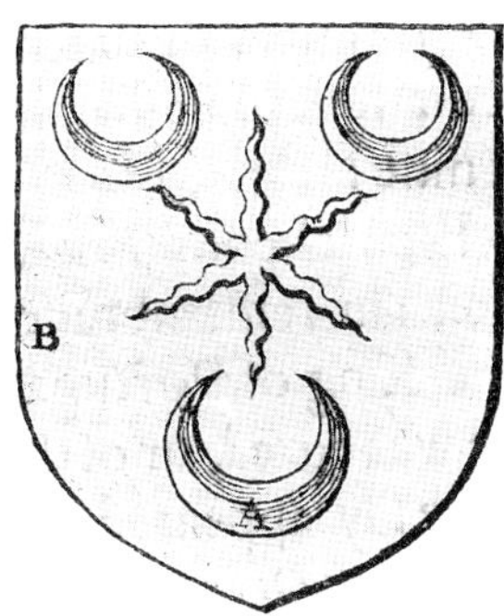

16. Thorpe's coat-of-arms, from Henry Peacham's *Graphice*, 1612, a book published under various titles, containing the only known personal reference to John Thorpe, 'my especiall friend, and excellent Geometrician and Surveiour'

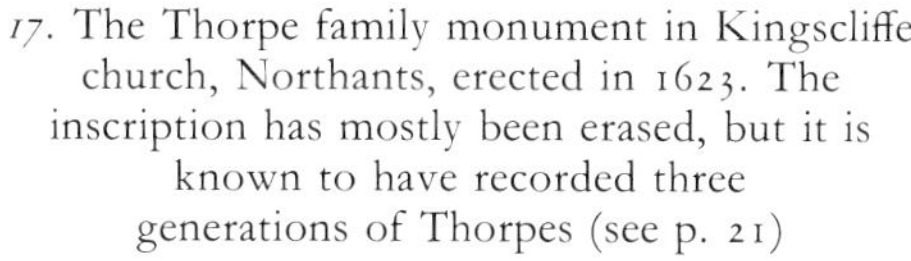

17. The Thorpe family monument in Kingscliffe church, Northants, erected in 1623. The inscription has mostly been erased, but it is known to have recorded three generations of Thorpes (see p. 21)

occurs on the Thorpe monument in Kingscliffe Church. John Thorpe adopted a personal motto. It is not given by Peacham but is noted in the Visitation. It reads: *Supervidens non videns.* Obviously it alludes to Thorpe's profession of *supervisor* or surveyor, the meaning being that, through the surveyor's skill a land-owner could visualize and administer his property without actually setting foot on the soil. He can *survey* the land without *seeing* it.

1612 was the year of the death of the brilliant and adored Henry, Prince of Wales. Prince Charles, succeeding to his titles, succeeded also to estates held by him, and we find Thorpe, with Norden and Norden's son, periodically engaged on the survey of these. The Prince's Surveyor-General was a placeman, Sir Richard Smith, for whom Thorpe deputized. We find both of them, with Sir John Denham (the judge, father of the poet-architect) presiding at a Manor Court near Egham in 1618.[86] Three years later there is a warrant to Sir Adam Newton, the Prince's Receiver General, to pay £50 to Thorpe in respect of surveys of a number of the Prince's estates;[87] while later in the same year (1621) a warrant of a like nature for £72 is mentioned in Sir Adam Newton's Account Book.[88] From these documents we also learn that the Nordens and Thorpe were receiving a joint salary of £20 a year in the Prince's service.

This work for the future Charles I is the last we hear of John Thorpe's professional activities.[89] He was about fifty-eight, owned, perhaps, considerably more property than we are aware of and may also have adventured to some extent as a speculative builder.[90] This latter possibility is suggested by an extremely interesting incident recorded in the Acts of the Privy Council for 1616. On 18 September of that year, instructions were sent to the High Sheriff of Middlesex to demolish certain houses which contravened the Proclamations forbidding the erection, without permission, of new buildings around London. A few cases of 'principall offenders' were selected for instant demolition as a deterrent to others; and among these principal offenders was John Thorpe. His case is instanced as follows:

> John Thorpe hath begunne to erect three tenements so neere St. Martin's [in the Fields] Churche as if they goe on, will much hinder the lights of the same church, and give greate annoyance to the same. They are to be pulled downe.

The Sheriff later reported that this had been done.

This is almost the only specific evidence we have of Thorpe being associated with building work. There is nothing, of course, to suggest that the houses were to be of the slightest architectural importance, or anything more than common London houses erected for leasing or for sale. But this evidence does enormously increase the likelihood that some, at least, of the plans for London houses given in Thorpe's book are his own work. Indeed, there is actually a plan[91] for '3 houses for the cytty or for a country house' which may have some relation to the three tenements so defiantly begun hard by St Martin's church.

The demolition episode, combined with what we know of Thorpe's other property interests in Surrey, Berkshire and Northamptonshire and the absence of his name from records of official survey work after 1621, suggests that in later middle age Thorpe turned from professional life to the development and increase of his personal estate. The last recorded payment to him for professional services comes not from the government but from the Earl of Rutland. It was a fee of £5, 'all in gold', as 'Surveior of the contractinge' for a gallery on the south side of Belvoir Castle. His old age was spent in the austere London of the Civil War and the Commonwealth. We know that he went on living in his house in Little Church Lane, and we catch a last oblique glimpse of him right at the beginning of the troubles. Early in 1643 his father-in-law, Simon Greene, died.[92] He left a substantial estate, his son Richard being executor and residuary legatee. To John Thorpe he left a token gift – 'ten pounds in gold to make him a ring'. The will was proved by Richard, but trouble was to follow. Richard, although an elderly man, took up arms and joined the King at Oxford.[93] This was discovered when Parliament began to turn the financial screw on the inhabitants of London and Middlesex. A compulsory loan was levied, the instrument created for this purpose being the Committee for the Advance of Money. Simon Greene must have been assessed before or about the time of his death, for his estate came under the scrutiny of the Committee. Richard Greene's whereabouts was discovered, he was classed as a delinquent and his share of the estate sequestrated. Two other legatees, John Thorpe and a certain William Dalton, probably a servant of old Greene's, were hailed before the Committee and ordered to show, within a fortnight, what the deceased had died worth, what debts were due to him, how much of the estate was already in Richard's hands and what charges and legacies had been paid. That was at the end of 1644. Apparently Thorpe and Dalton were able to satisfy the Committee, because in the following July it was ordered that, apart from the sequestered residue, all the legacies should be paid.[94]

Ten years of life remained to John Thorpe. Of his large family, almost all had died, most of them in the plague epidemics so clearly reflected in the zig-zag statistics of the St Martin's registers. In 1643 he probably had only one son, John, and one married daughter, living;[95] and the son probably died in 1646.[96] For the last years, only the Parish rate-books and the Court Rolls of Egham certify his continued existence. He paid his rates regularly until 1650 when he was able to pay only 3s. 6d. in 14s. In 1651 he paid nothing. The rate-book for 1652 is missing and in that for 1653 his name no longer appears. The following year, 1654, is the last in which he is found in the list of tenants at Egham. The date of his death is thus fairly clearly shown. He was not buried where we should expect, in the churchyard of St Martin's; but in the register of the adjoining parish of St Paul's, Covent Garden,[97] for February 1654 (1655 N.S.), we find the following entry: 'Feb. 14, John Thorpe, buried in the church-yard.' As no Thorpes are discoverable in the rate-books of that parish it looks as if John Thorpe, in the last years of his long life, moved to the house of some friend or relation in St Paul's parish and his bones lie, therefore, under the shadow of Inigo Jones's famous church. He must have been about ninety-one or ninety-two.

I have not found John Thorpe's will and, as in the case of so many Commonwealth wills, the quest is probably a vain one. If it ever comes to light it will not, perhaps, tell us more than we already know about his life. But it will resolve one tantalizing problem. At Kingscliffe, there is a tiny row of three almshouses, one of which bears the following inscription:

Aedificavit charitas
Inhabitabit paupertas
Ornabit honestas
Durabit omnis aetas
Ex Dono Johanis Thorp arm̃ año 1688

Can this John Thorp be our John Thorpe, who died thirteen years before the almshouses were built? I think it possible. Thorpe possessed land and houses at Kingscliffe; a survey in the Public Record Office[98] shows that in 1609 the property yielded £4 4s. 1d. per annum. He may well have provided in his will for the building of almshouses out of revenue; if so, it would account for the period of years which elapsed between his death and the building of the almshouses. No other John Thorpe, likely to have made a gift or bequest of this nature, is discoverable and it would be wholly characteristic of the times for a man in Thorpe's position to provide for a benefaction of this kind: a token of loyalty to the soil which bore him and at the same time a personal monument to endure, as the inscription so confidently asserts, for a whole age.

18. Wollaton Hall, Nottinghamshire. Thorpe's record, probably copied from a drawing by another hand, of Robert Smythson's masterpiece of 1580–88

19. A fantasy house by John Thorpe, planned on his own initials, I-T. The covered way, linking the two blocks, is borrowed from Du Cerçeau

20. Sir John Danvers' house at Chelsea, built c.1623. Probably the latest design in Thorpe's book and the only one which shows, in the fenestration and balustrades, the influence of Inigo Jones's new classicism. The house was demolished c.1720.

The man and the book

Having now got a reasonably clear picture of John Thorpe, his origin, life, work and death, what are we to think of him as a character in the history of his time? We know now exactly how to class him professionally. As Blomfield shrewdly guessed, he was a land-surveyor, a man of the same type as John Norden, the map-maker and topographer about whose career there has never been any mystery. Beside these two names we could place many others, for surveyors were no rarity in Jacobean England. They were, indeed, swarming all over the countryside, to the considerable advantage of their employers and the no less considerable fury of small tenants comfortably holding house and land on some vague basis of manorial rights which nobody ever troubled to define or confirm.[99]

But Thorpe was not wholly typical of his class. More accurately, the class to which he belonged (I mean, surveyors in general) had not yet produced a uniform type, and Thorpe was one of the many variants within his own professional group. What makes him different from most other Jacobean surveyors is the exceptional knowledge of architecture shown by his book. This is easily accounted for: in the first place by his parentage, and in the second by the fact that he spent the first part of his career as a Clerk in the Queen's Works. He might easily have succeeded to the Comptrollership and eventually even to the Surveyorship, had opportunity and patronage moved in a different pattern. As it was, he became a successful land-surveyor, with a strong personal and professional interest in buildings, an interest richly reflected in that remarkable volume which, when his life as a land-surveyor had been wholly forgotten, caused him to be honoured for a whole century as the great 'Elizabethan architect'.

Finally we come to the famous book: a small folio of 282 pages filled with plans and elevations of nearly 200 buildings, mostly in ink, on a basis of scorer and/or graphite, some highly finished, others lightly sketched. There is no title-page, nor any specific statement as to the book's compiler. That it is John Thorpe's book can be safely inferred from the presence of his name on a limited number of drawings and a general

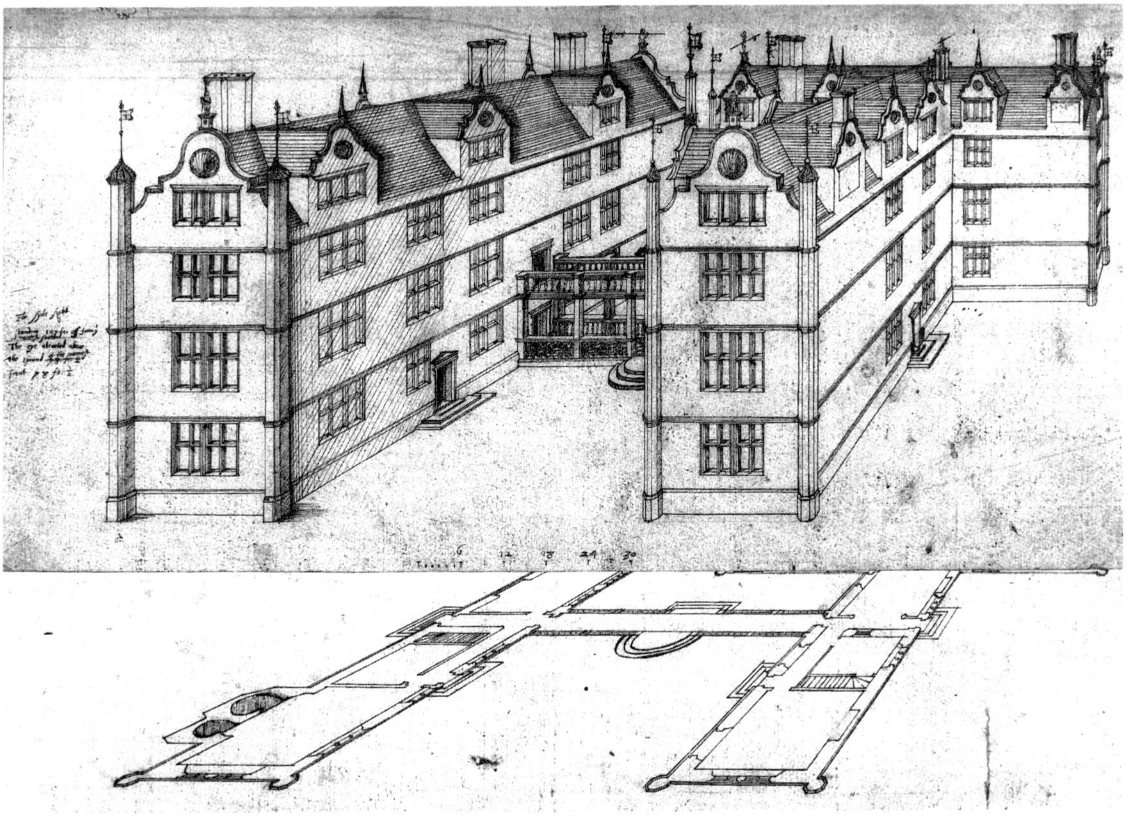

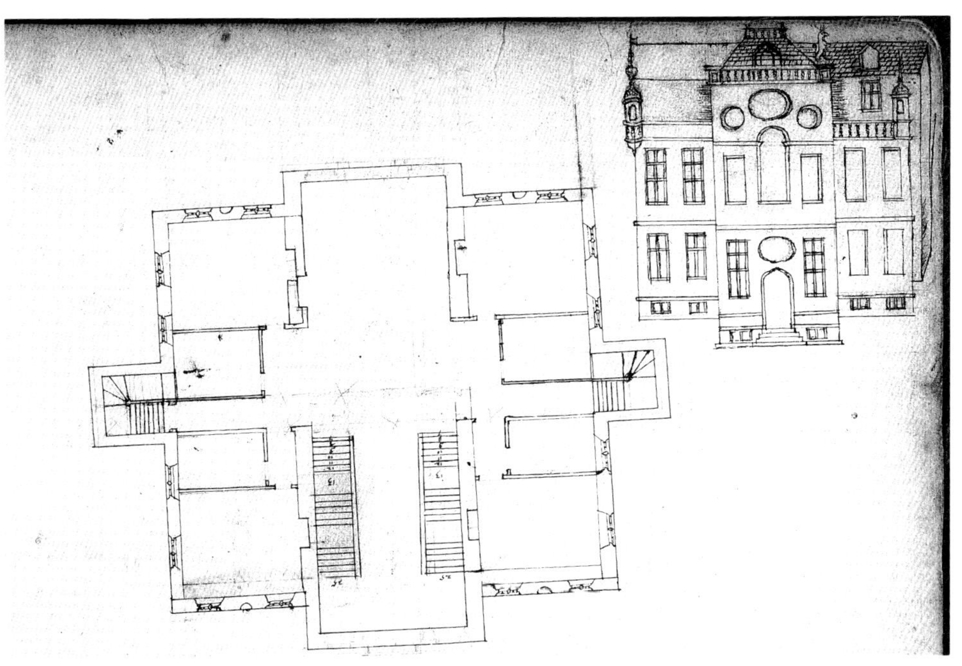

consistency in style of draughtsmanship and calligraphy corresponding with these. He seems to have used the book from about 1596 to 1623, a period of twenty-seven years, from the age of about thirty till nearly sixty. 1596 was the date of his father's death and a few extraneous drawings, including an early plan of Kirby, mounted on pages of the book, must have belonged to him. A curious thing about these is that they are nearly all *upper* floor plans, which suggests that on the father's death his plans were divided, the principal floor plans being perhaps taken by the elder son, Henry, John being left with the upper-floor plans which he pasted into his book.

The first nine pages of the book are filled with large-scale profiles of Tudor types of mullion, transom, corbel table, cant pier, water table etc., evidently approved types in the Thorpe practice. Then follow highly finished drawings of the five Roman orders. These are accurately copied from Hans Blum *Quinque Columnarum Exacta descriptio atque deliniatio*, a close imitation of Serlio, first published at Zurich in 1550 in Latin but translated into English by John Thorpe himself and printed in London 1608. After that come the designs and surveys. They come in no particular order and seem to have been placed quite arbitrarily in different parts of the book. They have been documented and, so far as possible, dated in the Walpole Society's catalogue (1966).[100]

The drawings can be divided into four classes. 1. Drawings copied from printed works, notably Blum (as above), Du Cerçeau and Vredeman de Vries. 2. Drawings of a few English and French buildings copied from unknown sources. Important examples
18 are Wollaton and Longford in England, and the Palais du Luxembourg in France. 3. Surveys of English buildings, earlier than Thorpe's time, to which he has made or proposed alterations and extensions, e.g. Somerset House and Henry VII's chapel. 4. Designs for houses by Thorpe himself. This is by far the largest class but also the most problematic. In the whole collection of designs only four bear Thorpe's signature. One
19 of these is the famous design for a house planned on his own intials, I-T;[101] another is a plan of Holland House, 'p'fected by me JT';[102] a third a plan for a reconstruction of Ampthill as a royal residence: 'enlarg^{ed} p. J. Thorpe';[103] the fourth is on an unidentified plan. These are not much to go on and it has to be admitted that attributions of other plans to Thorpe himself are never without risk. The safest attributions are those where a client's name is given; the most risky, the ideal plans and ingenious conceits, which may have been in circulation in Thorpe's time but whose sources are lost.

Thorpe's patrons or 'clients' were of very varied social status, descending from Lord Treasurer Dorset (a plan for rebuilding Buckhurst), by way of secretaries of state, minor court officials and unheard-of country squires who had managed to acquire knighthoods in the early years of James I. There is no evidence of Thorpe ever having supervised a building in construction. To supply a 'plat', with or without an 'upright', was probably the limit of his professional function. Nevertheless, his designs did sometimes come satisfactorily to fruition. Two existing houses where we can accept
21 Thorpe's authorship with reasonable confidence are Aston Hall, Birmingham, *c.*1618 (now a museum) and Somerhill, Kent, *c.*1613. Both vary somewhat from the plans in the book but the derivation is unambiguous.

How should we assess Thorpe's achievements as a designer? There is an almost irresistible tendency to see him as 'quaint'. Viewed in the light of Inigo Jones's performance which overlaps Thorpe's by some twenty years, this is understandable;

21. Aston Hall, Birmingham: the entrance front. The plans in Thorpe's book approximate to the house as built for Sir Thomas Holt from 1618 onwards. Thorpe gives no 'uprights'.

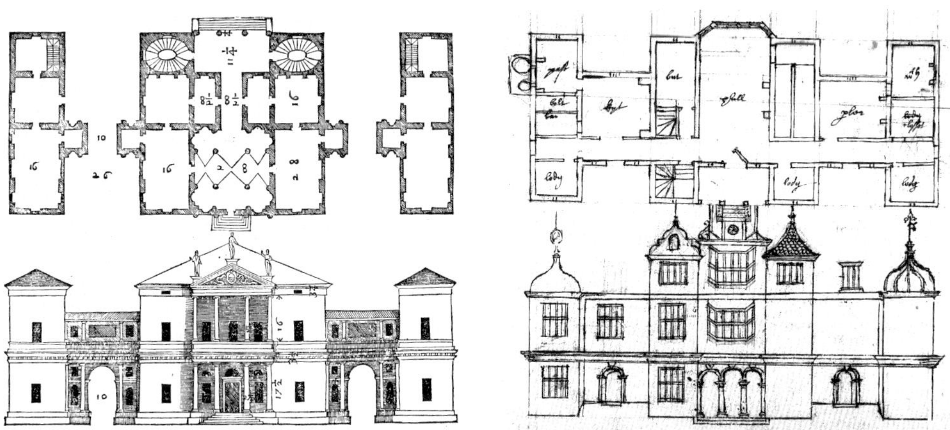

22, 23. Left: plan and elevation of the Villa Pisano, from Palladio's *Quattro Libri*. Right: Palladio turned into English. The main lines of Palladio's plan are preserved but the elevation is free and the rooms are given familiar English names – parlour, kitchen, larder, buttery, etc.

but the more one studies Thorpe's designs the less 'quaint' and the more intellectually remarkable they become. The plans, far more than the elevations, leave this impression. Sir John Soane, echoing Walpole, esteemed them as 'very ingenious and whimsical studies', but some of them are more than that. Thorpe was one of the first English architects to discover Palladio. Robert Smythson, to be sure, got in first at Hardwick (1590), certainly planned with reference to the Villa Valmarana; but Thorpe's Palladian plans are no later than 1605 and he studied the villa plans in Book 2 of the *Quattro Libri* with real appreciation. A specially interesting case is an unidentified house whose plan derives from the Villa Pisano.[104] Thorpe copied Palladio's engravings into his book, line for line, and to the same scale, and then worked over it, changing everything except the basic lines and 'domesticating' it in English terms, but preserving always the Palladian ratios. Palladio's elevation he utterly ignored, giving us oriel windows, towers with ogee roofs, a curly gable and a soaring lantern turret. About half a dozen plans in the book show the influence of Palladio in this way and in his plan for the new palace proposed for James I at Ampthill in 1605 he goes further towards classical planning on a monumental scale than any other English architect of that date.

Thorpe's elevations or 'uprights' are in a very different class from his plans. There are only about thirty of them as against five times that number of plans. Of these elevations, nine were drawn on separate pieces of paper and pasted into the book, which suggests that they belong to the years before 1596, and this is confirmed by their decidedly 'Elizabethan' character, ornamented in the Flemish way with pediments, consoles, pinnacles and obelisks clustering profusely and with tall masts issuing from vase-like terminals and carrying vanes. Chimneys invariably take the form of Doric columns and porches and doorways have classical columns to give them consequence. There can be no doubt that these elevations are by Thorpe himself but with certain exceptions they do him little credit and make an almost ludicrous contrast to the ingenious, hard-headed plans which are the main substance of the book. They convey the impression that Thorpe's serious concern was with the plan and the plan only. The uprights could be settled on the site by the owner, his masons and carvers. Elevations were probably gratuitous suggestions which might or might not be followed by them in whole or in part. As the years pass, datable elevations become less 'Elizabethan' and there is one which even takes a Du Cerçeau design as its model. One of Thorpe's oddest designs (if indeed it is his) is that for Sir John Danvers' house at Chelsea. The outline of
20 the plan repeats a shape which Thorpe was using twenty-seven years earlier; but the internal arrangement is extravagantly odd. One very long hall runs from back to front of the house, giving a view of the Thames at one end and the garden at the other. The hall is at two levels with a stair leading from the lower to the upper part and then sweeping up against the sides of the hall in true 'imperial' style. The elevation is no less idiosyncratic. Of all the designs in the book it comes nearest to actualizing the rise of the court style of Inigo Jones. The triad of windows, the oval windows and the balustrades almost persuade us that Thorpe has noticed the 'new wave'. Built in 1622–3 the Danvers house could well be the last design recorded in the book.

Inigo Jones was making designs for the Earl of Salisbury from 1608 and was Surveyor of Works from 1615. He and Thorpe must have come into frequent contact, though perhaps only on matters of administration. One would not expect Inigo to be much interested in Thorpe and, the Danvers house apart, one looks in vain in Thorpe's book for the least flicker of interest in Jones. They had one thing in common – Palladio; but Jones saw him in three dimensions, Thorpe only in two. There could hardly be a more divisive factor. Thorpe, having laid the foundation stone of one of the greatest Elizabethan houses in his infancy, remained 'Elizabethan' for the rest of his life.

III · Inigo Jones: Covent Garden and the Restoration of St Paul's Cathedral

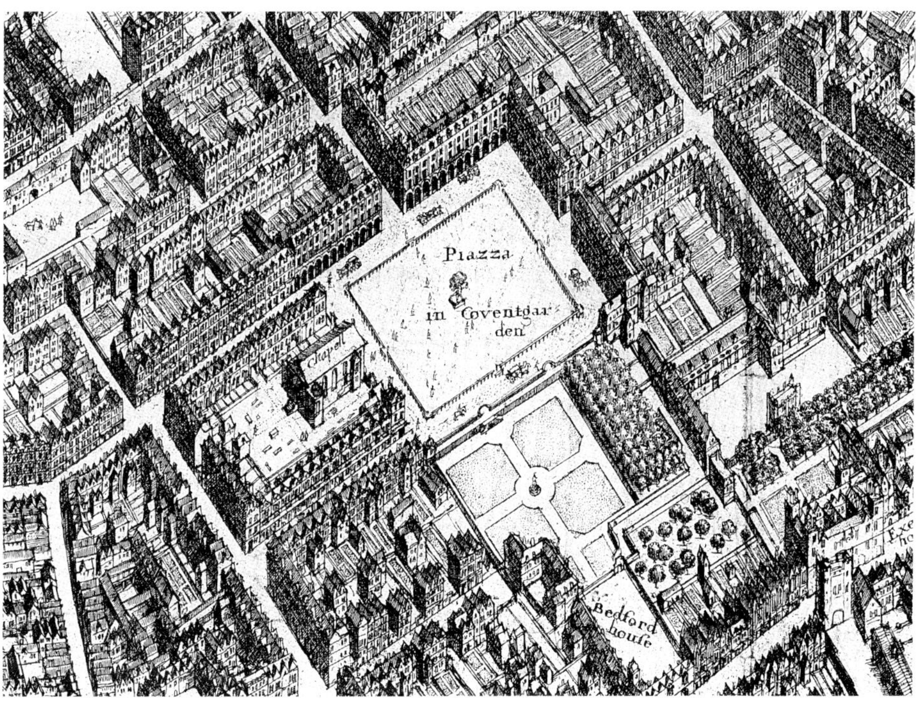

24. Bird's-eye view of Covent Garden, with St Paul's church (labelled 'Chapell') to the left. Detail of a print by W. Hollar

25. Houses on the east side of Covent Garden, seen through the arcades of the north side.
E. Rooker, 1768, after T. Sandby

I PROPOSE to consider here two buildings by Inigo Jones, one of which exists only in part, the other not at all, and neither of which has received the critical attention it deserves.[1] The first is the Covent Garden complex of church and square; the second is the remodelling of old St Paul's Cathedral. These buildings belong to the zenith of Inigo's career as an architect, when he was in his late fifties and early sixties. They show him, I believe, as one of the most independent architects in the Europe of his time, an artist of uncommon intellectual probity who declined to submit to the sway of any continental school and sought criteria which should have an absolute value independent of time and place. Such a quest can have been understood by only a handful of his contemporaries. At his death it was all but lost to sight. The 18th century rediscovered it in rediscovering Jones and made thereby, in spite of some misunderstanding and distortion, a special contribution to the anti-Baroque revolution from which Neo-classicism emerged. Indeed, a short and perhaps rather risky way of characterizing Jones would be to call him the first Neo-classical architect. The description could easily be dismissed as something less than a half-truth but it is none the less useful so long as we resist the temptation to let concepts belonging strictly to the 18th century filter back into our idea of Jones and his age. His performance must be assessed within the ambience of its own world.

Of the two buildings which I propose to examine, the Covent Garden work comes
first, belonging to the years 1631–5. The work at St Paul's Cathedral belongs to 1632–
42. At Covent Garden we are confronted with a totality comprising not only the *24*
church but the open space, houses and streets axially related to it. Historically and
architecturally, church, space, and houses are interdependent – part of a single project;
to understand any part of Covent Garden it is necessary to know something of the
whole and of the motives which brought it into being.

It is well known that Covent Garden resulted from a challenge to what we should call town-planning restrictions and the due rejoinder of authority to that challenge.[2] The ground belonged to Francis, 4th Earl of Bedford, a man of large business capacity and initiative, not a favourite at Court and in fact tending to hold dangerously independent views.[3] In face of the proclamation prohibiting building in the neighbourhood of London he had attempted to build for profit in Long Acre and been stopped.[4] Any attempt to develop Covent Garden would have been stopped but the earl approached this major project with more circumspection. By what stages he attained his goal we do not know but on 10 January 1631 the Attorney-General was ordered to prepare a licence for the earl to build as many 'howses and buildings fitt for the habitacons of *Gentlemen* and men of abillity' as he should think proper.[5] There was no mention of any payment by the earl but we know in fact that the licence cost him £2,000.[6]

How Inigo Jones, the King's Surveyor, came to be employed on the work is not obvious from the documents but inferences can be drawn. The proclamation of 2 May 1625 was in the nature of an absolute prohibition of any building whatever except on old foundations – i.e. rebuilding.[7] The commission appointed to implement the proclamation, however, was given some latitude.[8] Nothing was said about building on old foundations and authority was given to any four commissioners, *of whom the King's Surveyor of Works was to be one*, to allot ground for the rebuilding of houses in such a way as to achieve 'Uniformitie and Decency'. This still does not allow for any increase in the number of houses but it does facilitate planned redistribution. More significantly, it establishes the principle that any new-shaping of London's streets shall come under the eye of the King's Surveyor – in other words, Inigo Jones. The text of the licence itself is entirely in line with that of the commission.[9] It applies itself specifically to the demolition or alteration of existing structures (there cannot have been many), the building of new structures in brick or stone, and the alteration of existing ways to accommodate the new buildings – rather as if the new Covent Garden was to be a matter simply of rebuilding and redistribution. The principle that the Surveyor of Works should exercise control would clearly apply.

In the licence there is no mention of a church, but there is a strong suggestion elsewhere that the church got into the scheme because the Earl of Bedford was shrewd enough to see that the scheme would not work without one.[10] It was a matter of expediency rather than piety. It rendered possible the creation of a new quarter, ready
26 stamped with the seal of social acceptability. Church, open space, and streets were thus a single concept economically. Jones, brought into the project by virtue of his office and accepted, no doubt, by the earl as a condition of its viability, saw that it became a single concept architecturally.

The idea of church and square as a calculated ensemble is remarkable for this date but its derivation need not, I think, be in doubt. John Evelyn picked up the information that it was the church and piazza at Leghorn (Livorno) which 'gave the first hint to the building both of the Church and Piazza in Covent Garden' and this seems highly probable. Under Ferdinando Medici, who succeeded to the dukedom of Tuscany in 1587, Leghorn was rapidly transformed from almost nothing to the great international sea-port which it was to remain for two hundred years.[11] The building of the cathedral (designed by Cantagallina after Buontalenti) and the piazza were part of this planned development – at the time, possibly the most ambitious town-planning project to be found anywhere. Jones would certainly have seen it on his first Italian visit and the Earl of Bedford would have heard of it. Now, Duke Ferdinando's niece was Marie de Médicis, Queen of Henri IV of France and *his* initiative in creating the Place Royale (now Place des Vosges) and Place Dauphine in Paris in 1605 probably derived from Leghorn.[12] The Place Royale, which Jones will have seen in progress in 1609 has a distinct bearing on Covent Garden. And the long arm of the Medicis stretches even further when we consider that Henrietta Maria, Charles I's queen, was Marie de Médicis' daughter. The dynastic network apart, however, links between London and Leghorn, direct and *via* Paris, are not far to seek. The architectural common factors in the three schemes are less important than the idea, common to all three, of rationalizing a residential quarter on symmetrical as well as profitable lines. In the first two cases the initiative was that of the sovereign; in the third, characteristically for England, that of a subject at loggerheads with his sovereign.[13]

Coming strictly to architecture, the vaulted arcades of the Place Royale have more

26. Covent Garden looking north, T. Bowles, 1751. By this date the market had taken over the open space

to do with Covent Garden than the rather ordinary cinquecento loggie at Leghorn (mostly destroyed in the Second World War). Jones's vision was to be more classical than either and while we are considering sources we must not forget the combination of temple and cortile which Palladio found and recorded as an almost flattened ruin near San Sebastiano outside Rome.[14]

Church and houses were begun almost simultaneously. Sites in Henrietta Street were let from March 1631;[15] the church was started in July.[16] The form to be taken by the church raised a curious question. No church had been built on a new site in London since the Reformation. There had been rebuildings, like St Katherine Cree, on more or less traditional lines. Jones himself had built one Chapel Royal and was building another – both for Catholic worship, however. No new pattern had ever been proposed for an absolutely new Protestant church. What should its form be? No echo has reached us of the debates which must have been held on this question. We have only the result on which to base our own speculations; and the result is, approximately, a temple. The Earl of Bedford, not a high churchman, would require simplicity; Jones would need to seek specific architectural terms. As it happens, the attitudes of both men are neatly folded in an anecdote – an anecdote pregnant with more meaning than is generally ascribed to it. It was told to Walpole by Mr Speaker Onslow and if it was an Onslow family story it may have come down from Richard Onslow, the parliamentarian; that would make it four generations old, so we must not regard it as verbatim reporting. Walpole's version is as follows:[17]

> When the Earl of Bedford sent for Inigo, he told him he wanted a chapel for the parishioners of Covent Garden, but added he would not go to any considerable expense; 'In short', said he, 'I would not have it much better than a barn.' 'Well! then', said Jones, 'You shall have the handsomest barn in England.'

The manifest point of the story is the antithesis between the financier's dour economic challenge and the artist's gay, paradoxical response; and that is good enough. But there may be a little more to it. The anecdote may, I think, have been in origin an anecdote about the Tuscan order.

Inigo Jones's feeling for the Tuscan order, manifesting itself at various stages of his career, is one of the most interesting clues to his thought. The Tuscan has always been recognized as the most primitive of the five orders – the closest to the vernacular. Vitruvius gives a very incomplete formula but makes it clear that it is suitable only for timber beams and must have an enormous, truly sheltering, eaves-spread – one-quarter the height of the columns.[18] Alberti did not think the Tuscan worth mentioning. Serlio fitted it into his arbitrary gamut of five rising orders by making it the dunce – squat and coarse, recommended for military architecture, city gates, arsenals, and prisons.[19] Palladio does not see it so but, taking into account the timber beams and wide-spaced columns, says that it is appropriate to country buildings where the passage of carts is to be considered.[20] Scamozzi describes it as maintaining 'the plainness of primitive times'.[21] Where all the authorities agree is on its plain, robust character. A church which was to be of the simplest, cheapest kind could not inappropriately be a temple structure incorporating the Tuscan order. As such it would have classical dignity at the vernacular level: it would be the 'handsomest barn' of the anecdote.

The Tuscan was not a stranger to London. A striking example (perhaps the only one) was the York House water-gate, today stranded in Embankment Gardens but originally the riverside entrance to the Duke of Buckingham's London palace.[22] It was built by Nicholas Stone in 1626–7 and the design has long been attributed to Inigo Jones.[23] If that is correct it shows him consulting Serlio as his authority[24] and loading his order with several varieties of rustication and a good deal of sculpture, somewhat alien to the Tuscan *persona*. The result has been compared, not unreasonably, with the Fontaine des Médicis in Paris.[26] It is all very well for a palace entrance, but hardly for a Protestant place of worship.

If Jones designed the water-gate, he switched to a very different Tuscan loyalty when the Covent Garden church commission was put in his hands – i.e. Palladio. Palladio took the Vitruvian text[26] with true archaeological seriousness, drawing it out
27 first for Barbaro's translation of 1567, which he illustrated, and later for his own work[27]. Palladio called this order, with its wide spacing and hugely projecting eaves the purest and simplest (*il più schietto e semplice*) of the orders, created in the noblest region of Italy – Tuscany. Here was, indeed, a primitivism appropriate to a reformed Christian church seeking radically simple forms of worship, unpolluted by the symbolism and ornamental indulgences of Imperial Rome and the closest to natural ideas of construction.

Nowhere is there precise evidence of this but I think we must infer something of the sort from his attitude on that interesting occasion when, in 1620, King James asked him for an interpretation of Stonehenge. Stonehenge, he claimed (or so John Webb would have us believe) was a Tuscan temple built by the Romans.[28] By this he can only have meant that Stonehenge was Roman architecture at the most primitive level – a 'natural' architecture subject only to the discipline of rational spacing.

Palladio's and Barbaro's Vitruvian version of the Tuscan was expounded by them as a piece of theoretical archaeologizing rather than as a specimen for imitation. But it was as real architecture that it appealed to Jones and over 1629 to 1630, a year before

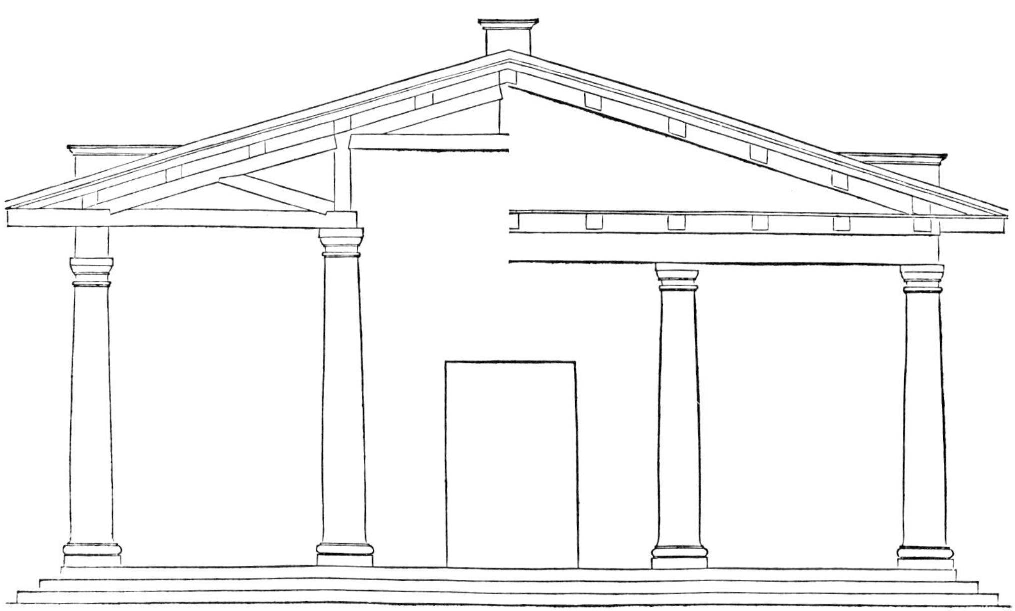

27. Palladio's reconstruction of the Tuscan order, following Vitruvius's description. From Barbaro's edition of Vitruvius, 1556

the beginning of Covent Garden church, he exploited it perhaps for the first time. He was building a sculpture gallery in the orchard at St James's and made it consist of a colonnade of fifteen columns, supporting the eaves of a roof which extended back to the park wall. But the joists extending from colonnade to wall he cantilevered out into the park sufficiently to make a covered area where the king could ride in bad weather.[29] This derives from Vitruvius's account of the Tuscan atrium.[30] Then came Covent
Garden. Here Jones constructed a full-scale approximation to the Vitruvian temple *29*
model – columns $7\frac{1}{2}$ diameters with mutules one-quarter the height of the columns, columns widely spaced and connected by massive timber beams. It is an extraordinary performance, this Covent Garden portico, an archaeological essay probably unique in the architecture of its period[31] and at the same time prophetic: prophetic of the theory and practice of Neo-classicism as it was to be understood more than a hundred years later. The extent to which Jones was aiming at archaeological exactitude is illustrated by a note he made in his copy of Barbaro's Vitruvius.[32] Barbaro, he says, had missed the meaning of *antepagmenta*, which he considers to be in the nature of casings to hide the ends of the mutules. The theorist had made the mistake of leaving the mutules exposed, 'and so I did in Covent Garden'.

The portico is not the whole church. It is, in fact, not even the main approach but only a monumental shelter with one sham and (originally) two real doors at the east end of the church and under the same roof. The church proper is a simple rectangular cell, a double square with a ceiling-height two-thirds the side of the square. It is lit by very large round-headed windows with moulded architraves but no impost mouldings – a type which belongs to the quattrocento and in particular to Michelozzo but which

33 Jones seems to give us for the naked logic of the thing. The west end is a copy of the
east but without portico and therefore overwhelmingly severe. Vestries project on
either side, that on the south having been built as a belfry, and there were originally
two-storeyed pedimented porches against the north and south walls. Internally there
was a perspective ceiling with a painted cove by Matthew Goodrich and Edward
Pearce.[33] There were no galleries.

The church, all but the portico, stands in a churchyard. The approach to this – and
thus to the great west door – was originally through two separately standing gateways
on each side of the church, each consisting of an arch between pilasters, all rusticated,
carrying an entablature and pediment. These arches have disappeared but must be
31 carefully considered in evaluating Jones's design and they are well recorded in Hiort's
drawing. They were Tuscan, not of the order of the portico but freely based on a
variant recorded by Serlio and, more carefully, by Palladio: the lower order of the
amphitheatre at Verona.[34] The connexion seems text-bookish but it does give rise to
the speculation whether, in designing Covent Garden, Jones consciously adopted a
Tuscan 'mood' for the whole. If we now turn from the church to the arcades and
houses enclosing the space in front of it we may perhaps conclude that he did.

The two houses on the west side, to north and south of the church and separated
from it by intervals in which stood the Veronese Tuscan gateways, are something of a
mystery. That on the south was the vestry-house; that on the north probably the
29 vicarage. Hollar's view and the engraving in *Vitruvius Britannicus* show houses of
30 obviously Jonesian proportions with pitched roofs containing dormers; but these
must have disappeared before or soon after 1700, for all 18th-century views show
25 entirely commonplace houses on these sites. We have therefore no exact record of what
Jones built and must pass at once to the ranges so well recorded by Sandby and Malton,

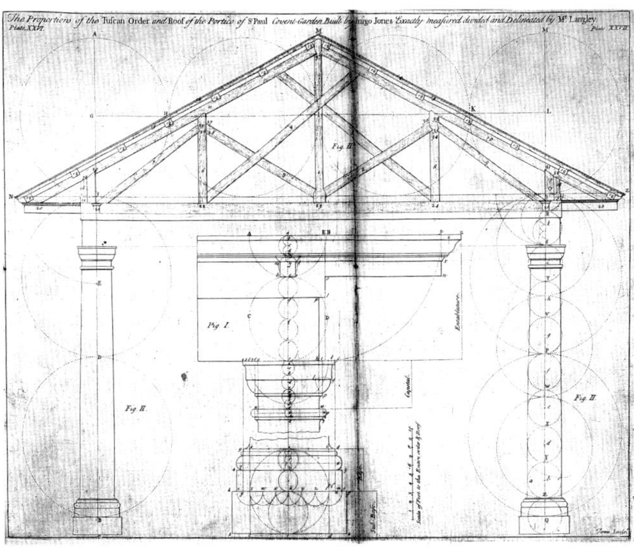

28. St Paul's, Covent Garden: section showing the roof construction with, in the centre, enlarged details of the Tuscan order. From Batty Langley, *Ancient Masonry*, 1736

29. The west side of Covent Garden, with St Paul's church. W. Hollar, c.1640

30. The same side in 1717. From Colen Campbell, *Vitruvius Britannicus*, vol. I

31. Measured drawing of St Paul's church by John W. Hiort, 'taken before the Restoration in 1788'

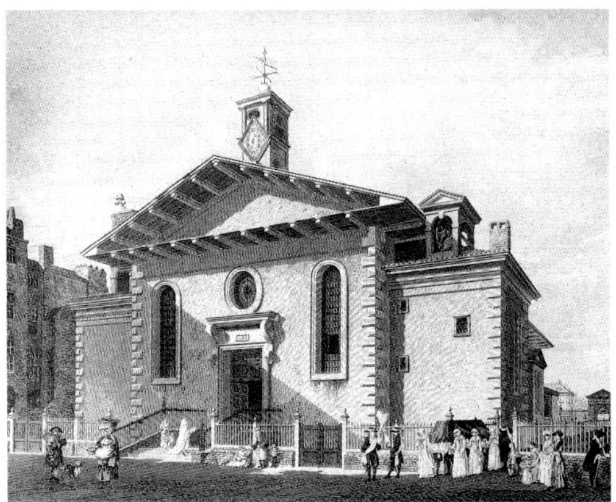

32. St Paul's, the east end as it was before 1788. T. Malton, *Picturesque Tour through. . . London*, 1796 *33.* St Paul's church, the west end. E. Rooker after T. Sandby, 1766

on the north and west sides, the houses whose fronts stood on open arcades within which were the vaulted walks which, absurdly, became known as 'piazzas'. On the south side were, in the first instance, no houses, only the walls of the Earl of Bedford's garden.[35]

After the highly sophisticated use of sources in the design of the church it is
36 puzzling at first to find that the main source of the houses is one of Serlio's rather coarse wood-cuts.[36] Yet it is natural enough. Jones uses Serlio here, as he had used him for twenty years, as a source not for technique but for ideas. As long ago as 1608 he had based the design for the New Exchange in the Strand on a Serlian design for a similar type of building.[37] Now he went to Serlio again for the sake of an idea expressed in a design for a great town house – 'Una habitatione per far dentro alla Città in luogo nobile.' Serlio's house has a steep roof with dormers, 'alla Francese', and in its ground floor and mezzanine the sort of arches which Jones was to build at Covent Garden, though in Serlio they are partly filled in and fitted as shops, 'fatta al costume di Roma'. These arches Jones built not exactly as in the Serlio design but with reference to a
37 diagram in Book iv of the same author,[38] in a section dealing with rustication and in fact demonstrating rustication as one of the attributes of the Tuscan. If we wish to regard Covent Garden as a continuous exercise in the Tuscan it seems that we may, nor does the design of the superstructure discourage the idea. Where Serlio put an Ionic
38 order with pedestal, Jones merely uses plain pilaster strips running up to an eaves cornice equipped with brackets which belong to no particular order and are in fact a miniature variation of the mutules of the primitive Tuscan. Covent Garden, therefore, seems to have been Tuscan from beginning to end, a comprehensive essay in the Tuscan mood – Tuscan all the way from the high sophistication of the portico to the vernacular of the houses – a new vernacular, the first statement of what we naturally think of today as the Georgian house.

Jones's prophetic role as a forerunner of 18th-century Neo-classicism is impressively vested in the church and we can judge how strikingly his prophecy was

34. St Paul's after the fire of 1795. Medland after Dayes *35.* St Paul's as it is today, restored by Thomas Hardwick and slightly altered at various dates. A rise in the ground level has buried the masonry platform on which the portico stands

fulfilled by the intense admiration awarded to it exactly a century after it was built. It was in 1734 that Ralph, the architectural critic, described Covent Garden church as 'without a rival, one of the most perfect pieces of architecture that the art of man can produce';[39] while to Thomas Malton, at the near end of the century, it was still 'one of the most perfect pieces of art ever produced in this country'.[40] Such expressions may seem exaggerated but they are not difficult to understand in the light of 18th-century architectural thought.[41] Covent Garden church would seem to Ralph to be architecture 'founded' – to quote Lord Shaftesbury – 'in truth and nature';[42] to Malton its bold simplicity would seem to justify the Abbé Laugier's enthronement of the primitive and his insistence on direct, uncomplicated expression.[43]

Today, what exactly do we find at Covent Garden? In spite of the 19th-century market buildings which fill the square, the presence of that portico is still tremendously felt. How much of this and of the church is original? It is certainly Jones's columns that we see and Jones's tough Tuscan version of a classical door-case inside. For the rest, it
is mostly Georgian or Victorian reconstruction. In 1795 the church was gutted by fire. *34*
Restored by Thomas Hardwick, it retained its original appearance till far into the 19th
century but by the end of it had suffered severe damage, the side walls of the portico *35*
being replaced by arches, the church-yard gateways removed, and the ground-level raised in such a way as to cover the plinth on which the whole church originally stood. This latter deprivation, of a feature echoing Alberti's sentiment as to the raising of temples above the common level, is perhaps the most serious mutilation of all.[44]

To enter the church today we must walk round into Bedford Street or go through a hole in the wall in Henrietta Street. As for the houses and the 'piazzas', all are gone: the last of them went in the early 1930s and nobody raised a hand in protest.[45] On the north side, however, is a block, originally a hotel, called Bedford Chambers, built by the ninth Duke of Bedford in 1878 to the design of his architect, Henry Clutton.[46] The lower storey is a very adequate version of the original 'piazzas', vaulted much as in the original. The upper part of the building is no more than a paraphrase of Jones, though

36, 37, 38. Left: two sources for the houses at Covent Garden from Book VII and Book IV of Serlio. Right: the last of the original 'piazzas' photographed before its demolition in the 1930s. The Doric pilasters are inaccurate replacements of Jones's plain strips. A rise in the ground level has distorted the proportion of the arched openings

38 a good one. A few photographs survive of the old building on the eve of demolition.[47]

Covent Garden as a whole was finished by 1635 or thereabouts. Inigo Jones was then sixty-two and had behind him a wonderfully productive five years. Since 1629 he had completed, besides Covent Garden, the Queen's House at Greenwich and the new chapel at Somerset House. The Cockpit at Whitehall had been made into a theatre, the sculpture gallery had been added to St James's, an arbour to Oatlands, and the new front of Wilton House was building from his designs under Isaac de Caux. He had designed nine masques, including some of the most lavish of his career, and had been ceaselessly occupied with questions arising from the restrictions on building. He had quarrelled with Ben Jonson. He had arranged the King's collection of medals. And, all the while, Jones was concerned with a task which had come into his hands long before, which had been delayed but never quite abandoned and which in 1634 at last began to be seriously promoted. That was the repair and partial reconstructon of St Paul's Cathedral.

Inigo Jones's actual work at St Paul's belongs to the years 1633–42, but to understand the nature of his task there and the approach he adopted it is necessary to look back a good many years.[48] The cathedral had been in some structural disorder ever since 1561 when the spire was struck by lightning and completely destroyed together with the nave and aisle roofs. Repairs were undertaken with funds contributed by clergy and laity on a national scale and with exemplary assistance from Queen Elizabeth in cash and timber. The new roofs were finished in 1566 but there was still no spire and enthusiasm had lapsed. Ten years later the queen pressed for renewed action but nothing was done. In 1582 designs and estimates were prepared but still nothing happened and when James I came to the throne he found his metropolitan cathedral uncapped and in tatters. To this reproach James was not impervious and in 1608, at the instance of the Earl of Salisbury, he had letters sent to the Lord Mayor and the Bishop of London requiring them to have the cathedral surveyed and estimates obtained for a general repair and a new spire. An estimate was procured and amounted to £22,500. For this large sum – three times what had been collected and spent under Elizabeth – there was no obvious source and the project lapsed. Nevertheless, it must have been at this time and in this connexion that Inigo Jones produced his first cathedral design. He was not then Surveyor of the King's Works but the cathedral was not in any case a royal responsibility. The initiative lay with the bishop and the City. Furthermore, the Earl of Salisbury was behind the project and he was already an active patron of Jones.[49]

At Worcester College, Oxford, is a drawing of the central tower of old St Paul's *39*
surmounted by an arcaded stage covered in turn by an octagon dome of ogee profile terminating in a gallery and spire.[50] It is undoubtedly by Inigo Jones and may be compared with his design for the New Exchange in the same collection, a design firmly dated to 1608.[51] It is a nice drawing but as a design decidedly immature. The arcaded stage is a diminutive copy of the arcades in the Basilica Palladiana at Vicenza; the spire and pinnacles are incongruously collected from Labacco's illustration of Sangallo's design for St Peter's; the dome, presumably a concession to Tudor tradition but with the curvature of a classical scroll, comes awkwardly over the arcades, with four of its eight edges standing on them and four sidling off behind the pinnacles. Historically, I suggest that the importance of the design lies in the overwhelming proof it supplies that in 1608, when Jones was thirty-five, he had no real experience of building and little of architecture and was in fact a painter and draughtsman to whom architectural forms were still nothing but a special mode of decorative design.

In the Burlington-Devonshire collection of the RIBA is another drawing for St *40*
Paul's, this time of the west front – a drawing often reproduced and usually assigned to a date shortly preceding the execution of Jones's work at St Paul's or at earliest to a scheme of 1620 (see below).[52] In its general distribution of columns and scrolls the design paraphrases, weakly enough, the façade of the Gesù church in Rome. On the two ancient but remodelled towers are lanterns which seem to be based on those of the lesser domes at St Peter's, Rome. But whatever the date of the design, it has, as we shall see, a direct bearing on what was actually built.

In 1620, when James I ceremoniously inaugurated yet another scheme for the restoration, Jones, by this time Surveyor of Works, was placed on the King's

39, 40. Two designs by Inigo Jones for St Paul's cathedral. Left: top storey of the central tower (1608). Right: west front (c.1630)

commission. On this occasion quantities of Portland stone were brought to the site but once again money failed to materialize in sufficient amount and the work stopped. Jones must have had designs in hand but of these we have no knowledge.

Finally, we come to the episcopate of William Laud. He was bishop only from 1628 till 1633, when he went to Canterbury, but in those five years he procured finance sufficient to put in hand the first stage of a comprehensive restoration of the cathedral, a restoration so vigorous that, seen from some points of view, it was to appear virtually a new building. In 1631 a new commission was set up, this time without Jones, who was made honorary architect with a paid 'substitute';[53] a new subscription was opened[54] and measures were taken to remove the houses which cluttered the flanks of the building.[55] Money did not come in easily. There was, indeed, the princely generosity of Sir Paul Pindar but his was a unique case.[56] Gentry in the counties were very cool and sometimes ill demeanoured, and in 1634 the Lord Mayor and Aldermen of London had to be prodded to improve their effort by a reminder that the King had promised no less than £500 a year for ten years and had taken the whole west front under his care.[57] From Canterbury, Laud exhorted the bishops and they in turn harangued their clergy.[58] Fines for profanity, adultery, incest, and such like were diverted to the cause.[59] But it was not an easy cause. There was delay and obstruction by the citizens whose houses were pulled down.[60] Seamen bringing stone from Portland were constantly being pressed for the navy and specific protection had to be secured for them.[61] There was trouble at the Portland quarries and the stone itself had to be protected from unauthorized use.[62] On the cathedral site workmen were constantly defecting. Only Laud, perhaps, could have forged his way through so much discouragement and hatred. Jones, meanwhile, set himself to produce the most refined and exact performance of his career.

What did Laud and his architect, Inigo Jones, achieve at St Paul's? Quantitatively, the accounts tell us exactly.[63] By 1642, when the works were stopped, the whole exterior of the cathedral, except for the central tower, had been in one sense or another renewed. The 14th-century choir had been renewed by careful replacement of decayed masonry, including mouldings and carved ornaments.[64] The accounts make it clear that the Gothic work was highly valued and there was no thought of modernization. With the Romanesque transepts and nave it was very different. Renewal here meant complete recasing of the exterior in Portland stone, the elevations being so far as possible redesigned in the process. As for the west front, this was in part demolished and completely remodelled to become the background against which was disposed what was, in effect, a new limb of the cathedral – a gigantic Corinthian portico.

41. John Webb: design for a church. One of several church designs by Webb presumably under instruction from Inigo Jones

Internally, very little was done. The choir, as we have seen, was lavishly furnished at the expense of Sir Paul Pindar but we have no date for this work, it is not mentioned in the accounts and was probably unconnected with Jones. Not only the choir but the Romanesque nave were left in their original condition and there is no evidence that any stylistic conversion of the nave interior was envisaged. What certainly was intended was the complete demolition of the central tower, the provision of new piers at the crossing, and the building of a new tower.[65] Of Jones's ideas for a tower we have no evidence later than the quaint proposal of *c.*1608. There is, however, an admittedly
41 rather speculative clue in one of John Webb's church studies.[66] Manifestly based on Jones's ideas and teaching, it shows a structure of two stages surmounted by a tempietto spired by an obelisk, very much on the lines of Sangallo's twin towers for St Peter's and still with something of the profile of the *c.*1608 design.

The restored cathedral in the form in which Jones left it presents us with problems of style which have never been brought into focus – let alone solved. It has usually been the practice to dismiss the recasing of the nave as a compromise in impossible conditions and to pay a cool, conventional tribute to the portico. I fear I have done something of the sort myself.[67] It is quite wrong. A close study of the evidence makes it obvious that Jones's work at St Paul's is at least as exact and subtle as anything he had previously done. Both in the general conception and in the detailing of the component parts it is of the greatest interest.

Consider the general conception first. We may start by bringing together the preliminary west-front design and the same front as executed from 1634 to 1642 and
42 preserved for us in what I believe to be a substantially accurate elevation drawn by Flitcroft for William Kent.[68] Leaving aside, for the moment, the portico there are radical differences in the two treatments. Considering that they may be as much as twenty-five years apart one would expect no less, but the nature of the differences is instructive. The early design has an arrangement of applied orders in two storeys with rustication suggested rather casually as infilling. In the executed design the only order is that of the portico; the front itself is a mass of accurately rusticated masonry uncommitted to any one of the orders. Again, the *c.*1608 design is surmounted by an attic storey and a shaped panel with pediment, between two candelabra. In the executed design all this has gone; the primitive gable shape is frankly accepted, and instead of the candelabra we have two obelisks standing on massive pedestals. The difference between the two designs in this. In the first Jones is thinking of a pretty architectural frontispiece to hang, as it were, on the old fabric. In the second he is thinking himself into the fabric, converting the fabric itself into a powerful new design.

Let us look at it more closely, relating the west front to the elevation of the
43 clerestories and aisles. The shallow Romanesque buttresses have lent themselves to a system of broad plain pilasters going up into a plain parapet to finish with huge Roman pineapples.[69] The pilasters of the aisles are echoed by similar pilasters in the clerestory, similarly breaking through a parapet. Across this system run two cornices, that of the clerestory, which carries across the west front and ties the whole design together, being 6 feet deep, the other, belonging to the aisles, rather less. Both these cornices are based on Roman 'block' cornices (as Chambers calls them) –i.e. cornices where closely

42. The west front of St Paul's with the portico as executed, 1634–42. From W. Kent, *Designs of Inigo Jones*, 1727

spaced ogee corbels support the corona. Such cornices the Romans used to trim off plain masses of masonry; Jones himself used one at the chapel at St James's and a similar one, probably, at the chapel at Somerset House. Here at St Paul's his treatment makes them again appropriate. The aisle cornice seems to have been a simple adaptation of that on the precinct walls of Castor and Pollux ('Mars Vindicatore' in Palladio),[70] but the great upper cornice was joined with an architrave and the architrave had carved upon it lion masks alternating with sets of three vertical motifs – motifs which the accounts call 'drops', which Sir Roger Pratt[71] was rude enough to call 'bobbins' but which in fact seem to have been inverted (as if hanging) leaf forms. This is a strange and wholly unorthodox form of decoration. It recalls Michelangelo's perversely adorned entablature in the courtyard of the Farnese,[72] and there is certainly an association. But Jones's rhythmic arrangement is quite different; what was in his

43. St Paul's; north side of nave, W. Hollar, from Dugdale's *History of St. Paul's Cathedral*, 1658. Illustrations 44–46 are from the same source

mind? The triolets of 'drops' or 'bobbins' made Pratt think of triglyphs and I think that may be exactly the answer. The 'drops' betoken triglyphs and the masks, with which they alternate, metopes. We have here, in short, an attempt by Jones to create out of animal and vegetable motifs a kind of 'proto-Doric' or, if you prefer it, a 'quasi-Tuscan', something appropriate to the massive astylar character of his walls – appropriate also, perhaps to the generally archaic, primitive character of the Romanesque nave he was enveloping.[73] Such a deliberate quest for the primitive brings us close to the mood of Covent Garden.

Of Covent Garden, indeed, we are reminded at once when we look at the clerestory windows with their utterly plain architraves, and at the circular windows in the aisles. The great aisle windows below are a little more complicated but not much. Here the architrave is relieved by a fillet at its outer edge while over the keystone is the
45 winged head of a cherub which seems to give central support to a cornice whose ends rest on consoles. This arrangement certainly comes direct from one of Michelangelo's windows at St Peter's but it is rigorously simplified, blocked-out one might say, to suit the quasi-Tuscan mood. Of Jones's deliberate scaling-down to a robust and dour mode of expression there cannot, I think, be any doubt. Pratt observed it and thought it overdone – he would have been happier with sunk panels in the parapets and balustrades in the windows.[74] I doubt if we should share his view. Jones, involuntarily, was looking 120 years ahead to the dour magnificence of Newgate Prison, one of the great monuments of Neo-classicism.

If we allow the recasing of the nave to be in a quasi-Tuscan mood, we must now

44. South transept of St Paul's, as refaced and altered by Inigo Jones
45. Cloister and part of the south transept of St Paul's

46. St Paul's Cathedral from the west. Compare Ill. 42

47. Palladio's reconstruction of the temple of Venus and Rome, from the *Quattro Libri*, 1570
48. St Paul's after the Great Fire of 1666. Drawing perhaps by T. Wyck

44 consider the fact that in the two transept ends were lodged Ionic portals, that the north
49 and south doors of the nave had pronounced Doric accents, and, finally, that the most memorable feature of all, the west portico, was Corinthian. A cathedral is a very big thing and it seems to be that in his handling of St Paul's Jones deliberately thought in linked episodes within a range of stylistic moods – near-Tuscan for the body, Doric for the lesser doorways, Ionic for the greater and, for the royal approach, the great western portico, the Corinthian.

46 This famous portico had a material if rather mean application to practical requirements; it was intended to harbour the mob of loiterers, touts, and hucksters who made the cathedral nave their habitual rendezvous and had created the standing blasphemy of 'Paul's Walk'.[75] A loftier and doubtless the real incentive was to preface the metropolitan cathedral with a royal offering of the most sumptuous kind. It was in 1634 that Charles I undertook to pay for the whole of the new west front out of his own revenue[76] and the work was begun in October of the following year.[77] The idea of a great porch, ten columns wide, without a pediment, projecting from the end of a
47 structure twice its height Jones took from Palladio's reconstruction of the temple of Venus and Rome.[78] The order, both in shape and size, he based upon that of the temple of Antoninus and Faustina, an order which, to the modern eye, is at once the least elaborated and most eloquently profiled of the Corinthian orders of Rome.[79] Its height is 57 ft. 4½ in. That of Jones's St Paul's was 56 ft. In modular terms his columns were a trifle thicker than the Roman temple, his cornices identical, but his frieze and architrave both shallower. The intercolumniation was extraordinarily subtle. A range of columns like this, lacking the gathering effect of a pediment, has a tendency to

weakness at the ends: the columns want to fall outwards. At St Paul's, Jones's solution was to give a pronouncedly greater intercolumniation to the centre bay and then to close the ends with a penultimate column standing up against a square pier.

At the time of its erection there was probably no other portico of comparable dimensions north of the Alps; and when we consider that in modern London only the British Museum colonnade mounts to the same height it will be seen what a miraculous performance this was in the England of Charles I and what a tragedy it is that it now lives for us only in a few tiny etchings, one architectural elevation, and a hasty topographical sketch.[80] Of the rich coffered timber ceilng we know nothing; of the three marble doorways behind the portico only what we can see in Flitcroft's elevation.

Inigo Jones at sixty-one was an implacable perfectionist. The cornices and window ornaments at St Paul's were all tried out *in situ* with full-scale prototypes in timber with the carved features modelled.[81] Similarly the whole entablature of the west portico was erected in timber, the enrichments carved, the inscription painted in, and the statues cut out in board before a stone was cut.[82] In the construction nothing was left to chance. John Webb who, as clerk engrosser, was on the job from beginning to end, discloses that Inigo reached an interpretation of Vitruvius's obscure passage about *scamilli impares* and had the portico set out with what he concluded to be the Roman method of optical correction.[83] At the Portland quarries the same remorseless standards were upheld. It was only after two years' quarrying that the perfect stone for the architrave at the wide central intercolumniation was extracted.[84]

When Webb boasts that with this portico Jones 'contracted the envy of all *Christendom* upon our Nation, for a Piece of Architecture, not to be parallell'd in these last Ages of the World', he is not being silly.[85] He is exaggerating only in that 'all Christendom' had precious little chance of seeing or even hearing of so enviable a work. It was barely finished before civil war clashed over the cathedral, disrupting the corporate body which governed it, dispersing its property, and raping its fabric. The portico, Dugdale tells us, was filled with gim-crack shops and lofts, the columns hacked to house their joists; the statues were thrown down.[86] The portico did indeed survive and, at the Restoration, could have been and, doubtless, would have been rendered into something near its original perfection. Then came the fire and and the
ruination of the whole body of the church. Still the portico stood and there is one *48*
design by Wren for the new St Paul's which contrives to preserve it.[87] But in the end it had to go; it was demolished in April 1687, having existed for forty-five years, but perhaps for only three or four of these in unmolested serenity.

Inigo Jones's St Paul's never received from the 18th century the acclaim which glorified Covent Garden. It was, of course, no longer there to be acclaimed. In any case, its profound innovations had already been recognized by a greater architectural mind than any which the 18th century produced – Sir Christopher Wren's. That Wren admired and envied the portico and would willingly have saved it goes without saying. That his own St Paul's owed much in its initial stages to the remodelling of its precursor is well known. Not so obvious, perhaps, is the fact that the simple, vernacular terms of many of the City churches derive from what I have called the quasi-Tuscan of old St Paul's. Those trios of plain round-headed windows, those cherub's-head keystones, those circular holes with plain architraves, even one or two of the lantern-topped towers have their origin in the Jonesian style. Not that they do that style full justice: they merely avail themselves of its simplicity. In intention it was something more profound, reaching back to the fundamental sources of the dignity and splendour of architecture in the service of religion.

In these accounts of two great works of Inigo Jones's mature years I am conscious of having included an amount of detail which may seem excessive. My reason has been an extreme reluctance to generalize about an artist for whom detail – in proportion, in ornament, in the whole procedure of architecture – was of such exquisite importance. Jonesian studies are not so advanced today that we can afford to take anything for granted. Like his contemporary and rival, Ben Jonson, he is rather difficult for the modern mind to seize – chiefly, I think, because his relationship to the antique, his love affair with Rome, was of a kind and an intensity which belongs peculiarly to 17th century England and are hardly to be recaptured emotionally today. I have called Jones 'the first Neo-classical architect' and I think you may agree, after looking deeply into Covent Garden and St Paul's, that it is a label coloured with some real meaning. There he stands, on the threshold of the Baroque age, looking (as it seems to us) right through it to what was to happen on the other side. Of course, he is not looking our way at all – he has his back to us. But these illusions of prescience always cast a halo round the master-minds.

49 Inigo Jones's design for north and south nave doors of St Paul's

IV · Christopher Wren: Why Architecture?

50. Sir Christopher Wren. Ivory relief by David Le Marchand. (National Portrait Gallery)

51. The Sheldonian Theatre, Oxford. Engraving by D. Loggan, 1669

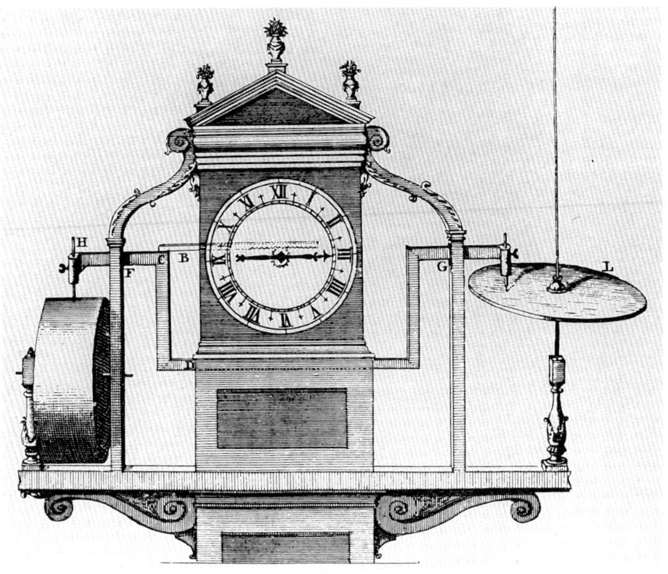

52. Weather clock designed by Wren, 1663. From T. Birch, *History of the Royal Society*, 1756

If Christopher Wren had died of the plague in 1665 or been trapped in a burning house in 1666 he would still have merited at least two columns in the *Dictionary of National Biography*. He would have been thirty-three or thirty-four, and his only building would have been the Sheldonian Theatre at Oxford, begun in 1663 and not finished till 1669. He would have been described as a professor of astronomy and his concern with building would have been briefly noticed at the end of the article. What in fact happened was that, having survived the plague and the fire, Wren not only completed the Sheldonian but involved himself in the restoration of St Paul's Cathedral and subsequently in the design of the new cathedral and the rebuilding of the city and its churches. He retained the post of Savilian Professor of Astronomy at Oxford till 1669 when he was appointed Surveyor of the King's Works. Of the many reasons which can be given for his turn from the sciences to architecture, the sheer pressure of opportunity is perhaps the most obvious. But it is possible to look a little deeper and to hint at the workings of his mind as they relate to the unfolding of events over the years 1660 to 1669.

In 1660, Wren was at the very centre of the group to which the Royal Society owes its origin. It was after his astronomy lectures at Gresham College in 1660 that the meetings took place at which the Society was created and it was to him that the composition of the preamble to the charter was entrusted. He participated regularly in the Society's activities in the first three years of its existence and always maintained his interest in it. He was President from 1680 to 1682.

There exists no authoritative account of Wren's scientific work: indeed, there is as yet no biography of him which is anything like definitive. In the absence of such a work the study of Wren is haunted by an enigma which may well seem more formidable than it really is. This enigma is the relationship of what are held to be his two quite distinct careers; his career as an experimental philosopher, in the course of which he made fairly substantial contributions in the fields of biology, astronomy and physics; and his career as an architect, in the course of which he reached a level of artistic performance unique in the England of his time and of European consequence. The question arises: were these two careers distinct in origin, developing from two sides of a personality, or did Wren's architecture develop naturally out of or alongside his scientific studies?

For us today the problem is bedevilled by those distinctions between 'scientific' and 'artistic' which were erected in the course of the 19th century and which it is extremely misleading to attempt to apply in the 17th. It is equally bedevilled by the element of rationalism which has crept into our notion of architecture, so that the idea of a 'scientist' becoming an 'architect' immediately suggests the application of some special rigour of a 'functional' kind to design problems. If we are to be realistic about the two aspects of Wren it is important to dismiss both these misapprehensions.

If we search the records of Wren's scientific work, beginning with his boyish experiments in dialling at thirteen or fourteen, for clues to his subsequent architectural interests we shall find nothing of direct significance before the time when, at thirty-one, he was actually building the Sheldonian Theatre at Oxford. We shall, however, find two indirectly relevant facts: that he was a natural draughtsman of exceptional ability and that he devoted much time and trouble to the making of models. Of the quality of his draughtsmanship we have some early evidence: it was of the kind obviously acquired from a study of engravings rather than in a studio. It lacks depth of sensibility but has a crisp elegance and, quite evidently, was a natural gift. Of the models, none has survived but we hear of so many of them and they were so highly rated that Wren's ability in this direction may be taken for granted.

The predilection for drawing and model-making becomes apparent in all the spheres in which Wren worked. Beginning with boyhood days, at the rectory at Bletchingdon, we hear of the solar system 'modelled on Pasteboard, illustrated with curious Astronomical Delineations in proper Colours'; and this is followed by the reflecting dial of 1648 'embellished with divers Devises, particularly two Figures representing Astronomy and Geometry, and their attributes; artfully drawn with a pen'.[1] These may be considered as juvenilia but the work he did for Dr Scarburgh's lectures in making models in pasteboard, demonstrating the working of the muscles, was scientific in intention and led on to his work for Thomas Willis for whom he made the series of drawings of the human brain which were engraved and eventually published in Willis's *Cerebri Anatome* of 1664. Model-making became a special part of his astronomical work. In connexion with his observations of Saturn he made models in wax, pasteboard and copper to test his hypothesis and for Charles II he constructed a relief model of the moon. Even in physics Wren's contribution was specifically concerned with visual demonstration. In 1662 he devised an apparatus of suspended balls wherewith to study the question of impact and Newton in the *Principia* pays tribute to its importance as confirming the theoretical results first arrived at by John Wallis.

If we turn to Wren's purely theoretical achievements in the sciences it is more difficult to define any special capacities except indeed a capacity for participating in every field of research – and in that Wren was not, perhaps, in the circumstances of his time, unique. We are very short of information as to Wren's *results* and for this he is more to blame than anybody because he showed a singular lack of interest in the publication or even the final exposition of his discoveries. Of his work on Jupiter we have no details; his methods of recording eclipses and determining the paths of comets lay among his papers till rescued and published years later by his friends; his solution of the problem of Saturn's rings he put aside as soon as he had seen Huygens's results. We have indeed, full accounts of the blood transfusion experiments undertaken with Boyle and of the symposium, with Wallis and Huygens, on impact; and we have his methods of generating the hyperbolic cylindroid and of rectifying the cycloid. But there is really nothing to which one can point as a crowning achievement in Wren's career as a scientist. The diffusion of his abilities is amazing and frustrating to us as it very possibly was eventually to himself. What we can see as a consistent bias in all his work is the disposition to visual demonstration and the construction of working models and with this in mind it becomes somewhat easier to understand why, when he had turned thirty, he threw himself wholeheartedly into architecture.

One circumstance with a strong bearing on the pattern of Wren's career is that he was much younger than most of his colleagues in the Royal Society group. In 1660 Wren was twenty-eight, while the average age of his associates was about thirty-seven;

the average age of men in the provisional list of Fellows drawn up, in that year was about forty. Men of that age had matured before the Civil War and their interests were firmly set by the time of the Restoration. Wren at twenty-eight was still skirmishing among the various lines of enquiry which his elders had opened up. If he could equal or surpass most of them in their special provinces it seems that there was no one province which he was passionately anxious to make his own. There is evidence that Wren had an aversion to already trodden paths. If somebody else was going that way, then let them go. None of his seniors had paid very much attention to architecture, nor had any of them his innate artistic ability. Architecture, which had been nearly dead since 1642 but which showed instant promise of revival in 1660, provided an avenue which he would have entirely to himself.

A desire for exclusiveness is not uncommon in men of genius and in architecture one is reminded of Brunelleschi, who, having been rated below Ghiberti in the competition for the new Baptistry doors at Florence, declined to collaborate with him, 'desiring' says Vasari, 'to be the first in some other art, than merely an equal, and perhaps secondary in that undertaking'.[2] The quick diversion from a path where somebody else was in possession is very like Wren. And one is reminded of Brunelleschi in another and perhaps more significant way. We know that, physically, Wren was a very small man. So was Brunelleschi, and Vasari's comment may be applicable to both: 'There are many men who, though formed by nature with small persons and insignificant features, are yet endowed with so much greatness of soul and force of character that unless they can occupy themselves with difficult – nay, almost impossible – undertakings, and carry these enterprises to perfection to the admiration of others, they are incapable of finding peace for their lives.'[3] It may well be that this sentence holds an important psychological key to the problem of Wren's search for his destiny.

The period of transition from science to architecture belongs to the years 1661 to 1665. In the former year Wren was invited to look after the harbour and fortification works in Tangier. He excused himself on health grounds but this is the first indication we have of his being considered an appropriate person to direct building works. He was very soon building Pembroke College Chapel, Cambridge, for his uncle Matthew and the Sheldonian was started in 1663. A model of the Sheldonian was exhibited to the Royal Society on 29 April of that year and Wren was asked 'to give in writing a scheme and description of the whole frame of it to remain a memorial among the archives of the society'.[4] It was the first and the last of his buildings to be exhibited to the Society in this way. The Sheldonian demonstrates perfectly the parting of the ways. Its *51*
architecture and decoration are immature and remind one a little of the decorative trimmings which Wren applied to his diagrams of weather-clocks. The hidden roof *52*
structure, on the other hand (not now existing), was a most interesting study in the problem of designing trusses for the considerable span involved – a real piece of 'Royal Society' research. So here in one building we have Wren working in both his capacities at once – as a neat decorative draughtsman and as an 'experimental philosopher' attempting to solve a practical problem in a new scientific way. Now it seems obvious to us that these two capacities lie quite apart from each other – that the decisions involved in determining the projection and recessions (the 'modelling') of the

Sheldonian façade are of quite different order from the decisions involved in determining the scantlings and spacing of the components of the Sheldonian trusses. To our modern way of thinking the first is 'art' and the second 'science'.

But these two capacities of Wren's, fundamentally separate as they are, were not by any means in conflict. It would never have occurred to him or to any of his contemporaries to think of the designing of a classical façade as being anything very remote from designing a new sort of roof-truss. The fact is that to them the natural *equivalent* of scientific thought in architecture was classical design. The bond was in the latinity which was the ultimate background to both. Latinity meant grammatical clarity, basic reasonableness – a point which Wren himself tried to convey to Dean Sancroft in the discussions about St Paul's before the Great Fire: 'I hope you will goe to the charges of trew Latine . . . Take one consideration; How that gives you a well-projected Designe, opens his heart to you, and tells you all at first.'[5] Vitruvian architecture, like Euclidean geometry, was basic and clear.

In Wren's subsequent career his mastery of the 'trew Latine' of architecture, its expansion and variability in the light of what modern Italian and French masters had done with it, was far more important than his ability to devise new structural methods. Nevertheless both capacities are present in St Paul's just as they are in the Sheldonian. The hidden cone of brickwork in the cathedral dome and the hidden flying-buttresses over the aisles are the kind of empirical devices which a meeting of the Royal Society would have appreciated. Note, of course, that both devices are hidden, just as the Sheldonian trusses are hidden. There was no question of structural innovations producing formal arrangements which could in themselves be considered architecturally valid – that is a rationalistic notion of a kind which only began to dawn in the 18th century and only to disturb the course of architectural history in the 19th. There was no sense of conflict. Clear and logical structural solutions were the appropriate concomitants of clear and logical (i.e. grammatical) classical design. In the climate of 17th-century England there was nothing there about which anyone would want to argue.

So it seems that the enigma of Wren's dual capacity as scientist and architect is not really a very profound one. A young man of exceptional gifts, with natural abilities as a draughtsman and model-maker, was drawn into a circle of men considerably older than himself. His remarkably elastic mind enabled him to come abreast with most of them in their own fields when, on nearly every occasion, his propensity for visual expression was made evident. Temperamentally dissatisfied, however, his energies were diffused into innumerable different channels. Ultimately, architectural opportunity (dormant before the Restoration) came his way and offered an immediate and satisfying focus for his energies. Notably, architecture offered an outlet for the capacities for his visual expression which he had always shown; it offered a field of work in which there were no rivals of any consequence; and it offered the opportunity to embody theory in difficult, costly and conspicuous undertakings. Finally, it solved the psychological problem of a man whose physical endowments were conspicuously below average.

V · The Penultimate Design for St Paul's Cathedral

53. The Penultimate design for St Paul's. Wren's section on the diagonal of the central space. (A. S., ii, 34)

54. The Warrant design, 1675. The central space as shown in the longitudinal section. (A. S. ii, 14)

AMONG the many problems attending the evolution of the design for St Paul's Cathedral perhaps the most critical is the relation of the so-called Warrant design to the executed structure. On the face of it the two conceptions seem so utterly opposed that some writers have been tempted to wonder if the official adoption of the Warrant design was not a mere device to close discussion and leave Wren free to develop and execute other plans which he was maturing.[1] On the other hand the Warrant plan is, as Professor Geoffrey Webb pointed out in 1937, 'certainly the basis of the existing plan' and the ground plan of the dome space 'very nearly as at present'.[2] The question arises whether it is possible to explore the transition further and to trace the stages by which the naïvely direct and crudely detailed Warrant design was converted into the mature and superbly modelled cathedral which we know. There is, as it happens, some evidence on the subject which has hitherto passed unnoticed. By associating one of the drawings at All Souls College with one (hitherto unpublished) in the library at St Paul's, it is possible partly to reconstruct a design which forms a sort of 'halfway house' between the Warrant design and the executed work. It may fairly be called the Penultimate design because, while much of it is as executed, it retains a strong individuality of its own and includes some features not found in any other of Wren's designs.

Before going further it may be as well to recall the attendant circumstances. The Royal warrant ordering the commencement of the new cathedral is dated 14 May 1675.
The Warrant design is stitched to it and is described therein as one of 'divers Designes *54*
which have been represented to Us' and which 'Wee have particularly pitchd upon . . . as well because Wee found it very artificiall, proper and usefull, as because it was so Ordered that it might be built and finishd by parts'.[3] Although the Warrant design is certainly the design referred to here it should be noted that there is no reason to assume that it was designed in 1675; it was one of 'divers designs' any or all of which may have been under consideration for a matter of years. It is as well to remember this, because the next important date is the signing of contracts with the masons, Marshall and Strong, for the foundations of the South side of the choir on 18 June.[4] These contracts would hardly have been drawn up without exact knowledge of the dimensions of the work to be built. Thus it would appear that a period of only thirty-five days was available to Wren in which to work out the whole of the changes from Warrant through Penultimate to Executed! This would not be mechanically impossible; but neither is there any objection to supposing that by the actual date of signature of the warrant Wren was already well away with his first revisions. As to the propriety of these revisions *vis-à-vis* the warrant, it is evident that Wren had the entire confidence of the King who, we learn from *Parentalia*, preferred 'upon After-thoughts' the revised design and 'was pleas'd to allow [Wren] the liberty in the Prosecution of his Work, to make some variations, rather ornamental, than essential, as from Time to Time he should see proper'.[5]

The Warrant design has been described and illustrated often enough and I may perhaps be forgiven for omitting any description of it here and proceeding directly to
its successor, the Penultimate. This design, shown here in drawings by Mrs Ison, *55*
commissioned with the assistance of All Soul's College,[6] depends on two drawings *56*

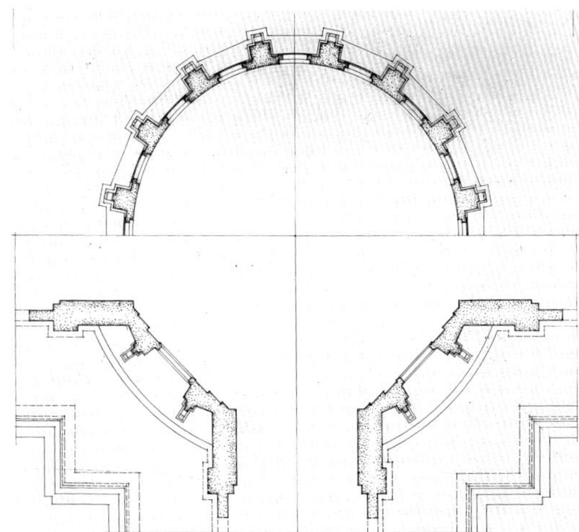

55. Above: Reconstruction based on A. S. ii, 34, turned through 45° so that the central space is seen from one of the cardinal directions. The left-hand half shows the exterior down to aisle level, the right-hand the section through the interior

56. Above right: reconstructed plan of the central space based on St P., i, 14. showing (top) the level of the oval windows of the drum and (below) the level of the windows on diagonal arches of the central space.

57. Right: Wren's quarter plan of the central space with plans at three levels superimposed. (St P., i, 14)

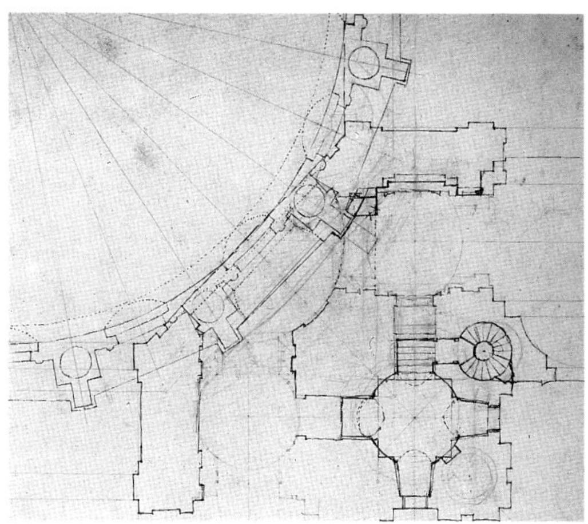

53 which appear to be in Wren's hand. The first and most important is a section on the diagonal of the central space (A.S., ii, 34).[7] The second is a quarter plan of the dome (St
57 P., i, 14). The two drawings do not correspond with absolute precision and in the section there are some passages which are in themselves 'unworkable' so that their intention has to be construed in the light of grammatical probability.[8] But as a whole the design can be developed without ambiguity.

The first thing to be noted about the Penultimate design is the extent to which it coincides with the cathedral as built. Up to the top of the entablature of the great interior order *all* dimensions are as executed.[9] Thus, at the date of this design the ground plan of the central space and the bay-design of the arms were finally settled. Above entablature level the interior correspondence is still close though the attic storey (and thus the springing-line of the great arches) is lower by 5 ft 6in. than in the executed work.

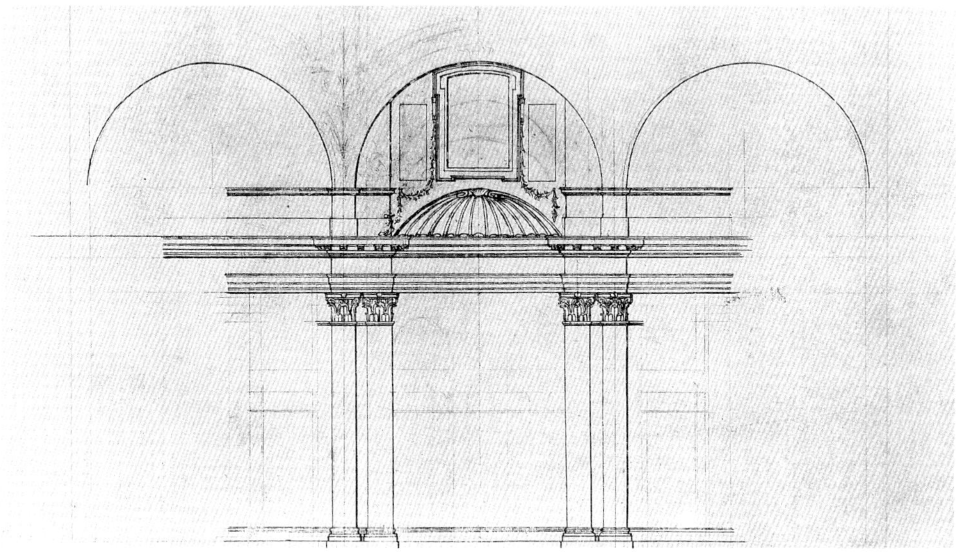

58. Developed elevation of a diagonal and two cardinal arches in the central space, preceding the Penultimate design (St P., i, 67)

The final settlement of the ground plan meant, of course, the introduction of that ratio between nave and aisle widths which had the effect of making the eight openings into the central space unequal – *i.e.* alternately wide and narrow.[10]

This was a departure from the Warrant plan, in which all eight openings were equal. It has never been clear why Wren posed himself the extraordinarily difficult problem of the unequal openings. It may have had something to do with the statics of the structure as a whole.[11] What is certain is that it raised a most acute design problem in the treatment of the (narrower) compartments on the diagonals of the central space. Wren never arrived at a wholly satisfactory solution of this but in the Penultimate design he came very near to it. His treatment here is bound up with the idea of lighting the central space from four large windows placed in the diagonal compartments – a very logical method recalling in principle the octagon at Ely, a building whose bearing on the plan of St Paul's has often been noted.[12]

These windows first make their appearance in a Wren drawing in the St Paul's Library (St P., i, 67),[13] a drawing which becomes, on close examination, unexpectedly *58* eloquent. It is an elevation on the diagonal of the central space showing one of the narrower openings and, on either side, the arches over the wider openings developed (*i.e.* bent back into the same plane). The drawing must be earlier than the Penultimate design as represented by our reconstruction, for in one important respect it adheres to the Warrant design and to the unfinished design which follows the Warrant (A.S., ii, 17). Some pencilled decorations in the spandrel on the left show that this spandrel was to be, in effect, one of the points of origin of a dome rising from around an octagonal figure, as in the Warrant design and its successor.[14]

The relationship of St P., i, 67 to these earlier designs is of great significance. The

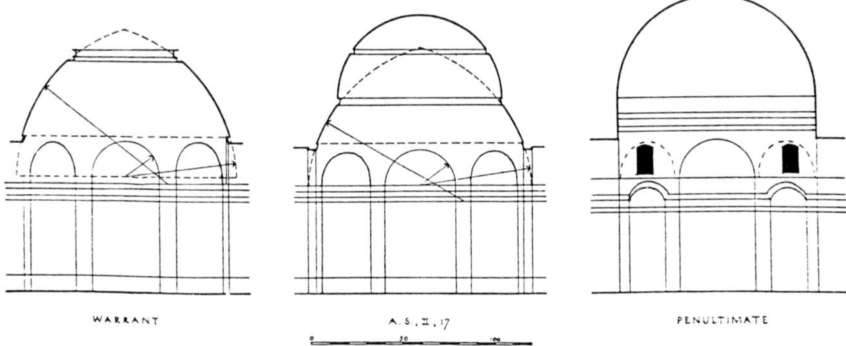

59. Diagrammatic sections of three consecutive central-space projects, showing the transition from Warrant to Penultimate designs. In the first two designs the dome springs from the same base as the arches but takes a different curvature from above the arches. In the Penultimate design the diagonal arches are lowered and flattened and windows are pierced in the wall above. The former diagonal arch-forms are retained only in order to articulate the pendentives subtending the circular plan-level. The dome is now a perfect hemisphere springing from above a circular entablature over an octagonal space

geometry of the Warrant dome is not as simple as it looks but for the purposes of this argument it is convenient to regard it as hemispherical.[15] It is obvious that a hemispherical dome whose base is described round an octagon, as here, is cut by the sides of the octagon in such a way that eight vertical semicircular planes are formed. Where the octagon rises as a wall the semicircle is established by the intersection of dome and wall. Simultaneously the semicircle may represent the intersection of the dome with an arch. In the Warrant design conditions provided for eight equal arches (four cardinal openings and four semi-domed recesses over the junctions of the aisles) and this arrangement was entirely natural. As soon, however, as the nave-aisles ratio was altered and the semi-domed recesses became narrower than the cardinal openings, a new and more complicated architectural scheme had to be devised. St P., i, 67 shows how Wren arrived at it. He retained the old dome-octagon relationship but lowered the recesses, filling in the space above them with wall rising to intersect with the dome and pierced by windows. Faint pencillings show that he considered retaining the semi-domes of the recesses (he tried this at two different levels) but he finally resolved on the segmental niche-head with the shell ornament, leaving room above for a segmental-headed window pressing up against the semi-circle formed by the lines of intersection between dome and walls. The inspiration is obviously from Maderna's aisles at St Peter's. The result is ingenious and the introduction of decorative swags assists it to a rhythmic elegance.

Here then, in St P., i, 67, we see the origin, under pressure of the geometrical idea first adopted in the Warrant design, of the elevational scheme on the diagonals of the central space, a scheme which we meet again in the Penultimate design and which persists, as we shall see, under changed conditions in the executed structure. At the Penultimate stage, however, the pressure of this particular geometrical necessity is suddenly withdrawn. The dome is removed from the arches and made autonomous at a higher level. It is now a complete hemisphere resting on a cylinder. But this raises a new problem because a transition still has to be effected from the octagon of the ground plan to the circle above the arches. Wren solves this by retaining all eight arch-forms with as much of the old dome as makes, in the spandrels, eight pendentives of extremely slight inclination. Thus all eight arch-forms still in theory represent geometrical intersections though the four arch-forms on the diagonals are now virtually pieces of architectural modelling designed to make a neat transition from octagon to circle.

The part played by the corner windows in all this cannot be accurately assessed; their presence depends on many other moves to which Wren may or may not have awarded more importance. But these windows are most skilfully integrated into the Penultimate design. Externally they are emphasized by lateral projectures terminating as consoles and supporting the ends of segmental pediments which develop naturally out of the clerestory cornice as it reaches the window. Internally, they make sense of the diagonal elevations of the central space – a sense which was disastrously lost when in the executed structure, for reasons we shall see later, the windows were replaced by openings into cavernous and dismal 'tribunes'. The segmental arches covering the openings below the windows presented an awkward problem. Wren's first solution (St P., i, 67)[16] is the simplest and, on paper, the prettiest. In the Penultimate he mitres the cornice of the main entablature and carries it over the arch, which again is direct if cumbersome. In the executed design he was to return the cornice against the face of the arch, excepting only its top member which was to ride over the arch as part of a segmental repeat of the whole cornice resting on the first – a forced solution which it is difficult to accept as satisfactory.

Why did Wren abandon these corner windows? The answer is in every sense a weighty one. Having fixed every dimension up to the top of the main interior entablature and having virtually settled the whole design up to the base of the dome he suddenly made one of the most momentous decisions in the whole evolution of the cathedral. This was to raise screen walls on the outer aisle walls from end to end of the building. It is only in the elucidation of the Penultimate design that the fact has emerged that these screen walls were in the strictest sense an afterthought – *i.e.* that they were added to a design which was dimensionally complete. It is tempting to wonder if the cathedral was actually *begun* on the basis of the Penultimate design in 1675. There are strong reasons against this,[17] but it is not inconceivable – in fact as late as 1686 the screen walls and their implications could have been accepted without modification of anything already built.[18]

What is most probable – indeed inevitable – is that the decision to build the screen walls was connected with the equally weighty decision to substitute for the low Penultimate dome a drum and dome of the present immense stature. Such a structure could involve greater lateral thrusts and a need for correspondingly greater abutments, which is precisely what the screen walls supply. These walls further enabled Wren to introduce (but conceal) the present flying-buttresses. The Penultimate design certainly had flying-buttresses but they were concealed below the aisle roofs and were therefore of low inclination and relatively weak effect.[19]

With the addition of the screen walls and a drum and dome of the existing type the Penultimate design becomes the Ultimate.[20] The square returns (vestries) in the angles

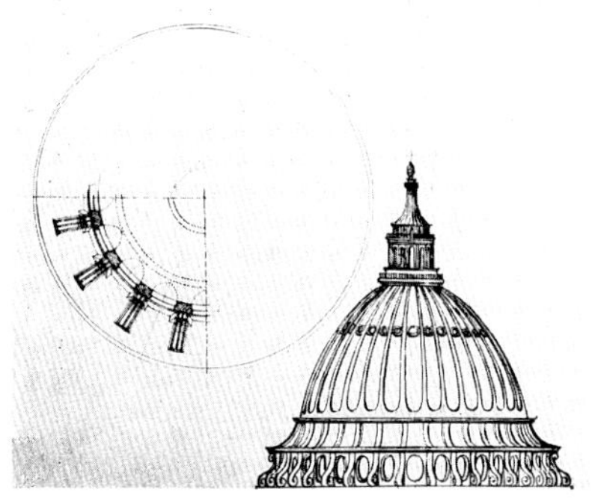

60. Design for a domed basilican cathedral (A. S., ii, 31). The dome is raised on a low drum containing 32 oval windows. *61.* Design for a dome (A. S., ii, 25), probably an alternative to A. S., ii, 31. The plan beside it relates not to this project but to the one illustrated in the next two drawings.

of the transepts have to be built up another storey to range with the new walls and take their share of the thrusts, at the same time blocking the space from which the corner windows of the Penultimate were to receive their light. Something had to be done with this space so the useless 'tribunes' were formed and the corner windows annihilated by the creation of full-width openings from the tribunes into the central space. The tribunes 'admit' darkness where the windows admitted light. The logic of the Penultimate arrangement is completely disrupted and there is a sense of over-complexity and frustration. The gain is in the richly modelled bulk of the exterior and the triumphant dome.

We are concerned here only with the Penultimate design itself and it is now time to consider its most conspicuous feature, the sixteen-sided drum from which rises an external dome whose termination is unfortunately lost. This design is much indebted to the dome of the Val-de-Grâce,[21] which Wren will have seen in Paris in 1665, but its general outline and character originate elsewhere. We must go back to the Greek Cross design which preceded the Great Model and which was probably drawn in 1672 (A.S., ii, 21–23).[22] This has a low drum with thirty-two bays of arches between pilasters. Above this is a concave sweep to a cornice and then the convex fluted dome surmounted by a lantern. If we compare this with the Great Model which has all the same features we are struck at once by the immaturity and poor articulation of the earlier design. Exactly the same uncertainty of the handling is observable in two other dome designs which one is therefore inclined to date close to the Greek Cross design but which are intended for basilican-cruciform plans. One of these designs is given
60 here (A.S., ii, 31).[23] It shows what may be an equal-armed basilican cross or a Latin basilican cross with equal nave and choir. The dome is raised on a drum containing, apparently, thirty-six oval windows. Above this is a stage decorated with swags, a feature deriving from the pre-fire design of 1666. The dome itself is close to the Greek Cross design. Associable with this is an alternative dome on a separate sheet of paper

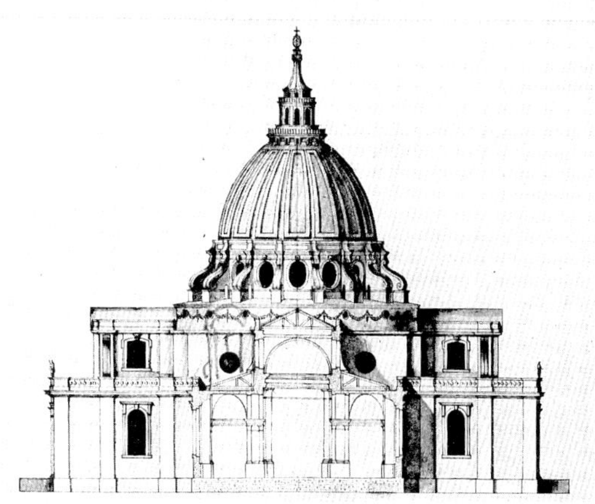

62. Section through the central space of a domed basilican cathedral. (A. S., ii, 17) *63.* Section through the nave of the same cathedral, showing the exterior of the dome and transepts. (A. S., ii, 32)

(A.S., ii, 25).[24] Here again there is a low drum with thirty-six oval windows but they are *61*
separated by consoles. Again, the handling is crude.

Now, on this last drawing is a well-drawn plan which is not a plan of the dome
shown but of a different dome altogether, given in elevation and section on two further *62*
drawings (A.S., ii, 17 and 32).[25] These drawings show a design to which reference has *63*
already been made in connexion with the dome-and-wall intersections in the central space. That they are later than the Warrant design is almost certain, the main clue being the adoption of segmental-headed windows in the clerestory, a feature which persists in the Penultimate and executed designs. Here the grotesque steeple of the Warrant design is abandoned and replaced by an outer dome of great delicacy which does in fact lead directly to the outer dome of the Penultimate. But it also looks back to the series associated with the Greek Cross design.

What this seems to prove is that in proceeding from the Warrant design Wren went back to sketches made at least three years earlier, and re-thought the ideas so crudely and amateurishly expressed in them. To this re-thinking he brought a confident technique based on Mansart and Lemercier. On the face of it, it is curious that his full appreciation of the French masters should have been so long delayed after the Paris visit of 1665 but the fact is that it took eight to ten years for the *modénature* of the Frenchmen to sink deep into Wren's personal style. One factor which may well have prevented an earlier acceptance of it was a conscientious preference for the antique, seen chiefly through Palladio. The Pantheon, the *Templum Pacis*, the Theatre of Marcellus and the Palladianism of Inigo Jones claimed Wren's loyalty and are reflected in most of the designs preceding the Great Model. From the Great Model onwards, the language of Mansart and Lemercier, restudied no doubt through engravings, became a part of Wren's own. The dome of the Penultimate design is an intricate fusion of influences. The general profile goes back, as we have seen, to the Greek Cross design and thus to Sangallo. The oval windows were an early predilection, doubtless inherited from Inigo Jones who used them in his west towers; but now they are ordered in the manner of the roundels at the Val-de-Grâce with consoles reaching to a cornice, above which is a blocking-course carrying candelabra – another Val-de-Grâce inspiration. But behind Wren's candelabra is an attic storey which comes from the Great Model and thus ultimately from Bramante's cupola for St Peter's.

The recovery of the Penultimate design helps considerably in making historic sense out of the last phase in the designing of St Paul's. It shows that there is no mystery about it and that Wren did in fact wrest his final results out of continual modification of the Warrant design, bringing into play some new ideas and others which had evolved years earlier and been laid aside. The Penultimate is worth recovering for its own sake and especially for the fine handling of the diagonal lighting. It also serves to explain, if not to excuse, those features of the central space which have hitherto seemed incomprehensible examples of hard-driven ingenuity.

Postscript (1989)

Up to this point we have been looking at the design from inside outwards. We have followed it nearly all the way to structural completion but without considering what sort of a building would meet the eye of an external observer. The drawings so far perused do not help. Kerry Downes, however, in his catalogue of the cathedral drawings (1989), has made a case for three, or possibly five more drawings in the St Paul's Collection as forming part of the Penultimate set. The most important of these is St P. 27 which shows the upper part of a transept with an array of Corinthian pilasters under a segmented pediment. It is clear from this drawing that the pilasters continue round the corners to left and right and are to be paraded on the east and west sides of the transept. That being so, where do they stop? It seems inevitable that when Wren drew St P. 27 he had in mind a pilaster order at clerestory level going all round the cathedral, its entablature uniting with the cornice which rides over the windows in the diagonal bays. What is more nearly certain is that the aisles were to have an exterior Corinthian order of their own – it is shown in St P. 59 (a half-section through the choir). These would be in pairs as in the existing building.

Pilasters on the aisles and a secondary pilaster order on the clerestory is not an arrangement which Wren would be likely to accept. It ran against the classical tradition of church-building and would involve an ugly hiatus and a loss of integrity.

Anyway, it was not, so far as we know, drawn out, and may have been seen at once as a vulnerable aspect of the Penultimate design. But what settled its fate was, of course, the decision to build the screen walls. With these the whole exterior character of the cathedral changed: it became a composition of great rectangular masses, governed by a system of superimposed Corinthian orders (the upper order later becoming Composite). The diagonal lighting of the central space was destroyed and the central space itself prepared for a dome and drum of much greater height. The Penultimate was lost to sight in the Ultimate.

VI · The Classical Country House in 18th-century England

64. Ideal Anglo-Palladian villa. From Robert Morris, *Essay in Defence of Ancient Architecture*, 1728

65. Claremont, Surrey, in its park. (See also ill. 96)

Patronage and performance 1710–40

THE STUDY of the 18th-century country house is at present somewhat lop-sided.[1] Although much has been printed on the subject, all the best work is in the form either of studies of individual houses or studies of the lives and works of individual architects. I know no history of the English country house which attempts to give an accurate, connected account of its changes of form through the 18th century. Indeed, the data required to give such an account have scarcely as yet been adequately surveyed. Nobody, I believe, has attempted to estimate the number of country houses built, the amount of money spent on them, or their distribution throughout the kingdom – elementary desiderata, surely, if country-house building is to be considered historically; and essential if changes in architectural character are to be properly observed. This state of affairs arises from obvious causes. It is only fairly recently that architectural history has come to be considered a 'legitimate' study and, where the 18th century is concerned, it is still dominated by the idea of a succession of architectural personalities; the study of *types* of buildings, their economy and distribution, is very backward. Then again, the study of the country house is still largely conditioned by what one may call 'guide-book' interest. Existing houses have received more attention than houses known only from records; houses accessible to the public (a category happily much increased in the past ten years) receive more attention than the inaccessible.

Within these limitations the work done on the 18th-century country house is substantial. It is now nearly seventy years since the late H. Avray Tipping began writing country-house articles for the weekly magazine, *Country Life*.[2] Tipping, with Christopher Hussey, his successor, and other contributors, have built up an incomparable library of information on English houses, their builders and architects, the cream of which (the architectural cream) has been republished in separate volumes.[3] In the architectural-biographical sphere the outstanding modern achievement is H. M. Colvin's *Biographical Dictionary of English Architects 1660–1840* (1954; 2nd ed. 1978), a work which draws together the information in all the older printed sources and adds to it a mass of original research. Colvin and the *Country Life* files together provide an excellent basis for the study of the country house. There is, however, a long way to go before a perspective of the whole subject can be set up. It means among other things giving to patronage and the economics of patronage at least as much study as has already been given to architectural performance.

I cannot, in these essays, take the matter of patronage and its relation to performance very far, but I propose to try at least to start on the right foot by examining it within the vital period 1710–40. If we obtain even the roughest idea of what was happening in those years the architectural issues then and later become readily comprehensible.

A numerical assessment of country houses built between 1710 and 1740 will be very difficult to reach. Even if all the facts were at our disposal we should have to ask ourselves what exactly we mean by 'a country house' in point of size and use, and how much or how little of an old house has to be re-built to constitute something significantly new. A survey on the basis of expenditure would be the most satisfactory, but that is obviously out of the question from lack of data. All we can do at present is to scrape together as many instances as possible of buildings or substantial re-buildings within those years and regard the aggregate as something from which we may draw tentative conclusions, remembering that our sources are nearly all tainted by the tendency to record houses of architectural or historical distinction in preference to others.

It is quite easy to compile a list of about 150 large country houses built in England between 1710 and 1740, the majority being securely dated and their builders and sometimes their designers known.[4] If we arrange these houses in chronological order (date of commencement being preferred to date of completion) we are faced at once with a most striking phenomenon. Out of 148 houses, 21 are datable to 1710–14, 22 to 1715–19, but no fewer than 50 to 1720–4. Continuing by five-year periods, the next figures are 22, 21 and 11 (average 18 up to 1740) and on an aggregate of 83 houses assembled on the same basis for the next twenty years, the average is between 20 and 21 right up to 1760, the outside figures being 15 and 23.

Even allowing for the inadequate basis of our assessment and the merely approximate dating of some of the houses, it does look as if there was a startling onset of country-house building enterprise between 1720 and 1724. The remoter causes of this are embedded in economic and social history and cannot be dealt with here, but there are architectural implications, and these are also to a certain extent causes. At the beginning of a building boom it is reasonable to suspect a latent stylistic factor. There is likely to be some fashionable architectural issue which becomes identified with the spirit of enterprise of the moment. A new style expands with the boom and is even, to a certain limited extent, one of its psychological causes, the desire to build being enhanced by the vanity of building in the new, the challenging style of the moment.

That this was the case over the period 1720 to 1724 is obvious. Those were the years of the first upsurge of what is called the 'Palladian' movement, and although by no means all the houses built then are 'Palladian', it was certainly that boom which carried the style to its long tenure of authority. Conversely it is possible to cite cases where the spirit of Palladianism quickened the desire to build.

The economic implications of the country-house boom of 1720–4 are of obvious interest, especially in view of the fact that 1720 was a year calculated to stop building enterprise rather than to start it. It is the architectural implications, however, which are my sole business here. These are fairly complicated and it is necessary to consider the English attitude to the country house and the change in that attitude which had taken place since the end of the 17th century.

In England after the Civil War country-house architecture was, by and large, reserved and repetitive. There was one basic type of house being built, the type conspicuously exemplified in Clarendon House, Piccadilly, built for Lord Chancellor Clarendon in 1664. This famous model was the culmination of a series of houses built by its architect, Roger Pratt, since about 1650 in various parts of England and containing some elements carried over from the Court architecture of Inigo Jones.[5] Clarendon House having been demolished in 1675, the type can most conveniently be
66 studied in a house like Belton, Lincs. (1685–8), which is a contracted version of it.[6] The

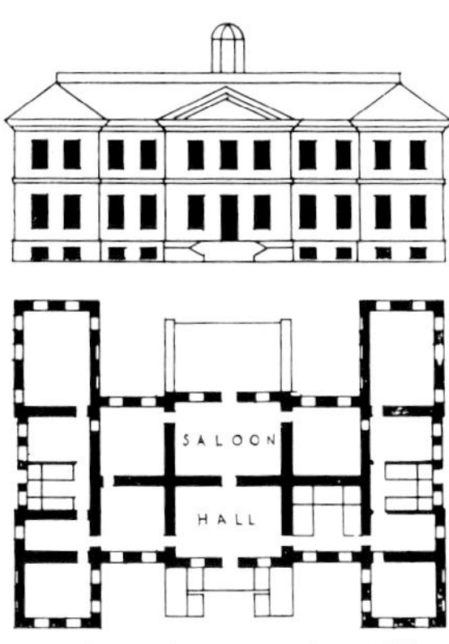

66. Belton, Lincolnshire, plan and front elevation

house consists essentially of a 'double pile' – i.e., an oblong divided along its long axis by a 'spine' wall. On the short axis are the two main apartments of the house – the *hall* and the *saloon*, the latter entered from the former. Attached at right angles to the main body of the house are four wings, projecting farther on one side than on the other. Finally, the centre part of the body of the house (the part containing hall and saloon) projects very slightly on both sides.

What is absolutely essential to this type of plan is the central combination of hall and saloon together with the compartments on either side. This part of the plan alone makes a characteristic 17th-century house of the smaller type, with a seven-window front and a pediment over the three-window projection in the centre. This nucleus can be elongated and remain complete; and to the elongated version wings may be added – two pairs (as at Belton) or one pair or, instead of wings, mere projections corresponding with that at the centre.

The 'bones' of this plan, and its easy expansion or contraction, must be constantly borne in mind, for it is the diagrammatic basis of the English country house for about a century – say from 1665 to 1765. During that period all departures from it are significant; while radical stylistic changes hardly succeed in distorting it.

The repetition of this type of house – short or long, two storey or three, brick or stone, enriched or unenriched, constitutes the standard country-house architecture of the later 17th century;[7] and it is against this repetitive background that we can study the architectural events which lead to the change of attitude in the new century. After the restoration of Charles II three houses stand out in sharp relief. First comes the house, dramatized as a 'capitol', which the first Duke of Newcastle began to build on the site of Nottingham Castle in 1674.[8] Second comes Thoresby, built for the fourth Earl of Kingston about 1683–5.[9] And thirdly, and most important, comes Chatsworth, begun by the fourth Earl (later first Duke) of Devonshire in 1686.[10] The first two of these houses are striking enough as architecture. The third, Chatsworth, is something more. It inaugurates an artistic revolution which is the counterpart of the political revolution in which the earl was so prominent a leader. The continental grandeur of Chatsworth was a challenge not merely to the Belton style of house-building but to the Court style itself – or to what would have been the Court style had Webb's Greenwich and Wren's

Winchester palaces been completed in addition to May's work at Windsor. Chatsworth was the first flaunting symbol in architecture of territorial Whiggery.

Chatsworth was finished in the year of the duke's death, 1707. By then Castle Howard had been begun (1699) by the young third Earl of Carlisle, a Whig of the second generation. If Chatsworth threw down the challenge to Court patronage of architecture, Castle Howard celebrated the capture of that patronage and did so in a most literal sense, for Castle Howard can be shown to have evolved, in plan and silhouette, from a scheme for Greenwich hospital designed by Wren in 1694.[11] Wren in the whole of his long career built, probably, no more than one country house,[12] and that was of small consequence. Both Chatsworth and Castle Howard were designed by men twenty and thirty years younger than he and who at one time or another held office under him in the Royal Works, but whose reputations were made not in the Works but in the building of country houses. In the period 1689 to 1718, the years during which Wren's career at the Works overlaps those of Talman and Vanbrugh, one could demonstrate in detail the transfer of authority in architecture from the Court to the landed oligarchs. By Wren's dismissal in the latter year it was completed; but the critical phase was around 1700 when a series of important houses, all by Court architects, began to rise in different parts of the country – Secretary Blathwayt's house at Dyrham, Glos., in 1698 (Talman); Castle Howard in 1699; Lord Leominster's at Easton Neston, Northants, in 1702 (Hawksmoor); the Duke of Shrewsbury's at Heythrop, Oxon., *c.* 1705 (Archer): and the Earl of Manchester's at Kimbolton, Hunts., 1707–9 (Vanbrugh). These were the biggest, except of course for Blenheim. The building of Blenheim Palace, from 1705, by the sovereign for a subject, under the supervision of a Crown architect appointed by Royal warrant at the subject's own request, rounds off the picture with symbolic appropriateness.[13]

By 1710 it may be said that the building of country houses in England was assuming a new significance in the minds of those who were able to build them – a national, even a patriotic significance. This had been considerably encouraged by the publication, in 1707, of the first volume of *Britannia Illustrata*, a collection of engraved bird's-eye views of country seats by two Dutch artists, Kip and Knyff.[14] Previous to this publication there had been only the most meagre facilities for assessing country houses and their gardens on a comparative basis as a *national* performance. Great houses were known to those who got about the country but otherwise only by descriptions in letters and very occasional engravings. Kip and Knyff put the English country house 'on the map' for Englishmen as well as foreigners. It is true that their first selection of houses (conditioned, no doubt, by the willingness or otherwise of owners to subscribe to the work) missed some of the most architecturally important; and the general impression given is that England's landed estates were dignified by reason of their formal gardens and avenues rather than by their often antiquated rambling architecture. Nevertheless, here was the English country house on parade, with a few important architectural beginnings, like the south front of Chatsworth, like Eaton, Lowther, Stansted and Uppark, conspicuous against the homely gabled miscellanea. The picture presented was one of opportunity as well as achievement.

In 1708, the year after the appearance of Kip and Knyff's first volume, Vanbrugh was writing to Lord Manchester: 'All the World are running Mad after Building, as far as they can reach.'[15] By 'all the World', Vanbrugh will have meant the circle of politically important Whigs in which he and his correspondent moved, and it was there that the new, patriotic building enthusiasm originated. But a much wider world was getting into a frame of mind to build, and in 1715 another collection of engravings appeared to feed their national pride as builders. This was volume 1 of *Vitruvius Britannicus or the British Architect*, the first book strictly on British architecture (as distinct from topography) ever to be published. This was no speculative venture like Kip and Knyff, but a carefully planned and sponsored collection of plans and elevations of English classical buildings, dedicated to the King and subscribed to by twenty-two dukes and nearly every great officer of state. Of its author, Colen Campbell, and his patrons there will be more to say presently. Of its influence we shall be able to judge by events. Of its immediate success there can be no doubt. After the appearance of volume 2 in 1717 (with a revised list of 461 subscribers) there was a reprint of volume 1,[16] while in 1725 came a supplementary volume 3, not originally envisaged. *Vitruvius Britannicus* had arrived at the psychological moment. The initiatives of which it is the manifesto, the patronage to which its text pays monotonous tribute, were to lead on directly to the extraordinary boom phase of country-house building noted earlier on. We shall need to return to *Vitruvius Britannicus* presently, but for the moment we must resort to our experimental aggregate of 148 houses built between 1710 and 1740 and ask the vital question: who were the builders?

In more than three-quarters of the cases on our list the new house was built on the site of an old house on an inherited property. In a minority of cases the property was acquired and the house rebuilt by its new owner. The incentive to replace inherited Tudor and Stuart manor houses by houses of a modern type was obviously very strong – by 1710 the contrast between the one and the other would be so sharp as to be, to a man with Court connections, decidedly painful. After all, the accepted 'modern' plan of 1710, with central hall and saloon, was already more than fifty years old. A re-building was done if the money could be found, and one can understand that a spreading interest in architecture would often tip the scales in favour of a bold decision.

Especially so if the builder felt an obligation or ambition to figure in public life. In 120 suitably documented cases we find that 27 builders were peers and that of the 93 commoners 54 were, at one time or another, members of Parliament. This represents 58 per cent over the thirty-year period. What is more significant is that in the first fifteen years of the period (1710–25) no fewer than 71 per cent of the building commoners were MPs. This fact suggests a connexion between architectural enterprise and political activity which is borne out by the study of individual cases. The houses were undertaken with a view to success or as a corollary of success in public life. Their distribution is remarkably even throughout the English counties, and it is obvious that a main object was to enhance the owner's position in the constituency which he might represent at Westminster. The houses were, of course, part and parcel of landed estates and must always be considered as such; but it is doubtful whether their function as the administrative headquarters of a great estate was ever in itself an incentive to costly rebuilding. Landed possessions automatically involved political interests – the manipulation of patronage; if the land produced a surplus of wealth it usually led to political ambition and thus to the need for a new house as a prestige-symbol; not merely so as to dispense large hospitality but as a visible witness of surplus, and thus of influence.

House builders who were commoners but not MPs cannot, of course, be assumed to be nonentities. A general might build a house for the purpose of retirement; so might a man who had made a fortune in trade or in legal practice. Or an estate might be bought as an investment and a house built thereon with a view to the assumption of political responsibility by the next generation. And if political ambition emerges as the strongest incentive it is seconded closely by the idea of leisured retirement. This idea had always been associated with the country house, and in the 18th century it became particularly identified with the kind of house which we shall call the villa. By association with the classical authors – especially the younger Pliny – the idea of the villa as a centre for the cultivation of friendship and leisure gained currency and in the course of the 18th century it gained at the expense of the political idea. It could probably be shown to have gained most significantly towards the end of the century, when the bourgeois townsman tended to invest in government stock rather than in land and to build in the country principally, if not solely, for leisured retirement.

Among the builders of 1710–40 it is possible not only to distinguish various sources of wealth but even, rather tentatively, to associate architectural attitudes with this source rather than that. Thus the political adventurers and the inheritors of city fortunes are, far and away, the most disposed to innovation. Lawyers are, almost without exception, conservative or, more probably, merely indifferent to architectural showmanship. Among inheritors of landed wealth circumstances vary greatly. A sudden accretion of wealth by successful marriage may produce the shock necessary to inspire a lust for architectural adventure. A man coming into his estate early in life may be more intrigued by architectural novelty than an older man. And so on. But among the myriad chances of circumstance attending the building of a country house none was more architecturally decisive than the choice of the architect.

The architects of the houses have been the subject of much research (much more than the patron) and can be fairly clearly analysed. Among the 148 houses 112 have satisfactory attributions and represent the artistic work of 42 designers. The most obvious division here is between those designers who were artisans (chiefly masons) and those who were gentlemen. Very roughly speaking, one can say that the aim of the artisan was to make money out of successful contracting, while the aim of the gentleman was to obtain or retain a place at Court, probably in the Royal Works, with its appropriate pickings. This division, it will be seen, leaves no room for the gentleman architect in independent professional practice, and in fact as a *type* he did not exist till about the middle of the century. If we analyse our list of 42 names we find that 17 of them held office at one time or another under the Crown, while 16 can be identified as masons conducting contracting businesses in London or the provinces. This leaves a balance of 8 names, made up of 2 peers and 4 gentlemen who must be set down as genuine amateur-architects, one gentleman who held a non-architectural office under the Crown and one foreigner practising professionally. Naturally an analysis of this kind is too crude: it is full of distortions and in fact it is the distortions which show us what was happening. To take an extreme instance: Nicholas Hawksmoor and James Paine both built country houses during our period and both held offices in the Works. But in Hawksmoor's case his official duties and performances outweigh his private practice, while in Paine's case his private practice was enormous and his official work negligible. The two men were born 55 years apart: they practised at the beginning and end of our period. Hawksmoor belonged to an age when place was everything and private commissions rather in the nature of chance profits; Paine to an age when professional connexion among wealthy landowners was everything and official employment a collateral (though still highly desirable) source of prestige and income. Hawksmoor, in fact, was a genuine Court architect; Paine was for all practical purposes a private professional architect – one of the first in England.

Our crude analysis also fails to take into account the changes which often occurred in a single career. The 'gentlemen' of the Office of Works had sometimes begun, like Kent and Flitcroft, as artisans and were raised to gentility by a combination of talent and patronage. Again, contracting masons like Townsend of Oxford or John Wood of Bath could 'leave off their aprons' and figure in society as gentlemen-architects in their own right and their own localities.

In the course of the period 1710–40 the professional picture moves steadily towards the crystallization of a more or less stable architectural profession – that is to say, a body of men practising on a recognized fee-taking basis and recruiting new members to the profession by apprenticeship. The transitional character of the period is very clearly reflected in the character of its architectural performance.

By performance I mean the actual building output of the period and its architectural character. Of the general plan-form of the houses we need say little at this stage because the typical plan was inherited from the Restoration type of 'double-pile' house, already described. If we bear in mind an oblong with hall and saloon interconnecting on the short axis, formal rooms to left and right of the saloon and a grand staircase somewhere adjacent to the hall, it is sufficient to go upon. But this rough traditional basis was always capable of different kinds of architectural expression and different degrees of discipline, and these require more careful discrimination.

The houses of 1710–40 can most usefully be divided in much the same way that we have divided their designers – i.e., between the architecturally top-ranking houses designed by the officers of the Works and their near equivalents; and houses designed by the contracting masons or bricklayers who built them. One can list about eighty houses by architects having Court connections without feeling that there is any serious liability to error. If, on the other hand, one lists eighty houses not by such architects, one knows very well that the list could be doubled or trebled if lost houses and houses unnoticed because of their negative architectural interest were duly enumerated. Thus the architecturally important houses can be dealt with as a total achievement; the masons' and bricklayers' houses can only be dealt with by the sample. Not until after about 1780, by which time the architectural profession had so far expanded and established itself as to control design throughout the building trade, does the difference between the two classes become unimportant. In the period 1710 to 1740 it is still of great importance if a true picture of country-house building is to be obtained, and it is convenient to deal with the builders' houses first.

67. Buckingham House, Westminster

In general, builders' houses are not original: they are almost all copies of other houses, or combinations of features of other houses, under the direction of the building owner. Many of them take routine 17th-century types as their models, but there is a large group – the characteristic group of the period – which affects the rhetoric of the orders in an ambitious way. There is some mystery about the early examples of this kind, and their probable prototypes. At Hanbury, Worcs.[17] (1701), we have a palpable imitation of the Duke of Kingston's house at Thoresby, Notts., with Corinthian columns in the round flanking the centre and a pediment such as Thoresby almost certainly had before its reconstruction after a fire. But Thoresby's influence elsewhere is unconvincing and in a house like Cound, Salop,[18] said to have been finished in 1704, the 38-ft composite pilasters seem to relate rather to what was going on under Wren and Hawksmoor at Greenwich and under Hawksmoor at Easton Neston. Cound is the work of a local architect-builder, John Prince of Shrewsbury. Hardwick Hall, another Shropshire house, built from 1705 to 1713,[19] has the same sort of towering order framing the centre and the same theme is found in some of the houses of Francis Smith of Warwick, notably the front he built at Stoneleigh Abbey, War., for the third Lord Leigh over the period 1714 to 1726.

The one really convincing prototype for a very large number of houses at this
67 period is Buckingham House, Westminster, built from 1703 to 1705, for John

68. Wotton House, Buckinghamshire

69. Chilton, Buckinghamshire

Sheffield, Duke of Buckingham. This was designed by Captain William Winde and by its conspicuous position on the western edge of London must at once have made a great impression – just as Clarendon House in Piccadilly had done forty years earlier. It is not in the least like Winde's earlier houses (which were much on the Clarendon model) and is perhaps the crystallization of a type which sprang from Thoresby, when it had acquired its attic storey. It may have been handled by other architects before Winde sponsored it. In any case, the general proportions of Buckingham House with its attic storey, its pilasters at centre and ends of the front, its quadrant colonnades and wings flanking a court, set a pattern which was followed for thirty-five years after its completion in 1705.[20]

Wotton House, near Aylesbury,[21] begun about 1704 by a mason, John Keene, for *68*
Richard Grenville was one of the earliest and, before its alteration in 1821, the most complete imitation. After 1710 houses of this type are found every few years, though with diminishing frequency in the 1730s. A late example is Chilton, Bucks.,[22] built after *69*
1739 for Chief Justice Richard Carter; here the pilasters have become mere strips and the colonnades mere curved walls. There are fripperies of a later vintage but diagrammatically the source is as obvious as ever.

The houses built by the Court architects and their equivalents during the period 1710–40 make a much more complicated story. In the first place, the expression 'Court architect' only applies accurately to a certain group who were in practice in 1710 and all but one of whom were dead by 1740. In order of age these were Talman, Hawksmoor, Vanbrugh, Archer, John James and Thornhill. All these men were closely connected with royal works of one sort or another under William III and Anne. Their buildings have strong personal characteristics but, in the case of the first four, so much in common that, in a broad sense, it is reasonable to talk of a 'Court style' or 'Office of Works style' as prevailing throughout the group. The people for whom they designed houses were almost always people of high standing at Court or else moving within a circle of which the architect was himself a member.

Of the architecture of this extremely important group little can be said here. Its sources are in the royal works of William III; its greatest country-house achievements – Talman's Chatsworth, Hawksmoor's Easton Neston, Vanbrugh's Castle Howard and Blenheim, and Archer's Heythrop – were all designed earlier than 1710. In the picture of 1710–40 this is a once great but now rapidly shrinking school of design, leaving no heirs. The two youngest members of the group, John James and Sir James Thornhill, built, it is true, their only important houses during the 1720s, where they occupy a rather curious position, half loyal to old, half to new ideas. In this they have something in common with a very important figure who would have counted as a Court architect but for certain peculiar circumstances. The career of James Gibbs is out of step with everybody else's, partly because he was rather younger than the leaders of the Court school but mostly because he obtained advancement through Tory patronage and was in fact (though not openly) a Roman Catholic. Gibbs held a Court appointment for a very short time, being one of the surveyors for the new churches under the Act of 1711; but thereafter relied entirely on private patronage.[23] He was very distinctly the Tory architect in the great age of Whig ascendancy and his personal style is correspondingly out of the swim. Like all good Tories he stole radical ideas promptly and unblushingly and presented them as his inimitable own.

Apart from Gibbs, the architects just mentioned form, as has been said, a diminishing school and its diminution was accelerated by the fact that from 1710 a very different school was in the ascendant. This is of course the 'Palladian'. It did not originate in the royal works, and if its adherents eventually filled all the important posts there, it would be anachronistic to think of Palladianism as a 'Court style'. But after George I's accession, the idea of a Court style is anachronistic anyway.

Who, then, were the progenitors – the first patrons and exponents – of Palladianism? By far the most conspicuous character, as it seems to us now, was Colen Campbell, the author of *Vitruvius Britannicus*: but this hitherto obscure Scot who had, so far as we know, built nothing but a small house in Glasgow, must have had patrons of considerable influence and perspicacity by the time he found himself in London, in or before 1712, assembling the material for his book. A 'very early' patron, he tells us, was Charles Montagu, Earl of Halifax, of Bank of England fame;[24] another was the Whig politician Edward Southwell;[25] Campbell was able also to invoke the high, but possibly nominal, patronage of the chief of his clan, the great second Duke of Argyll.[26] All one can say is that a wide and important circle of Whigs, in the latter years of Queen Anne's reign, must have been sufficiently interested in architecture to encourage Campbell and enable him to launch his book in tremendous style – almost, indeed, as a national manifesto – in the second year of the new reign.

The movement inaugurated by Campbell's book has long been and is now irrevocably denominated 'Palladian', and this is slightly misleading. The initial intention was not so much to celebrate Palladio as Inigo Jones and the movement was, in its earliest years, quite specifically an Inigo Jones cult. The 'British Vitruvius' of the title is in fact probably allusive to Inigo[27] who, in Campbell's preface is 'opposed' to the great Palladio in possessing not only the Italian's 'regularity' but, in addition, unique 'Beauty and Majesty'.[28] The revived respect for Inigo Jones can be traced to 1710, when an ambitious young Whig, William Benson, who already had the ear of the future George I, designed himself a house at Wilbery, Wilts., on an Inigo Jones model.[29] In the following year, one of the younger Works officers, John James, alludes to Inigo in the course of a report on new churches, in a sense which suggests consciousness of the revival.[30] Whatever the origins of the movement, it is clear that by the time Campbell took it up it contained a strong patriotic element and therein lay one of the sources of its success.

Volume 1 of *Vitruvius Britannicus*, 1715, illustrates sixteen country houses and the selection is illuminating. Notwithstanding the somewhat doctrinaire and purist tone of the introduction, it really is wonderfully representative. Campbell gives the greatest space to the works of Vanbrugh, acknowledging Vanbrugh's help in lavish terms. Castle Howard has 9 plates, Blenheim 8, and King's Weston – the Vanbrugh house of Campbell's own patron, Edward Southwell – also appears. 'Classics' of the previous century include Talman's Thoresby and the same architect's Chatsworth. The standard 17th-century product (the Belton type) is represented by Stoke Edith. There is Buckingham House. There is Benson's Jonesian design for Wilbery. And there are representative houses by distinguished Works officers such as Hawksmoor, Archer and John James. This is all very fair and equable, but the house which occupies the psychological summit of the book – adroitly placed just after the preliminary parade of new churches and Inigo Jones masterpieces – is a house by Colen Campbell himself: Wanstead, Essex, just then approaching completion for the heir of an East India fortune, Sir Richard Child.[31] Without too obvious egotism, Campbell managed to use his book to display himself as the architect of the purest, most classical and, excepting Blenheim and Castle Howard, probably the largest house of the day.

Campbell is the outstanding figure at the beginning of the Palladian episode. He died in 1729, however, and the biographical pattern of Palladianism up to 1740 is made up of other names. The next of consequence are those of two young Whig noblemen – the third Earl of Burlington and Lord Herbert, the future ninth Earl of Pembroke. Burlington's name appears among the subscribers to *Vitruvius Britannicus* in 1715, when he was twenty-one. Herbert was a year younger and his connexion with architecture seems to start with the building of his own house at Whitehall on a site acquired in 1717, when he was 22.[32] Both Burlington and Herbert employed Colen Campbell – Burlington in the remodelling of Burlington House, Herbert in the building of his house at Whitehall, and both took their architectural principles from him. Soon after 1720, however, both these young lords stood on their own feet as architects and gathered about them professionals of their own age, forming two small circles of architectural talent which constantly overlap. Burlington seems, on the evidence, to have been the most intimately concerned with design and his influence and authority became paramount. He brought William Kent into his household, converted him from painter to architect and launched him as a carrier of the Burlington style. He took Henry Flitcroft, a young joiner, into his service and launched him, too, into practice and a career in the Royal Works. Herbert took as his professional lieutenant a mason, Roger Morris, and Roger had a relative, Robert Morris, who was the author of the only serious theoretical exegesis of Palladianism. The names of Campbell, Lord Burlington, Lord Herbert, Kent, Flitcroft and the two Morrises provide us with the Palladian constellation of 1710–40. Those men virtually created the 18th-century country house, and all the significant steps in the process were taken within a decade.

At this point it is necessary to make a distinction between two classes of houses found at this period. There is what I shall call the *greater house* – the house which, in general conception, is in the 17th-century tradition, with a plan following either Wanstead or the older Belton type, and with suites of 'rooms of parade'. And there is the *villa*, a house not necessarily very small but very necessarily compact. The distinction is an artificial one to the extent that it is sometimes quite possible to see the greater house as an enlarged villa or the villa as simply a re-dressing of the lesser type of great house. Nevertheless, the ideas are separable and the separation is valuable in a general investigation of 18th-century country houses.

Wanstead, obviously, belongs to the category of the greater house and it was followed by a series of houses of this order, most of which were the product, as Wanstead was, of new wealth issuing from South Sea or East Indian enterprise. Sir Theodore Jannssen's house at Wimbledon (1720; never finished),[33] Robert Knight's at Luxborough, Essex (1716–20)[34], Benjamin Styles's at Moor Park (after 1720),[35] Sir Gregory Page's at Wricklemarsh (after 1720)[36] were all *nouveau riche* houses. Not all were of Palladian design. Campbell designed Jannssen's house and we may assume it to have been Palladian. Thornhill, the painter, designed Moor Park, but it is Palladian only in the possession of a pure Roman Corinthian portico – an answer to Wanstead. At Wricklemarsh, John James, one of the younger Works architects, derived the façade from Jones's Wilton but added a portico – again, perhaps so as not to be inferior to Wanstead.

In a more aristocratic flight, we have the Duke of Chandos' house at Cannons,[37] finished in 1723 after nearly ten years chopping and changing of architects, and very far from Palladian; we have the second Earl of Lichfield's Ditchley, Oxon. (*c.*1720–4),[38] where the conservative Gibbs built in a conservative style for a descendant of the Stuarts; we have the new front added to Lyme Hall, Cheshire, by Sir Peter Leigh, whose architect was Giacomo Leoni;[39] and we have Robert Walpole's Houghton, designed by Colen Campbell about 1720 and completed by Gibbs.

These are among the more prominent of the greater houses which cluster round the year 1720. Of them all, only Wanstead and Houghton proved to be effective as prototypes for the future; both designed by Campbell but wholly different in their interpretation of the Palladian idea.

Now the *villa* is a totally different thing from these and it is Palladian or nothing. It derives from the designs given by Palladio for what he called *case di villa* or country houses. The English type is square or nearly square in plan, with a symmetrical arrangement of rooms on both axes. The front and back façades are divided into three, the central part having a portico (pilasterwise or in the round), the side parts one window each. The window-rhythm one-three-one is essential to the type. A house of this type has all the formality of a greater house but the window-rhythm renders it totally opposed to the idea of long ranges of intercommunicating rooms. Its accommodation is necessarily modest and its character therefore more in the nature of a retreat than an advertisement of its owner's standing or ability to entertain. Hence we find the type developing in relatively small country houses, especially round London, where the great found it convenient to have secondary houses, or those in retirement from a metropolitan career to seat themselves modestly. The Thames Valley is the real home of the English villa, as we shall see when we come to deal with its later evolution.

The first villas all come between 1719 and 1724 and all are by members of the Palladian constellation. The biggest is Campbell's enlarged copy of Palladio's Villa Rotonda at Mereworth, the smallest Lord Herbert's town villa at Whitehall, also by Campbell. Probably the most influential were Lord Herbert's Marble Hill, Twickenham, built for the Countess of Suffolk, and Lord Burlington's own elaborate villa at Chiswick.

Now these two classes of houses – the greater house and the villa – subdivide into various types, all of which were fully developed within the period 1710–40 and some of which achieved greater longevity. It is the thesis of this essay that the idea of the villa is the essential innovation of the century and that the development of the country house can most readily be elucidated as a struggle between the greater house and the villa in which the villa first achieves the disintegration of the greater house and then supersedes it, but in doing so becomes something totally different from what it started as. It is not a struggle simply between the large house and the small house but between one idea of a country house and another. To present this story it is necessary to follow the history successively of each idea.

Progress and decline of the greater house

Of the great houses of the early 1720s, two became prototypes of far-reaching consequence in English architecture: Wanstead and Houghton. Wanstead was designed by Colen Campbell, Houghton by Campbell and Gibbs.

Wanstead must have been largely finished by the time of the publication of *Vitruvius Britannicus*, volume 1, in 1715, for Campbell gives both the original plan and elevation and those which, he says, were executed.[40] The latter, however, were not regarded as absolutely final for in volume 3 Campbell gives the elevation again with the addition of end towers (never built),[41] while a writer of 1768 records that the house 'was intended to be made still more magnificent, by wings raised with colonnades answering to the grandeur of the front.'[42] For these no designs survive, but it seems that the intention was not lost on some of Wanstead's subsequent rivals.

The growth of Campbell's conception of Wanstead must be studied in relation to the main block of Castle Howard and its garden elevation. This was, apart from Blenheim, the grandest performance in English architecture of the time and Campbell illustrated it fully in his first volume. In the first Wanstead design, the association of the two buildings is remote. The Wanstead plan is a long 'double pile' with hall and saloon on the main axis and six rooms inter-connecting on each side, providing about as many rooms *en suite* as there are at Castle Howard, though not (as there) in one long vista, but doubled back. The elevation is an unbroken rectangle from which the hexastyle

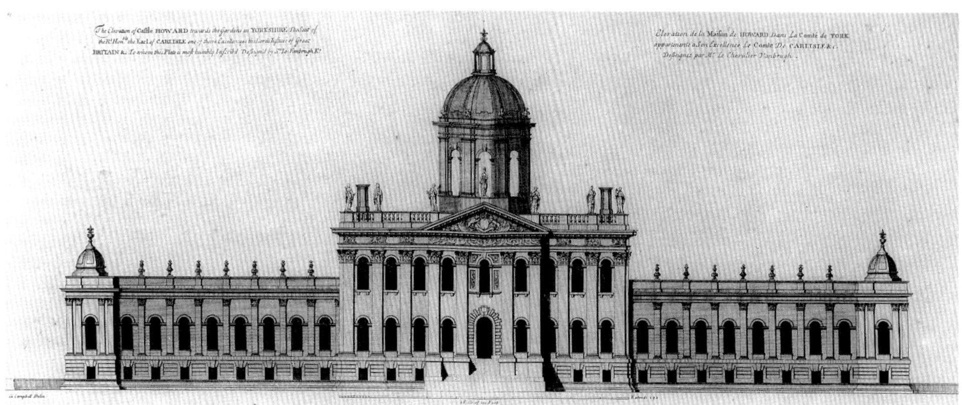

70. Castle Howard, Yorkshire, garden front

portico projects in the centre. There is an obvious revulsion from the mobile and plastic character of Castle Howard (there are, for instance, no pilasters) and the ground, first and second storeys are placed in Palladian ratio.

72 The second Wanstead design approaches a little nearer to Castle Howard. It is lengthened from 200 ft to 260 ft, and is made to consist of a centre and lower wings. Furthermore, in the design (though not in execution) there is a cupola over the hall, an
70 equivalent in silhouette to the dome at Castle Howard. Finally, in 1720, Campbell designed towers to fit on to the end of this elevation giving a total length of about 312 ft, and reproducing the Castle Howard composition pretty completely, though now
73 without the cupola. This complete design, consisting of a centre block with portico, lower wings and towers at each end was engraved in *Vitruvius Britannicus*, volume 3, and was to prove a classic statement by which English country houses were influenced, directly or indirectly, for more than a century.

Wanstead was tremendously admired and, being near London, much visited. Its size and the lavish splendour of its grounds impressed all. To the connoisseur the beautiful novelties will have been (*a*) the horizontal divisions of the façade, basically Palladian, but detailed with knowledge of Inigo Jones[43] and (*b*) the portico – 'a just Hexastyle, the first yet practised in this manner in the Kingdom'.[44] The portico was not merely an applied effect; the roof behind the pediment rode right across the house and the interior Corinthian order of the hall was nearly identical in size and nearly ranged with that of the portico, so that the temple idea was pretty forcibly implanted. No previous English house had displayed such spectacular and rational loyalty to Rome.

Wanstead was not immediately imitated – unless, indeed, we consider the porticos of Wricklemarsh, Moor Park and Lyme (all smaller) to be emulations of Wanstead's. But round about 1733–5 three houses were begun which consciously derived from it.
74 The earliest of the three is Wentworth Woodhouse, Yorks.[45] This house had been under reconstruction since soon after 1716 in a dramatic, highly ornate style by Thomas Watson-Wentworth, who became Lord Malton in 1728. By 1733 he had started the eastern block which is a building in itself, extending right across and concealing the older parts and continuing in long outlying wings to a total length of

71. Wanstead, Essex. First design, c.1714

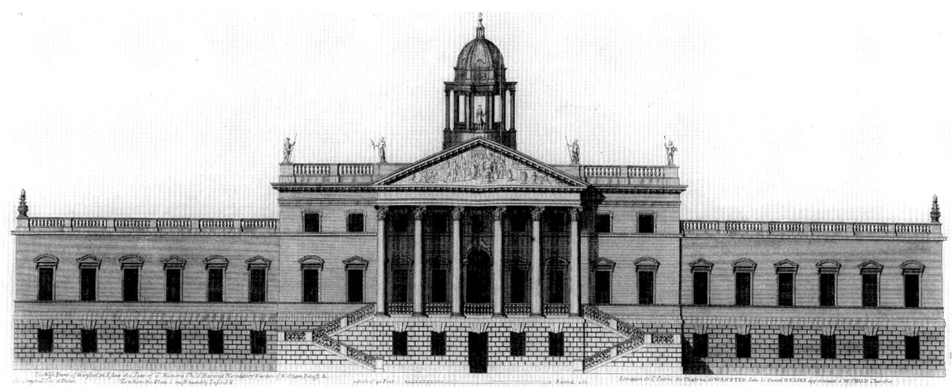

72. Wanstead, Essex. Second design, c.1714–15

73. Wanstead, Essex. Third design, 1720

74. Wentworth Woodhouse, Yorkshire

606 ft.[46] In the centre of this enormous range is a very close imitation of Wanstead. Among the three or four modifications in detail, the most important is perhaps the advancing of the portico by one intercolumniation to give it greater effect in perspective. Next to this centre block, on either side, are blocks of offices with pedimented centres, and these blocks are linked by short curved portions to towers, no doubt suggested by those designed by Campbell for Wanstead. The total composition carried the idea of an extended Wanstead just about as far as it could be taken without a collapse of architectural coherence.

Begun almost at the same time as the great east range of Wentworth Woodhouse
75 was Nostell Priory, Yorks.[47] (*c.*1733 onwards), built by Sir Rowland Winn from designs by the amateur Colonel Moyser and with the assistance of a very young architect, James Paine. Here the main block of the house is a derivative, both in plan and elevation, of the *first* Wanstead design, but curtailed, with thirteen windows instead of seventeen to the principal floor, and the portico (here Ionic) flattened against the house. Here the appendages were originally intended to take the form of four square pavilions linked to the house by quadrant passages in the manner of Palladio's

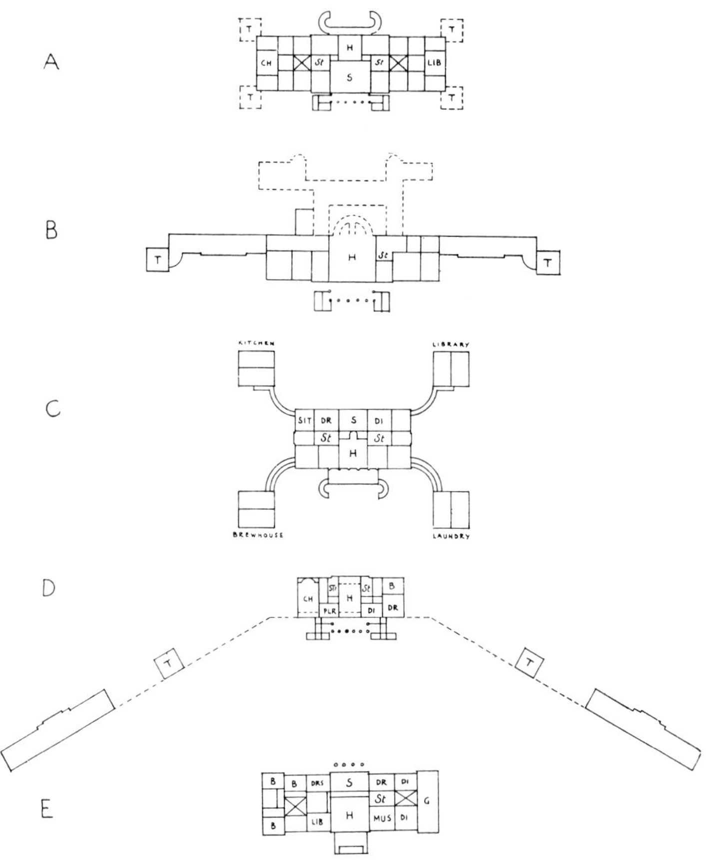

75. Wanstead and four derivatives. A: Wanstead (ill. 73). B: Wentworth Woodhouse (ill. 74). C: Nostell Priory, Yorkshire. D: Prior Park, Bath (ill. 76). E: Harewood House (ill. 92)

76. Prior Park, Bath

design for a Mocenigo villa; only one pavilion was built and the whole scheme was later revised by Adam.[48]

The *first* Wanstead design was again the inspiration at Prior Park, Bath.[49] Ralph *76*
Allen began this house in about 1735, primarily to assert the value of his Bath stone quarries and to surmount the London prejudice against the material. He was conscious of rivalry with Wanstead, for he insisted on the diameters of his columns being 1½ in. greater than Wanstead.[50] The length of the main block here, as at Nostell, is curtailed, though only by two as against four windows. Allen and his architect, John Wood, may also have known what was going forward at Wentworth Woodhouse, for the wings of Prior Park comprise rather similar components. They were to consist, as at Wentworth, of two pedimented service blocks and two towers. But these (in the original design) are separated from the main block, though linked to it by low walls; and the whole composition is bent round three sides of an elongated dodecagon – a form suggested to Wood by the contours of the combe in which the house is built. Furthermore, the towers come between the house and the pedimented blocks. Thus, the overpowering continuity of Wentworth Woodhouse is disrupted.

Wentworth Woodhouse, Nostell Priory and Prior Park, all building simultaneously, all owe their inspiration to Campbell's Wanstead designs. One might go farther and say that any house of the 30s, 40s and 50s having a hall-and-saloon plan, a regular three-storey multi-windowed front of Palladian ratio and a portico contains at least a streak of Wanstead. Having said this one may go as far ahead in time as 1759 and consider the relation to Wanstead of another major house – Harewood, Yorks., begun *75*
in that year for Sir Edwin Lascelles by John Carr.[51] Harewood in its original form was certainly indebted to Wanstead, but its debt was to the *third* Wanstead design, with added towers. And at Harewood this design was not so much curtailed as compressed. The whole silhouette of Wanstead III was got within the space occupied by Wanstead II (as built) – 240 ft as against 260 ft.

Now here, in this gesture of *compression* in lieu of *curtailment*, we have something new. The nature of the novelty cannot be fully explained until we shall have dealt with the development of the villa. But it may be said here that the bulk composition of Harewood may be considered in two lights – either as a *reduction* from Wanstead III or as the *expansion* of a villa by the addition of wings and pavilions. One glance at Carr's plan for Harewood shows that it was as a reduced Wanstead that he saw it. But
91 equivocation is in the air and one glance at Isaac Ware's Wrotham Park, built only five years before Harewood, shows how readily the same silhouette was achieved from the other standpoint. Wrotham and its antecedents, however, belong to the next section.[52]

Next to the three Wanstead designs, the great model for major houses up to 1760 was the house built by Sir Robert Walpole on his family estate at Houghton, Norfolk, with Campbell as his architect.[53] Campbell's association with Walpole begins (so far as we know) with a design dedicated to him in *Vitruvius Britannicus*, volume 2 (1717).[54] This is a highly interesting and, in a way, prophetic design. It consists of a square centre block whose front and back are in effect octastyle porticos, with mural infilling, fenestrated. This block is linked by wings (which are mere two-storey corridors) to narrow pavilions of the same depth as the centre, as in Palladio's villa for Francesco Pisano. The 'villa with wings' is here forecast, though the centre is less a villa than a temple, the design being calculated in Campbell's words, 'to introduce the *Temple* Beauties in a private Building'.

Of this design nothing, except the window ornaments, survives in the house
79 begun to be built at Houghton in 1722. For this Campbell took a type of plan which
80 had been floating about in architectural circles for a long time – a type consisting of something very like the Belton model but with square towers at each of the four corners instead of wings. The antecedents of this plan are somewhat obscure but a

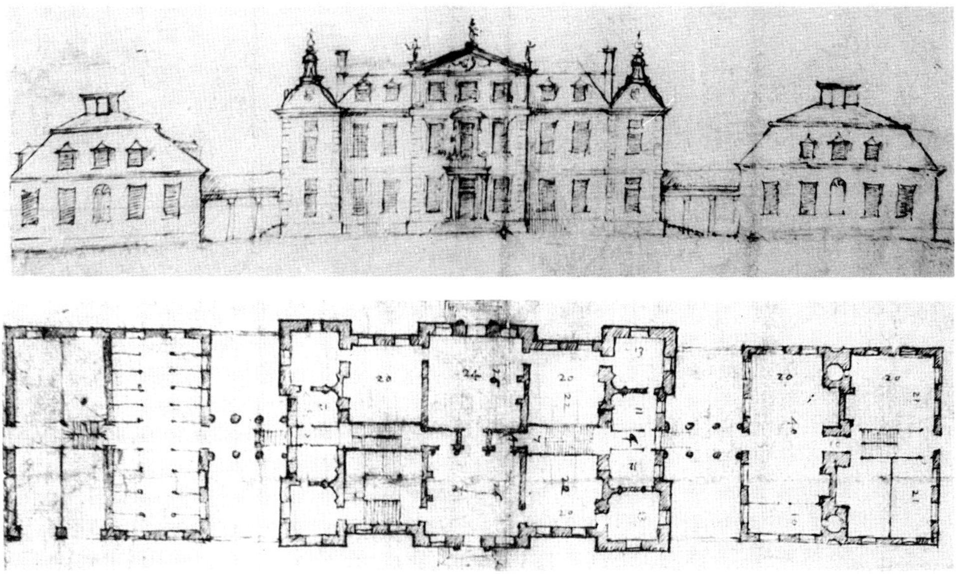

77. Sketch design for a country house, probably by William Talman

78. Wilton, Wiltshire: south front, begun in 1636

79. Houghton, Norfolk: south front, an illustration by Colen Campbell in *Vitruvius Britannicus*

remarkable forecast is found in the form of a free sketch among Wren's drawings at All 77
Souls College and the sketch is almost certainly by Talman.[55] A plan on these lines was adopted at Shobdon, Herefordshire,[56] which being for Sir James Bateman, a Bank of England, South Sea and East India magnate,[57] may well have been procured from a Royal Works officer. In any case Campbell took the idea and rehabilitated it for a new
purpose. He married it, in fact, to one of his favourite Jonesian classics – Wilton. The 78
two Wilton towers became the four corner towers of this four-square mass. Houghton, as designed by Campbell, is a complete amalgam of an English 17th-century plan and themes selected from Inigo Jones. If it is Palladian, it is so only by virtue of Jones's own indebtedness to Palladio.

Houghton was so important for the future that it is as well to analyse some of its parts more closely. Although the plan seems to be a novelty it can be read, up to a point, as a compression of Wanstead. And the towers are, in fact, the towers of Wanstead III, designed (Campbell tells us) in 1720, just before Houghton was begun. But both plan and towers have been thought out in more Jonesian terms. The cubic hall (40 ft as against 30 ft at Wanstead) is conceived as an imitation of the hall (40 ft) of the Queen's

House at Greenwich. The towers become more like Wilton by having their attic storeys pedimented. The horizontal divisions are much as at Wanstead and so are many of the details, but in the east (entrance) front the windows of the principal floor are heavily rusticated in a manner deriving ultimately from the Palazzo Thiene but most probably studied from the end elevation of Webb's building at Greenwich.[58] To Webb's designs, however, are added some variations of Campbell's own, notably the application of the Thiene system of rustication to 'Venetian' windows, with the blocked architraves carried up the mullions and round the arch, a device which achieved great popularity at all levels during the middle decades of the century.[59]

Houghton was not completed to the designs given in *Vitruvius Britannicus*, volume 3. The west portico was flattened into pilaster form; the two service blocks were linked by curved colonnades in the manner of Buckingham House and not in a reverse of this, as shown in the engraving; and, most noticeable of all, domes were substituted for the high attics of the towers. This latter change was made by Gibbs after Campbell's death and the substitution may be partly explained by the fact that Gibbs had himself made and published a version of the Talman (?) plan above-mentioned and had followed its author in capping the corner towers with domes.[60]

80 The plan of Houghton was to become a standard type in the 1740s and 50s. Lydiard Tregoze (1743–9),[61] a partial rebuilding of an old house, Croome Court (1751–2),[62] Hagley Hall (1754–60)[63] and Fisherwick (1766–74; demolished)[64] all reflected its general composition and corner towers (Gibbs's domes seem never to have been imitated). Even in later years, the 'bones' of the plan were adopted for some large houses.

But the earliest and most important derivative of Houghton is its Norfolk neighbour, Holkham,[65] and the derivations here are none the less important for being
81 partial. Holkham Hall was begun by Thomas Coke, Lord Lovell (later Earl of Leicester) in 1734 and is generally regarded as the product of his own and Lord Burlington's deliberations in conjunction with William Kent as drafting architect and Matthew Brettingham as executive on the site. The plan shows obvious connections with Burlington's plan for Tottenham Park, Wilts.,[66] made in 1721, and still more so with Burlington's Chiswick villa of 1723–9.[67] Yet the main block is obviously based on Houghton. It is nearly the same length as Houghton, but considerably thicker to allow for open courts where at Houghton there are staircases. At Holkham the main staircase is worked into the apse of the hall. The towers with their Venetian windows and high attics go back to Wanstead III (1720), though Burlington had already

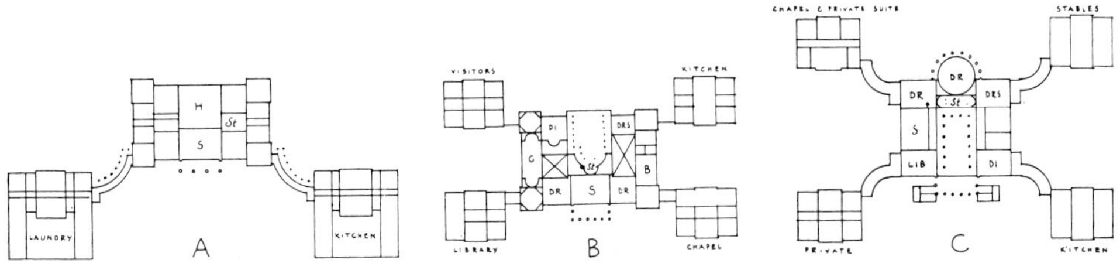

80. Houghton and its derivatives. A: Houghton (ill. 79). B: Holkham (ill. 81). C: Kedleston, original plan (ill. 82, 83)

81. Holkham, Norfolk

imitated them in his Tottenham Park drawings (1721). The projecting portico is, of course, in the Wanstead tradition. In short, the main block of Holkham owes more to Campbell than to any other source. The most striking departure from Houghton, but really a very natural one, is this. At Houghton Campbell made his hall a fairly exact copy of Jones's at Greenwich. The designers of Holkham, more ambitiously, made their hall an imitation of a Roman basilica mounted on a podium.

As regards the wings of Holkham, the case is different. The general idea of a four-winged house is always, and no doubt rightly, referred to Palladio's Mocenigo project.[68] But the attachment of the wings to the main block by short straight passages instead of quadrants is unlike the Mocenigo design and appears first in the Tottenham Park drawings. The actual design of the wings is, again, unPalladian; it could hardly be otherwise, for the wings of Palladio's villas consists of granaries, stables and the like, while those at Holkham are in effect subsidiary residences or contain such important apartments as the chapel and library. Their triple-pedimented façades seem to be Burlington's invention: they occurred previously in the façade of the remodelled house next to the villa at Chiswick and in a façade (now demolished) at the end of Savile Row, on Burlington's London estate. They are not very far from being *villas* in the sense in which that word will be used in my third section; and when we come to look at their next appearance on the Holkham scale – i.e., at Kedleston – we shall find that Brettingham, whose design they were, did in fact use the villa formula for this purpose.

Kedleston,[69] though begun twenty-four years after Holkham, is the next obvious land-mark in our history for its general indebtedness to Holkham needs no underlining. Sir Nathaniel Curzon (Lord Scarsdale from 1761) started to build, with Brettingham from Holkham as his architect, in 1758. But he soon exchanged Brettingham for James Paine. Paine accepted Brettingham's villa-like wings and designed the main block, but whether on a plan determined in outline by Brettingham we do not know. In any case, the main thing to observe about the plan of the main block as designed by Paine is this: it is quite unlike either Holkham or Holkham's source – Houghton. Those plans were more broad than deep; Kedleston is more deep than broad. In both directions it is divided into three by main walls. In other words it is much closer, in principle, to the villa plan as shown at, say, Stourhead than to Houghton, Holkham or, of course, Wanstead. This tendency to reduce a house of the greatest size to the compactness of the villa formula is a more important indication of the extent to which the villa idea had obtained a hold by 1759. And this tendency at Kedleston had an issue to which we shall come presently.

Apart from this important change in the proportion and plan divisions of the main block, Kedleston as designed by Paine follows Holkham and, in addition, casts a look
82 further back to Wanstead – by this time over forty years old. The main front with its portico and steps is a slightly modified Wanstead I. The great hall conceived as a basilica is an emulation of Holkham, and the villa-like wings, as we have seen, are only a step away from the Holkham conception.

Paine's design for Kedleston was never completed. In 1761 Lord Scarsdale changed his architect again, Robert Adam taking charge and making substantial modifications. But Paine's design requires a little further scrutiny for it contains a novelty of considerable importance.[70] In addition to fashioning the hall as a basilica, Paine proposed to introduce on the same axis a circular drawing-room of Pantheon-like character, three-quarters of which should project from the building and give the
83 appearance of a peripteral temple. Adam curtailed this proposal but Paine exhibited his design at the Society of Artists in 1761,[71] so it was not unknown in the profession. Not that the idea of a circular chamber part-embedded in a rectangular block was new. Its source is in Roman bath planning and it seems to have been in familiar use, at least on paper, by 1755.[72] But its appearance in a design for a major house would certainly be memorable.

Paine's whole design for the south front of Kedleston can now be used to demonstrate exactly what happened to the idea of 'the greater house' when, after 1760, sheer size and show began rapidly to lose their appeal. We have only to juxtapose Paine's front and that of a house designed more than ten years later – Heaton Hall, near Manchester – to see the same main elements dealt with in a totally different way by a patron and an architect of a younger generation.

84 Heaton Hall[73] in its present form was begun in 1772 by Sir Thomas Egerton, Baronet and Knight of the Shire, who in that year was only twenty-three. The architect he employed was James Wyatt, who was twenty-six. A controlling factor in the design was the need to incorporate the plain brick house erected by Sir Thomas's father about 1750. This older house, wholly remodelled, Wyatt made the centre of a new composition whose south front consisted of a centre block with projecting segmental bay, connected by colonnaded wings to octagon pavilions. It is the south front which provides an instructive parallel with Paine's proposed south front of Kedleston. It is not really necessary to suppose that Wyatt knew Paine's design or was consciously influenced by it. He would be fifteen when it was exhibited at the Society of Artists; he may or may not have had later knowledge of it. The fact is, however, that the components of the Paine design nearly all recur at Heaton but with modifications which, taken together, epitomize the change of climate in English architecture and the change of attitude towards the country house. These modifications are worth particularizing.

The main difference between the Kedleston and Heaton fronts is, of course, that Kedleston is a monumental composition with a total length of 350 ft while Heaton measures only 258 ft. Then, at Kedleston the wings are separate buildings connected to the house by curved members which are mere passage-rooms. At Heaton, the 'wings' are not wings at all but rooms integrated with the house; neither are the connecting links articulated except as colonnades in front of the body of the house. In short, the

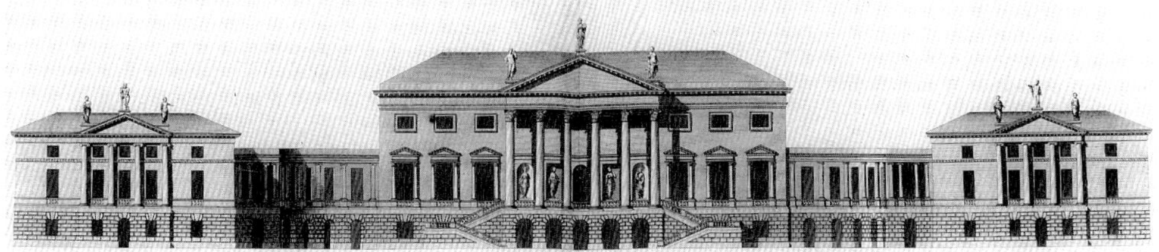

82. Kedleston, Derbyshire: entrance front

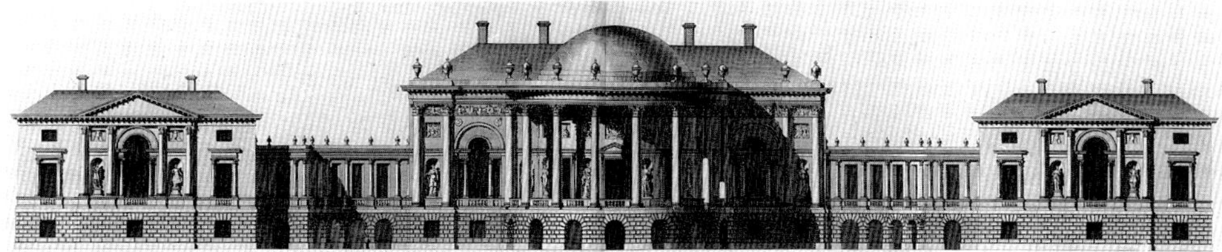

83. Kedleston, Derbyshire: garden front as designed by Paine

84. Heaton, Lancashire

whole composition is reduced and its units articulated only to the extent necessary for architectural effect. Finally, whereas at Kedleston the orders are raised on a high rusticated base in the Wanstead tradition, at Heaton there is only a 2ft 6in. plinth below them.

Nevertheless, in both compositions we have (*a*) the centre block with a domed bay flanked by Venetian windows under relieving arches, and (*b*) a subsidiary order in the linking units leading to (*c*) wings in which the Venetian windows are echoed.

Looking deeper into the differences between the two compositions, the first thing to observe is that a new scale has been accepted and that this has been helped by a new freedom in the detailing and proportioning of the orders. This is the freedom of Robert Adam.[74] It is to Robert Adam, too, that we must refer the lowering of the order to ground level. Adam's screen at the Admiralty in Whitehall[75] (1760) introduced into the London scene a small-scale order in the round standing virtually on the ground – a gesture which might seem of small consequence were it not that it contradicted the established feeling for raising the order whenever possible on a high plinth if not on a higher rusticated basement. In country houses, where the typical Palladian villa ratios, mostly involving an order at first-floor level, were so firmly established, the placing of the order at ground level was a really striking innovation. It gave a new sense of intimacy and accessibility to the house. It also involved a major planning factor. For if the old-type rusticated basement was eliminated, accommodation for the kitchen and other services had to be found either on the same level as the principal rooms or in a separate wing, tucked away from the front or screened by shrubs. At Heaton, the first alternative was adopted, the kitchen occupying in fact the octagon pavilion on the west which balances the library on the east.

At Heaton it will be seen that the young Wyatt produced for his even younger patron a country house of a wholly different character from those with which we have so far been dealing – a house containing, on its main floor, almost as many rooms as the main block and residential wings at Kedleston taken together but all reduced in size and in architectural scale. This does not mean that Heaton Hall in itself effected a revolution in country-house design. It was, rather, the end of a revolution which had begun with the situation which I described earlier on in connection with Harewood (1759). Harewood, I suggested, could be viewed as a reduction of Wanstead III, in
91 contrast to the earlier but more adventurous Wrotham (1754) which was clearly a Burlingtonian villa *plus* wings. It is very likely indeed that Heaton owes something to Wrotham which, by 1772, had been twice published.[76] The octagonal form of the wings certainly suggests this.

Wyatt's design for Heaton was shown at the Royal Academy in 1772 but was never published in an architectural form and it is difficult to assess how far it was responsible for the various echoes of its composition and individual features in later years. The design for Putney Park, Roehampton (built about 1794), given in *New Vitruvius Britannicus*[77] is an obvious derivative, but that is explained by the fact that the architect, William Porden, had been in Wyatt's office.[78] Much later, between 1823 and 1826 the Heaton composition reappears at Holmwood, Kent, designed by Decimus Burton;[79] here all the details are translated into Greek. The centre block of Heaton, with its columned bay, was followed in several later houses by James Wyatt and his brother
97 Samuel,[80] but it is also prophetic of Soane's Tyringham of 1793,[81] and Soane would certainly have studied Wyatt's drawing in the Royal Academy of 1772. But whatever the responsibility of Heaton for subsequent developments, its main importance for us is as a symptom. Here is the sevenfold composition (three parts to the porticoed centre; two links; two towers or pavilions) which we can trace back to Wanstead III, which has become differentiated in winged houses like Holkham and Kedleston and whose centre has come to adopt the scale and plan of the villa. For if we clip the wings from Heaton we have what is in effect a perfectly typical villa as that word was understood from the time Heaton was built till the end of the Georgian era.[82]

Before turning to the villa, however, it is necessary to say something about the passing of what I have called the 'greater house' from the architectural scene. What I mean this expression to stand for will by now have become apparent: it is, in the main, the group of very large houses including primarily Wanstead and Houghton and then all houses dependent on them and on their chief procreations, Holkham and Kedleston – a very large family of houses of fairly homogeneous character. The building of such vast and emphatic piles as these reached its climax with Kedleston. The house at Worksop which Paine, after leaving Kedleston, started to build over the period 1763 to

1769 for the Duke of Norfolk would have over-reached Kedleston, but – significantly – it was never finished.[83] Stowe, Bucks., as remodelled with a new front by Adam and Borra from 1771 to 1779[84] might claim to be the last major effort in the old tradition; and other and later claimants might well be nominated. But the evidence for diminishing interest in this kind of building adventure seems to gather round the year 1760. It is not, of course, a question of a lapse of interest in building, for the number of country houses built, year by year, after 1760 is certainly greater than before that date. It is a question of the diversion of interest from sheer size and correct grandiloquence to other aspects of house-design – notably to interior arrangement and decoration. The early career of Robert Adam and his brothers, after Robert's return from Italy in 1758, illustrates this in a remarkable way. In the first ten years of their practice, the brothers built only one new country house (Mersham-le-Hatch) and that of no very great importance. They did complete or continue a number of half-built houses (Harewood, Kedleston and Nostell among them) but rarely with any great display of invention. All their originality and much of their patrons' enthusiasm and wealth was directed towards interior installations, including furniture, textiles and even plate. Two of their most lavish performances – Osterley and Syon – were undertaken within the scarcely modified shells of an Elizabethan and a Jacobean house.

If we turn from the Adams to the almost exactly parallel career of Sir William Chambers we find that although he did in fact build half a dozen new houses between 1758 and 1768, not one of them approximated to the 'greater houses' of the previous decades. And, what is even more significant, all or nearly all, were on the villa model. To Chambers therefore we shall need to give considerable attention in the next section. Here it is only to be noted that neither he nor Adam – the two most courted architects of the 1760s – was invited to expend his talent on the established form of country-house enterprise.

Underlying this sudden lapse of interest in long-practised types is an inclination to relax the aristocratic and politically conscious attitude to country-house building. This is reflected in the world of architectural publishing. Campbell's *Vitruvius Britannicus* is essentially an aristocratic work. It is not till 1749 that a design manual appears which is essentially non-aristocratic, but William Halfpenny's *New and Compleat System*, published in that year, makes a special point of giving suggestions for cheap houses: he even gives the prices. Robert Morris, in 1750, descends from the lofty plane of his theoretical writings of twenty-five years earlier and complains that most authors 'have raised nothing but *Palaces* glaring in *Decoration* and *Dress*; while the *Cottage*, or *plain little villa*, are passed by unregarded'.[85] Both John Crunden[86] in 1767 and Thomas Rawlins[87] in 1768 show themselves much more interested in making house designs for gentlemen or merchants than for noblemen. Rawlins says that most published plans are for houses that are far too big and which have the offices underground – which he says is 'useless in the country'. By the 1780s the greater house is beginning to be looked back upon as a place of 'melancholy magnificence'[88] and as the books proliferate they are more and more concerned with bourgeois-type villas, cottages and houses for 'gentlemen of moderate fortune'.[89] Finally, in 1802 James Malton sees the greater house as a white elephant: 'How few of the extensive mansions of the great and opulent, particularly the more modern ones, are properly inhabited, or kept up'.[90] And he instances the demolition of Cannons and Wricklemarsh and the dilapidation of Eastbury.

Thus, by the end of the century, the great Palladian mansions were already seen as hulks stranded from the past – very much in the perspective in which such houses are often seen today. The typical and representative country house of the last three decades of the 18th century was something quite different. It was not necessarily small – it might have as many rooms as Wanstead and many more than Houghton; but its scale was smaller, its contrivances for 'conveniency' greater and its sense of 'parade' much modified. As to architectural character, this varied considerably, and by the end of the century the varieties were manifold and complex. But behind it was a single, positive idea which had taken root at exactly the period when Wanstead and Houghton were building, an idea planted in England chiefly by Campbell, the architect of those houses – the idea of the *villa*.

The idea of the villa

The word 'villa' has frequently been used in this essay, but as the present section is to deal exclusively with the villa type it is necessary to say at once that what we today may think of, architecturally, as a villa was not necessarily so called by its builders. In fact, in the 18th century the word was never used with any *architectural* precision at all and in identifying a certain type of early 18th-century house as a villa I am going a little beyond the warrant of contemporary usage. So long as this is understood no harm will be done. It may, however, be as well to know how, in the 18th century, the word villa was used.

Palladio himself, from whom the English villa idea ultimately derives, does not call his country-houses villas; he calls them *case di villa*, which allows to *villa* the meaning of a country estate as distinct from the owner's house. Throughout the three volumes of *Vitruvius Britannicus* (1715, 1717 and 1725) Colen Campbell uses the word villa once only[91] and then with the exact Palladian meaning of a country estate – not just a house. When Kent, in 1727, published plans and elevations of Lord Burlington's villa at Chiswick he did not call it a villa but Lord Burlington's 'building' at Chiswick.[92] Gibbs, on the other hand, in his *Book of Architecture* of 1728, calls two of his designs *villas* (italicizing the word) and they happen to be designs for houses in the Thames Valley intended for the Duke of Argyll and his brother, Lord Islay,[93] so that Gibbs seems to recognize the villa both as a nobleman's secondary seat and as more or less suburban – a meaning it certainly possessed later on. Robert Castell's *The Villas of the Ancients* (1728) may have given further currency to the word but one does not meet it often till the 1750s when it is a frequent synonym for the lesser kind of house. Robert Morris, as we have seen, alludes to 'the cottage or plain little villa' in 1750[94] and Horace Walpole was using 'villa' as a diminutive in 1752.[95] Nevertheless, in 1768 it was still possible for a provincial architect to use 'villa' to mean village as against town.[96]

In the last three decades of the century 'villa' became a very common word indeed, probably for the snobbish reason that it seemed to give an air of distinction to a house which was not quite big enough to earn distinction by its dimensions. James Lewis published *Original Designs . . . for Villas, Mansions and Town Houses*, etc., in 1780 and insisted on the peculiar need for harmony in the design of villas, 'a species of building exposed to so many points of view'.[97] He had in mind the squarish, compact house which had by then established itself as the leading type of English gentleman's country abode. In 1793 we have at last a really explicit conception of what 'villa' conveyed to an architect of that time and it is worth quoting in full. It is by Charles Middleton, a London architect who had been closely associated with James Paine, Henry Holland and Sir Robert Taylor, and so may be supposed to have seized the villa idea where the most accurate conception of it prevailed. In his *Picturesque and Architectural Views for Cottages, Farm Houses and Country Villas* (observe the ascending order) he writes as follows:

> Villas may be considered under three different descriptions – First, as the occasional and temporary retreats of the nobility and persons of fortune from what may be called their town residence, and must, of course, be in the vicinity of the metropolis; secondly, as the country houses of wealthy citizens and persons in official stations, which also cannot be far removed from the capital; and thirdly, the smaller kind of provincial edifices, considered either as hunting seats, or the habitations of country gentlemen of moderate fortune. Elegance, compactness and convenience are the characteristics of such buildings . . . in contradistinction to the magnificence and extensive range of the country seats of nobility and opulent gentry.[98]

Here, the small compact character of the villa is established; it is also firmly established as a middle-class type of house – a type to which the nobility may retreat but intrinsically secondary to the great country seat. It is also seen to be, with some latitude, suburban. But it will be noted that no specific architectural character is ascribed to it.

Middleton's definitions are valuable as showing the kind of social status at which the villa was to arrive by the end of the century. But what everybody called a villa then was in direct descent from a type of house which was not at first denominated 'villa', and to which we now attach the word simply for convenience. It is a Palladian derivative, selectively modified, as will be seen by a study of its earliest English manifestations.

Around the years 1720–5 we know of six houses being built more or less on the *85*
model of Palladio's *case di villa*, four of the six being designed by Campbell. They must all have been building more or less together and it is impossible to arrange them chronologically. The most obvious and complete derivative from Palladio is Mereworth Castle, Kent,[99] designed by Campbell for the young Colonel Fane and roofed in 1723; it imitates the Villa Rotonda very closely but the body of it is 90 ft square as against the Rotonda's 80 ft. Fane used it at first only for a few weeks in the year, to entertain parties from Tunbridge Wells, so Mereworth has distinctly the secondary character which the villa was early to acquire.

Then there is Stourhead.[100] Henry Hoare, second son of the great banker and *93*
incidentally brother-in-law and cousin of William Benson, the first promoter of the Inigo Jones revival, acquired Stourton, Wilts., in 1720, and 'immediately bought Mr. Campbell's books'. The design he then obtained from Campbell derives both in plan and elevation from Palladio's villa for Leonardo Emo at Fanzolo. About the same time Sir William Robinson, the MP for York and former Lord Mayor, was also building

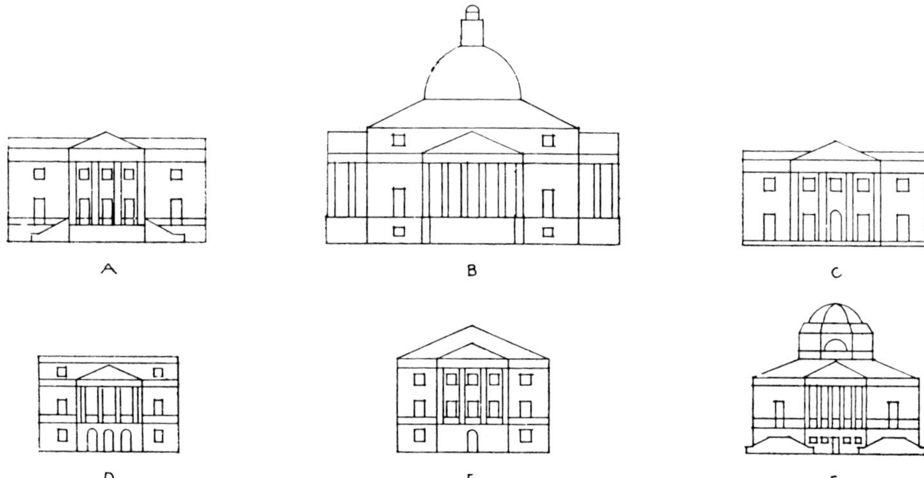

85. Anglo-Palladian villa prototypes of 1720–24. A: Stourhead (ill, 93). B: Mereworth, Kent. C: Newby-on-Swale (Baldersby), Yorkshire. D: Lord Herbert's Villa, Whitehall. E: Marble Hill, Middlesex (ill. 86). F: Lord Burlington's Villa, Chiswick, Middlesex.

from a Campbell design at Newby-on-Swale (now Baldersby) near Ripon;[101] here the same Palladian prototype is followed.

Alongside these three Palladian derivatives there is something rather different – Lord Herbert's house at Whitehall: in effect, a villa, but smaller than any of the three just mentioned. He acquired the site in 1717 and the house was built by 1724.[102] The design was again by Campbell and it introduces the horizontal divisions most characteristic of the Anglo-Palladian villa. The principal floor is raised high and the portico is carried on piers connected by three arches – a device which occurs nowhere in Palladio, but was ready to hand in the Jonesian gallery at Somerset House.

When Lord Herbert acquired his Whitehall site in 1717 he was twenty-two. His near contemporary, the Earl of Burlington, at twenty-three, was not only in process of transforming the forecourt of Burlington House with the assistance of James Gibbs, but building a bath-house in his grounds at Chiswick from his own design, though evidently under the influence of Campbell. Herbert followed Burlington in becoming actively interested in design, and within a decade the two young lords had been largely responsible for the three main prototypes of the English villa – all within a two-mile radius, at Twickenham, Chiswick and Richmond Park. Lord Herbert had the services of a minor Court architect, Roger Morris; and he in turn had a relative called Robert Morris whom he appears to have trained and who became the only profuse theoretical writer of the Palladian circle (Campbell was a designer and illustrator rather than a theorist). Burlington was a more thoroughgoing architect than Herbert and his innovations, as we shall see, were far-reaching. The Herbert–Morris combination, however, was hardly less important.

86 Marble Hill, the house built at Twickenham by George II's Countess of Suffolk, was probably begun as early as 1721 though not finished for eight years.[103] The

86. Marble Hill, Middlesex

surviving accounts show that Lord Herbert was in charge of the house and that Roger Morris was paid for the work through him, and one can imagine the kind of collaboration which prevailed. The main horizontal and vertical divisions and the pyramidal roof derive from Palladio and Scamozzi, without being assignable to any one prototype. The main apartment is a cubic saloon on the first floor towards the river. The elevation to the Park is shown plain by Campbell who illustrates it in *Vitruvius Britannicus*[104] with the date 1724; but as completed in 1729 there was an Ionic pilaster-portico over a rusticated base. This elevation corresponds very nearly to that of an ideal house illustrated by *Robert* Morris, the theorist, in his *Essay in Defence of* 64
Ancient Architecture, 1728, and in his text we have the only printed exposition of the rational philosophy which was conceived to be the justification of this kind of house.[105] It is unnecessary here to follow Morris into his extremely interesting explanations and analogies, but the fact that this particular design – in effect, the design of Marble Hill – was given a philosophical exegesis, goes some way to explain its great and persistent success as a model. Robert Morris followed up this work with a series of theoretical lectures, delivered between 1730 and 1735 and published (*Lectures on Architecture*) 1734–6, in which the villa model is given the greatest prominence.

Roger Morris built in 1724–5 a house at Whitton Park, Twickenham, for Lord Islay which was probably of the villa kind and then, from 1727, the White Lodge in Richmond Park as a hunting lodge for George II.[106] This was a development from Lord Herbert's house at Whitehall and contained no further innovations of consequence.

A Thames-side villa of the very first importance was, of course, Lord Burlington's at Chiswick.[107] This is a more complicated thing altogether and contains much – perhaps overmuch – architectural study and experiment. It can hardly have been begun

87. Bower House, Havering, Essex

later than 1724 and follows therefore hard upon the completion of Mereworth. It takes the same plan-model as Mereworth – the Villa Rotonda at Vicenza – but uses it very differently. Campbell deliberately *enlarged* the square body of the house; Burlington deliberately *reduced* it and did so in an odd way, adopting a square of 68 ft, which is very nearly the dimension in Palladio's engravings in Venetian feet (considerably bigger than English). The result is a toy-like unreality which must have contributed something to the English notion of the miniature nature of a villa.

The Chiswick villa contains many novelties of detail and arrangement but none more important than its plan. Within the limits of the 68 ft square, Burlington packed ten rooms of interesting and varied shape, including a domed octagon in the middle and along the garden side room with end apses leading to circular and octagonal rooms, the suite of three forming a gallery. This suite, deriving from the plan of Palladio's Palazzo Thiene, but compacted into a miniature house, was the beginning of a kind of planning which had immense influence in English country-house design, which Adam exploited without very much developing and which permeates the villa type of the latter part of the century.

Other things at Chiswick which entered the English architectural vocabulary were the domed octagon appearing through the roof, the Venetian windows within relieving arches in the garden front and the steps to that front and to the portico. The interiors, as at Mereworth, are largely based on Inigo Jones, though without the fanciful plaster reliefs and with more research, as by 1727 many of Jones's drawings were in Burlington's possession and being studied by his collaborator, William Kent.

Mereworth, Stourhead, Newby, Pembroke (Lord Herbert's) Lodge, Marble Hill, Chiswick and White Lodge: these are the prototype villas in the English 18th-century tradition. Of these, the first five were published in plan and elevation by Campbell in

88. Frampton Court, Gloucestershire

1725; Chiswick by Kent in 1727 and White Lodge by Campbell's successors, Woolfe and Gandon, in 1767. Publication apart, the last four – all easily seen by a visitor to London – were, of course, the most likely to be influential. Marble Hill became at once a classic. Chiswick proved not so much a classic as a treasury of invention; its parts were borrowed freely and became part of the language of English Palladianism.

It will be seen that the villas we have discussed were something very different from the great houses being built at the same time. Not only were they relatively small but they were compact. Suited for what in fact most of them were – suburban retreats for the very wealthy – the type could not easily be enlarged into the regular country seat without losing much of its character. Nevertheless, so captivating was the villa as an architectural idea that some small country houses began to be built in this form rather than on one of the versions of the old 'Belton' plan. James Gibbs seized on the idea very quickly; in fact, the villa-type house he designed for Matthew Prior at Down Hall, Essex (not built owing to Prior's death) is dated 1720.[108] It might seem to have priority over Campbell's villa for Lord Herbert at Whitehall (finished 1724), which it much resembles; but taking Gibbs's practice as a whole he seems to have been a prompt snapper-up of Palladian ideas rather than an innovator, and his Palladianism is always diluted.

A villa of the simplest kind on the perimeter of the Burlington-Herbert group is
Bower House, Havering, Essex, designed by Flitcroft for Serjeant John Baynes in 1729 *87*
and built explicitly, as an inscription records, for the owner's hospitable retirement.[109] The façade has the villa arrangement of pedimented centre and single windows at the sides; the interior details reflect Chiswick.

Frampton Court in Gloucestershire, built from 1731 to 1733 for the Stroud wool *88*
family of Clutterbuck,[110] is an imitation of Stourhead, at the hands of a not very learned

Bristol architect, John Strahan. He has squeezed the design and given it a vertical stress foreign to Campbell. He has also taken Campbell's 'Thiene' system of rustication and crammed it busily on to the Stourhead elevation. And he has added wings to the house, though they hardly seem to be intended to be read with the main block and look like an after-thought.

89 A much more out-of-the-way interpretation of the villa idea is Linley Hall, near Bishop's Castle, Salop, built from 1742 to 1743 for Robert More, MP, FRS, the botanist and friend of Linnaeus.[111] His architect was Henry Joynes, of the Office of Works, but Joynes had spent most of his early life in the service of Vanbrugh and Hawksmoor at Blenheim and elsewhere. The result is that, while Linley adopts the compactness and main divisions of the villa and details which might almost be Campbell's, its recessed planes and varieties of opening are of an older school.

These three – Bower House, Frampton and Linley – are scattered manifestations of the villa idea and it would not be easy to find many more in the 30s and 40s. It was not until the 50s – a generation after the prototype statements – that the villa idea really broke through. After 1748 it certainly did, to the extent that one is tempted to speak of a 'villa revival'. This revival – if we may so call it for the moment – is best dealt with by considering the practices of three architects – Isaac Ware (d. 1766), Sir Robert Taylor (1714–88) and Sir William Chambers (1723–96). In the hands of these three, over a period of some twenty years, the English country house underwent a fundamental change of character, based on a reconsideration of the villa and financed not by county magnates but, very largely, by moneyed men from the towns.

Ware was the oldest of the three and he is easy to deal with because his entire vocabulary derives from the Burlington-Herbert circle with which he was closely associated. His Clifton Hill House, built for a Bristol merchant, Paul Fisher, from 1746 to 1750 is, externally, on the lines of Marble Hill, though without pilasters and raised on a terrace, with steps of the Wanstead kind.[112] It might be dismissed simply as a competent derivative but for its plan which, one is surprised to find, is not in the least

89. Linley Hall, Shropshire

90. Danson Hill, Kent

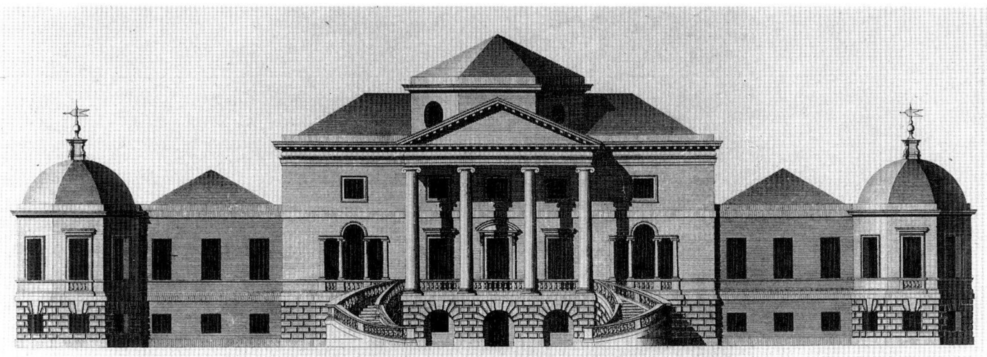

91. Wrotham, Middlesex

like Marble Hill but, in fact, one of the commonest bourgeois types of plan, consisting of a corridor running through the centre of the house with rooms on either side. No hall; no saloon. Here is the aristocratic Marble Hill idea, recast to make the suburban dwelling of a merchant. It is something of a portent.

Some time before 1756 Ware designed two houses in Scotland,[113] both of which consist of central blocks on the villa model, with service wings attached thereto by passages – colonnaded quadrants in one case and short straight links on the other. Then, Sir Robert Taylor built Harleyford Manor, Bucks.[114] (1755), and Danson Hill, *90* Kent[115] (1756), both for moneyed men with City backgrounds. All these houses are distinctly villas and all but one (Harleyford) have attachments which make them like miniature editions of Holkham or Kedleston. Taylor's are perhaps a trifle more original than Ware's. Taylor made great play with the canted bay – a feature almost certainly of Burlingtonian origin, with a long history before that, but which only became popular shortly before 1750;[116] and at Asgill House, Richmond,[117] built for the banker Sir Charles Asgill over the period 1758 to 1767, he combined canted bays with another Palladio–Burlington theme, the half pedimented wing, to make a villa type which achieved a long run of popularity.[118]

These houses by Ware and Taylor are manifestations of the villa 'revival' of the 1750s. But there was more to it. In or around 1754, thirty years after Palladio's Rotonda had been copied at Mereworth, two new versions were being built, in different parts of the country: one was Nuthall Temple, Notts., built for Sir Charles Sedley by the rather obscure Thomas Wright,[119] the other was Foot's Cray Place, Kent, built for Bourchier Cleeve, the financier, probably by Isaac Ware.[120] Foot's Cray almost certainly prompted Sir William Chambers' design for Lord Bessborough's Roehampton villa to which we shall come presently.

But probably Ware's most important and certainly his largest house was Wrotham, Middlesex, built around 1754 for Admiral John Byng.[121] Here we have *91* something of a land-mark in the history of the country house, for Wrotham consists of a centre which is palpably a villa (strongly marked by Chiswick influences), to which wings terminating in pavilions are added, the whole thing from end to end being, however, a single continuous house. In my second section I alluded to Wrotham as a

92. Harewood House, Yorkshire

92 significant contrast to Harewood, which is superficially the same composition but arrived at by telescoping the plan of Wanstead III. Wrotham (1754) and Harewood (1759), observed together, indicate the point at which the descending 'greater house' crosses the ascendant path of the villa. Wrotham proposed a new type of winged house and there is little doubt that Wyatt's Heaton and many following houses owe something to it.

It is obvious that the works of Ware and Taylor were creating a new situation in country-house design. The villa, with or without attachments of one sort or another, was in the ascendant. Other architects were following: for instance, John Wood II of Bath, in the oddly proportioned villa with long wings and octagon pavilions at Buckland, Berks.[122] (1757), and John Carr at Burton Constable, Yorks.[123] (*c.*1762). And when a newcomer, William Chambers, arrived on the scene fresh from Italy in 1755 it was the villa theme which offered itself as the obvious path for an aspiring talent.

93. Stourhead, Wiltshire

94. Duddingston, Edinburgh

Chambers, in spite of his five years abroad and his almost immediate success at the English Court, seems (unlike Adam) to have had no particular desire to revolutionize English house design. Just as his *Treatise on Civil Architecture*, first published in 1759, took its departure from Isaac Ware's *Complete Body of Architecture* of 1756, so in his early houses he drew upon Ware's architectural performances. His first house (*c.* 1758) was a villa for the Earl of Bessborough at Roehampton.[124] Bessborough was a brother-in-law of the Duke of Devonshire to whom Burlington's Chiswick villa had descended. He was himself a virtuoso and collector of antiquities and at Roehampton seems to have proposed to himself something analogous to Chiswick. The house which Chambers designed for him has one façade (towards Richmond Park) closely modelled on Ware's paraphrase of the Villa Rotonda. The plan, however, is not centralized but an ordinary oblong villa type and the entrance front is plain. Service wings are placed round the forecourt, thus avoiding interference with the 'villa' effect of the park front.

Of Chambers' subsequent houses up to 1770, the three that we know are all interpretations of the villa idea. Castle Hill (now Duntish Court), Dorset (*c.* 1760), has a plan deriving from Stourhead or Newby with single-storey attachments like orangeries.[125] Duddingston, near Edinburgh,[126] built in the years 1763–4 as a Scottish *94*
pied-à-terre for the bachelor Earl of Abercorn, is more interesting. The main front
comes very close to Campbell's Stourhead, but with the important difference that the *93*
rusticated basement is eliminated. The plan is quite different, involving a very spacious hall with a grand staircase with two returning flights on the main axis (Ware had built such a staircase for Lord Chesterfield). And the services – there being no basement – are incorporated in an independent block, loosely linked to the house. Then, in the period 1765–75 comes Peperharow, Surrey,[127] for Lord Middleton, where the plan is very close to one of Ware's which, in turn, depends on Stourhead.

The main fact about these early houses of Chambers (and he built few others) is that all are on the villa model, with full appreciation of both Ware and Campbell. They

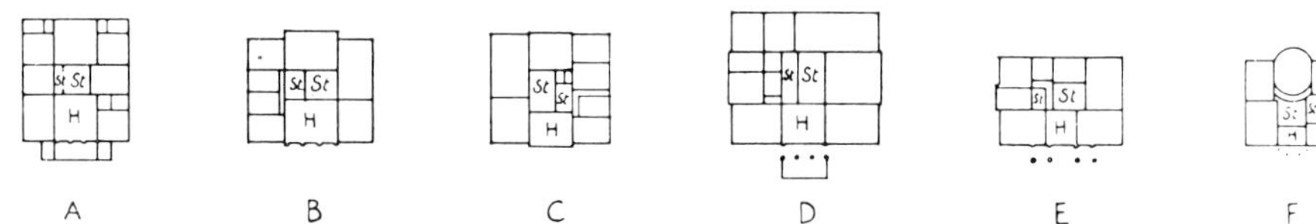

95. The villa idea in house plans from 1720 to 1780. A: Stourhead (ill. 93). B: a plan from Isaac Ware's *Complete Body of Architecture.* C: Pepperharrow, Surrey. D: Claremont, Esher, Surrey (ill. 96). E: Berrington Hall, Hertfordshire. F: Tendring, Essex

confirm that the 'villa revival' which Ware seems to have inaugurated in the 1750s set the fashion for country-house building in the following decade. This can be supported by a glance at the work of two of Chambers' younger contemporaries. Robert Mylne's Tusmore House, Oxon,[128] 1766–9, was on the Marble Hill model. James Wyatt's Gaddesden Place, Herts., 1768–73, is on the Stourhead model.[129] Only the older men – John Carr and James Paine – were still building houses with long many-windowed façades and in his Thoresby Park, Notts,[130] 1768, Carr at least seems to have joined the moderns. Robert Adam's attitude was equivocal; neither the strict villa fenestration (one-three-one) nor the idea of the villa as a compact independent mass had much appeal for him. There is, however, among the Adam drawings in the Soane Museum a substantial group of small house designs which are sometimes villas, sometimes miniature castles and sometimes quite simply small houses.[131]

65 An obvious land-mark in English country-house building is Claremont, in
96 Surrey.[132] Built for Lord Clive from 1770 to 1774, it inaugurates the imperialist age of

96. Claremont, Esher, Surrey

97. Tyringham, Buckinghamshire

building by Nabobs. It cost over £30,000; and four interesting architectural personalities, belonging to two generations, were involved in it. Clive was always building; and at his two Shropshire houses, Styche and Walcot, he had employed Sir William Chambers. For Claremont, he again invited Chambers to prepare a design, but he also invited Lancelot Brown, the landscape-gardener, to submit one, and to Chambers' fury, it was the latter that he chose. Now the odd thing about this is that the plan of Claremont, as eventually built, is very close indeed to Chambers' Peperharow. Are we to conclude that Brown having, like Chambers, consulted Ware's published plans, adopted the same model? Or can it be that Lord Clive, having both Brown's and Chambers' drawings in his hands, selected Chambers' plan and instructed Brown (whom he had already engaged as landscape-gardener) to develop and execute it? Whatever the truth of the matter, the fact is that this very large and important house near London was built on what is essentially a villa plan – the plan, indeed, of Stourhead, broadened and somewhat elaborated.

Being a very large house, the main elevations of Claremont are forced away from the one-three-one fenestration of the villa and resemble a very much diluted and abbreviated Wanstead I. They are of no particular significance for their date. The plan, however, is of great importance if only because it was adopted and propagated by two younger architects who were working at Claremont under Brown – Henry Holland, who was twenty-five when the house was begun, and John Soane who, at seventeen, was in Holland's service (and claimed, later on, to have been entrusted with the design of the entrance hall).

The principle of the Stourhead–Peperharow–Claremont plan is very simple. Campbell derived it from Palladio's Villa Emo and paraphrased it both at Stourhead and Newby (where it is closer to Palladio). The plan is squarish and is divided into three both ways. In the resulting centre compartment are the main staircase and a subsidiary staircase. This leaves eight spaces for rooms all round and communicating, if desired, with the staircases. In England, quite obviously, the main central stair had to be top lit – and this provided an architectural opportunity. Thus at Claremont there is an interesting arrangement of columns and niches at first-floor level. At Berrington Hall, Herefordshire,[133] built from 1778 to 1781 for a former Lord Mayor of London, Holland used the same plan and splendidly elaborated the staircase treatment.

And from Henry Holland this type of plan passed to his pupil, John Soane. In Soane's first country house, Tendring Hall, Essex,[134] built for Admiral Sir Joshua Rowley between 1784 and 1786, the plan was united with a modified villa-form exterior. Soane used it again at one of his largest and most felicitous houses,
97 Tyringham[135] (1793–*c.*1800), built for the banker William Praed; and again, on a miniature scale, at Sydney Lodge, near Southampton[136] (1794) for the widowed Mrs Yorke. In both these latter instances, however, there are important distortions and departures from precedent. At Tyringham, the main staircase has been pushed out of its place in the centre (though not precisely placed anywhere else) to make room for a hall which Soane called a 'tribune', rising into the first floor.[137] This, with the introduction of Greek Doric columns and a cross-vault in the hall and the 'shaping' of the drawing-room makes the interior highly idiosyncratic. As for the exterior, instead of a portico we have a shallow columned bay – a modification of what James Wyatt did at Heaton – and on either side of it two windows, with double end-pilasters, all modelled with the most minute subtlety. This is a very long way from Colen Campbell, but it is most essentially a *villa* of the 1790s.

At Sydney Lodge, with an undistorted plan, we find that the main elevation is divided into three and the centre part is *recessed*, a complete reversal of villa practice and almost certainly prompted by some French model. But Soane's freedoms were legion. And in any case this is work of the 1790s, when the architectural situation had changed very much from what it was when Claremont was being built. It is necessary to retrace our steps.

By 1775 the country house situation may be stated as follows: (*a*) Although very large houses often compromised with older types of plan, the villa form, with or without wings, was the advanced type. Its patronage was less aristocratic than wealthy middle class. (*b*) The high basement containing services had gone out of fashion. If an order was used it stood on a mere plinth, thus conforming both with the fashion brought in by Adam at the Admiralty, and with the new rationalist theory announced by the Abbé Laugier. (*c*) The basement having disappeared, a service wing was often necessary, but this was not to interfere with the compact wholeness of the villa. It could be attached to the house symmetrically at a low level or as a rear court; or simply as an appendage kept away from the best views and concealed by shrubs. (*d*) The ornamental detail of the house followed the example of delicacy and freedom set by the Adams and by Wyatt – especially (after 1775) Wyatt.

Taking this as the position and then looking ahead to any collection of house designs of the 1790s, we shall see that in the intervening fifteen or twenty years something had happened which had the effect of dissolving the sharpness of this 1775 picture and rendering country-house design altogether more fluid and more personal.

98. Bletchingdon, Oxfordshire

The obvious over-all answer is either 'romanticism' or 'neo-classicism', whichever you like; but such words do not help to define what really happened. We have to proceed by looking at evidence, and the most useful evidence to hand is in the form of books.

Shortly after 1775, two books were published which tell us a good deal about the changing attitude to design among younger architects at that time. The first is John Soane's *Designs in Architecture*, published in 1778 when he was twenty-five. The designs are not for houses but for pavilions, garden seats and such things, and they display a curious mixture of Burlingtonian themes and decorative abstractions in the manner of Neufforge and Delafosse. The intention is obviously to 'let loose the imagination' and to invent. Terribly immature, these designs were regretted by their author, but their very immaturity tells us of a condition of mind characteristic of the moment. The second book is more important. James Lewis was perhaps a year or two older than Soane and, like him, went to Rome. His book, *Original Designs in Architecture . . . for Villas, Mansions, Town Houses, etc.*, is dated (on the plates) 1779. The text makes it clear that the intention here, as in Soane's book, is an imaginative release. The first design is most significant from our point of view. It is for a villa based on a square plan and elevated as a geometrical block, in which two Greek Doric columns are inset at the entrance, with a relief panel (copied from Stuart and Revett) above, and some wildly unorthodox ornaments.

These two books forecast what could, and did, happen to the villa in the next twenty years. It became an object round which the architect's vanity might play and which would be infinitely subject to his invention. In Soane's case we can see his feverish imagination at work in the remarkable series of houses published in his *Plans,*

Elevations and Sections of 1788 and *Sketches* of 1793, three of which I have mentioned. Lewis's case is different. He never became the revolutionary figure which his first villa
98 designs seemed to promise. But he did build, in 1782, Bletchingdon House, Oxon[138] (for Arthur Annesley), in which we see the Stourhead model handled yet again, loyally in plan and outline but with idiosyncratic modelling, not unrelated to the French romantics. If Ware's designs of the 1750s may be said to have started a 'revival' of the Campbell villa prototypes, Lewis's Bletchingdon may conveniently be chosen as a representative last word in that revival.

It is beyond the scope of this essay to explore in detail the variations and innovations presented by the mass of country houses built between 1780 and 1800 – a period of great middle-class prosperity and one in which the architect achieved full status as an independent professional man: likewise as an independent artist and man of genius. In the latter rôle he found himself with a galaxy of themes at his disposal and his preoccupation with 'invention' meant, in effect, that he was continually seeking new combinations within the currency of themes from the English past, as well as new themes from France. John Nash's extremely eclectic practice, dating from the early 1790s onwards, is a conspicuous case. Starting with villas modelled on those of his master, Sir Robert Taylor, he proceeded to play with themes taken from Adam, from Wyatt and from Henry Holland; and from the Hôtel de Salm.[139] Before the end of the century he was building Gothic castles deriving from Payne Knight's Downton, and an Italian vernacular type of villa, inspired perhaps by the buildings seen in Claude's landscapes. Nash was a celebrity; but an analysis of Mr Colvin's country-house entries indicates that at least fifty-five architects of repute were engaged on country-house building in England between 1780 and 1800; while in the last decade alone there were as many as forty-two. Nearly all of the latter group were playing, within narrower spheres, the same eclectic game as John Nash.

A detailed study of country-house building in the last twenty years of the century would be of great interest, but it would have to be prefaced by an investigation of the social background on the lines attempted in the first section in relation to the earlier period. Both the distribution of wealth and the conditions of patronage had changed radically since the days of Colen Campbell and *Vitruvius Britannicus*. Furthermore, the limits set to these by the intrusion of the word *classical* into their title would have to be infringed. After 1780 the factor of stylistic choice – Palladian, Greek or Gothic (or, indeed, Indian) becomes vital to an appreciation of the whole picture.

VII · Sir John Soane and the Furniture of Death

99. Soane's design for a tribute to his friend James King, exhibited at the Royal Academy, 1777

100. The mausoleum of the Dulwich Art Gallery, as rebuilt after partial demolition in the Second World War

In the summer of 1776, John Soane, aged twenty-three, was working against time on a design for a triumphal bridge. He was competing for the Royal Academy's gold medal for the second time and desperately wanted to win. Earning a wage in the office of Henry Holland he could apply himself to the triumphal bridge only after office hours and on Sundays. Accordingly, when two friends asked him to join them in a boating party at Greenwich, to celebrate the birthday of one of them, he declined. The boating party took place. There was an accident and one of the lads, who could not swim, was drowned. Soane could not swim; he, too, would have perished.[1] Thus, providentially, the young architect escaped death by drowning and was duly awarded the Royal Academy's Medal. Moved and perhaps not a little exalted he expressed his feelings in a design dedicated to the memory of his dead friend and in the Royal Academy exhibition of 1777 appeared a drawing entitled 'Design for a Mausoleum to the *99*
Memory of James King Esq, drowned June 9, 1776'. The design was not in the nature of a structure to enclose Mr King's remains (if indeed they were ever recovered), but an architectural composition, seeming to be offered much as a poet might offer a funeral elegy in similar circumstances. The mausoleum was on the grandest scale with a central domed chapel on a podium joined by diagonal wings to four pyramids and containing accommodation for 84 coffined bodies, with, in addition, 24 receptacles for ashes. The design was engraved and occupies two of the plates in the slim octavo *Designs in Architecture* which Soane published in 1778.[2]

There was nothing very extraordinary about this performance. Mausolea were favourite subjects for young architects airing their talents and inviting patronage, and the reasons for this are obvious. The mausoleum is a classical type capable of infinite variation. Since the dead do not require air, light and warmth but only shelter and veneration, the mausoleum is a theme round which the imagination can freely play. Soane's design was not, by standards of the time, novel or extravagant. It owed much to a series of designs which Sir William Chambers had made, twenty-five years earlier, on the occasion of the death of Frederick Prince of Wales in 1751, when Chambers himself was looking for notice in high quarters.[3]

In 1778 Soane went to Italy as the Royal Academy's travelling student. He was there for two years, during which his taste moved towards a more severe and restrained classicism, with a Greek content which Chambers would not have tolerated. A mausoleum design, dated 1779, takes the upper part of the King design and recasts it with a new horizontal emphasis in Greek Doric;[4] a companion design varies it again in Greek Ionic. These were perhaps the designs exhibited at the RA in 1781. The list of Soane's Academy exhibits in subsequent years includes a design for a mausoleum in 1784, another in 1792 and a design for a 'national' mausoleum in 1799.[5] To 1800
belongs a beautifully rendered drawing, based on a design published in the same book *101*
as the 'King' design in 1778.

All were imaginary projects, for in those years Soane was increasingly busy designing and building houses for the living and no commission as yet contained anything in the nature of a tomb-chamber. Soane's only three-dimensional exercises in
the funerary field up to 1800 were the elegant little sarcophagus for Miss Johnstone *103*

(1784) in St Mary Abbots churchyard, and a mural monument in the now lost church of St Stephen, Coleman Street.[6]

But the mausoleum, the sarcophagus and the cinerary urn were becoming objects of reference of increasing importance to Soane as a designer. At the first house he built
102 for himself in Lincoln's Inn Fields (No. 12) in 1792 there is already a back room on the ground floor which has a low, vaulted ceiling like a Roman tomb-chamber.[7] And when we come to his country house, Pitzhanger Manor, Ealing, built in 1800, we see that the classical furniture of death was indeed taking hold of his imagination.

When Soane bought Pitzhanger it consisted of a plain box of a house with a more recent wing containing two beautiful rooms designed by his first master, George Dance. Soane preserved the wing but rebuilt the main house. In doing so he was, again, his own employer. He was forty-seven. He was fairly rich from the property left by his wife's uncle. He was an ARA and architect to the Bank of England. Secure in wealth and status, he built for his own pride and pleasure.

104 The visitor to Pitzhanger enters the drive through an arch which at once arrests. The red brick arch springs from stone imposts lodged between piers of markedly funereal character. Each pier consists of coupled pilasters of rough flint rising from a pedestal, joined at the top by a delicately moulded stone band and then capped by what

101. One of a series of ideal designs for mausolea by Soane. The commemoration of the Earl of Chatham, who died in 1778, gave the subject special appeal. This highly finished design, related to a much earlier one, is dated 2 February 1805

102. The tomb-like breakfast room of No. 12 Lincoln's Inn Fields, Soane's first London house, built in 1792

103. Tomb of Elizabeth Johnstone in St Mary Abbots churchyard, Kensington, 1784

is evidently the lid of a cinerary urn.[8] The mixture of brick, stone and flint is very strange for London. (Did Soane perhaps discover this combination in Norfolk where he was much employed in his early practice?) It is intended to strike a 'primitive' note, like some of the cottage designs he had published in 1793.[9] The urn lids, however, are nothing if not sophisticated. Each has a tiny wreath with flying ribbons carved on each face. Each lid was originally surmounted by a vase but these have vanished.

Sophisticated, again, is the object which crowns the arch – a scrolled *acroterium* such as is often found on the sides or ends of antique sarcophagi. An eagle within a wreath is carved on the front.

The Pitzhanger gateway is of no little significance in the history of the Soane style but for the moment we must leave it and pass on to the house. Here we are confronted by an architectural set piece, in brown brick and Portland stone. The principal features are four detached Ionic columns supporting restored versions of the Erectheum caryatids. There are no windows in the upper storey, only carved panels with antique motifs. There is a high central attic, again with a carved panel. If there are no specifically mortuary features here the façade warns us that a more than ordinary solemnity is likely to be discovered within.

We enter the house and find ourselves in a barrel-vaulted corridor. The vault is interrupted, half way along, by a vertical shaft with windows which admit almost no light because they look into rooms. The top of the shaft is like an urn lid, turned inside out – a theme which obsessed Soane and which we shall meet in another context.

105 On our right is the front parlour, a room 17 ft square, the size dictated by the

104. Gateway to Pitzhanger Manor, Ealing, 1800; sketch by C. J. Richardson

105. The front parlour of Pitzhanger Manor, Ealing; drawing by J. M. Gandy, 1803. The principal ornaments are cinerary urns, bought a few years earlier at the sales of older collections

foundations of the old house. The ceiling is an extremely flat dome with incised ornaments and, in the spandrels, angels in low relief, carrying wreaths in their outstretched hands. The wall-arches which carry the dome rest on piers which incorporate draped mourning figures. To complete the picture of the room as it was in Soane's time, we must refer to the darkly lit perspective drawing made for him by J. M. Gandy. Here we see that the walls were decorated in the style of a Roman villa excavated in 1777 and recorded in coloured engravings which Soane possessed.[10] We see also that the walls on either side of the fireplace were fitted as columbaria, containing Roman cinerary urns and vases. We know where these came from because Soane had been buying such things, evidently with an eye to Pitzhanger. The Cawdor sale in 1800, the Bessborough and Duke of St Albans sales in 1801, the Clerk and Mendip sales in 1802 provided nearly all.[11] In Gandy's drawing the great Cawdor vase stands on its own pedestal opposite the fireplace.

Opening from this room is the back parlour, with a vaulted ceiling painted with *106*
trellis, much like the back room, just mentioned, at 12 Lincoln's Inn Fields. To dado height the walls are lined with book-shelves. Above these are niches, each containing an urn surmounted by a marble vase. Both rooms, but especially the front parlour, give something of the feeling of a tomb chamber. With the great store of urns still in place the sense of present death must have been suffocating.

Shortly after the building of Pitzhanger, things like sarcophagi with *acroteria* as at the Pitzhanger gateway began to appear on the new skyline of the Bank of England. In *107*

1804 an obelisk, commissioned by a Mr Simeon, was built in Reading market-place; it had three sides with an urn lid at the summit carrying a colonette with a pineapple.[12] In 1806, Soane built a massive tomb, an overgrown sarcophagus with a square urn and vase on top, over the grave of Samuel Bosanquet, a bank director, at Leyton (this, alas, has vanished in the past few years).[13] Then in 1807 he was drawn into a situation where death and burial opened new and rather special vistas for funerary invention. This was occasioned by the death in that year of Noel Desenfans, art collector and man of letters, and the Desenfans story is of sufficient interest to be told in full.[14]

Desenfans had come from Paris to England as a young man, apparently as a teacher of languages but already with some small reputation as a writer. This he increased somewhat in England, but the main thing in his life was a love of pictures. He was introduced to the Prince Primate of Poland, King Stanislas's brother, who obtained for him the post of Polish consul-general in Britain and, more significantly, a commission from Stanislas to form a collection of pictures which should constitute the nucleus of a Polish national gallery. In this, Desenfans was very successful. However, in 1795 came the third partition of Poland and the abdication of Stanislas. The Russian government repudiated the King's debts to Desenfans and the pictures were left on his hands. He sold some of them in 1800 but continued collecting at his house in Charlotte (now Hallam) Street and entertained very handsomely in a dining-room hung with superb Poussins.

The Desenfans household was rather curious. Desenfans had an English wife but no children, and a third member of the household was an artist of Swiss extraction,

106. Back parlour of Pitzhanger Manor: another drawing by Gandy, lit in a way that emphasizes the room's funereal character

107. The Lothbury front of the Bank of England with its blind windows and skyline of sarcophagi and vases; a drawing of 1807

Peter Francis Bourgeois. Bourgeois was eleven years younger than Desenfans who had known him since he was a boy and had, in fact, made his career for him. He had persuaded him to study painting instead of taking a commission in the army and it must have been Desenfans who obtained for him in 1791 the post of painter to the King of Poland. This was followed by conferment of some sort of Polish decoration which Bourgeois persuaded himself was the equivalent of a knighthood. Three years later Bourgeois was appointed landscape painter to George III who sanctioned the anglicized use of the title. Sir Francis Bourgeois, as he then became, never married. He lived with the two Desenfans till Noel Desenfans's death. He then inherited, jointly with Mrs Desenfans, the house in Charlotte (Hallam) Street with all the furniture, linen and plate. More important, he himself inherited the whole of the great collection of pictures.[15]

The legacy of the pictures was unconditional. There was, however, a strong moral obligation on Bourgeois to deal with them according to his friend's often expressed wishes, which were that they should be kept together and made available to the public. Bourgeois very properly identified himself with his deceased benefactor's intentions.

There was a further obligation on Bourgeois and this brings us back to our central theme. A sentence in Desenfans's will, made nearly four years before his death, runs as follows: 'I desire to be laid in a leaden coffin and kept in my own House till the Executor of this my last will shall have prepared a vault where I may be removed';[16] the executor, of course, being Bourgeois. There are no further directions but one can hardly doubt that an understanding had been reached in Desenfans's lifetime as to the nature and location of the 'vault'. It was to be, in fact, a domestic mortuary chapel on the premises at 38 Charlotte (Hallam) Street. For such a work Soane may well have seemed to Bourgeois the most proper architect. As fellow academicians they knew each other well and Soane, obviously, had the right feeling for the subject. Bourgeois would no doubt remember a design of Soane's in the Academy of 1801, for 'a Sepulchral Church' (probably intended for Tyringham).[17]

Desenfans had died on 8 July 1807. By 15 August Soane had made preliminary designs, one of which was accepted. The chapel, which was to accommodate not only Desenfans but, eventually, his wife and his friend, was begun in that month and completed by November.

Desenfans's desire (if, indeed, it was his and not Bourgeois's) for the domestic conservation of his corpse in unconsecrated ground which was not even freehold may strike us as strange, but there does not seem to be any great mystery about it. Desenfans was not irreligious, though his beliefs probably were of the somewhat abstract deistical kind, common among intellectuals of the period. There are phrases in his will concerning God, the soul and forgiveness; and it seems that religious services were conducted in the mausoleum by a minister of the Church of England. If an explanation is required it lies, perhaps, quite simply in an aesthete's desire to be as fastidious in his own disposal as he had been or would have wished to be in the selection and disposal of fine works of art. He may well have felt a distaste for interment in the over-full churchyard at St Marylebone or the uninviting parochial cemetery at Paddington Street.

Whatever the case, Soane interpreted Bourgeois's wishes to the entire satisfaction of all concerned. On the ridiculously cramped site of an old stable, he planned a circular
108 temple with an interior peristyle of six Greek Doric columns supporting a low dome with an oculus. The chamber was otherwise windowless, but a segment of it was cut away to join a smaller rectangular chamber, the mausoleum, brilliantly lit from a lantern light in the roof. The mausoleum provided accommodation for three sarcophagi. From the dark, circular chamber one looked through an arch into the irradiated mausoleum – a Baroque effect contrived in the severer terms of the age which had discovered Greece.[18]

After the building of the chapel, Bourgeois turned his thoughts to the realization of Desenfans's ambitions for his collection. One possible solution was to keep the pictures where they were. Desenfans had owned the leases not only of the Charlotte Street house but of two adjoining houses numbered in what is now Great Portland Street.[19] All three houses had passed to Bourgeois and Mrs Desenfans. If the freehold of these properties could be acquired, Desenfans's collection could be rooted in perpetuity in the St Marylebone soil. And it must have occurred to Bourgeois that this would also solve the problem of maintaining a corpse, or corpses, in a mausoleum which, as things stood, would in 1874 revert to the ground landlord, the Duke of Portland. Bourgeois therefore wrote to the Duke, begging to be allowed to purchase the reversion of the properties. Promptly and curtly, without even the courtesy of acknowledging the assumed knighthood, the Duke replied that he would do no such thing.

Bourgeois's letter to the Duke is dated January 1810. On 20 December of the same year he made his will.[20] He was probably then suffering from the effects of a riding accident of which he died two weeks later, aged fifty-five. In the short year between the Duke's refusal and the accident he had made up his mind as to the future of the pictures. J. P. Kemble, the actor, an old and close friend of Desenfans, is said to have prompted the decision; but the Rev. Robert Corry, a Fellow of Dulwich College who had conducted services in the chapel at Charlotte Street, may also have been an influence. The decision, in any case, was to leave the whole of the collection to the College of

108. Design for the Desenfans-Bourgeois mausoleum in Charlotte (now Hallam) Street, London, built in 1807

God's Gift at Dulwich, with the addition of £10,000 for its suitable maintenance and £2,000 for improving the west wing of the college, where a gallery already existed, for the reception of the pictures. Bourgeois had hinted to the Warden of Dulwich, that Soane would be the right architect for these improvements.

Bourgeois's body was presumably enclosed in the second of the three sarcophagi at Charlotte Street, but it was not to remain there for long. It soon became obvious that 'improvement' of the existing gallery at Dulwich, however extensive, would not make adequate provision for the collection. Mrs Desenfans, now an old lady, living alone with the bodies of the two men in the back yard, offered to put down £6,000 at once, to be put to another £6,000 found by the College, to pay for a separate picture gallery at Dulwich combined with a mausoleum – a replica, more or less, of that existing at Charlotte Street. Soane was commissioned by the College and produced an estimate, comfortably within the imposed limits, on 12 July. The building was begun. On 19 April 1813 Mrs Desenfans made her will, directing that her remains be deposited in the Dulwich mausoleum and making Soane one of her executors.[21] She died before 9 August 1814 by which time the building was well advanced. In September, the pictures were removed from Charlotte Street and displayed in the gallery.

109 The chapel and mausoleum at Dulwich are, internally, virtually duplicates of what was built at Charlotte Street. Externally, they are something new for the simple reason that the building at Charlotte Street, jammed between three boundary walls, had no

109. Mausoleum at the Dulwich Art Gallery; Soane's design for the interior. It was somewhat simplified in execution

110. One of the three false doorways in the mausoleum at Dulwich *111.* Interior of the Dulwich mausoleum as rebuilt after the Second World War

exterior in the architectural sense. At Dulwich, Soane had to invent one.[22] For the
gallery as a whole he had adopted, partly for economy and partly as a gesture towards
the old college buildings, alleged to be by Inigo Jones, the 'primitivist' style we noted
in the Pitzhanger gateway. The mausoleum followed the same style and may be *100*
thought of as a Roman tomb type reduced to bare essentials, Robert Adam's towers at
Mistley providing a significant link. Built of ordinary London stocks with little stone,
it is, nevertheless, precise and subtle; sombre, too, with those three doors which not *110*
only never open but have nothing behind them. Three cenotaphs on the parapet
demonstrate the building's purpose. The lantern, taut, thin and luminous, carries
funeral vases and terminates in yet another sarcophagus motif. The Dulwich
mausoleum was hit by a bomb in the Second World War and half ruined. But it was
loyally restored and today the visitor is allowed to enter the chapel. The compartment *111*
beyond, with the porphyry-painted sarcophagi, is bathed in yellow light filtering
through stained glass in the lantern – the *lumière mystérieuse* which so much impressed
Soane in churches he had seen abroad.[23] It is all very melancholy and there is not a
Christian symbol to be seen.

During the years when Soane was engaged on these two successive funerary monuments he was busy in Lincoln's Inn Fields, first with an extension to his house, No. 12, to provide an exhibition space for antique marbles and casts and, later, building a new house next door to the old, the house which was in due course to become the Soane Museum. The whole process lasted from 1808 till 1813, a period exactly parallel

112. Tomb of Philip James de Loutherbourg, the painter, in Chiswick churchyard *113.* Roman cinerary urn illustrated in B. de Montfaucon, *L'Antiquité Expliquée*

with the Desenfans-Bourgeois enterprise. We need not follow the story in detail. What concerns us is the extent to which associations with death and sepulture enter into it. The earliest sketches for the extension to No. 12 are dated 11 June 1808.[24] They show the exhibition space as extending from the basement up through two storeys to a lantern light. The basement portion is marked 'catacombs'. On a basement plan of 28 July, 'catacombs' are relegated to a passage-way to the north of the main space;[25] the central area has become 'model room', while on the south is a chamber marked 'mausoleum'. This measures only 8 ft 5 in. by 2 ft 7 in. and could have been intended to be top-lit. What was it for? It is, I suppose, just possible that Soane, having so recently assisted in the interment of Noel Desenfans's corpse on his own premises, was considering equivalent accommodation for himself. If that is so, it was a passing thought. In later drawings the 'mausoleum' has vanished.

The basement of the new structure had, nevertheless, begun to be thought of as a place for exhibits of a melancholy kind. In 1810, Soane gave up his country house at Ealing and brought the antique urns and other treasures which he had there to Lincoln's Inn Fields. In 1812, his neighbour at No. 13, a Mr George Booth Tyndale, whose stables he had already acquired and demolished, agreed to sell to Soane the whole of his house on condition that Soane leased to him *his* house at No. 12. The exchange of houses was settled on 13 July 1812 and Soane immediately demolished No. 13 and rebuilt it as a house-museum, very much as it still exists.[26] The exhibition space of 1808 was cut off from No. 12 and entered from No. 13. Today we call it 'the dome'. The basement continued to be the receptacle for sepulchral objects but it was not for another ten years that its character as a tomb-chamber was ratified and confirmed by the arrival of the Belzoni sarcophagus. Of that more presently.

In 1813, the year that Soane, with his wife, moved into the new house, he was sixty. The building of the De Loutherbourg monument at Chiswick, a tall, elegant and *112*
slightly sinister chest-tomb, with an affinity to the false doors at Dulwich, belongs to this year.[27] Just after Christmas he became seriously ill and in March 1814 underwent an operation. In the following year he had the satisfaction of being appointed one of the three architects to the newly-constituted Board of Works and, as architect to the Bank, received flattering attentions from the Emperor of Russia. But trouble came in 1815 with Mrs Soane's illness, exacerbated by the behaviour of her son, George, who saw fit to ridicule his father's architecture in some magazine articles. Mrs Soane, deeply hurt by this, died on 22 November 1815. She was buried nine days later in the burial ground of St Giles-in-the-Fields, which adjoins old St Pancras church. The date of burial, 1 December, is the date on a drawing (not in Soane's hand) for a brick vault, to which we must assume that the coffin was transferred in due course.[28] It measures 7 ft 3 in. by 4 ft 9 in. Over this vault, Soane was to erect one of his most bizarre and idiosyncratic monuments.

The memory-threads woven into this monument are various. A cinerary urn illustrated in Montfaucon[29] is one source. The monolithic head-piece of Soane's *113*
canopy is an enormously enlarged version of the lid of just such an urn. The cylindrical terminal, in the form of a pineapple is a classical symbol of eternity and so is the self-devouring snake curled round the base of the terminal; so perhaps also the undulating line etched along the edges of the head-piece. Taking the canopy and the space it covers together they can be interpreted as the breakfast room at 13 Lincoln's Inn Fields turned

114. One of the many projects for the Soane monument; a drawing by J. M. Gandy, 1816

inside out, the domical surface of the room's ceiling being externalized. (Soane's domed clock, still in the breakfast room, neatly demonstrates this inversion on the spot.) The heavy piers which support the canopy have been refined from the early design with sunk panels and delicately etched capitals, modelled on those in one of Campanella's engravings of decorations at the Villa Negroni, Rome.

Within the canopy and protected by it is a white marble monument, itself in the form of a canopy carried on four Ionic columns, but filled internally with the inscription-bearing marble block. Among the many preparatory designs for the monument, the earliest dated drawing is of 14 February 1816, but there are undated drawings which are certainly earlier. As all the designs are on the same general lines it is fair to assume that the basic idea had been adopted very soon after the event which called it forth. In the simplest terms the idea is of a monolithic convex canopy supported on four square piers, all in Portland stone, sheltering a more delicate monument in a more precious material – marble; the whole standing within an enclosure facilitating access to the vault.

116 One of the early drawings shows the canopy as brutally crude and primitive –
almost like a dolmen.[30] By stages it becomes more refined but still is in determined
contrast to the delicate Ionic monument within. All sorts of variations occur. In two
114 drawings a figure of death is shown emerging from the pedestal of the canopy and
hurling a spear at the marble monument, as does the wild Rococo skeleton in
Roubiliac's Nightingale monument in Westminster Abbey.[31] Another considered
feature was a gateway before the enclosure, carrying a pedimented lintel. This was
115 eliminated, and a modest iron gate substituted. Beyond this gate is a sunken area, a pit,
where one would expect to find steps leading down to the vault. But there are no steps
and probably never were. The entrance to the vault is, and probably always was, walled
up. There is not even a symbolic door.

115. The Soane monument in the former St Giles's graveyard (now St Pancras Gardens), as executed. An iron gate admits to a path leading abruptly to the sunk courtyard of the tomb-chamber *116.* An early design for the Soane monument made soon after Mrs Soane's death in November 1815. A powerful evocation of the 'primitive.'

117. Section of the Pitt cenotaph in the National Debt Redemption Office, Old Jewry, 1818. Demolished c. 1900

The commemorative inscriptions are on the marble monument under the canopy. At one stage Soane was considering an epitaph for the lintel of the proposed gateway and in March 1816 he wrote to his old friend Rowland Burdon of Castle Eden for advice.[32] His own suggestion was Vergil's *His saltem accumulem donis et fungar inani munere* (let me, at all events, pile up these funeral rites and perform vain offices). This had appeared on one of the Dulwich drawings and so may have been Mr Bourgeois's suggestion. Burdon advised something less laconic, from *Proverbs* or *Ecclesiasticus*, but Soane's choice seems to reflect all too sadly his sense that what he was doing was to erect a large and elaborate monument for no other purpose than to demonstrate his own grief and loneliness. But there was another purpose and one of which Soane can hardly have been unconscious. At his own death he would be buried there with his wife and the mausoleum would become the monument to a great architect – himself.

The balustrades of the enclosure carry those scrolled *acroteria* we have met before. They seem oddly misplaced. The curious 'drops' on the dies can be traced to the Roman painted ornaments which Soane imitated at Pitzhanger. In combination with the mourning putti lodged in two of the dies they seem to have caught something of the strangeness of Michelangelo in the Lorenzian Chapel. The only totally conventional elements in the building are the balusters – all too probably ordered from a Coade stone catalogue.

Soane's obsession with the furniture of death may seem to have reached, in this deeply personal and intense creation, its ultimate phase. Perhaps it had. But it was not long before circumstances conspired to involve him in another commemorative
117 enterprise, this time of a more public sort – the erection of the so-called Pitt cenotaph at the National Debt Redemption Office in Old Jewry. In 1818 the Commissioners for the Redemption of the National Debt leased from the Bank of England a property on which to build their office, for which the architect was to be the bank architect, Soane. It happened that at the same moment a committee appointed to erect a monument to William Pitt was considering where it should be placed and nothing seemed to them more appropriate than that it should be associated with that part of the nation's administration of which he had been the greatest promoter. The Commissioners agreed and the bank approved.[33] Soane was therefore required to include in his plans for the building an appropriate place for the reception of a robed and enthroned figure of Pitt in bronze, the work of Richard Westmacott. Models and drawings in the museum show with what seriousness Soane took this memorial to a man who was not only the greatest political figure of his age but had been a patron and benefactor of himself. In April 1818 he submitted plans and they were accepted.

The minutes of the Commissioners are terse and one wonders if they fully realized what Soane was giving them. This was, in effect, a Pitt shrine, consisting of a domed space, the dome opening upwards into a domed lantern with a ring of columns. There were recesses on three sides with the Westmacott figure in the recess facing the public hall, into which the fourth side opened. It was all much in the spirit of the two Desenfans/Bourgeois mausolea and is related also to Soane's 'tribunes' at Tyringham and elsewhere. There were no corpses so Soane called the structure a 'cenotaph', thus conveying the idea of a symbolic tomb-house. In an early design he shows cinerary urns, lodged on shelves in the lateral recesses, as if for a whole family of Pitts. These vanished, however, to be replaced by two hollow, vertical three-sided objects with urn-like tops, not unlike the Reading obelisk in miniature, marking the entrance to the shrine. The purpose of these is not very clear. Models for them, in the Soane Museum, are described in the inventory as 'pedestals'. But they support nothing.[34] They must be read, presumably as commemorative obelisks. But why two? The cenotaph took up a quite disproportionate amount of the site area and vanished, along with the office, in about 1900. The Westmacott statue survived and may be seen today with its back to Alfred Waterhouse's library at Pembroke College, Cambridge.

At the time of the building of the Pitt cenotaph, Soane was buying very liberally for his museum: in 1818, casts and marbles from Robert Adam's collection, in 1821 the marbles collected by Heathcote Tatham for Henry Holland, in the same year an important Reynolds, and in 1823 Hogarth's *Election* cycle. In 1824 came the

118. The 'Belzoni Sarcophagus'. The sarcophagus of the Pharaoh Seti I, discovered in 1815 by Giambattista Belzoni and bought by Soane in 1824

opportunity to eclipse all these by the purchase of the rarest and most spectacular piece of all – the Belzoni sarcophagus.

This fabulous work of funeral art, to be known in due course as the sarcophagus of *118* Seti I, had been discovered by Giambattista Belzoni, under the patronage of the British Consul-General in Egypt, Henry Salt, in 1817. Salt had shipped it to England in 1821, where it was deposited in the British Museum, pending arrangements for its purchase by the government. As the price required by Salt was £2,000 and the museum trustees were disinclined to give even half that sum the arrangements, after more than two years of waiting and haggling, came to nothing.[35] In February 1824, Soane approached one of the trustees whom he knew well (his neighbour, Mr Tyndale) begging him to procure for him the reversion of the sarcophagus, should the government not purchase. The reversion was obtained and Soane paid £2,000 to Salt's agent. An opening was made in the back wall of the museum to receive this monster coffin which was lowered into the crypt on 12 May. It was the most costly acquisition Soane had ever made.

The space in the crypt under the dome was, of course, the only place in the museum where the sarcophagus could possibly go and its eligibility for this position must have

gone far in recommending its purchase. 'Catacombs' and a 'mausoleum' had been in Soane's mind when he planned this area and here was a justification of such themes ampler than he could have imagined. Nevertheless, in a curiously oblique way, it had been imagined for him. Some nine years earlier, his eccentric perspectivist, Joseph Gandy, an artist no less concerned than Soane with funerary themes, had offered him as
119 a gift a fantastically elaborate drawing he had made called 'The Tomb of Merlin'.[36]

It showed the magician's sarcophagus in a crypt, clustered with curious monuments, a pale glow emanating from the translucent sarcophagus itself. Soane either did not accept the gift or passed the drawing on to his friend Westmacott. But when, at a reception he gave in 1825, he placed lamps inside the Belzoni sarcophagus to display its translucency and sent out invitations 'to see the sarcophagus by lamp-light', he must surely have reflected on the uncanny prescience of Gandy's proffered gift.

The acquisition of the sarcophagus was Soane's greatest triumph as a collector. It must amply have satisfied his vanity. Its extreme (though then still unascertained) antiquity extended his romantic experience of the archaic. But there is perhaps more to it. In making an empty tomb the centre-piece of his domestic museum, Soane was creating what would inevitably be seen as a monument to himself. It was already a monument to its discoverer, Belzoni, and remained so until Egyptologists gave a more prominent role to the Pharaoh, Seti I, for whom the sarcophagus had been made. But if it was 'the Belzoni sarcophagus' it was also, by virtue of its architectural enthronement in the museum, very much the Soane sarcophagus – almost, indeed, a Soane cenotaph.

I am not suggesting that any ideas of this sort passed through Soane's mind. But in relation to the chain of circumstances which I have recited the installation of the sarcophagus becomes an act of some biographical and psychological significance. It was now forty-seven years since the drowning of James King had set off the series of designs for ideal mausolea. The rooms at Pitzhanger followed; then the crypt and catacombs at Lincoln's Inn Fields and, at the same time, involvement in the burial enterprises of Sir Francis Bourgeois; then Mrs Soane's tomb; then the Pitt cenotaph and, finally, the acquisition of the Belzoni sarcophagus.

I say 'finally' because the occasion seems climactic. But it is not quite the end of the tale. In the same year, or very soon afterwards, another place of burial appeared at 13 Lincoln's Inn Fields – the tomb of the 'monk'. In 1824, Soane bought No. 14 Lincoln's Inn Fields and rebuilt it as an independent dwelling-house for leasing. He used the site of the stable at the rear, however, to extend his galleries. The extension comprised a top-lit picture-room on the ground floor and below, at crypt level, a low-ceilinged
120 room which was to become the 'Monk's Parlour'. A space between this and the rear of the new house became the 'Monk's Yard'. In this yard Soane built two arches made up of Gothic stonework from Westminster and called it the monk's 'cloister'. Lastly, beneath the window of the parlour he assembled a variety of odd fragments to form the monk's 'tomb'.

Who was the monk? Soane, in his *Description* of the museum, calls him 'Padre Giovanni' – Father John. Who was this 'Father John'? Was he John Soane? Not quite. A passage in the *Description* contributed by Mrs Barbara Hofland seems to show that the monk was a fanciful proto-Soane who had lived and suffered in a vaguely remote dark age. In creating him Soane was, I am afraid, being coyly humorous. He quotes

119. The Tomb of Merlin, 1815, by J. M. Gandy, offered by him to Soane 'as a mark of my esteem and gratitude.' It forestalls the installation of the Belzoni sarcophagus by nine years

Horace's *Dulce est desipere in loco* – it is pleasant to be nonsensical in due place. In the Monk's Parlour and its adjuncts, including the tomb, Soane was being nonsensical. He had done something of the sort at Pitzhanger, with a 'monk's dining-room' in the basement, vestiges of which survive. At Lincoln's Inn Fields, things were more elaborate but equally nonsensical. We must not make the mistake of seeing the Monk's Parlour as a serious attempt at antiquarianism. It is a *bricolage*, made up almost entirely of old and modern junk. It is a parody of the Strawberry Hill vision and it mocks the earnest kind of antiquarian studies which, in 1824, were making serious advances. So what of the monk's tomb? To build, at the age of seventy-one, out of junk, a pretence tomb for a likeness of oneself in one's own back yard may seem to us a rather dreary kind of joke – a kind of self-mockery. Nor is it much enlivened by the actual burial there of a pet dog and the addition to the head-stone of the inscription 'Alas! poor Fanny'. It all sounds a bit silly; and, as described in the sentimental and platitudinous prose of Mrs Hofland, which Soane must, I suppose, have approved, the silliness plunges to bathos.

Soane's interest in the furniture of death passed through four successive phases. In the first phase Soane uses the mausoleum theme dispassionately to exercise and display his powers of original composition. The King mausoleum, the studies for mausolea for William Pitt serve this purpose. Then comes an archaeological phase, the collecting mania of *c.*1800, the creation of the urn-filled rooms at Pitzhanger and the use of cinerary urns to enrich the sky-line of the Bank of England. This phase is followed by a third one in which he is involved in actual places of burial: the two Desenfans mausolea, at Hallam Street and Dulwich, the Loutherbourg monument at Chiswick and immediately afterwards the monument for the burial place for his own wife. These all show a new emotional attitude, a use of imagery of an evocative kind – the locked door, the drawn blind, the impenetrable recess, culminating in the vault and monument for his family and himself. In all these there is a sense of abstraction, an exploitation of the 'primitive', combined with the 'antique'. There are no Christian symbols, only symbols of eternity. In the fourth and last phase there is a return to archaeology, introduced by the acquisition of the Belzoni sarcophagus and continued in the creation of the Monk's yard, cloister, parlour and oratory. Here, however, archaeology dissolves into antiquarianism: senile play-acting in the scene of his own approaching death.

After the creation of the monk's apartments, Soane lived on for another thirteen years, nine of them as a distinguished public architect, engaged on the new Law-courts at Westminster Hall and a new State Paper Office. His very last exercise in funereal composition was a gratuitous suggestion for a 'sepulchral church and military chapel' to be erected in St James's Park for the Duke of York who died in 1827. The designs are of no great interest, one being merely an elaboration of the design for a church at Tyringham, made some twenty-five years earlier.

Soane was knighted in 1831. In 1833 he obtained the Act of Parliament under which the museum and its contents were to be vested in trustees after his death and preserved for ever from alteration or rearrangement in consideration of an endowment left by him. In 1835, a committee representing the architectural profession met at Lincoln's Inn Fields to present him with a laudatory address and a gold medal. On 20 January 1837, Sir John Soane died and, at mid-day on 26 January, the remains were deposited with those of his wife and son under the monument at St Pancras. The funeral was 'strictly private'.

120. The 'Monk's Tomb' in the 'Monk's Yard', constructed by Soane in 1824 at the back of No. 14 Lincoln's Inn Fields. Its only occupant is Fanny, a pet dog. The adjoining 'cloister' is composed of fragments of Gothic masonry from Westminster Palace

VIII · The Evolution of Soane's Bank Stock Office in the Bank of England

121. Soane's Bank Stock Office as completed in 1792. A perspective view by J. M. Gandy.

122. Sir Robert Taylor's Bank Stock Office, demolished 1792; aquatint by T. Malton

123. Soane's Bank Stock Office photographed in the early 1930s

In the Bank Stock Office at the Bank of England, built in 1792, Soane created an interior of a kind previously unknown in England and not found elsewhere except in a type of Byzantine church with which few English architects were familiar and which none would have regarded as an acceptable model for imitation. The building, demolished about 1925 and re-built in facsimile as part of the Bank of England
Museum in 1988, may be described as follows: it is cruciform, consisting of a square *136*
central area or 'crossing', extending from which are two deep arms (north and south) and two shallow arms (east and west). Each of the deep arms is covered with a segmental cross-vault, each of the shallow arms with a segmental barrel vault of the same radius. The four vaults meet at the 'crossing'. In the four angles of the cross are chambers, barrel-vaulted, but at a lower level than the vaults of the adjacent arms. These chambers open through wide semicircular-headed openings into the deep arms and through narrow 'passage' openings into the shallow arms, an arrangement somewhat resembling the aisles of a church. Lighting is from a circular lantern-light over the 'crossing' and from lunettes in the sides of the deep arms.[1]

How this interior evolved is the subject of the present paper. A controlling factor was the plan and substructure of the building already on the site and whose foundations were re-used by Soane. Soane's predecessor as architect to the Bank was Sir Robert Taylor who, at various unrecorded dates between 1766 and 1788, built at the corner of Threadneedle Street and Bartholomew Lane a rotunda and four halls. Two of the latter ran north and south along Bartholomew Lane, with a vestibule to the rotunda between them; the other two, running east and west, stood north and south of the rotunda respectively. The northernmost of the halls in Bartholomew Lane was
used as the Bank Stock Office; that is to say, the public hall where the purchase and *122*
registration of Bank Stock and the issue of dividends was conducted by the appropriate clerks. This was the hall which Soane re-built in 1792. The other three halls and the rotunda were re-built by him between that date and 1823.

Taylor's four halls were all on the same model, borrowed, in principle, from Gibbs's St Martin-in-the-Fields, i.e. a rectangular plan with sixteen columns separating the central area from side and end passages. Each column supported an articulated entablature and from these sprang arches intersecting a barrel vault covering the 'nave', while the 'aisles' or passages were crossed by arches between which were small domes, carried on pendentives. Lighting was from three partly glazed openings in the crown of the nave vault and also from the aisle domes just mentioned. The columns in Taylor's halls appear to have been of stone with capitals and entablatures of carved wood (a specimen is in the Soane Museum) fixed round a load-bearing core. The vault was timber, plastered. Above the vault was a framed timber roof covered with lead.[2]

Taylor had found it necessary to make very deep piled foundations both for the main walls and for those carrying his sixteen columns, the tops of the piles, in both cases, being 14 ft below floor level. To distribute the weight of the columns, inverted brick arches were formed between each pair. As Soane's drawings show, he preserved the whole of Taylor's foundation work. He excavated the area between the walls, however, and constructed brick vaults to carry a new floor.[3] The new vaults had the

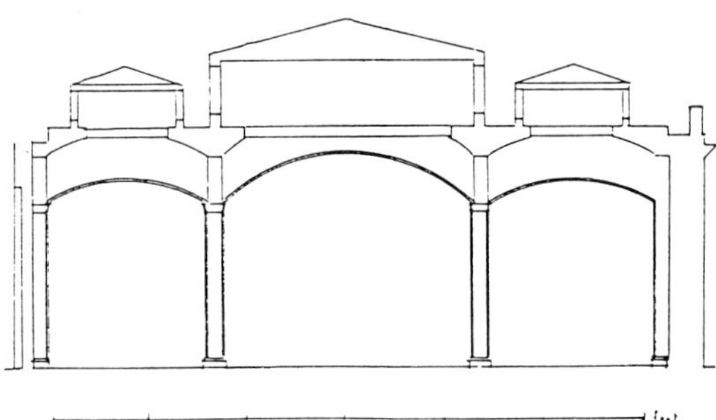

124. Long section of Soane's first design for the Bank Stock Office, abstracted from the detail on the right-hand side of the drawing opposite *125.* Taylor's Bank Stock Office, plan and section dated 19 November 1791, with Soane's design for rebuilding superimposed in broken lines. Marginal sketches for a stove and column are attributed to George Dance. (Pf. 3/1)

effect of binding this lower part of the building into a continuous, homogeneous structure.

125 The first drawing on which Soane's intentions for a new superstructure are seen is Portfolio 3/1. This shows the plan and four sections of Taylor's hall, drawn presumably by Soane's pupil, Thomas Chawner, who, according to the office Day Book, had measured the building on 19 November 1791 (this date appears also on the drawing, though it can hardly have been executed on the same day). Over this is drawn, in broken lines and by the same hand, what appears to be a first proposal for rebuilding. Isolated from Chawner's drawing it is shown in Pl. 124. Soane here proposes to remove all Taylor's columns but to replace them in four instances by piers, thus completely altering the spatial character of the building. The new piers mark four corners of a central square and this has the effect of dividing the hall in the ratio 2:3:2 longitudinally and 1:3:1 across. The new piers are joined to one another by very flat segmental arches springing at 16 ft above floor level. Segmental arches also join the piers to the end walls. A circular lantern on pendentives appears to be intended for the central bay. This design is very little more than a diagram though it does comprise the essentials of the building as executed in the following year.

We must now turn our attention to certain freehand sketches and annotations added to Chawner's drawing at an unknown date. These are not by Chawner or Soane but almost certainly by George Dance. They include, bottom left, a sketch in black ink of a spiral column with a palm-leaf capital and the enriched springing of a vault, against which is written 'Oak leaves, Acorns, Birds'. Presumably also by Dance are pencil sketches of a triangular stove with three open fireplaces. This stove is shown to be, in fact, the pedestal upon which the column stands.

126 The meaning of the sketches becomes clear when we turn to Pf. 3/18. In this longitudinal section the arrangement of piers, arches and roof-lights is very close to Pl. 124 but in the middle of the square central bay is a column standing on a stove. From the capital of the column springs a vault which rises to the top of the central roof-light, while the shaft of the column provides a flue for the stove, emerging in a chimney above roof level.

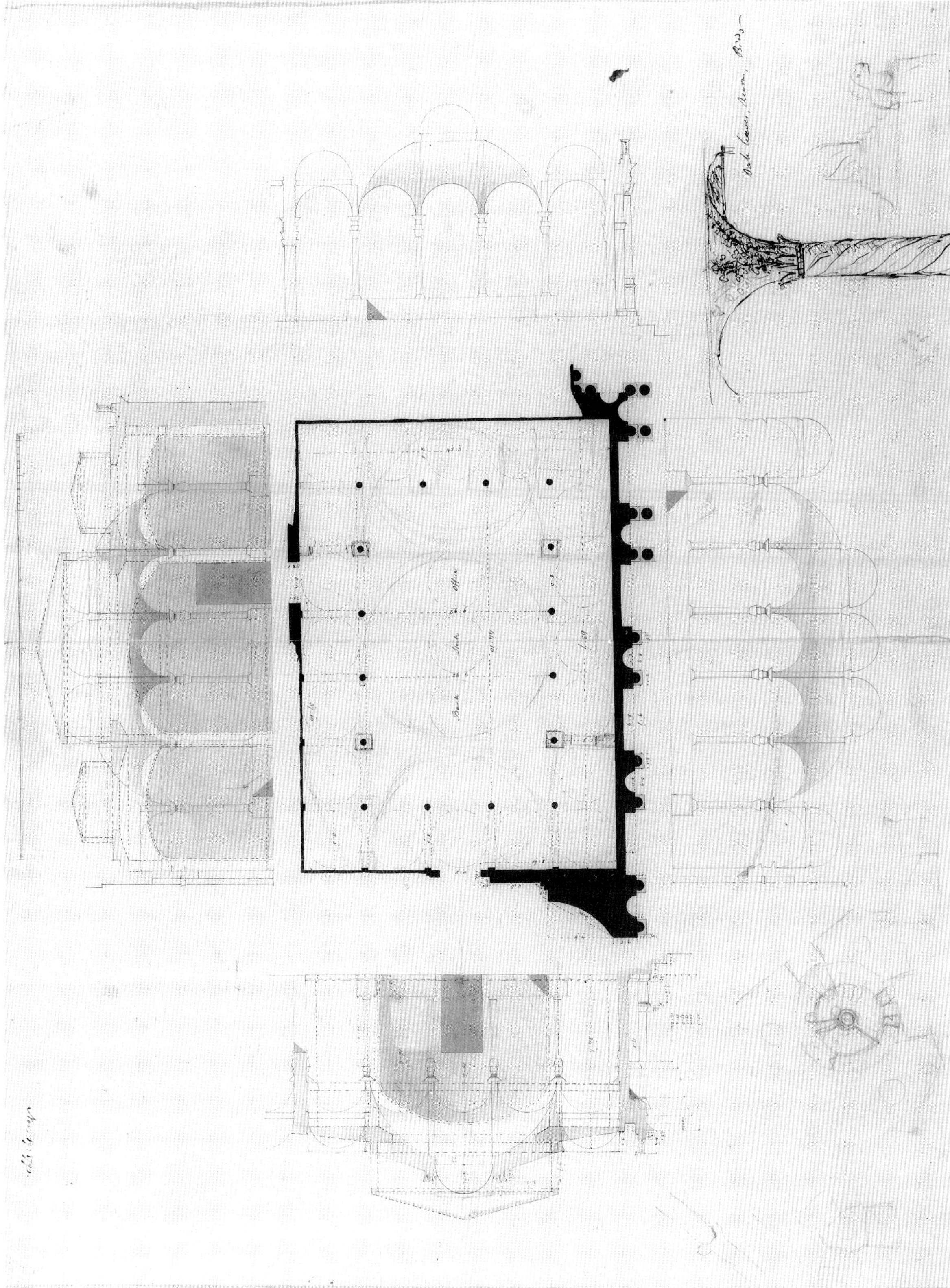

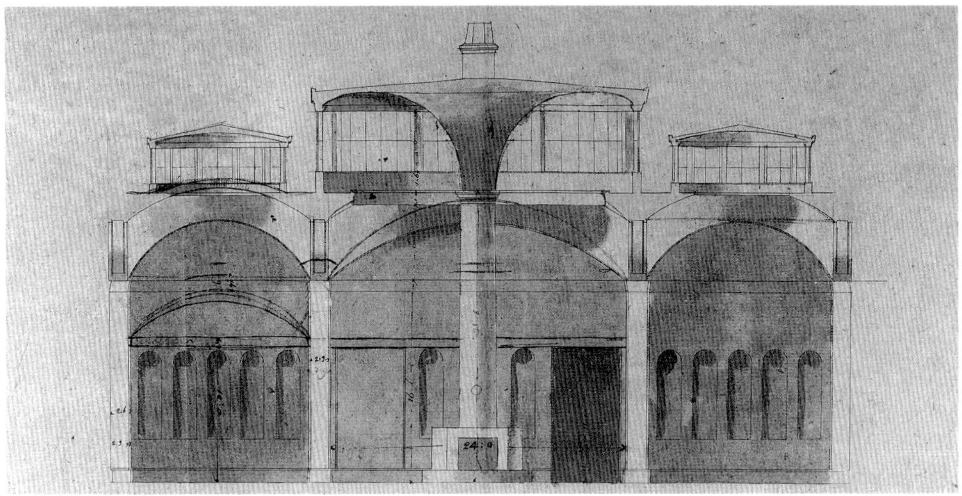

126. Long section of Soane's Bank Stock Office with stove-pipe column. (Pf. 3/18)

The obvious conclusion to be drawn from all this is that the stove-pipe column was a suggestion by Dance which was adopted by Soane. The suggestion may seem to us grotesque and the character of Dance's annotated sketch almost suggests that it was intended to be humorous.[4] But Soane adopted it with great seriousness and the stove-pipe column occurs in a series of five sections (Pf. 3/18, 17, 15, 16, 19), the last of which (if my order is accepted) is dated 1 March 1792.[5] Four of these sections are shown in Pls 125, 130, 131 and 132.

Before proceeding we must consider some further evidence of the participation of George Dance in the building's design. This consists of a series of sketches pasted into an album marked on the spine 'Original Sketches'[6] (hereinafter OS). One of the sketches (OS 175) bears the inscription 'Recd. at Bank Dec. 11 1791' and another (OS 170) simply 'Recd.' with the same date. This is a fortnight after the date on Chawner's drawing. Dance's name nowhere appears and the sketches are here attributed to him wholly on the style of the sketches and the handwriting.

The sketches show a series of connected ideas for a three-bay vaulted hall with
127 aisles. In one design the three bays are identical, with semi-circular (or, in a marginal version, segmental) arches between the piers and semicircular lunettes intersecting the continuous barrel-vault of the 'nave'. The lunettes recall Dance's All Hallows, London
128 Wall. Another design proposes a combination of segmental arches and lunettes but with cross-vaults in the end bays and, in the centre bay, pendentives subtending a
129 circular lantern-light. In a trio of sketches on one sheet this idea develops rapidly. The centre bays are opened up as 'transepts' to the central space and we have, in principle, the 'Byzantine' space mentioned earlier. The building is now cruciform above the level of the roofs of the end bays. Semicircular arches are adopted for the openings from the deep arms into the 'aisles' and, in fact, all the essentials for the executed building are present.

127. Sketch design attributed to George Dance dated 11 December 1791. (OS 170)

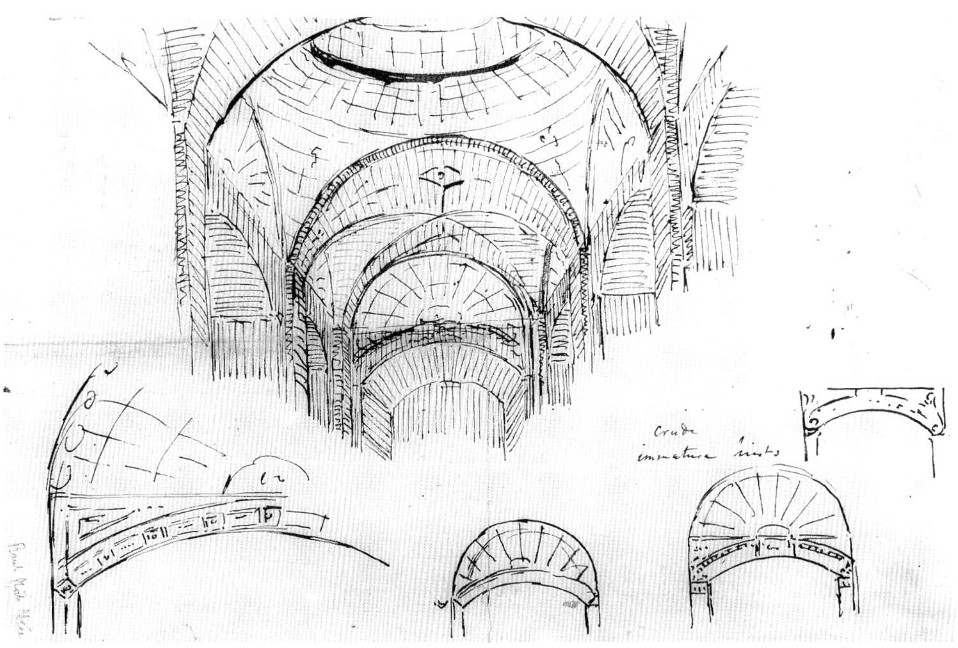

128. Sketch design attributed to George Dance, inscribed 'crude immature hints' and 'Recd. at Bank Dec 11 1791.' (OS 175)

129. Sketch designs attributed to George Dance. (OS 171)

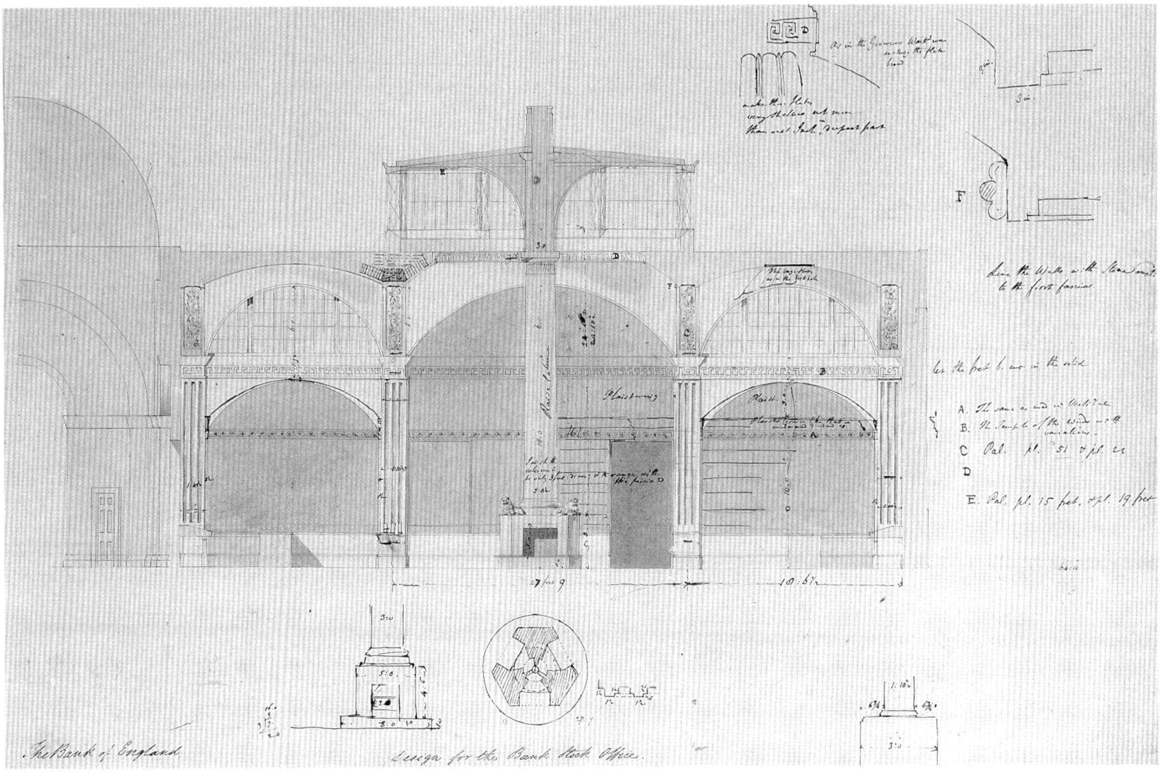

130. Long section of Soane's Bank Stock Office with a central column which contains the flue from a triple stove forming its base. (Pf. 3/15). This is developed from Dance's tentative sketches on Pf 3/1. (ill. 125)

131. Long section of Soane's Bank Stock Office with stove-pipe column. (Pf. 3/16)

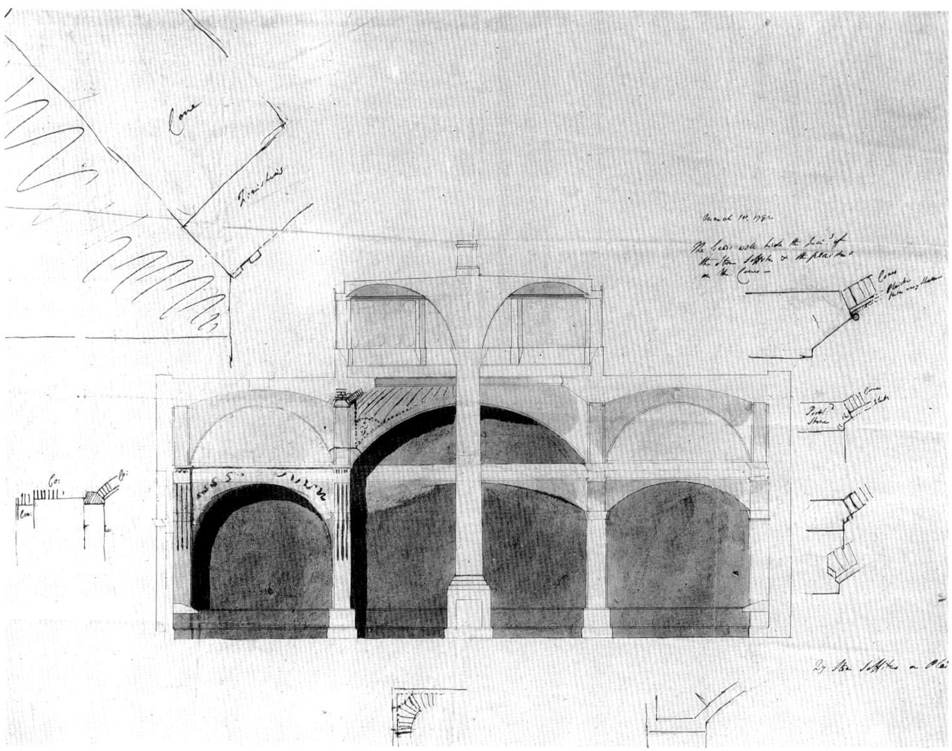

132. Long section of Soane's Bank Stock Office with stove-pipe column. Marginal sketches dated 1 March 1792 showing construction with fire-clay cones. (Pf. 3/19)

In these sketches one has the strong impression of a single mind passing from phase to phase in an exploratory ramble. Dance's note on OS 175, 'crude immature hints', reflects the spirit in which the sketches are offered. They seem, as does the sketch for the stove-pipe column, like an invitation to Soane to adopt a bold approach to the problem and to exercise the sort of stylistic freedom which Dance was demonstrating in some of his own works. What Soane made of his invitation will be seen in what follows.

None of Dance's designs takes account of the points of support surviving from the old hall. They are free conceptions of a totally new building on the site. Nevertheless, there can be no question that the designs had a decisive effect on Soane's final solution.

An interesting aspect of the Dance sketches is the type of ornament indicated. It appears to consist almost entirely either of incised lines or very low relief modelling. There is no 'order' in the canonical sense, either real or implied, nor is there any conventional enrichment. Here and there is an approximation to a Greek fret and in one instance a plant-form, borrowed from a ceiling engraved by Bartoli (and paraphrased, incidentally, by Dance at Cranbury).[7] This deliberate avoidance of conventional modes of expression is, of course, found in Dance's Council Chamber (1777) and Chamberlain's Court (1787–89) at Guildhall[8] and these sketches for the Bank Stock Office are in the same mood of stylistic liberation.

Returning now to the sequence of office drawings, we have already noticed the
strong connexion of the 'stove-pipe column' sections with the primitive design shown
on the Chawner survey. All the 'stove-pipe' sections except the first omit the lantern- *125*
lights over the end bays, while the aisle vaults in these bays are dropped to a lower
level. This, in principle, is very much what we have (without the stove-pipe column) in
the last of the Dance sketches. Soane, however, has not accepted the total freedom *129*
from convention proposed by Dance. The piers have fluted pilasters in relief
representing a token 'order' and in Pf. 3/15 are notes prescribing antique sources for *130*
certain enrichments including references to Wood's *Palmyra*.[9] In Pf. 3/16, however, *131*
this combination of the segmental arches with the lunettes in the end bays obviously
owes something to the marginal 'hints' in Dance's OS 175. *128*

The last of the 'stove-pipe' sections appears to be Pf. 3/19. Here it is proposed to *132*
lower the vault of the central aisle bays to the level of those of the end bays as is shown
by the very flat segmental arch which now crosses the central bay at the lower level.
The purpose of this will be explained when we come to the next drawings in the series.
Meanwhile it is important to note that Pf. 3/19 is the first drawing which shows the use
of fire-clay 'cones' for the vaults.[10] The system is illustrated in six small and one larger
sketch section with annotations. It is to these sketches and annotations that the date 1
March 1792 seems to apply.

Nearly contemporary with the 'stove-pipe' series are two designs containing important changes. The stove-pipe column disappears; and arrangements are proposed for enclosed spaces on an upper level. The first design (Pf. 3/30 and 31; not illustrated) obviously takes its departure from Pf. 3/19 and explains the interposition of the lower segmental arch in the central bay tentatively sketched in the drawing. The lunette above is shaded dark which seems to mean that it admits no light in the main interior but does admit 'borrowed' light to a room over the centre bay of the aisle. This is confirmed in the cross-section.

In the second design (Pf. 3/26 and 28), the cross-section is initialled and dated 'J.S. March 10th. 1792' (it is the only autographed drawing in the collection). In this design, the long section of which is shown in Pl. 133, the vaults of the end bays of the nave are brought down to the level of the vaults of the aisle bays. So now we have a central area rising full height to the dome and lantern light and surrounded on all four sides by lower spaces. The object of this seems to be to occupy the whole of the space over the aisles with rooms and to light the central area from lunettes on north and south instead of from east and west. The rooms at the upper level would receive 'borrowed' light from the main hall in the central bay and direct light in the two end bays. There is no indication of what purpose these rooms would have served or how access to them would have been gained.

The unsatisfactory character of this design with its muddled use of lunettes and weak and jarring curvatures, is obvious. We can only suppose that there was pressure to provide these upper rooms and Soane saw this as the only way of doing so. Happily the design was abandoned.

The ultimate solution of the problem seems to make its first appearance in Pf. 3/22, *134*
a crude statement lacking the final adjustments and ornaments. The ornaments of the
Bank Stock Office seem to owe something to Dance though they are never quite as free

133. Long section of Soane's Bank Stock Office with continuous enclosed spaces over the aisles, (Pf. 3/26). (The companion drawing of the cross-section, Pf. 3/28, is signed 'J. S. 10 Mar. 1792')

as in his sketches. Soane evidently wished to preserve a rudimentary 'order' and fluted pilasters occur in all but the first of the 'stove-pipe' series and are retained in the
130 executed work. The channelled treatment of the walls is also first seen in Pf. 3/15. The serrated treatment of the pendentives in the crossing and the antique paterae or roundels with lion heads are seen for the first time in large-scale working details.

It remains to consider whether, in the evolution of the Bank Stock Office, experience of Byzantine church types can have played any part. Such architecture did not pass wholly unnoticed. Santa Sophia, Constantinople, is illustrated in various travel books and was taken by James Wyatt as the basis of his Pantheon in Oxford Street, 1770. That, however, is not much to our purpose. Probably the only illustration of a simpler Byzantine type which could have influenced Soane and Dance at the Bank
135 is an engraving of the monk's choir adjoining the church of the Holy Sepulchre in Jerusalem, in Corneille Lebrun's *Voyage au Levant*, 1714.[11] This illustration was copied and used by Thomas Sandby in his Royal Academy lectures and would certainly be familiar to Soane and Dance before 1790.[12] Sandby used it 'to exemplify or show from whence what is called *Saxon Architecture* took its rise'. The double-page engraving shows the 'crossing' of the church with its pendentives and a circular ring of windows above; beyond the 'crossing' is a vaulted bay and through the side arches 'transepts' are
121 seen. In general outline this is the shape of the Bank Stock Office as erected.

Dance, with his strong eclectic leanings and his periodic probing of the primitive and the exotic would be more likely than Soane to discover value in a curiosity of this

134. Long section of Soane's Bank Stock Office, the penultimate stage. (Pf. 3/22)

135. Corneille Lebrun's illustration of the monks' choir adjoining the church of the Holy Sepulchre, Jerusalem, in *Voyage au Levant*, 1714. (Compare with ill. 123)

kind dredged up from the dark ages; and his perspective sketch (OS 175) certainly suggests an acquaintance with the Lebrun engraving. It is also worth observing that the church shown by Lebrun was associated with the great rotunda of the Holy Sepulchre, which Lebrun also illustrates; a relationship which would inevitably evoke the relation of the halls to the rotunda at the Bank of England.

Obviously, no conclusion can be drawn and a Byzantine derivation remains highly speculative. We have seen that the first steps towards the creation of Soane's Bank Stock Office were taken when it was decided to retain and re-use four points of support on Taylor's foundations. From that decision sprang the original diagrammatic sections. Then we have Dance's sketches, starting with the fairly formal round-arch design and continuing with versions of increasing freedom till something approximating to the final arrangement is reached; it is in these sketches that the design acquires its
123 quasi-Byzantine form. The Bank Stock Office, as built, was the prototype of Soane's later Bank halls: the Old Shutting Room (1795–6), the Consols Office (1797–9), the Old Dividend Office (1818–23) and the Colonial Office (1818–23). The type was never adopted elsewhere, perhaps because of its complexity and perhaps because interiors of this form have no obvious functional merit. The form arose from the special circumstances present at the bank and remained the bank's exclusive contribution to English architecture.

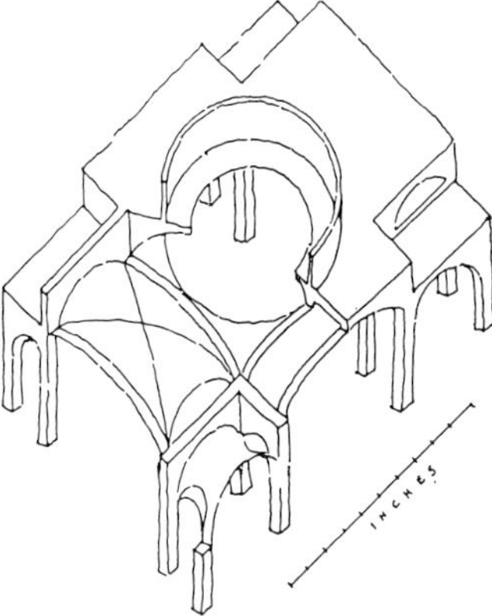

136. Diagram of Soane's Bank Stock Office, based on the model of 1793 in the Soane Museum, showing the arrangement of domes and vaults

IX · Charting the Victorian Building World

137. Dulwich College, by Charles Barry Jnr., 1866–70, using terracotta from J. M. Blashfield's factory. The first application in England of terracotta on a monumental scale

138. Offices at 65 Cornhill, designed by Edward I'Anson, 1870. The front is constructed entirely of terracotta, with a backing of brickwork in Portland cement. The builders were Cubitts and they modelled the terracotta in their own yard at Grays Inn Road

IN THE PAST FIFTY YEARS much has been written on Victorian architects and architecture but almost nothing on Victorian *building*. Raymond Postgate's *The Builders' History* (1923) deals exclusively with trade unionism. Marion Bowley's works are concerned with the economics of the industry in the present century. There is, so far as I can discover, not a single work describing what the industry consisted of in the 19th century and plotting the innovations which so profoundly changed its character. The essay which follows is an attempt to sketch the kind of book which might be written on this subject – its outline and contents. It would not be a book about the building 'industry' but about a wider and vaguer area, which, to avoid precise definition, we may conveniently call 'the building world'. The expression commits us to no boundaries but suggests a radiation of activity from the central act of construction. Obviously there are no absolute boundaries.[1] Building draws upon many human activities and resources, from digging clay and importing timber to writing books and manufacturing pencil-sharpeners. The economics of building engage with the economics of property-holding, transport, insurance and much else not necessarily exclusive to building. It therefore seems improper to confine it, as we sometimes do to architects, builders and their employees or, at least, to do so without at the same time trying to extend our view outwards and to chart at least some of the territory which lies beyond the building site. To do so leads us into regions relatively unexplored which require research to illuminate, but it is not difficult to throw out some hints as to what to look for in these regions and that is what I propose to do.

We are talking about the *Victorian* building world and the first thing to enquire is whether the Victorians themselves were conscious of that world as an area of Victorian life, how they saw it and what they felt about it. The answer to this question is at least partly answered for us by the founder and first editor of *The Builder*, Joseph Aloysius Hansom. Hansom started on that famous enterprise in 1842 when he was thirty-four. He had built the Birmingham Town Hall, which he won in competition, but little else and he had taken out a patent for a type of Hackney Carriage, thus demonstrating an uncommon breadth of interest in technological problems. His conception of *The Builder* was not of a magazine for architects (there were, or had been several of these) nor for builders in the sense merely of building contractors but for anybody who had anything to do with building. The title of the first issue (the 'Precursor' issue of 31 December 1842) is as follows: *The Builder: an illustrated weekly magazine for the Drawing-Room, the Studio, the Office, the Workshop and the Cottage*. This picturesquely defines an extensive band of the social spectrum without telling us much. However, at the end of this issue is a manifesto of the paper's aims, accompanied by two lists, which give us what we want. One is an alphabetical list of building trades with figures extracted from the 1841 census. The other list is far more important. It is a rough list of various classes of people – tradesmen, manufacturers and others not necessarily within 'the trade' who are or should be interested in the new periodical; 'interested', says the editor, 'both as a medium for obtaining information and for advertising their own productions and requirements'. This list, compiled for the express purpose of defining the probable sales area of an advertising medium called *The Builder*, seems as good a starting point as any for a study of what 'the Victorian building world' should mean.

Before we attempt a break-down of this list it is worth following the editor's arguments a little further. The second issue (18 February 1843) carries a leader describing the scepticism which he encountered in starting the project. 'Grave and experienced men', he says, 'hold up their hands in astonishment at the rashness of our enterprise. They say the Builders are not a reading class, nor a class at all either in themselves or their connection'. Editorially, it may be said that these critics were proved right, for *The Builder* was to become, under later editors, primarily an architectural paper. The social spread from drawing-room to cottage was never achieved – or only nominally, perhaps. But they were proved wrong in that they underestimated the importance of advertising and it was advertising that floated *The Builder* on its majestic course and made it an indispensable organ for so many participants in the building world who were neither architects nor builders. It goes without saying that it is the advertisement page of *The Builder* (and, of course, its later rivals) which must be studied if we are to apprehend what Hansom meant by 'the Building class', or what we are calling the 'building world'.

To return to the list aforementioned. There are 102 items, alphabetically arranged. If we scramble the list and reconstruct it in some sort of logical order, we shall begin to have a diagram of the picture we are seeking. Perhaps the best way to do this is to re-arrange the items under headings which reflect as nearly as possible the building process. The headings I suggest are as follows. 1. Builders' plant. 2. Supplies of building materials. 3. Supplies of building components. 4. Supply and installation of equipment and services. 5. Artist craftsmen. 6. Drawing Office supplies. These headings do not cover everything in Hansom's list, which includes, for example, railways, canals and carriers, estate agents, booksellers, brokers, insurance companies, schools of design, loan societies, mechanics' institutes, and patent agencies. The relevance of all these to the building world is obvious but they are not wholly and entirely of it so we may dismiss them.

There would be little point in developing the subject from Hansom's list alone. It was compiled in 1842 and a great deal was to happen in the building world in the next thirty years. The image of the building world as a coherent area of British industrial life is reflected more elaborately than by Hansom in a massive publication of 1868 entitled *The Architect's, Engineer's and Building-trades Directory, a Business Book of Reference for the various Industries Connected with the Art of Construction*, published by Wyman and Sons.[2] Here are twice as many trades as are listed by Hansom and there is a nation-wide directory for each trade. In passing, it is worth noting which trades claim the greatest share of space. Builders, not suprisingly, head the list with 37½ pages. They are followed by plumbers (19¼), mechanical engineers (17½), gas fitters (14), iron-founders (10½), and brass-founders (7¾), in that order. These priorities suggest that metal-workers involved in mechanical construction and services were, after contracting, the most prominent businesses within our world, the older crafts having become increasingly absorbed into the builder's own organization. At the end of this admirable directory is a good, thick section of classified advertisements with many useful wood-cuts.

From such sources as these, together with the descriptions of currently completed buildings in *The Builder* and other building periodicals, the Post Office Directories, the

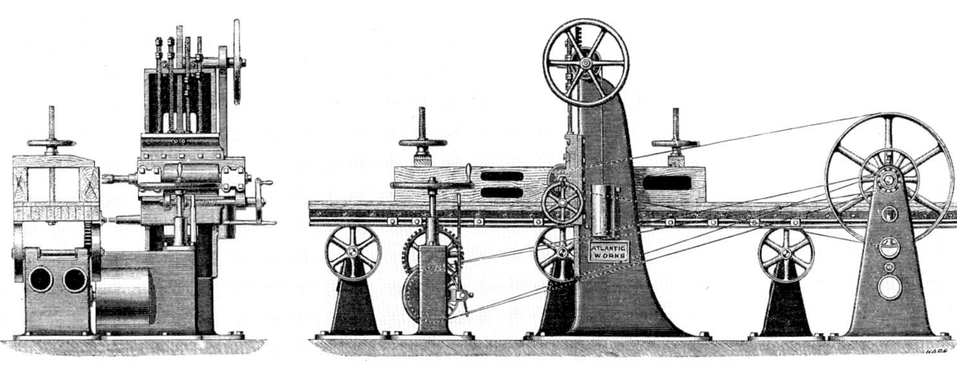

139. Wood-working machine. From J. Richards' *Treatise on the Construction and operation of wood-working Machines*, 1872

census returns, the files of the Patent Office, the contemporary literature of building technology and the articles in the Architectural Publication Society's *Dictionary* (not forgetting the editor's own richly interleaved copy in the Soane Museum) a very satisfactory picture could be put together of what, as its shape becomes clearer, we may venture to call the Victorian building industry. Surprisingly, such a picture has never been drawn and let me say at once that I have no intention of drawing it. All I am doing here is sketch very roughly, in the manner of a scrap-book, *some* of the things it might contain.

First, builders' plant. Under this head I have assembled from Hansom only these few categories: tool-makers; machine-makers; mill-wrights and millstones; grindstones; steam-engines and boiler makers; and, rather oddly, builders' cards and advertisements. What were the steam-engines for? Hermione Hobhouse answers this question in her book on Cubitt when (chap. 14) she gives an account of the Cubitt works at Millbank (where Dolphin Court now stands).[3] In 1845, steam power was being applied to sawing timber, polishing marble, pumping water, preparing food for the horses and clipping iron bars. There were other forms of steam-driven mechanization at that date at Cubitts and elsewhere, two of the most notable being machines for brick-making and machines for the preparation of joinery.

The wood-working machines developed first, timber-framed types being in *139*
common use in America before they were taken up in Britain where they were re-designed on more sophisticated lines, with metal frames. Cubitts used wood-working machines for joinery components in their Isle of Dogs factory[4] and they featured conspicuously in Corbett and McClymont's rapid development of the Redcliffe estate, Kensington, in the 1860s and 1870s.[5] John Richards, whose treatise on the subject was published in 1872, tells us confidently that by that date machines had completely supplanted hand-labour.[6] Their main use was for ordinary repetitive joinery but there were also machines which could accurately copy carved work. As early as 1845 Taylor, Williams and Jordan's carving and copying machines were hired for use at the Houses of Parliament.[7] Jordan set up at Belvedere Road, Lambeth but by 1860 the business had passed to Cox and Co. who, finding that opinion was veering away from the ideal of the

'mechanical copy', claimed only that their machines executed approximate outlines, leaving scope for the artist's touch in the finishing.[8]

Brick-making machines came in with Cook and Cunningham's patent of 1839,
141 followed by Ainslie's of 1841, 1843 and 1845.[9] Cubitt was using Ainslie's machines when, in 1851, he acquired land at Burham on the Medway where, within two years, he had established a model brick-works with many improvements.[10] In the 1840s, contracting builders were still making their own bricks, often on or near the site of whatever they were building; but after the repeal of the brick tax in 1850 there was an irresistible incentive to increase the speed, quality and uniformity of brick production. Moreover, rail transport made it profitable to establish independent brick-making works on a large scale, brick manufacture becoming an industry in itself.[11] The Great Northern Brickmaking Company, operating at Arlesey in Hertfordshire from 1866, produced 20–25 million bricks a year.[12] Cawte's of Fareham provided the 25 million bricks required for St Thomas's Hospital in 1871 and all the facing bricks for the Albert Hall and the South Kensington Museum at about the same time. In fact, 'Fareham reds' seem to have been among the factors responsible for the change in the colour of London streets from brown to red in the 1870s. At St Pancras Hotel, Scott used Gripper's very close-textured bricks which came by rail from Nottingham. Gripper (Jack Simmons tells us) had acquired the rights in a new type of kiln and set up his works at Mapperley in 1867, only just before the hotel was begun.[13]

There were many experiments with new types and sizes of brick. Cubitt tried some hollow bricks in Pimlico.[14] Beart's of Bedfordshire patented perforated bricks and also moulded white bricks used in 1864 in Southwark Street, that great parade ground of Victorian brick-work.[15] Gumlin's patent moulded bricks are still to be seen at

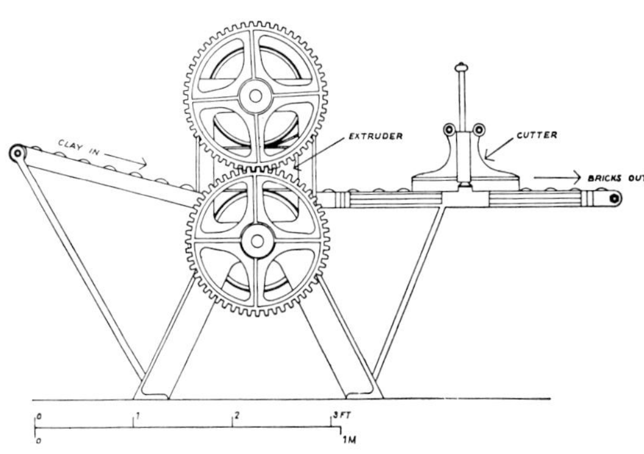

140. Hypothetical structures illustrating Parr and Strong's cellular bricks. They were hexagonal, with circular holes filled with concrete *141.* Ainslie's brick-making machine. It could be driven either by steam or horse power

142. The upper part of a house in Gloucester Road, roofed with John Taylor's patent tiles. Insets show the tiles in detail

Kenwood Towers, Highgate (1870).[16] Parr and Strong's bricks were hexagonal with a *140*
hole in the middle filled with concrete.[17] I remember boundary walls built on this curious method at Delarue's printing works in Bunhill Row but the blitz got the building and the walls have vanished.

From bricks to tiles. For roofing there were innumerable patent tiles; the *APSD* article selects nineteen as in use by 1889. An early and very successful patent was John Taylor's which he sold to the Broomhall Brick and Tile Company in 1865. Taylor's *142*
tiles are instantly recognizable – a flat, Italian-looking affair with an interlocking device; described as indestructible but now rarely to be seen. The stations on the old London, Chatham and Dover line, which Taylor designed, had them; so had Charles Gray's peculiar houses at the corner of Gloucester Road and Queen's Gate Terrace; also 'The Logs', Hampstead, but they have all been replaced.[18] He patented a type of concrete walling with brick facing for cottages; also a damp-proof course consisting of perforated earthenware slabs. He sold the latter to Jennings, the sanitary people, in 1860.[19]

For floor tiles there were two great Victorian firms – Minton's of Stoke-on-Trent and Maw's of Broseley. Post-mid-Victorian buildings of any consequence had encaustic tile flooring by one or other of these firms. Herbert Minton's story is given in the *Dictionary of National Biography*, where Matthew Digby Wyatt calls him 'neither a man of profound research nor a dedicated artist, neither an economist nor an inventor' but a man who assembled people of ability to work for him. His connexion with Pugin and his work at the Houses of Parliament are famous.[20] He made tiles for Osborne,

Lichfield Cathedral and the Capitol at Washington. Of George Maw, Wyatt took a different view.[21] He was both artist and antiquary. His firm seems to have caught up with Minton's in the 1870s. Already in 1867 they had a two-page coloured insert in the *Building News*, while their London agents, W. B. Simpson and Sons, continued to advertise in the building press with a well-designed wood cut, the work of H. W. Lonsdale. Simpsons were really decorators[22] but they specialized in tile work and I seem to remember that the splendid refreshment room at Holborn Viaduct Station Hotel was theirs.

From tiles to terracotta is an easy transition and terracotta was, of course, one of the most spectacular developments in Victorian building technology. There were three or four great manufacturers and many small ones. J. M. Blashfield, after nearly ruining himself by speculating in Kensington Palace Gardens in the 1840s set up, in or before 1859, a terracotta manufactory at Stamford.[23] In 1863 a terracotta porch by him in Cumberland Street, London, was noticed,[24] but his greatest performance was the
137 nearly all terracotta Dulwich College building of 1866–70 for Charles Barry junior. This was a challenging contract, heavily weighted against the manufacturer, who undertook not only to provide but to fix the material and make good any faults due to shrinkage. It was the first successful application in England of terracotta on a monumental scale.[25]

143. Osborne House, Isle of Wight. Encaustic floor tiles by Minton and Co. in one of the corridors, c.1850. The colours are blue, brown, red and black.

144. Doulton's advertisement in *The Builder*, 21 January, 1871, illustrating some of their products in architectural terracotta

At South Kensington the leading terracotta firm was M. H. Blanchard's. He got most of the work, from the Horticultural Gardens of 1861 to the South Kensington Museum (i.e. the inner parts of the V and A) of 1870.[26] At the Albert Hall, however, the contract went to Gibbs and Canning of Tamworth.[27] They employed a different technique from either Blashfield or Blanchard, their moulded terracotta blocks being chambered at the back so that the structural brick-work could be built into them. This method evidently appealed to Alfred Waterhouse who nominated Gibbs and Canning as sub-contractors for the Natural History Museum.[28] *145*

The most prominent advertisers of terracotta ware in the 1860s and 1870s were Doulton's of Lambeth. This celebrated firm had started in a small way in 1815 but it *144* was Sir Henry Doulton (1820–97) of the second generation who saw, in the 1840s, what could be made of it.[29] Pinning his faith to the movement for improved sanitation he produced glazed earthenware pipes for sewers in huge quantities. Eventually he had factories not only in Lambeth but at Rowley and Smethwick in Staffordshire whence their products were dispatched by canal or rail all over the country. Doulton's edged into the art field in the 1870s and by 1871 had an enormous range of products. In the sanitary line, pipes, basins, sinks, urinals; in the architectural line terminals, copings, dentil or dog-tooth courses, key-stones, capitals, as well as flues, air-bricks and damp-proof courses.[30] They also tackled sculptural groups and successfully executed the two allegories of 'Instruction' on the skyline of the South Kensington Museum.[31]

Not wholly unrelated to the clay products are the cements, in which there were highly important developments in the 1840s. Portland cement and Keene's cement were specially significant. Portland cement, so called because it was supposed to look like Portland stone, was 'artificial' cement, so designated because it was a combination of selected chalk and clay and not, as in Roman cement, a natural combination found in calcareous nodules. Portland cement superseded Roman: it was harder, more durable

145. Terracotta dormer on the Natural History Museum, London (Alfred Waterhouse) *146.* Pre-cast Portland cement enrichments on the Grosvenor Hotel, London (J. T. Knowles)

and was thought by many to be acceptable without paint. James Pulham of Broxbourne, was already making it in 1821.[32] Aspdin's and Maude's patents came a few years later but it was in the 1840s that John Bazley White developed the industry at Swanscombe, Kent, using the blue clay of the Medway.[33] For a brief period Portland cement was regarded, as was iron, as a great new material for the architect and one in
146 which he could model to his heart's content at an economic rate. J. T. Knowles and Charles Gray, those notable stylistic latitudinarians, handled it with enthusiasm but it got into the hands of the jerry-builder and the cheap-jack purveyor of ornaments and was soon despised except as a utilitarian recourse.

Keene's cement, made of gypsum steeped in alum before heating, was another product of J. B. White's in the 1840s.[34] It was hard as nails and made the perfect finish for the floors of prisons, hospitals and workhouses as well as smart interior decorative work.

With cement we are close to artificial stone; indeed, a whole range of earthenware and cement products tended to go under that name. Ransome and Parsons exhibited their 'artificial silica stone' at the 1851 exhibition and there were many other manufacturers whose names are less well-known.

But what of real stone and what of marble? Hansom lists Bath, Portland, granite, Yorkshire and other stone merchants, stone quarries and slate quarries. It is obvious that the increased mobility of raw materials throughout the country led to the exploitation of quarries on a large scale, by firms like, e.g. the Hopton Wood Stone Co. Ltd. of Wirksworth or Randall Saunders and Co. who advertised from the Bath Stone Office, Corsham. Some quarrymen, advertising in *The Builder*, had depots in London. The South Western Granite Co. was at Holborn Viaduct in 1870 and the Lizard Serpentine Co. was in Mark Lane in 1872. Ashton and Green, slate and slab merchants and quarry agents, who sold chimney pieces, had show-rooms in the City.[35]

Marble was mostly imported. To name just one importer, Bernardo Fabricotti, *148*
who owned quarries in Carrara, built an extremely handsome Thames-side depot in Grosvenor Road, designed (with plenty of marble) by Woodzell and Collcutt and illustrated in 1870.[36]

Under the heading of timber, Hansom gives us only two rather special applications of the material: bent timber manufacturers and wood paving companies. Bent timber would be for laminated trusses as used, for example, at King's Cross Station, and can hardly have enjoyed a very extensive market. Wood paving and flooring were more important. Wood paving for streets was tried in Whitehall in 1839 but failed in a week. There was a further experiment in Oxford Street before 1845 but it was not till the 1870s that satisfactory results were achieved with wood sets laid on concrete.[37]

147. Advertisements for rival makes of parquetry appearing in *The Builder* around 1870.
148. Premises of Bernardo Fabricotti; marble merchant, in Grosvenor Road, London designed in brick and marble by Woodzell and Collcutt, 1871

For internal floor surfaces the great innovation was parquetry. Steinitz established a parquetry works in London in 1840 and received the only award in this class at the
147 1862 exhibition.[38] In 1857, however, Arrowsmith had introduced their 'patent solid Swiss parquetrie', consisting of various woods, grooved and tongued in squares, each square tied at the back with strips of wood. This was used by many of the best architects, and Arrowsmiths floored, among other buildings, Burlington House and the Garrick Club.[39]

The timber trade in general was, of course, an industrial area largely but not wholly dependent on building and would require a very special investigation. For my present 'charting' purpose I merely quote an advertisement which suggests the type of business which developed in the direction which interests us. It is by William Oliver and Sons, of Bunhill Row, 1868:

> Wholesale timber, mahogany and wainscot merchants and importers; dealing in cedar, rosewood, walnut, satinwood, ebony, and all other kinds of wood. Veneers of every description. A large stock of all woods cut into planks and boards, dry and fit for immediate use; mouldings in every kind of wood; wainscot thoroughly seasoned in every thickness.[40]

And now, the metals. From Hansom's list I extract the following: brass founders, bronzists, coppersmiths and braziers, iron and steel merchants, iron and tin plate workers and zinc manufacturers. What did all these people make and contribute to the building world? That would be too long a story for this essay and I shall content myself with saying something about iron.

Both wrought and cast iron have a long history. Cast iron was in every-day structural use by 1837, Smirke and others even using it for girders in spite of its low tensile strength.[41] At the Polytechnic, Regent Street, 1837, there was a cast iron girder of 40 ft 6 in. span. Then came rolled iron, extensively used in the Crystal Palace, 1851. Rolled iron, i.e. rolled out of the lump into sheets, plates, girders and joists of various sections, swept the board. Fairbairn was the pioneer.[42] In 1866, W. & T. Phillips
149 introduced rolled iron beams of various shapes and strengths which, for efficiency, claimed to supersede Fairbairn.[43] Both Fairbairn and the Phillipses were manufacturers but the latter seem to have taken more trouble to cultivate the architect. Fairbairn's treatises were rather above his head. Phillips advertised themselves as follows:

> Engineers, contractors and patentees of solid flange girders, fire-proof floors; railway waggons . . . every kind of iron for building purposes. Patent girders from £12 per ton; fire-proof floors and roofs from £4 per square, iron and concrete included. Large stock of rolled beams in the ordinary sections. Girders required for immediate use can be designed, made and delivered in two days.[44]

'Designed, made and delivered.' They designed the stuff as well as making and marketing it. Phillips supplied the structural iron for Burlington House, the rebuilt auditorium of the Haymarket Theatre and Dulwich College. They published two excellent books for the use of architects who, they say in an introductory note, 'desire practical examples rather than theoretical deductions'. That was significantly true. Architects might talk airily about the great future of iron but in practice they showed

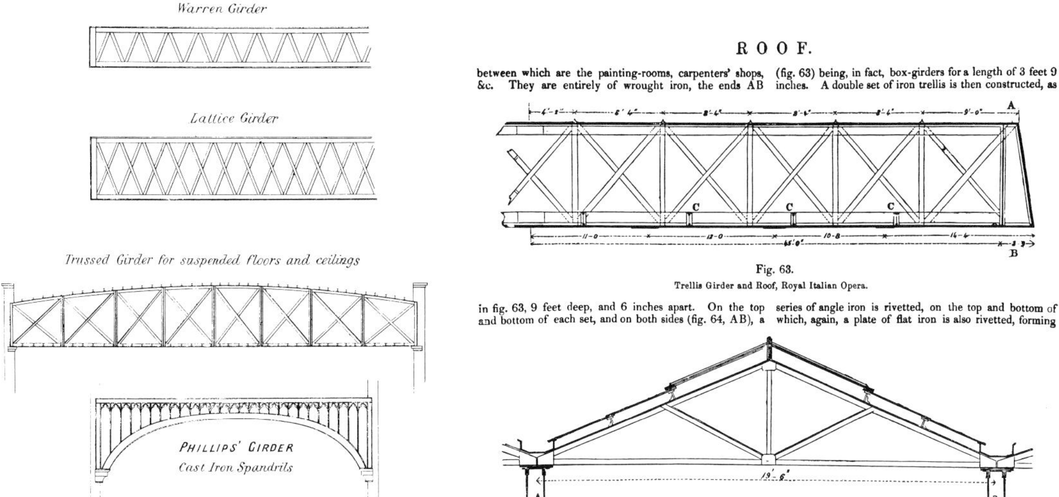

Illustrations from W. and T. Phillips, *Architectural Iron Construction*, 1870

149. Various types of rolled-iron girder. *150.* The roof of Covent Garden Opera House, showing (above) part of one of the eight 17-ton girders which carry the ceiling, and (below), one of the iron king-post trusses which bridge the spaces between the girders forming a 'ridge and furrow' roof structure. The whole roof was designed, manufactured, guaranteed and erected by Henry Grissell.

very little confidence in handling it. 'The hesitation to use iron', says George Aitchison, writing in *APSD*, 'is perhaps due to the little study hitherto bestowed by architectural students on mathematics, statics and the strength of materials'. This indifference and the superior prestige to be earned by manipulating the styles in good old brick and stone was characteristic of the profession. Aitchison himself certainly tried to break away, as his Mark Lane counting-house still stands to bear witness; but even he, as he became distinguished and successful, relapsed into fine artistry in traditional materials.

Thus, iron became essentially an engineer's material and figures in the building world mainly in the design of bridges, station sheds and exhibition halls, architects being employed only for the masonry trimmings. It is not easy to ascertain how far the typical architect was capable of calculating stresses but I suspect not very far. He probably relied heavily on the manufacturers. When E. M. Barry, from 1859 to 1860, built Covent Garden Opera House in the unbelievably short space of eight months, he *150*
entrusted the carrying of the auditorium ceiling to Henry Grissell of the Regents Canal Ironworks, Eagle Wharf, Hackney.[45] Grissell designed, manufactured and guaranteed the eight seventeen-ton girders which do the job. He also made the ironwork of the Floral Hall.

Grissell is one of the prominent names in iron construction from the 1840s onwards. Henry Grissell's uncle Thomas was, with his cousin and partner, Samuel Morton Peto, one of the contractors for the Houses of Parliament.[46] His nephew established the Regents Canal Ironworks in 1844, I suspect with a view to getting the contract for the iron roofs of the Houses of Parliament, which Grissell and Peto did in 1845 (they are, incidentally, of very advanced design). Like many engineering enterprises of the period, the Regents Canal Ironworks were incorporated under the Companies Act of 1862, Henry Grissell remaining for a time as managing director.

Many iron manufacturers were not content with purveying the bare structural elements of building. Like Doulton in the world of clay they poured out ready-made artistic objects of all kinds, from street-lamps to decorative finials. Walter Macfarlane & Co. of London and Glasgow called themselves 'architectural, sanitary and artistic ironfounders'. The firm was established about 1834, making gold and silver work, then hammered iron and finally, from 1854 mainly cast iron in quantities. They had a London depot under the arches of Cannon Street Station at Saracen's Wharf but the foundry was in Glasgow, the Saracen Foundry there being in Venetian Gothic.
151 Macfarlane catalogues of the 1870s are spectacularly vulgar and the very essence of what we think of as Victorian vernacular.[47] Many builders and some architects availed themselves of ready-made Macfarlane ornaments. The fantastic iron finials on the 'King Lud' at Ludgate Circus[48] look suspiciously like a catalogue item, rather than a creation of Henry Isaacs the architect. The great Macfarlane ventilator-lamp made for Bazalgette at Southwark Street, a masterpiece of its kind, has gone.[49] Public urinals by Macfarlane used to be conspicuous everywhere. Older readers may recall the one with a pierced floral dome on Hampstead Heath. I know very few survivors, but there is a modest one in Bell Yard off the Strand.

One highly important application of iron was to the fire-proof floor. In the period 1833–4, a physician, a Dr Fox, built a lunatic asylum in Gloucestershire and introduced a method of flooring of his own invention.[50] It consisted of cast-iron joists with concrete between them and battens to form the ceiling, the whole floor becoming in effect a monolithic slab with iron ribs. Fox patented this method in 1844. It was used by Wyatt and Brandon in a lunatic asylum of 1849–50 in Wiltshire. The Fox and Barratt
152 floor was in general use until the 1870s, when it vanishes in a flood of new patents.

Going back to the classification I suggested for a break-down of Hansom's list, it will be seen that my second and third categories – building materials and building components – have run together into one, which is natural enough. Reluctantly I leave out glass, lead and the whole world of plumbing and sanitation (for which see Lawrence Wright's *Clean and Decent*, 1960), paint, papier maché, asphalt and come to my fourth category: equipment and services.

Equipment covers an immense number of items. Hansom gives, among others, the manufacturers of brass fenders, blinds (Venetian and other), chimney-pieces, clocks and bells, safes, metallic sashes, locks, ovens, pumps, water-closets. He also gives ventilation and warming and gas-fitting, in other words heating and lighting services, and it is with a few observations on these that I shall conclude.

The subject of heating and ventilating was one of the most discussed, the most philosophical and, indeed, aristocratic in the Victorian building world. Authorities looked back to Rome, to the Cardinal de Polignac, Benjamin Franklin and Count von Rumford. The Marquis de Chabannes had successfully warmed the old Covent Garden opera-house with a hot-water system. Sir Goldsworthy Gurney was another contemporary pioneer. By 1837 a substantial literature was growing upon the subject and that year saw the publication of the first edition of Hood's *Treatise*, C. J. Richardson's *Popular Treatise* and W. Walker's *Comparative Merits*. The subject is ably

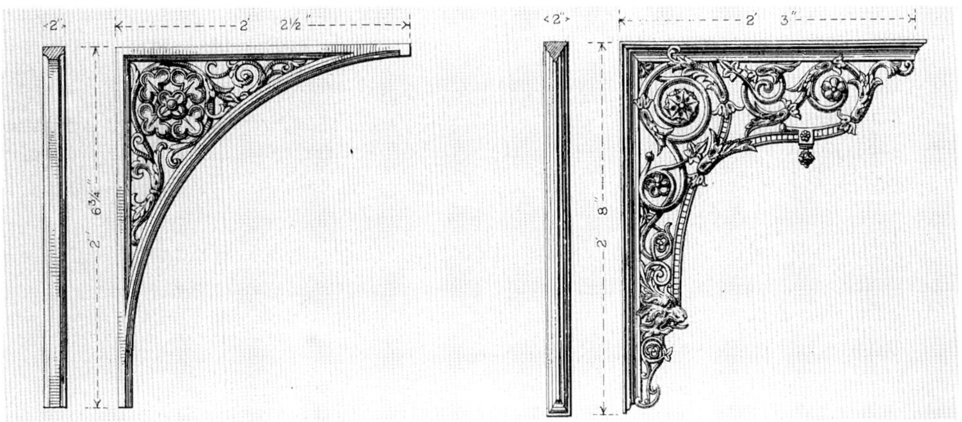

151. Cast-iron brackets from the catalogue of Walter Macfarlane and Co., London and Glasgow. (5th. edition, 1862)

dealt with in a long essay by Robert Burn in *APSD*, written about 1850. He examines the principles involved in open grates and stoves, then proceeds to describe hot-air, steam and hot-water (low and high pressure) systems, all in common use at that date.

The most sophisticated was Perkins's high-pressure hot-water system, depending on a directly-heated coil of water-pipes extended to other coils throughout the building and equipped with an expansion pipe. Soane had installed this in his museum before 1830. Smirke used it in parts of the British Museum, the Custom House and elsewhere. At the British Museum his coils or congeries of pipes were enclosed, Dr Crook tells us, in chests covered with marble slabs to look classical.[51] Other specialists in hot-water heating were Price and Manly, and Stratton and Oldham.

Hot-air systems were less common, but the Houses of Parliament were originally so heated in 1852 on a principle of Goldsworthy Gurney's, with a battery of steam boilers in the basement feeding warm air into an intermediate space called an 'equalizing chamber', whence the air percolated through cast-iron gratings in the floors, covered with hair carpet in the Lords and coarse hemp netting in the Commons – a nice distinction. This, of course, was subsequent to the great ventilation fiasco

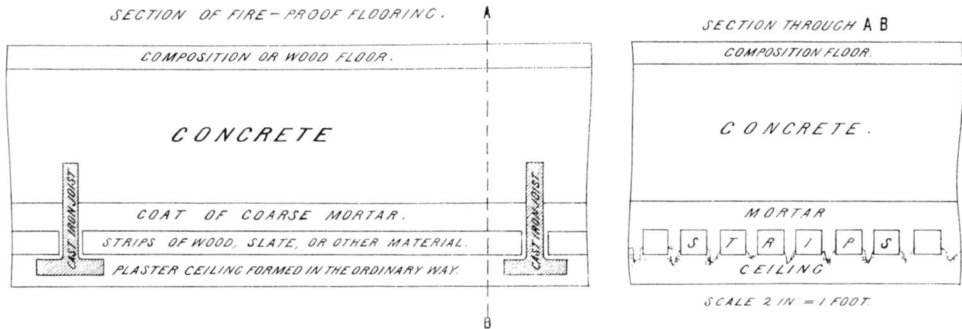

152. The Fox and Barratt fire-proof floor, first patented 1844 and in common use till 1870

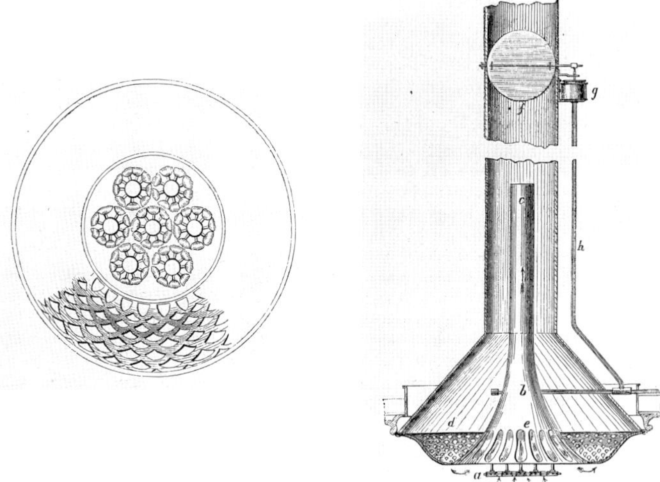

153. Clegg's 'sun-burner', combining gas-lighting and ventilation, patented 1866. The plan on the left shows the seven 'stars' consisting of fish-tail burners

conducted by Dr D. B. Reid, the man who made Barry build the huge (and, incidentally, very beautiful) steeple over the octagon hall to extract vitiated air from the entire building. The story of that is told in detail by Mr Port in the *History of the King's Works*, vol. 6 (1973) and, with more technical details, by Mr Denis Smith in Mr Port's book on the *Houses of Parliament* (1976).

A steam heating system was used by Sydney Smirke in the huge domed Reading Room of the British Museum in 1857. There were three 15 ft boilers in the basement feeding 3 in. and $2\frac{1}{2}$ in. pipes which ran through the radial desks, warm air emerging through gratings in the ends of the desks. A hand-operated fan to keep the air in motion at certain periods was part of the system, installed by Hadens of Trowbridge.[52] At the Albert Hall, 1870, there were again three boilers, supplying steam to nine condensers which in turn heated the water in 26,000 feet of 4 in. cast-iron piping in chambers distributed through the basement. Each condenser heated the water for two distinct systems of piping. The designer here was Wilson W. Phipson, a civil engineer who also took the contract not only for the heating but for the mechanically operated system of ventilation. Incidentally, the mean winter temperature stipulated in the contract was 58 Fahrenheit, which may strike us as spartan.[53]

Gas-lighting was no novelty at the beginning of Victoria's reign. William Murdock had lit his house at Redruth with gas in 1792. Murdock subsequently installed gas-lighting in Boulton and Watts Soho factory at Birmingham and, on the occasion of the peace celebrations of 1802, a young apprentice of Boulton and Watts,
153 James Clegg, was present. He became the leading gas man of the early Victorian age and died in 1861. Clegg's *Practical Treatise on the Manufacture and Distribution of Coal-Gas* (1st edition 1841; 4th by Clegg jn. 1866) is required reading for this subject. T. L.

Donaldson in his *Handbook of Specifications* of 1859 warns the architect to embody the 'tubings' in his specification and keep an eye on what the gas-fitter does to the brickwork. As to burners, the *APSD* article says there are three types – the fish-tail which is the worst, the bat's wing which is better and the Argand which is the best. With these three types and variations on the last Victorians had to be content till Welsbach, following Bunsen, invented the incandescent mantle, first seen in London in 1886, and saved gas-lighting from defeat by the electricians.[54]

The one great novelty in early Victorian gas-lighting was the 'sun-burner'[55]. Clegg says it was introduced by Alfred King of Liverpool. (King, incidentally, lit Cockerell's concert hall at St George's Hall.) It combined illumination with ventilation and was appropriate only for large interiors like bank halls, chapels and theatres. It consisted of a congregation of (seven) circular 'stars' each having six or more fish-tails. Over these stars were two concentric chimneys, the inner chimney closed so that the air entering above the flames was regurgitated to form a ring of flame round each jet before passing up the outer chimney. Inconveniences were the shadow cast by the chimney as it hung down into the room and the cold air coming down the chimney when the gas was not on. Cures were devised for both.

The leading gas-fitter in the 1850s and 1860s was Strode who lit the New City Club (1869), the National Provincial Bank (1865), the Haymarket Theatre (1869), Inner Temple Hall (1870) and St Thomas's Hospital (1871). Strode was very proud of his profession and would never consent to be a sub-contractor and always insisted on a separate contract.

Here I must call an end to this scrap-book survey which hardly even adumbrates what I have called a chart. My last two categories must go. I would like to have said something about the artist-craftsmen – the tribe of carvers: Earp, Seale, Dugman, Farmer and Brinley and Forsyth, the people whose skill, speed and accuracy, whether in classical entablatures or Gothic pulpits were dazzling. I would like to have said something about drawing office equipment. I omit with reluctance the vastly interesting sphere of architectural innovations. As for architects, it never occurred to me to include them. But that, I hope, was predictable.

There is one feature of the building world, not mentioned by Hansom because it had not emerged in his time but which I cannot ignore. This is Kirkcaldy's Testing Works, a private business which became, in the 1860s and 1870s almost a national institution. David Kirkcaldy came from Glasgow where he was apprenticed in the ship-building industry.[56] The study of the strength of materials became an obsession with him and after some setbacks he made it into a vocation and a successful business. He came to London in 1866 and set up a workshop in Southwark, building premises of his own at 99 Southwark Street in 1873. The building, which still stands, contained a testing room on the ground floor with an impressive variety of machines for testing building materials: cast- and wrought-iron girders, nuts and bolts, bricks, cement, concrete and ropes. Above was a machine room and three museums illustrating the results of various tests, all of which were tabulated with exemplary refinement. Kirkcaldy was an engineer rather than an architect but he was a sensitive graphic artist and an engineering drawing of a steam-ship was accepted by the Royal Academy and exhibited in 1861. Engineers and architects relied extensively on his reports; lawyers resorted to him for expert evidence. His machines are said to have been of uncommon ingenuity and elegance.

Earlier on, I asked the question how conscious the Victorians were of a building 'world', how they saw it and what they felt about it. To this last question there are doubtless several answers. The more sophisticated architects would, I think, look upon it simply as a tradesman's world, where judicious shopping was necessary and sometimes interesting. But in some quarters the scene was regarded in a more fanciful light and I want to end with a quotation from Banister Fletcher. *Not* Sir Banister (Flight) Fletcher of the great history book but his father who at various times was a member of Parliament, master of the Carpenters' Company, Colonel of the Tower Hamlets Volunteer Brigade and Professor of Architecture and Construction at King's College, London. In 1872, this Banister Fletcher (then forty-two) organized an exhibition for the Inventors' Institute. He showed patent bricks, pavement lights, locks and their fastenings, sash fastenings, door-springs and rollers, water bars, revolving shutters, electric bells, domestic telegraphs, cottage ovens, stoves, lifts, hoists, dust-shoot boxes, pipes, paints and enamels. In a lecture given at the exhibition, Banister Fletcher expressed himself as follows:

> There is a grand future for architecture, but it must be by striving to combine in building all the scientific inventions of the day, to do so continuously and with judgment, and herein new forms will be created by the use of new materials. We must earnestly strive to make the requirements of science express themselves in our works.[57]

'New materials . . . new forms'. This has a familiar ring! The idea was not, of course, entirely new even in 1872 and it still had a very long way to go: it is perhaps still with us. But it is interesting to find it here underlining the sense of evolutionary progress which some Victorians evidently felt in the flood of technological innovations which swept through the 1840s, 1850s, 1860s and beyond. In those decades, as Hansom of *The Builder* astutely foresaw, a new 'building world' came into being, a world created very largely by artisan initiative, a crude, ambitious fortune-seeking world which jostled the architectural profession with an unattractive combination of obsequiousness and arrogant self-confidence. To the historian of technology it is, I suppose, rather small beer. To the architectural historian it is background stuff. But I have a feeling that if we ignore it our whole picture of the Victorians and their building works is somewhat out of balance. In this paper I have merely switched on a few highlights in the scene. What we need is really careful charting of the Victorian building world and an exposure of the technological inventiveness of the period, the concentration and the speed of work – the *tempo*. Covent Garden Theatre built in eight months, girders designed, made and delivered in two days! That sort of thing. The building world was alive then as, I suppose, it never was before and certainly never has been since.

X · The London Building World of the 1860s

154. Bridge carrying the London, Chatham and Dover Railway across Ludgate Hill. Designed by John Taylor, architect, with Joseph Cubitt and F. T. Turner as engineers. The bridge was 'de-Victorianized' and stripped of its ornaments about 1960

155. 'Cut and cover' excavations for the Metropolitan underground railway at Baker Street, c.1863

IN THE SEVENTH DECADE of the 19th century, London was more excavated, more cut about, more rebuilt and more extended than at any time in its previous history. Consider the situation as Londoners of the time experienced it. Think first of the main drainage, with the deep trenches for four intercepting sewers ploughing across the town and its suburbs in long crazy zig-zags from west to east, an operation continuing through all the ten years. Then the cut-and-cover work for the Metropolitan Railway, 155
running the length of Marylebone Road and Euston Road, with the operations for the District Railway making more havoc as the two companies united in forging the Underground's inner circle. For the fifth great sewer and a superincumbent highway the Victoria Embankment was begun in 1862, but the southern stretch of the District got into it, too. Above ground, the main-line railways were forcing themselves into London. The Pimlico Bridge carried two companies' lines to Victoria in 1859; the double station and the Grosvenor hotel opened in 1862. From 1864 to 1866 two more railways crossed the Thames from the south. The South Eastern swung out from London Bridge and, with the help of 17 bridges, 190 brick arches and an iron viaduct, with the destruction of a hospital, the removal of 8,000 bodies from a graveyard and the construction of a new Thames bridge, got itself to Charing Cross. With less effort it lurched across the Thames into the great shed at Cannon Street. The LC and DR, meanwhile, drove north from Penge, crossed the river with yet another bridge at Blackfriars, paused at Ludgate Hill, then steamed on, across the very threshold of St 154
Paul's, to Holborn. In the north, the North London struck down from Dalston and built the Broad Street terminus in 1865, while the Midland came grandly down through the Middlesex fields to a new station called St Pancras whose cathedral façade belongs to 1870. Nor was this all. New highways were grooved into the old street pattern. Victoria Street in 1860 was still a long, open scar. Garrick Street, cut in the 1850s, was built up from 1861. Southwark Street started building in the following year and went on into the 1870s. The ruthless Queen Victoria Street, pickaxing the City all the way from Blackfriars to the Mansion House, and carrying in its belly a main sewer, the District Railway and gas and water subways, was partly opened in 1869; while the City conducted its own adventurous bridging of the Fleet Valley, with Holborn Viaduct built in 1866, the new meat market of Smithfield from 1867 to 1868 and the new Blackfriars Bridge in 1869.

These were the massive, crude constructional enterprises of the time. They accompanied and partly instigated a building and rebuilding of great richness and variety. For the City itself this was the critical decade of the residential exodus. In 1861 the City still had 113,000 inhabitants, in 1871 only 75,000. The old Stuart and Queen Anne mansions, long since deserted by their masters and made over to managing clerks, were giving way to strictly business buildings, offices or warehouses.[1] The breed of masters had gone to Bayswater or Kensington or perhaps to Hornsey or Clapham; now the breed of clerks was going to Camberwell or Peckham, Stoke Newington or Highbury. According to the District Surveyors' returns over 73,000 new structures were built in the metropolitan area in the decade, the majority being suburban dwellings.[2] But if it was a decade of sweeping change we must also remember the tracts that did not change: Bloomsbury and Islington, Marylebone and Mayfair, St James's and Belgravia. They remained almost as Georgian as ever so that, in spite of all, it can be said that in 1870 London was still the Georgian metropolis.

A great part of the scene I have just sketched came about through engineering enterprise, though there were architectural attachments at many points. In this paper I shall have nothing to say about engineering. The railway story has been superbly handled by Barker and Robbins[3] and if the history of 'improvement' above and below ground has yet to be written it is not something to which I will attempt a contribution here. I mean only to probe a little into the world of ordinary building where, year by year, architects, builders, surveyors and a host of tradesmen and labourers were constructing banks, offices, warehouses, hotels, theatres, music-halls, taverns, churches, chapels, schools, hospitals, orphanages, workhouses and all the other components of the London we call 'Victorian'.

The proportion of London's population concerned, in one way or another, with building was high. In 1861, the population of the capital was 2,800,000 and of these, according to the census returns, 91,000 were employed on 'houses and buildings'. Slightly more than 10 per cent of the male adult working population was so employed. The category is widely drawn for it includes house proprietors and house agents as well as architects, surveyors, builders and workers in all the building trades.[4] It includes – to name one trade only – 27,000 carpenters. Extracting the three most immediately responsible classes we have, in the 1861 returns, 3,845 builders, 1,459 architects and 749 surveyors.[5] These figures are grossly inflated as we shall see in a moment but, relatively to the national figures, they give us a striking measure of London's building capacity in relation to the rest of the country. Thus, London had 24 per cent of all builders in England and Wales, of architects 38 per cent and of surveyors 40 per cent. The ratios were not very different in 1871 – the same in respect of builders, but there had been a strong growth outside London in the profession of architect and still more in that of surveyor.[6]

The figures for people calling themselves builders in the census returns are misleading for reasons which may easily be guessed: any character with a set of tools doing some random jobbing could set himself down as such. Kelly's *Post Office London Directory* for the census year is more realistic, with a list of 1,116 names and addresses in the central area and 650 in the suburbs, totalling 1,766. A cautionary note says 'see also architects, bricklayers, carpenters and surveyors'. The appellation 'builder' remains still somewhat ambiguous, however, because of the varieties of function performed, ranging from the smallest-scale suburban land development at one end to public works contracting at the other. The people I would like to identify here are the contracting builders who were responsible for public buildings and churches, commercial and domestic buildings in the City and central area generally. Who were they? There are several ways of finding out. The main source I have used is the series of lists of competitive tenders published regularly in the building journals.[7] These cover only a small proportion of the construction activity proceeding in London at the period but they reflect, however imperfectly, that sector where architects were extracting from the building industry fair market prices for their clients' projects, a sector moreover in which builders had to be continuously competing to keep their businesses going.

If we take one year (1861) of the London tenders printed in *The Builder* we find 540 builders tendering for 263 works ranging in cost from a workhouse at £30,000 to alteration jobs at £100. An analysis of the lists gives the names of builders tendering for the largest-scale work and we find that of our 540 builders only 39 tendered for work over £10,000. Of these 39, only 7 tendered for more than one such contract in the year. We may reasonably suppose that these seven were among the largest and most active businesses at the moment. They were: Mansfield, Myers, Willson, Lawrence, Kirk and Parry, Hill Keddle and Lucas. Obviously if our analysis were carried through the whole ten years other names would come to the top while some of the seven would go down. A less laborious way of extracting the important names for the decade is by analysing a list of all those who built buildings sufficiently large or interesting to be illustrated either in the building journals, the *Illustrated London News* or the *Companion to the Almanac*. In this process Myers, Lucas and Dove Brothers come out top while all the other five in our previous list come in the first eighteen.

Yet another way of probing the building world of the 1860s is to look at such records as can be found of builders' organizations. The London Builders' Society was founded by a group of seventeen builders in 1834, with the object of protecting themselves against bad contracting procedures and the arrogance of the architect (the RIBA was founded in the very same year!).[8] Later they had to defend themselves from another quarter – trade unionism – and by 1860 they had brought the Central Association of Master Builders into existence.[9] In 1859 the membership of the Society was 'sixty or seventy', in 1867 it was seventy-six.[10] Perhaps that was roughly the number of top-ranking firms in the ten years with which we are concerned. The leaders of the Society, as also of the allied Builders Benevolent Institution, include several of the names already mentioned, notably Myers, Lucas and Lawrence.[11]

What do we know about these people? Very little. Nobody has ever written about them and their biographies and business methods have, by now, become almost impenetrably obscure. *The Dictionary of National Biography* gives only the giants of the contracting world. Thomas Cubitt is there, of course, but he died five years before our decade opens, while his brother William, having retired in 1854, had moved into public life, becoming Lord Mayor in 1860 and 1861. The contracting firm continued under his name. Samuel Morton Peto is there but his wealth and fame depended more on vast railway constructions all over the world than on the building contracting which engaged him in London during the 1840s. He, like Thomas Brassey, and a few others belonged to the heroic class of Victorian contractor, the class to which Trollope's unhappy Sir Roger Scatcherd also belonged. The fact is that the mid-Victorian builders of our city streets are, historically speaking, a lost tribe.

However, we can ask general questions and partly answer them. The type of builder we are dealing with was in a fairly exclusive minority. In the great mob of London builders the commonest was the builder employing up to ten men and capable of nothing much more than putting in a shop-front.[12] Above him there were firms of all sizes and, in the top layer only, those which were general contractors in the sense which Thomas Cubitt had pioneered as long ago as the 1820s.[13] That is to say, businesses which incorporated all the trades, each trade conducted by its own foreman. These firms contracted in gross. In principle, there was no subletting, a practice frowned upon by architects as leading to irresponsible cut-price workmanship, though separate contracts were made for such things as gas-lighting, heating and often for ornamental carving.

Building was, in the 60s, London's biggest industry and these all-in contractors required large premises with good communications, a plentiful supply of labour and a continuous flow of work.[14] As to premises, some of the builders had their yard and offices in the same place and perhaps even lived on the spot; others had a business address in central London, a yard or yards elsewhere, and resided in the suburbs. Water transport was important, if not vital, to a big building concern. Myers established himself in Belvedere Road on the South Bank in 1848. In 1853 Lucas Brothers arrived next door. By 1861, Richard Holland and Benjamin Hannen were there, too, with Lawrences just down the road at Pitfield Wharf where the National Theatre now stands. Cubitts had, besides their Gray's Inn Road works, a large establishment at the Isle of Dogs.[15] Builders in Islington like Dove Brothers of Studd Street and Hill of Charlton Place (who became Higgs and Hill) no doubt used the Regent's Canal.

A basic need for the as yet almost wholly unmechanized industry of the 60s was a large labour force. It is hard to ascertain precisely what numbers these firms employed, for the obvious reason that there was continual fluctuation, labourers, bricklayers and carpenters being taken on and laid off as the work required them.[16] We hear of Myers employing 2,000 men when he had to face a serious strike in 1851 and he cannot have been employing less than that number in the 60s when he was among the two or three busiest builders in London.[17] Cubitts were said to be employing 3,000 men in 1876 and for them, too, the 60s had been a busy period.[18] These round figures are presumably rough assessments of the labour force at work at a given moment and it is interesting that when Benjamin Dixon Dove, senior partner in Dove Brothers, filled in his census return in 1861 he stated (quite gratuitously) that he employed 210 men and 11 boys.[19] These very precise figures possibly represent a cadre of workmen continuously employed at the Islington works.

Most essential of all to the big builder was a continuous flow of work and this was obtained almost entirely by competitive tendering all the year round. The system was an old one but by the 60s had reached a fierce intensity which is reflected in the published lists. In *The Builder*'s lists of a typical year (1865) we find Myers tendering for forty-four contracts, with only five (presumed) successes; Dove Brothers for twenty-four contracts, with three successes and Piper and Wheeler, a firm of comparable standing, for thirty-one contracts with no successes at all. The estimating clerks must have been under continuous pressure to catch enough acceptances to keep the business afloat without inviting disaster by under-pricing – a practice all too common in the lower ranks of the industry as a last gamble under impending bankruptcy.

The tendering system is one of the vital features in the Victorian building scene, a touchstone of change not only in building but in architecture, and for this reason. No reputable builder would tender unless quantities were supplied by a recognized quantity surveyor.[20] The taking out of quantities required very full working-drawings and specifications from the architect who would thus need to take on clerks (or 'assistants' as they preferred to be called)[21] for the purpose. This kind of employment contributed to the inflation of the architectural profession in the 50s and 60s and tended to create a 'lower deck' of professionalism, partly an 'under-dog' breed of limited but useful competence and partly a class of hopefuls who would very likely join the Architectural Association, debate about styles and clamour for professional qualifications and the regulation of competitions. As building became more an industry than a trade, so architecture became more a business than a profession. As the big builders killed the master-craftsman by absorbing him into industry, so the relations between architect and builder became as faceless as a deed of contract. The 'art action', as H. Bruce Allen put it in 1865, became 'wholly expended on paper'.[22]

The builder's business was always economically hazardous but whereas bankruptcies were commonplace in the middle and lower reaches, the big building firms seemed rarely to have crashed. The spectacular failure of Peto and Betts in 1866 was within the larger contracting world of docks and railways. In the troubled 70s builders tended to merge with one another and often settled down to a hundred years of thriving existence. It is impressive to find how many of the great building names of the 60s are still current today. Concerning the founders and heads of the firms it is difficult to find much information. Obituary notices of builders, unlike those of architects, are rare and brief. One indubitable fact is that the big builder's business was conducted with ruthless efficiency. Notices of builders rarely fail to pay tribute to 'perseverance and strict integrity' – certainly true of the best.[23] If they add that the deceased had 'the welfare of his men at heart', this may have been true up to a point; but even the heartiest sense of workers' welfare would vanish on the approach of strike action, as was cruelly demonstrated by the solidarity of London builders in the great lock-out of 1859 when the nine-hour movement was, for the time being, smashed and twenty-four thousand operatives were adrift on the London streets for eight weeks.[24] The Victorian builder was tough. He was no remote board-room personage. If he was to survive he had to face his men, command them and, if necessary, endure their hatred.

If we think of the Thomas Cubitt generation as the first generation of great general contractors, most, though not all, of the builders of the 60s were second-generation men. George Myers, as it happens, was not. As he was perhaps the most conspicuous *158*
London builder of the 60s his story, or such little as I have gathered for this occasion, is of some interest here. Born in Hull in or about 1804[25] he was working as a mason in Beverley when Pugin visited there, probably in the early 30s. A pleasant anecdote comes in here. He helped Pugin with tackle to reach inaccessible parts of the Minster which Pugin was studying and was caught by his Gothic enthusiasm. By 1837 Myers was in business as a builder. He tendered for the new Catholic church at Derby without realizing that the architect was the young man he had helped at Beverley. Pugin recognized and embraced him and a long association followed. By 1844 Myers was established in Lambeth, where he gathered together a group of competent carvers, provided casts for study and was, according to Ferrey (who may exaggerate a little), responsible for the availability of so many good carvers at the period.[26] But Myers's building activities embraced every size, type and style. Two of his sons came into the business, which flourished at Ordnance Wharf, Belvedere Road till the father's death in 1875, when they disposed of it. Myers lived in modest affluence in the Clapham Road and left a comfortable but not spectacular fortune of £40,000.[27]

The story of Lucas Brothers also has provincial origins but begins later and runs *156*

what we may think a more spectacularly Victorian course. Charles, born in 1822, set up in business at Norwich, then joined his younger brother Thomas in developing an establishment at Lowestoft. Both brothers were on the staff of Samuel Morton Peto during his London contracting years. When Peto moved on to bigger things in 1847 the Lucas brothers took over his London business and built, among other things, two of Sir Charles Barry's great houses and his son's Covent Garden Theatre. The 50s and
166 60s were the firm's great London period. With John Kelk they were responsible for the International Exhibition of 1862.[28] Later they had a big share of the Underground railway work in which the elder John Aird was involved and with him they carried out the District Line.[29] In 1870 they went into business with the younger Aird and formed three separate firms, one of which, Lucas and Aird, built the Royal Albert Docks.[30] Thus, the Lucases, like Peto before them, moved into the wider field of public works contracting and became immensely rich. Charles left £300,000 at his death in 1895. Thomas was made a baronet and died in 1902, worth £750,000.[31] That sort of money was not made out of building banks, warehouses and model dwellings.

159 Dove Brothers of Islington came up at the same time as the Lucases but never issued into the more ambitious fields of contracting.[32] John Dove (d. 1823) was a carpenter-builder at Sunbury-on-Thames. His son, William, went to town and set up in Islington in the mid-20s. Of his four sons, three entered the business and were the original Dove Brothers, formal partnership being notified in 1862.[33] Throughout the 50s Doves were tendering, mainly for churches, chapels and schools, and from the first they seem to have specialized, as they still do, in these types. In the 60s they certainly

156. Sir Morton Peto's house, Kensington. Architect: James Murray. Builders: Lucas Brothers.
157. The Philharmonic Hall, Islington.
Architects: Finch, Hill and Paraire. Builders: Holland and Hannen.

158. Wesleyan Chapel, Brixton. Architects: J. Tarring and Son. Builders: Myers and Sons
159. St Mary Abbots, Kensington.
Architect: Sir George Gilbert Scott. Builders: Dove Brothers

built more churches and chapels than any other contractor. No fortunes were made and throughout our period the head of the firm lived modestly at the yard in Islington.

These three builders stand at the top of my list of those whose performances were most frequently illustrated. It may well be that Doves owe their position to the fact that churches make better illustrative material than some other things. There are big names further down the list – the firm of Lawrence, for instance, which had a solid City background, the founder being an Alderman in 1848 and his two sons, James and William, becoming Lords Mayor in 1860 and 1868 respectively, with a baronetcy for
James in 1869. The Cubitt contracting firm, William Cubitt and Co., stands high and so *160*
does that of Piper and Wheeler. Thomas Piper, a second-generation builder (his father had been Mason to the City), was conspicuously one of the aristocrats of the building world, with intellectual and institutional interests of a distinguished kind. He retired in 1867 and when he died in 1873 his obituarist noted significantly that it would be 'not uninstructive to examine into the reasons why he did not, like some of his contemporaries, make a large fortune as a contractor'.[34] As we learn from Piper's evidence before the Royal Commission on Trades Unions of 1867, his attitude to labour was hard. But perhaps not hard enough.[35]

160. Peabody Square, Westminster. Architect: H. A. Darbishire. Builders: W. Cubitt and Company

I have not attempted to discover the historic roots of other great contractors of the 60s. It would be a worthwhile exercise and there is a field for research here where one would like to see things done, following the lead given by Hermione Hobhouse with her book on Cubitt.

Very different from the contracting builders we have been considering were those who were primarily estate developers but using their own labour. Thomas Cubitt had set two patterns for adventurous builders – the all-in contracting pattern and the speculative development pattern. Both were followed, but never again to any considerable extent, by a single-family concern. As with the contractors, our present ignorance of the developers is profound. What, for instance, do we know of the virtual creators of the South Kensington area in and around the land acquired by the Commissioners for the Great Exhibition in 1851 – C. J. Freake, Charles Aldin and Thomas Jackson? The Kensington volumes of the *Survey of London* tell us a good deal about their undertakings but little about their lives or how their businesses developed. Their initiatives, which probably owe much to what they learnt from Cubitt, mostly belong to the 50s and so hardly concern us here. But they flourished through the 60s and Freake, anyway, became rich, got his baronetcy in 1882 and died in 1884. Freake was what we would call a developer but he certainly employed his own labour, for we hear of him prosecuting three of his labourers for intimidating men who accepted a wage rate which the three had rejected. The magistrate gave them three months' hard labour and a warning.[36] *The Times* obituary of Sir Charles Freake is disappointing. Nothing is said of building South Kensington and the points made are that he married the sister of a Brigadier-General and that his daughter-in-law was a great-grand-daughter of the sixth Earl of Lauderdale.[37] As Freake started at the bottom his social climbing was certainly an achievement but unfortunately it is not what interests posterity. One has the impression that a career in speculative building, however successful, was not a thing to be much doted on when a man had come through it and out at the top.

The generally, though not universally odious reputation of building developers comes out in *The Builder*'s obituary of John Spicer who operated through the 60s on the Gunter estate in Earl's Court. He was, says the editor, 'one of the class of conscientious builders that we have known and still know despite the popular idea that nothing but shiftiness and chicanery are to be found in the calling'.[38] The editor, George Godwin, was, as it happens, the surveyor to the Gunter estate and thus had a rather special relationship with the builders there. Godwin also reports approvingly of work proceeding on the adjoining Redcliffe estate where Corbett and McClymont had built 550 houses by 1868, a massive accretion to London of the 60s, with 400 more houses to come. They were using mass-production techniques of some interest, the planing, mortising, tenoning, tonguing and grooving of their joinery being mechanically operated.[39] This sounds like the sort of mechanization which, as Miss Hobhouse tells us, William Cubitt and Co. had been operating at their Isle of Dogs works many years earlier.[40] Here, as so often in the study of the Victorian building world, one finds that innovations in organization, technology and even design must be credited to the Cubitts.

The building history of North Kensington, like that of its southern counterpart, is now irradiated with formidable intensity by the *Survey of London* volumes.[41] If space allowed I would steal extensively from this work. I will allow myself one allusion, which is to the performance, through the 50s and 60s, of the Radford brothers in Pembridge Square and Holland Park. The Radfords, who came from Devon, were, it seems, prudent and respectable. They employed about sixty men. Their houses – some two hundred in all – were nearly all of one design, Francis Radford's: a design of the supercharged mannerist variety once thought disgraceful but now loved for its very ostentation. They are excellently built and the Radfords, who financed themselves by a long series of mortgages, arranged by attorneys, got reasonably and deservedly rich. For the story in detail and for others no less relevant to London of the 60s I refer you to the *Survey* volume, where you will find not only the best insights to date into the mechanics of London development but superb measured drawings and a galaxy of photographs.

Estate development and building in the outer suburbs I deliberately exclude from this paper. Professor Dyos of Leicester has opened up this huge and complex area of study, notably in his book on Camberwell of 1961, and it is a pleasure, in passing, to pay him tribute.[42]

It is time to leave the contractors and developers and look at the other major component of the building world, the architects. The architectural profession increased rapidly in the early Victorian decades. Robert Kerr, at an RIBA conference in 1874, observed that 'where there was one architect of fair pretensions half a century ago [i.e. 1825], there are at this moment literally twenty at the very least'.[43] This was not a bad guess. It presupposes a rate of increase of nearly four hundred in every decade.

The national census increases in the decades 1851–61 and 1861–71 average out at almost precisely that. Admittedly the three previous decades, for which there are no figures, must reduce this but not, perhaps, by very much. If we can trust the census figures for relative increases we cannot take their numerical totals as realistic, but here again Kelly's directories come to our rescue. In 1861, Kelly prints the names and addresses of 638 London architects and most considerately gives, by a system of symbols, an indication of those who called themselves architects *and surveyors*. This category constitutes over half the total, which seems to show that the increase in the profession was, as one would expect from what I said earlier, on the bread-and-butter rather than the aesthetic side. A number of these 'architects and surveyors' would be quantity surveyors, a profession which sprang out of the side of architecture under the pressure of the competitive tendering system, and obtained a standing of its own. Kelly also indicates which of the listed architects are fellows or associates of the Institute of British Architects. They number 209, or rather less than a third of the total and include most of the familiar mid-Victorian names. It must be added that Kelly's list of 'surveyors', as distinct from 'architects and surveyors', totals only 210 and covers a whole variety of functions such as land and estate agency, auctioneering and land surveying and is only remotely connected with our theme.

The RIBA in the 60s was a strong and distinguished institution, entry to which was by election after seven years in practice, and election to which was esteemed something of an honour, exceeded only by election to the Royal Academy, to which body only three architects were elected between 1847 and 1870. The Institute occupied beautiful 18th-century rooms in Lord Macclesfield's old house in Conduit Street with a salaried secretary and already a fine library and was permitted to be the 'Royal' Institute from 1866. Its presidents in the 60s were Cockerell, Tite, Donaldson, Beresford Hope and Tite again – men of considerable influence and, in two cases, of great wealth, but singularly different in personality and performance. Nor did they quite belong to our period. Cockerell, Tite and Donaldson were really early and not mid Victorians and the
161 rising men in the Institute in the 60s were George Gilbert Scott, M. D. and T. H. Wyatt and the younger Charles Barry. The RIBA was remarkable for a lively catholicity; it retained what one might call a 'literary and philosophical' character and the papers read show a consistent balance between archaeology, science, professional practice and fine art.[44] The intellectual side of the Institute at this time is reflected in that noble achievement of eclectic scholarship, the Architectural Publication Society's *Dictionary*, which was being edited all through the 60s from Conduit Street by Wyatt Papworth.

With seven years practice as a qualification for election, the RIBA membership was fairly mature. Sheltering under the same Conduit Street roof, however, at a nominal rent, was a junior and wholly independent body, the Architectural Association. Founded by some rebellious youngsters in 1847, it was in low water when it began to
162 use the Conduit Street building for its meetings but it quickly revived under a succession of notable young presidents, A. W. Blomfield and R. W. Edis especially, who contributed significantly to the London architecture of the 60s and beyond. Primarily, the AA was a self-help society, meeting once a fortnight for a design class and in alternate weeks for papers and discussions. Its membership of about two

161. The Foreign and India Offices, Whitehall.
Architects: Sir George Gilbert Scott and M. D. Wyatt. Builders: Smith and Taylor

162. Mission House, Bedfordbury, St Martin-in-the-Fields. Architect: A. W. Blomfield. Builders: Child, Son and Martin *163*. St. Giles National School, Endell Street. Architect: E. M. Barry. Builders: Mansfield and Son.

hundred, rising to nearly five hundred by 1890, came from the clerks and articled pupils who wanted more from architecture than a mere living. They wanted formal education and they wanted a properly regulated competition system and on both these issues they were able to give occasional prods to the senior body.[45] As a result the RIBA held the first voluntary examination in 1863: it was not a great success because it conferred neither membership nor anything else, but it was a signpost.[46] On the competition question the RIBA held debates but many years elapsed before it acquired the monopolistic authority which could dictate reforms.

The architectural profession in the 60s was a gentleman's profession – but only just. The RIBA upheld the tradition of the gentleman architect inherited from Sir William Chambers and maintained through the years by an irreproachable élite. But the recruitment in the 30s, 40s and 50s had a decidedly 'lower middle' tone. Never do we find sons of the gentry entering architecture as they did the Church or the Law, or even the fine arts. To a great extent the expanding profession was recruited from its own sphere of activity. Some of the top architects of the 60s came from honoured architectural dynasties, such as the Wyatts and the Hardwicks. The sons and pupils of Sir Charles Barry and Professor Cockerell distinguished themselves. At a lower level, many practitioners of the 60s had architectural, surveying or building backgrounds going back two generations, while at a lower level still, the sons of builders and builders' tradesmen, looking for a more genteel career than their fathers, helped to swell the ranks.[47] From outside, sons of clergy, like Scott, or of small solicitors, like Street, represent the social high-water mark. They were an important infusion, uninhibited by paternal tradition and happy to be innovators.

The architect's education, through articled pupilage, was, in the 1860s, becoming less and less satisfactory for the simple reason that, with the increasing drudgery involved in practice, pupils tended to be used as junior clerks and to spend their time tracing, copying or doing repetitive operations on standard products.[48] After pupilage, opportunity was sought either through social contacts, obtained very often by deliberate touting, or through competitions, but far more through the first than through the second. Open competitions, mostly initiated in the provinces, were a mere gamble, usually for dubious rewards, and only very young architects with time on their hands went in for them. The more promising competitions were mostly limited by invitation to a few architects of mature experience.

I can find no adequate method of representing the pattern of employment of London's six hundred architects. The prevailing type was the general practitioner who dealt confidently with any and every sort of building, though sometimes finding peculiarly fruitful patronage in a particular group or persuasion or by virtue of a surveyorship to some corporate body. A class of middling successful London architect can perhaps be identified by listing those who were elected to the District Surveyorships under the Building Act of 1844 and the Metropolis Management Act of 1855.[49] They were men in private practice who, after submitting to an examination, were authorized to collect fees for passing plans submitted by other architects for buildings in their allotted districts. In 1860 there were fifty-six of these officers covering the metropolitan area and the names of many are well known. Though never quite of the top rank, they form a representative body of acknowledged professional

164. Smithfield Meat Market, by the City Architect, Horace Jones. Builders: Brown and Robinson.

competence which the architectural historian should not overlook. These Surveyorships were much sought after so long as it was permissible to combine them with private practice; when that permission was withdrawn in 1891 nobody wanted them. The important districts brought in well over £1,000 a year in fees and the office carried a status which attracted clients. In the City, to take two examples, John Young and Edmund Woodthorpe, District Surveyors for the east and north divisions respectively, had conspicuously fine office and warehouse practices. Woodthorpe had the Surveyorship of Spitalfields into the bargain and was, in addition, Surveyor to the Girdlers' Company and to the Parish of St Giles Cripplegate: a combination representing a typically prosperous City practice.[50] John Young had probably the biggest warehouse practice of the time.[51] Outside the City and in the suburbs it is noticeable that substantial commissions accrued to District Surveyors. How, otherwise, did the relatively obscure F. W. Porter,[52] District Surveyor for Holborn and East Strand, come to build the magnificent £30,000 London County Bank in Chancery Lane; or Henry Jarvis[53] to be so busy with churches and houses and a vestry hall in Camberwell as well as having a good warehouse practice in the central area?

Office holding without facilities for private practice was, in general, a sad affair. The Metropolitan Board of Works, to whom the District Surveyors were responsible, had its own full-time Superintending Architect. The first to be appointed, in 1855, was Frederick Marrables who designed the Board's offices in Spring Gardens (destroyed) but was so overloaded with report-writing that he resigned after five years, though offered a 25 per cent rise in salary.[54] He was succeeded by George Vulliamy, the designer of the architectural parts of the Victoria Embankment including the famous lamps; he survived till his health failed in 1886.[55] In the City of London the ancient office of Clerk-of-the-Works (which became 'Architect' in 1847) was held by James Bunstone Bunning whose performance in the previous seventeen years had included such outstanding things as the Coal Exchange and the Metropolitan Cattle Market. But, grossly overworked and already consumptive, he collapsed on the steps of the

Mansion House in 1863 and died soon afterwards.[56] The short list for his successor was, understandably perhaps, not very brilliant and the office went to the genial and
164 portly Horace Jones, a man of tougher fibre but less talent.[57]

At Her Majesty's Office of Works, the position of the official architect was a sad one in another way. James Pennethorne, Nash's professional legatee and a designer of immense ability, had, after serving with Works and with Woods and Forests for many years, been given the title of 'Salaried Architect and Surveyor' to the Office in 1859. He was allowed to design such government buildings as were not handed out to private architects by competition or otherwise and he did achieve the remarkable London University building in Burlington Gardens. But in 1869, the First Commissioner, Sir Henry Layard, found the office of Salaried Architect otiose and retired Pennethorne with a knighthood and a pension.[58] After which the Office of Works sank very low.

The mid-Victorian hatred of official architecture and, indeed, the fear of seeing public money spent on architecture at all, was at its height in the 60s. We see it at its most intense in the conditions for some of the competitions arising out of the provisions of the Metropolitan Poor Act of 1867. In those for the Poplar and Stepney Sick Asylum, for instance, it was specifically provided that designs should possess 'no architectural pretensions whatever'. It is not unamusing that one of the unsuccessful competitors on that occasion was young George Gilbert Scott, Sir Gilbert's brilliant son – evidently trying his luck with Poor Law work as his father had done a generation earlier.[59]

165. The Langham Hotel, Portland Place. Architect: John Giles
Builders: Lucas Brothers.

166. The Albert Memorial, Kensington. Architect: Sir George Gilbert Scott. Builder: Sir John Kelk

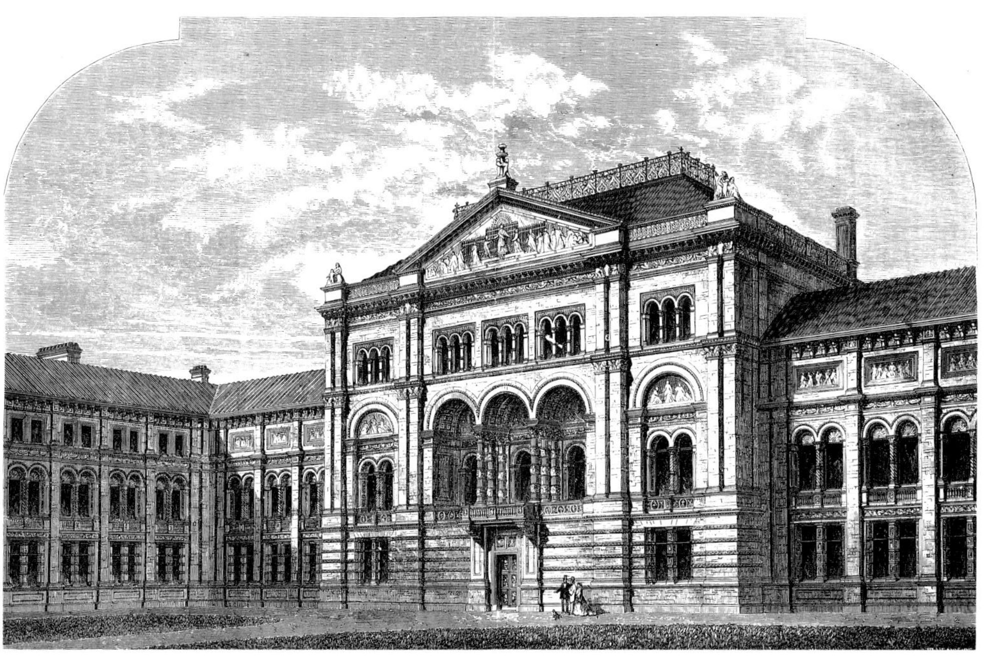

167. Courtyard of South Kensington Museum (now the Victoria and Albert). Architect: Francis Fowke. Builders: Smith and Taylor

What emerges from this brief consideration of office-holding architects is, of course, that nearly all the major architectural opportunities and achievements, all the glory and much of the profit is associated with the private practitioners. These I find impossible to set in any sort of order unless by their artistic parentage and stylistic affiliation. With categories of this kind we find ourselves on the threshold of art history, an area which on this occasion I want at all costs to avoid. I would like to conclude, however, with some visual evidence and of this I have made a rather frivolously controlled selection. Having compiled a list of illustrated buildings with a view to identifying the leading builders I thought it might be instructive to discover which architects came out top under the same test. You may care to hazard your own guess as to who was the most illustrated London architect of the 1860s. You will probably say Sir Gilbert Scott and I cannot seriously dispute this though in my count E. M. Barry does get one nominal point over him. In a total of 160 architects of illustrated London buildings, 17 earn more than three points. After Barry and Scott they are: Alfred Darbishire, G. Somers Clarke, the brothers Francis, James Murray, Horace Jones, John Giles (with or without partner), John Tarring, Francis Fowke, A. W. Blomfield, Henry Jarvis, John Taylor, J. T. Knowles (senior and junior), Basset Keeling, John Johnson and C. G. Searle. I am not inviting you to take this list very seriously but it does happen that by shuffling the illustrated works of these masters and rearranging them typologically a representative picture emerges of what was happening in the London building world of the 1860s.

You will have perceived by now that what I have been doing is to take a small slice of architectural history, stand it on its head and see what falls out. What, in fact, has fallen out? Almost everything, you may say, which, in the history of art, really matters. I have made no mention of London buildings by Butterfield, Street, Pearson, Burges, Waterhouse, Philip Webb or half a dozen other celebrities whom you could name. I did not exclude them on purpose, but my method of approach did not seem to require their presence. If an apology is required it is simply this. I believe that an architectural historian should, from time to time, look over the shoulders and under the feet of the conventionally accepted heroes and try to see what went on around them and on what they stood; and, furthermore, to see whether that hinterland may not contain some very adequate heroes of its own. This is what, in my brief excursion into London's building history, I have tried to do.

XI · The Victorian Rebuilding of the City of London, 1840–1870

168. The centre of the City of London in the 1840s. From left to right, a corner of Soane's Bank of England; the Globe Office, corner of Cornhill and Lombard Street; Hawksmoor's St Mary Woolnoth and, in the distance, Wren's Monument; the Mansion House by George Dance

169. Entrance to Munt and Brown's Warehouse, Wood Street, by G. Somers Clarke, 1857 (demolished)

THE CITY OF LONDON has always been in a state of more or less continuous rebuilding. There have, however, been three periods when the rebuilding was especially rapid, intensive, and visually transforming. The first was in the years after the Great Fire of 1666. The second was two hundred years later, when the City ceased to be the living place of a community and became an area almost exclusively of daytime business. The third period is our own in which the surviving products of the second are being rapidly suffocated or destroyed, so rapidly that it is now almost an archaeological exercise to reconstruct the appearance of the streets as they existed from the 1850s or 1860s to the outbreak of war in 1939.

Nobody has ever written the architectural history of the City of London in the Victorian decades, which is one reason why I am attempting here to put together some of the more obvious and even some of the less obvious material, and trying to interpret it. How it looks when it is put together I must leave you to judge. I do not claim to be revealing hidden treasure in a neglected corner of architectural history. I do claim, however, two things: first, that the dying architectural heart of a great 19th-century metropolis is worth a historian's attention anyway; and second, that the rôle of London was of such supreme international importance at the time of the Victorian rebuilding that the architecture can hardly fail to have some historic relevance. Walter Bagehot described that rôle with notable lucidity in a book whose title is the name of a famous City street, *Lombard Street* (London, 1873). 'The briefest and truest way of describing Lombard Street', wrote Bagehot in a famous sentence, 'is to say that it is by far the greatest combination of economical power and economical delicacy that the world has ever seen'. Bagehot was using Lombard Street to symbolize the City of London in its rôle as a centre of international finance. The period of which he wrote was that between Peel's epoch-making Bank Charter Act of 1844 and the years after the Franco-Prussian War, when London's economic authority had become unquestioned throughout the world. He expounded what had happened in those years and explained the invisible power structure and its tremendous efficacy. His book was written just at the moment the structure was complete. In the latter decades of the century it was extended, elaborated and refined; but it was the period of thirty years between 1844 and 1874 that saw its rise. It is that period that will concern us now, but as a matter of architectural rather than economic history.[1]

There was no obvious reason why the invisible structure described by Bagehot should at once be reflected in conspicuous architectural display. But so it was. When *Lombard Street* was written, the street itself was almost entirely lined with buildings built or rebuilt since 1857, all, as we shall see, in lavish style and with the assistance of some notable architects. The new buildings were very little higher than the tall brick houses that preceded them – passenger lifts still lay in the future – but frontages were wider, often embracing several old sites.

The rebuilding had in view three objects: not quite the Vitruvian triad of 'commodity, firmness, and delight'; but, firmness being taken for granted, commodity, prestige, and investment. The first was provided by a generous reception area on the ground and a handsome boardroom on the first floors, strong rooms, boiler rooms, and clerks' lunch rooms in the basement, and a caretaker's flat at the top; the second by a highly enriched masonry façade towards the street; the third by the allocation of all the remaining space to lettable offices, flexibly partitioned between the iron columns which, behind the solid stone façade, formed the main structure. This was the new pattern of the 50s, and in principle it has hardly changed in 120 years. It was immediately justified. In 1864 it was said that site values in Lombard Street had doubled within a year;[2] in 1866 £1,000- or £2,000-a-year rent could be asked for a single floor in a building that cost no more than £10,000 or £15,000 to build and had perhaps three lettable floors.[3]

Lombard Street, the street of the great bankers, was special, but in other main streets of the City much the same was happening. In the 60s and 70s, Lothbury, Cornhill, Threadneedle Street, Cheapside, Leadenhall Street, and Mark Lane were changing as fast as Lombard Street. A city still almost uniformly Georgian and domestic was being broken up into a city of competing commercial blocks. A city that lit itself by candles and oil lamps was moving into the world of gas sun-burners. The resident population, which had risen to 129,000 in 1851, began to slump. In 1861 it was 113,000; in 1871, 75,000; in 1881, 51,000; and at the end of the century, 26,000. The biggest drop, representing something like a mass migration from City streets to west end and suburbs was in the 60s and early 70s, which was also the period of the most spectacular and innovative new non-residential buildings. From time to time, the rebuilding was accelerated by factors other than the initiative of individual firms. There was the occasional local conflagration. There was also the City's policy of street improvement when the widening of thoroughfares created new frontages, as in the case of Threadneedle Street and Bartholomew Lane from 1840 to 1844, while the cutting of wholly new streets like Cannon Street (west) from 1852 to 1855 and, above all, Queen Victoria Street from 1866 to 1871 placed on the market quantities of valuable building land, which was never for long short of bidders.

The transformation of the City, a drama in itself, was prefaced by a dramatic accident – the burning of the old Royal Exchange in 1838. It was rebuilt in the years 1842–44, to a design elicited in the course of a competition of classic absurdity.[4] The new building, differently oriented from its predecessor, was given a huge temple portico, facing west. This, in combination with the Bank of England to the north and the Mansion House to the southwest, made up a scene that had, and still has, something of the character of a forum. On this space all the important City streets converged: Poultry, coming along from Cheapside, on the west; Threadneedle Street, Cornhill, and Lombard Street on the east: ancient streets to which the 19th century had already added King William Street on the south-east and was soon to add Queen Victoria Street on the southwest. It was around this convergence of seven streets that the City began to renew itself.

The main constituents of the new monumental scene were banks and insurance offices. An inspection of the chronology of the rebuilding shows at once which of these agencies led the way where architecture was concerned – it was insurance.[5] Insurance was highly competitive. Insurance depended, even more than banks, on the wide dissemination of confidence, and, moreover, on the propagation of a sentimental image, the image of upright, prudent men banded together to arrest the cruel hand of

170. Law Life Office, Fleet Street, by John Shaw, 1834 *171.* Atlas Assurance, Cheapside, by Thomas Hopper, 1838

fate. Insurance companies still sell us this kind of thing. They were selling it just as busily in the 19th century, and one of the effective ways of doing so was through architecture and sculpture. One of the oldest companies, the Pelican, got itself into Lombard Street very early in the century by acquiring an old banker's house. It announced the change of user simply by a sculptured allegory over the entrance.[6] Other insurance offices in the City housed themselves on much the same quasi-domestic lines. There was a great concentration of insurance offices in New Bridge Street, Blackfriars, a then modern thoroughfare, west of St Paul's, all – so far as I can find – in ordinary terrace houses. The idea of architectural demonstration by insurance companies started outside the City in London's west end, notably with the County Fire Office (1829), whose palatial façade was part of Nash's Piccadilly scheme and, a few years later, with Cockerell's Greek-Palladian Westminster Office (1832), in the Strand. The first self-announcing insurance office inside the City seems to have been the Law Life of 1834, just east of Temple Bar. Law Life, as the name implies, had a special line in *170*
soliciting the patronage of lawyers, a shrewd innovation that paid off. Situated in the precincts of the law, with the Temple just opposite and Lincoln's Inn around the corner, the age of Shakespeare was a plausible stylistic evocation. John Shaw was the architect.[7] His neat 'Jacobean' frontage is still there but has suffered from being more than duplicated by a westward extension.

The Law Life is one of a group of legally oriented insurance offices clinging around the Inns of Court, and to some of these I shall return. In the central area of the City, the first monumental gesture by an insurance company came in 1836 when the Globe, having seized a corner site between Lombard Street and Cornhill, employed the

172. Sun Fire Office, Threadneedle Street, by C. R. Cockerell 1849 (demolished)
173. Alliance Office, Bartholomew Lane, by Thomas Allason 1841 (demolished)

distinguished Philip Hardwick to build on it. His conventional Georgian treatment of stucco with shallow pilasters soon lost countenance, however, and by 1864 the building was being called an eyesore.[8] Stucco was going out; for confidence and moral stability, masonry offered the better medium. In 1838 the Marine Insurance refronted its premises in stone, with allegories of 'Navigation' and 'Hope' in spandrels and Britannia sitting on a keystone.[9] Also in 1838, Thomas Hopper, an architect one associates with the fantastic neo-Norman castle of Penrhyn, came into the insurance world, building an arched and pilastered front for the Law and General in the Inns of
171 Court group and, more important, the Atlas in Cheapside, a sensitive Inigo Jonesian design with a well-carved representation of Atlas and his load over the entrance.[10] This building, burned out in the war, has been preserved at the acceptable cost of the pedestrian causeway of a widened Cheapside running through its arches and the less acceptable cost of a pitched roof.

In the early 40s the rebuilding of the Royal Exchange caused the realignment of frontages in Threadneedle Street and Bartholomew Lane and this resulted in two important re-buildings – the Alliance in Bartholomew Lane and the Sun Fire Office at
172 the corner formed by the two streets. The Alliance (1841), for which Thomas Allason was the architect, had a well-organized columnar front (demolished 1932).[11] The Sun
173 commissioned C. R. Cockerell, who had succeeded Soane as the Bank of England architect, to design theirs.[12] Thoughtful and original as he always was, Cockerell tried to give his four-storey building a convincing architectural unity by combining the second and third floors within one order. Vignola's Castello Farnese accounts for some of the composition, and the detail was a sophisticated blend of Italian, Pompeiian and
213 Greek. The stilted segmental windows (or flat-sided arches) of the ground floor were

174. Alfred Life Office, Lothbury, by Henry Clutton, 1844 (demolished)
175. Imperial Assurance, Threadneedle Street, by John Gibson, 1849 (demolished)

to become one of the universal clichés of Victorian design. After Cockerell's time, the building was spoiled by the introduction of a mezzanine above the ground floor, the upper part being raised and somewhat altered. This so falsified Cockerell's whole intention that demolition in 1969 could not easily be resisted.

By the date of the Sun building (1841–43), insurance was a hugely expanding area of business enterprise. With the Joint Stock Companies Act of the following year, the launching of these companies was much facilitated, and ninety-two companies were registered in Great Britain in the year 1844–45 alone.[13] In London in 1851 there were 125 insurance companies, thirty-two of which were less than seven years old.[14] Among these were mushroom companies that either collapsed or merged with others. Competition was intense, and only the successful companies reached the stage of housing themselves behind Italian façades with emblematic *relievi*.

Italian cinquecento was nearly always the style. It was the style that Charles Barry had established with his two famous clubs in Pall Mall, followed by other club architects in the same street. To a considerable extent, Victorian City architecture took its stylistic colouring from Barry's clubs. There was perhaps a prestige element here. A
nice example was the Alfred Life Office in Lothbury, 1844 (now demolished), where *174*
Henry Clutton borrowed effectively from the garden front of the Travellers' Club.[15]
Another was the Imperial Office (demolished about 1960) at the sharp corner of *175*
Threadneedle Street and Old Broad Street. This was by John Gibson, a pupil of Barry, so imitation of the master's Reform Club was not surprising. The date was 1849.[16]

The 1850s saw the erection of at least ten insurance buildings in the City, important enough to receive comment in the press. All but three have vanished, and of only a few of the others have I been able to find records. Penfold's Scottish Equitable (1857) in the

176. Royal Insurance Office, Lombard Street, by John Belcher, 1857 (demolished)
177. Royal Insurance Office, Lombard Street, as rebuilt by Belcher, 1863–66 (demolished)

Poultry had shafts and panels of polished granite.[17] T. H. Lewis's Union Fire and Life Office (1858) in Cornhill has passed unrecorded, and John Foulon's Minerva (1852) was destroyed in the Second World War.[18] Sancton Wood's Queen's Insurance Office in Gresham Street (1858) survives – a sober composition with some borrowings from Cockerell.[19] The Mutual Life in King Street, by J. M. K. Hahn (1859), was a vulgar imitation of the neighbouring Atlas.[20]

More impressive than any of these were the two successive buildings of the Royal. This company, originating in Liverpool in 1845, was extraordinarily successful. Already its Liverpool headquarters, built in 1849, had the appearance of a public building. In London, the Royal got itself a site in Lombard Street, the sacred home of
176 banking, and its first building of 1857, by John Belcher, became at once the dominant
building in the street.[21] Six years later, however, this was disposed of, and a larger
177 office was built on the opposite corner of Clement's Lane by the same architect with his
son.[22] By this time, the Royal had discovered and tested the benefits of publicity and was unique among the offices in spending £20,000 or £30,000 a year on advertising.[23] The new building with its four panelled and plastered storeys and fulsome display of allegorical sculpture, was sheer advertisement. The Royal of 1863 marks the point where insurance companies began to use architecture less as a symbol of quality and integrity than as an effusion of conspicuous waste. The building was demolished in 1910.

Down Fleet Street way, in the legal cluster, some curious stylistic variations belong to the late 50s and early 60s. Penfold's Law Union (1857), in Chancery Lane, is, like its neighbour, the Law Life, Jacobean and doubtless for the same sententious reason.[24] A few doors away is Thomas Bellamy's Law Insurance (1859), conventionally composed but with uncommonly nice spacing and delicate detail[25] – which is more than can be said for W. C. Bartleet's funny little Promoter building (1860) in Fleet Street, a Parisian absurdity in variegated materials, stuck with texts and symbols.[26]

The most outlandish and exciting newcomer in the late 50s was the Crown Life *178*
Office in New Bridge Street.[27] Here the directors surprisingly placed themselves in the hands of the latest and most controversial exponents of the Gothic Revival, Thomas Deane and Benjamin Woodward. They had just finished building the Museum of Natural Science at Oxford, which was strongly influenced by Ruskin's ideas. In New Bridge Street they had a narrow site in a range of plain Georgian houses (mostly occupied by rival insurance offices), and they produced what might be described as the Ruskinian equivalent of such houses: more or less Venetian, with a delicate polychromy of Portland stone, brick, red and grey granite, and Sicilian and other marbles. The naturalistic carving was by the famous Shea brothers from Oxford, and inside were ceilings and friezes with foliage, birds, and animals painted by the Pre-Raphaelite, John Hungerford Pollen ('Very peculiar,' commented *Building News*). Unhappily, this important and innovative little building had a life of only seven years.

178. Crown Life Office, New Bridge Street, by Deane and Woodward, 1858–60 (demolished 1867) *179.* Crown Life Office, Fleet Street, built in the later sixties as successor to the building shown in ill. 178 (demolished)

The London, Chatham, and Dover Railway came with its Act of Parliament and sheared off the whole of the east side of New Bridge Street. Crown Life, duly
179 compensated, built itself a stylistically similar but more pretentious office in Fleet Street.[28] Benjamin Woodward, the more significant of the two partners in Deane and Woodward, had, however, died, and it was the earlier building which was the more influential and which initiated that round-arch, pointed-extrados type of medievalism with which so much Victorian commercial architecture is imbued. Of the many original gestures made by insurance architecture this is, historically, the most striking, and it is sad that, apart from a handful of woodcuts of the exterior, there appear to be no records.

The great wave of insurance promotion, halted by the crash of 1858 when twelve companies failed, began to wane in the 60s, but there were some important late-comers. The National Provident Institution, after flexing its muscles in second-floor rooms in Nicholas Lane, burst into Gracechurch Street and built, in 1863, a brilliantly overloaded façade by Robert Kerr (demolished about 1950) – Venetian renaissance with a modern twist.[29] Similarly, the North British and Mercantile (demolished 1970), in Threadneedle Street, next door to Cockerell's Sun Fire and designed by a former assistant of Cockerell's, J. E. Goodchild, shows a considerable relaxation from the formal Italian. But by the 60s there is very little point in distinguishing insurance architecture from any other kind of City architecture. What I have been concerned to do here is to show how the competitive, publicity-seeking spirit of the insurance world brought into the City a whole variety of architectural initiatives. It is now time to turn to another and more sober area of the City's business – banking.

Banking, at the beginning of Victoria's reign, was mainly in the hands of the great banking families. It was a private business, conducted by the very rich for the well-to-do. It did not need to advertise itself. The banking houses were the town residences of the bankers (there is still in Fleet Street a merchant bank, Hoare's, that is also a family residence). The classic instance of the banker's house was Sir Charles Asgill's in Lombard Street – already mentioned – designed in 1756 by Sir Robert Taylor, with just a hint of strong rooms behind its Doric order, but otherwise quite simply a gentleman's house. Later banking houses were no less gentlemanly, and the monumentalizing of bank architecture only came with the intrusion of the joint-stock banks into London. The least resented and most successful of these newcomers, the London and Westminster, took a site opposite the Bank of England in Lothbury.[30] They appointed William Tite as their architect but gave the design of the front block to Cockerell, perhaps out of respect for the Bank of England, whose architect he was. Built in 1839 and demolished in 1928, the façade was discretion itself. It was noticed at the time that, like some of the insurance offices, it seemed to derive from a Pall Mall club – Sydney Smirke's Oxford and Cambridge, then just completed.

The discreet intrusion of the joint-stock London and Westminster received what looks like an architectural rebuff when, on the next site, one of the great private
180 bankers and overt enemy of the joint-stock principle, Mr Jones Loyd, rebuilt his premises, employing Cockerell's successor at the Bank of England, P. C. Hardwick (son of Philip) to build what was more like a first-rate west-end mansion than a commercial building, with a Doric ground floor like the old Asgill house in Lombard

180. Jones Loyd Bank, Lothbury, by P. C. Hardwick 1857 (demolished) *181.* City Bank, Threadneedle Street, by William Mosely 1864 (demolished)

Street.[31] It towered over the joint-stock intruder. But time conciliates, and Jones Loyd was no fool. The merging of Jones Loyd with the London and Westminster as a joint-stock corporation was one of the sensations of 1864. The Jones Loyd building survived till about 1920.

Meanwhile, some brash joint-stock newcomers showed their hands. In 1854, the Bank of Australasia, founded in 1838 and now flushed with the optimism of the Australian gold rush, took a site on the corner of Threadneedle Street and Finch Lane.[32] Their architect, P. C. Hardwick, took the main idea of Cockerell's Sun Fire Office, the telescoping of four storeys into three by embracing the top two in a single order, and executed it in his own coarser but very handsome way.[33] Then, in 1857 came
the City Bank, a joint-stock affair only two years old, and it occupied the opposite *181*
corner of narrow Finch Lane.[34] The directors employed an almost unknown architect, William Moseley, who, it seems, was reluctant to cut less of a figure in Threadneedle Street than the senior man. His round-arched portal on a rounded corner is a nice Mannerist exercise, and I am happy to say that it is still there and has just been cleaned, while Hardwick's building is gone. Another colonial intruder was the Australian Chartered Bank by Henry Baker, flashing its polished granite columns in Cornhill.[35]

But the greatest explosion of bank building and rebuilding came, of course, in
Lombard Street. Of this rebuilding there is now almost nothing left, and we must rely *196*

182. Barclay and Bevan's Bank, Lombard Street, by P. C. Hardwick, 1864 (demolished)
183. London and County Bank, Lombard Street, by C. O. Parnell. 1860 (demolished)

on prints and old photographs. As we have seen, the Royal Insurance Office somewhat insolently made its home there in 1857 and a second, grander home in 1863, by which
183 time the London and County Bank had rebuilt its premises further along the street, using, as it happens, the stone from old Westminster Bridge.[36] The architect, C. O. Parnell, had already built two west-end clubs in the Barry manner, which we see here married to the Doric ground-floor theme of the Asgill house. In 1863, P. C. Hardwick built Robarts and Lubbock's bank in a reserved Italian style and, in 1864, Barclay and
182 Bevan's, where he couples his Doric columns (the Asgill tradition again) in an ingenious pier-and-window model to get as much light into the building as Italian convention would allow.[37] Then, in 1865, came a most peculiar stranger. The Scottish
184 banking house of Alexander Cunliffe and Company, the Clydesdale Bank, chose to bring into the City a young architect who had made his name by winning the competition for the Manchester Assize Courts in 1859, Alfred Waterhouse.[38] As the Assize Courts showed, Waterhouse was a Gothic man, an emancipated designer who, when he came to London, was not to be shackled by the conventions of 'club-land' or Lombard Street. Clearly, he had much sympathy for Deane and Woodward's breakaway at the Crown Life, but he was much less pious in his medievalism and expressed himself in a rough dialect that had an Italian base and details perhaps more Romanesque than anything else. The Clydesdale Bank (now demolished) made a great impression, and the style is reflected in many streets of commercial London. Waterhouse himself took it to the west end and actually built a club in St James's in much the same style – an ironic reversal of the older trend.

Outside Lombard Street the most prominent bank of the 1860s was P. C. Hardwick's Union Bank, opposite the Mansion House.[39] But by far the most exciting,

184. Clydesdale Bank, Lombard Street, by Alfred Waterhouse 1865 (demolished)

185. National Provincial (now the National Westminster) Bank, Bishopsgate, by John Gibson 1865

186. Royal Bank of Scotland, Bishopsgate, by Thomas Chatfeild Clarke, 1877 *187.* Ottoman Bank, Threadneedle Street, by William Burnet 1871

and perhaps really the queen of all the City banks since Soane, was, and is, the National
185 Provincial in Bishopsgate.[40] The National Provincial had, as its name implies, flourished in the provinces for thirty years and already had a London headquarters in Bishopsgate, not quite inside the inner sanctum of banking, but nearly touching Threadneedle Street. This was rebuilt in 1865, and for architectural effect there is no City bank to compare with it. The National Provincial here dispensed with the profit arising from office-letting and built a single-storey building of noble scale, bolder and grander than the Bank of England itself, with Corinthian columns running full height to a cornice ranging with the tops of the tall houses next door and even then pointing further into the sky with groups and statues. Within is a stately Corinthian hall lit from three domes. The architect was Barry's pupil, John Gibson. The rich profiles and fine distribution of ornament show how well he had learned the lessons of his master. Threatened with demolition a few years ago, the building has been saved by an adroit manipulation of the site and the erection of a high-rise building in close proximity.

After 1870, the great phase of Victorian bank building in the City was in decline. Initiative switched to branch banks in the suburbs and provinces. But two individual departures are worth noting – both in very narrow streets. William Burnet's Ottoman
187 Bank in Throgmorton Street (1871) is round-arched quattrocento Venetian.[41] Fred Chancellor's Bank of British North America in Clements Lane (1873) was flat-arched and rather unexpectedly Soanean.[42] Both used polychromatic masonry. Of the two only the Ottoman Bank survives. The last mid-Victorian gesture in the banking world

188. National Discount Company, Cornhill, 1856, by F. and H. Francis.
189. General Credit Company, Lothbury, by G. Somers Clarke, 1866.

was Thomas Chatfeild Clarke's Royal Bank of Scotland in Bishopsgate (1877), where *186*
the upper storeys ride on a series of arches springing from polished granite columns – a
spectacular performance but curiously thin and jaunty after the sterling classicism of
Cockerell, Hardwick, and Gibson.[43]

The success of the joint-stock banks led, after 1855, to the formation of joint-stock
discount companies with limited liability. Fifteen such companies were formed
between 1856 and 1870.[44] Their architectural requirements differed in no conspicuous
way from those of the banks, but it happens, nevertheless, that two of these companies
built premises rather distinct from the general run of bank architecture. The National
Discount Company was the pioneer. Formed in 1856, it lost no time in buying an *188*
expensive site in Cornhill and putting up a building perfectly representative of the new
norm in commercial architecture, with commodity, prestige, and investment all well-
provided for. It is the type that much City architecture was still adopting in the 1930s.

Very different indeed was the architectural adventure upon which the General
Credit Company entered seven years later. This company started in the grandest style
with a capital of £2.5 million, so that the question of prestige premises was no problem.
Immediately after incorporation, it possessed itself of a site in Lothbury and called in
G. Somers Clarke, who, like Gibson, was a pupil of Sir Charles Barry. With the
cinquecento modes having become, by 1863, a little stale, and with a site that dictated a
tall thin elevation to Lothbury, Clarke turned to Venetian Gothic.[45] He was not a *189*
philosophical Ruskinian like Deane and Woodward, and he handled the Venetian

190. Office building, 59–61 Mark Lane, by George Aitchison for the City of London Real Property Company, 1864 *191.* Office building, Fenchurch Street, by Edward I'Anson, 1857 (demolished)

material in the dexterous unsentimental way that an Italian training under Barry had taught him. He produced a beautiful building, unkindly criticized at the time for being too literal in its quotations from *The Stones of Venice*. If some details are, indeed, fairly literal, their combination is something new. The filing of quadruple sets of windows in a continuous vertical frame, the effectively judged contrasts between plain walling and enriched areas, the brilliant modelling of the doorway – all these things set the building apart as one of the most original of its time in the City.

Insurance offices and banks led the way in the renewing of the City's streets, and by 1858, most new buildings in these categories contained a quantity of lettable floor space. The building consisting *entirely* of lettable floor space and promoted solely for this kind of investment was a collateral development. According to Edward I'Anson, who specialized in such buildings, the first of the type was built as early as 1823.[46] I'Anson himself built Royal Exchange Chambers (1844–45) for Sir Francis Moon, the printseller who became Lord Mayor, in 1844.[47] It was a sound classical building in the New Oxford Street style with arches on the ground floor for shops and office space above. In the 50s, development companies began to proliferate, their sole function being to buy up City sites and cover them rapidly with ostentatious buildings containing nothing but office space. The architects working for such companies or for individual developers were rarely in the first flight. They were men with City connexions – often inherited – sound professionals with some artistic gifts. A few, like Edward I'Anson (1812–88), George Aitchison (1825–1910), and John Whichcord

(1823–85) rose to be presidents of the Royal Institute of British Architects; Aitchison even to be a Royal Academician. Others worked in relative, though by no means impecunious, obscurity. I'Anson's work is always interesting. In 1857 he experimented with an office block in Fenchurch Street that had a front more glass than wall.[48] *191*
That is gone, but his Corn Exchange Chambers in Seething Lane still stands: a palazzo type, as severe as Barry, but with quattrocento feeling and naturalistic ornament.[49] In a block in Mark Lane, also 1859,[50] he seems to have caught the Gothic mood of Deane and Woodward's Crown Life office, and this led on to the really charming rebuilding in brick and terracotta of 65 Cornhill in 1871.[51]

One of the leading development companies was the City Offices Company. In 1866 this company developed one of the biggest sites in Lombard Street with a £70,000 block – a huge property investment for the time. In the following year they built an £80,000 block on the site of the old Bull Inn, running through from Bishopsgate to Old Broad Street.[52] Undertakings on this scale were new and highly significant of what was going to happen to the City in the next hundred years. Architecturally, they aimed to overtake the banks and insurance offices in external show. A good address and an extravagant façade were justified by the sort of rents that would pay for the site and the building within a very few years. The architects employed on these two developments were the brothers Francis. Perhaps the nicest thing to say about them is that they gave their clients exactly what their clients wanted. One may add that while earlier blocks of offices were described as *chambers*, the second of the two monster blocks undertaken by the City Offices Company was called *buildings* – Palmerston Buildings – in commemoration of the prime minister who had died in 1865. The new nomenclature gradually superseded the old, *chambers* surviving mainly as a description of residential accommodation for lawyers and bachelors.

Another development company, the City of London Real Property Company, was active in Mark Lane, employing George Aitchison to build a block of lettable *190*
counting-houses there in 1864. A building resulted that was regarded then and is still regarded as one of the most interesting of its kind in the City.[53] Nos 59–61 Mark Lane has a Portland stone front with round-arched openings, subtly modelled, perhaps with a feeling for the Syrian researches of de Vogüé. Internally, it is an iron structure and includes a self-supporting iron staircase. We can compare it with an only slightly less remarkable building in Cannon Street, No. 103, built two years later by the Registered Land Company, the architect being Fred Jameson.[54] Here the style is more positively Romanesque and owes a great deal to Crown Life, but both buildings show how close the City medievalism of the 1860s, initiated by Deane and Woodward, could come to a reasonable and sympathetic modernity. In Jameson's building the fenestration is simple, rhythmical, and luminous, the modelling bold in relief and well able to defy the appalling accretions of soot, which, it was said, rendered conventional classical detailing void of meaning in five or six years.[55]

Good sense and simplicity of this kind were not, perhaps, always the best way of attracting the sort of custom that the development companies required, and toward 1870, office space was being enveloped by increasingly outlandish elevations. The problem was to give the customers plenty of light while still retaining a prestige exterior. Edmund Woodthorpe's Cornhill Chambers,[56] built on the site of four old

192. Albert Buildings, Queen Victoria Street, by F. J. Ward, 1873 *193.* Office building, Bishopsgate, by William Wilkinson of Oxford. 1861 (demolished)

houses for a small private company of investors in 1866, shows rather acutely the sort of compositional difficulties that arose, and one can see why T. Chatfeild Clarke, faced with a similar problem in Throgmorton Street in 1870, ran his lights together in unbroken horizontal rows of Gothic arcading.[57] Strictly Gothic fronts had, before that date, been rare in the City; in fact, the only one I can find is a building put up in
193 Bishopsgate in 1861 by a firm of seed merchants, for their own use and for letting.[58] It was designed by the Oxford architect, William Wilkinson, and owes much to Deane and Woodward – not to their Crown Life building, but to the daring design they sent in for the government offices competition of 1856. This was followed ten years later by Mansion House Buildings and Albert Buildings, both on awkward 'flat-iron' sites created by the new Queen Victoria Street. Mansion House Buildings, by John Belcher, is a vulgar piece of work, pointing a rude Gothic finger at the Mansion House
192 opposite.[59] Albert Buildings, by F. J. Ward and even more grotesquely coarse, has about it a monstrous reasonableness. A contemporary critic observed that 'the first floor has a not unpleasing air of Viollet-le-Duc about it,' and the reasonableness may indeed have issued from that source.[60]

The question of style in office buildings was much inflamed by a momentous challenge in 1873. It was in this year that Richard Norman Shaw, a total stranger to the
194 City, a country-house man, began to build New Zealand Chambers in Leadenhall Street and exhibited a drawing of the building in the Royal Academy.[61] Here there was no question at all of Gothic or Italian, Lombardic or quattrocento; the style was quite distinctly and impudently an improvisation on English vernacular products of the early or mid-17th century. Nothing remotely like it had been attempted, and it was as

194. New Zealand Chambers, Leadenhall Street, by Richard Norman Shaw, 1873 (demolished)

195. Cook's Warehouse, St Paul's Churchyard, by J. T. Knowles 1852–53 (demolished)
196. A £70,000 office block on the corner of Lombard Street and Gracechurch Street (demolished). Built by the City Offices Co. to the designs of F. and H. Francis, 1866.

improper in the City as walking into the Stock Exchange in knickerbockers and a Norfolk jacket. Old T. L. Donaldson, father of the profession and broad-minded in so many things, expressed what all of his generation and many younger must have felt about the new building. 'I cannot conceive what motive could have induced its author . . . to rake up a type of the very lowest state of corrupt erection in the City of London, of a period that marks the senility of decaying taste.'[62]

But there was another way of looking at it. City office buildings needed all the light they could get. This in straitlaced Italian was, as we have seen, difficult to provide. The medievalists had had their successes but to the accompaniment of rather precious forms of expression. Why not go back to the London of pre-1666, the brave bourgeois capital of merchants and craftsmen whose architecture was free and easy, richly ornamented but, above all, practical? The main features of Shaw's front in Leadenhall Street were three two-tiered bay windows directly imitated from an old house, not in London but in the High Street at Oxford; they were developed in such a way as to give considerable areas of glass between the four massive piers of Farnham brick that were the front's main uprights. On the ground floor were the entrance and, on either side, two bays with small square panes like early Georgian shop fronts (the Oxford house had such a shop front). At the top was a huge, plastered cove with coarse rhythmic ornament like the ceilings at Canonbury and, above that again, ample square-headed dormers.

New Zealand Chambers caused a stir and was one of the buildings that precipitated the so-called 'Queen Anne' revolution of the 1870s. It created a type and was a gesture of liberation. Once it became artistically acceptable, there was really nothing that was not acceptable. It should be noted, moreover, that Shaw's controversial building, whatever its artistic merits, was a commercial success. The ground floor of the back block commanded a rent of one thousand guineas a year. In the air raids of 1940 and 1941, however, the large area of timber and glass invited incendiarism too readily, and New Zealand Chambers was burned almost to the ground – not quite, however, and the beautifully modelled doorway and *oeil-de-boeuf* window in brick remained for many years in pleasing isolation.

The last and most multifarious type involved in the great rebuilding of 1837 to 1875 was the warehouse. A warehouse could be many things, from a gaunt dockside structure designed solely for the reception of heavy merchandise, to a building comprising offices and showrooms, as well as storage space, and showing an elegant face to an important street. Furthermore, there were different classes of warehouses, according to the associations of different areas. Off Cheapside, around Wood Street, there were the drapers and fancy warehousemen; off Eastcheap and Great Tower Street, around Mark Lane and Mincing Lane, were warehouses for foreign and colonial, as well as some native, goods.

197. Warehouse, Little Britain, by John Young, 1858. *198*. Hunt and Crombie's 38–39 Eastcheap, by John Young, 1864

An excellent tradition of plain brick and iron construction for warehouses had
long prevailed in the City, but a tendency towards architectural showmanship began to
195 be noticed after 1850. Cook's (drapers and outfitters) huge warehouse, staring at
Wren's cathedral from the south side of St Paul's Churchyard and built from 1852 to
1853, was a work of J. T. Knowles; its bulk in that position excited unfavourable
comments, and it was also observed that these things were done better in Manchester,
which was very true.[63] Then followed the far more elegant warehouses of the Wood
Street area where the drapery, lace, silk, and hosiery trades were concentrated. The
outstanding performer there was G. Somers Clarke, with an elaborately detailed Italian
169 front for Munt and Brown, built in 1857.[64] Over the next twenty years, Wood Street
and Milk Street were largely rebuilt, the Gresham Street fire of 1864 accelerating the
process. R. W. Edis, Herbert Ford, and Tillot and Chamberlain were among the
architects represented; but records of the street are scanty, and both have been totally
rebuilt since 1945.

In the eastern area there was a more adventurous approach. At 38–39 Eastcheap
198 stand the colonial produce offices, showrooms, and warehouses built by John Young
and Son for Hunt and Crombie in 1864.[65] The Youngs had already built in 1858 a small
197 but innovative warehouse in Little Britain: a five-storey piling up of round arches –
prophetic, in a way, of Aitchison's sophisticated block of counting-houses in Mark
Lane.[66] The Youngs were not for sophistication, however, and their decorative
originalities were on a popular level, as their Eastcheap building with its lively
rustication and playful ornaments shows. At No. 28 St Mary-at-Hill was, until
recently, a little warehouse by the same firm with charmingly eccentric details,
including capitals composed out of rope and flowers, very nicely carved.[67]

A more serious and influential experiment came from a famous medievalist
momentarily venturing into the City. This was the narrow warehouse front carried out
199 by William Burges for John Skilbeck in Upper Thames Street in 1866 (demolished).[68]
Burges brought up two pointed arches and a cinquefoil under a gable, made the cranes
operate through the jaws of grotesque lions, and, over the ground-floor shop, inserted
a Gothicized iron bressumer, with corbelled bearings. It was almost perfectly 13th-century and as perfectly suited to its purpose. The idea was seized at once and used on a larger scale in Bishopsgate and elsewhere.

In Eastcheap again, a costly and truly dazzling kind of Gothic arrived in the following year. R. L. Roumieu was an architect of determined individuality, strongly inflected by the current French fashion for making Gothic work overtime to catch up with the 19th century. His warehouse for Hill, Evans and Company, the Worcester vinegar manufacturers (they were selling two million gallons a year), is the most arresting building in the street.[69] In a brick and stone front of extravagant thickness, shafts ascend through two storeys of window to jutting canopies in two sets of three, each set under a pair of gables, each pair made to carry the sides of two enormous hooded dormers, between which dormers one tiny boxlike dormer, propped on the pinnacle of a central canopy, brings the composition – it may charitably be said – to rest. The result is quite unlike a warehouse, and, in fact, it became used as chambers.

This sort of nonsense was, of course, untypical, but the City around 1870 was full of untypical adventures, and one can set beside the Hill, Evans building a warehouse,

199. Skilbeck Warehouse, Upper Thames Street, by William Burges, 1866 (demolished) *200.* Peek Warehouse, St. Mary-at-Hill, by Ernest George and Vaughan, 1871.

equally untypical, in St Mary-at-Hill, designed by two dedicated young architects, 200
Ernest George and Vaughan, in what *they* conceived to be the modern direction for 1871, a severe and subtle interpretation of the style of George Edmund Street.

Of the many hundreds of warehouses built in the 40s, 50s and 60s, I have chosen these few because they excited interest at the time. An analysis of the whole mass of warehouse building would show a very different and far less entertaining picture. With so much destruction since 1945, I doubt whether such an analysis will ever be possible.

Such were some kinds of the architecture thrown up by initiatives in insurance, banking, office and warehouse building. This is the real stuff of the City's Victorian life, and I hope that such a compressed and selective survey as I have given has justified the rather bold title of this essay. A balanced account of the rebuilding would stretch over much more ground. Room would have to be found for such things as City clubs, the building or rebuilding of chophouses and taverns; the arrival in the City of five railway terminals, one of them (Cannon Street) equipped with a majestic hotel especially planned for the needs of City life; the widening of streets and the cutting of new streets, notably Queen Victoria Street by the Metropolitan Board of Works; the rebuilding of their halls by some of the City companies; and last, but by no means least, the public works of the Corporation of the City of London itself – the reconstruction of Guildhall with its library, the building of the Coal Exchange with an iron hall like a huge parrot's cage, the building of the fish market at Billingsgate, the meat market at Smithfield and the poultry market at Leadenhall Street, and the bridging of the Fleet Valley by the construction of Holborn Viaduct.

I began this essay with the observation that to reconstruct the City of the Victorian 1850s, 60s and 70s is now almost an archaeological exercise. To me this is a melancholy consideration because, although I am old enough to remember the City before even the spasmodic replacements of the 1930s, I remember in fact precious little of it. As a student I was conscious only of its sombre intricacies, its multiplication of sad and sooty ornament and, more than anything, its nauseating excess. To probe and discriminate never entered my head. I suppose that all architecture has to die before it can touch the historical imagination. The eye of the 1930s saw the City as dead: a petrified theatre of bad architectural rhetoric. Today, half demolished and overwhelmed by a harsh and shimmering modernity, it begins to live again and to move, less by its art than by the characteristic strangeness of the resurrected, the curiosity and even the admiration of our alien world.

XII · The London Suburban Villa 1850–1880

201. No. 1 and 2 Eton Villas, Chalk Farm. A semi-detached pair on the Eton College estate, built in 1849 by Samuel Cuming

202. 'Worcester Lodge', No. 1 Middleton Grove, Camden Road, designed by George Truefitt for himself in 1859

EVEN THE MOST despised Victorian villa derives from an architectural design; while those villas which pique us by their special monstrousness and (as it seems to us) their unique ugliness are almost always the cherished work of architects. These architects are the forgotten architects of the century, men who never aspired to greatness or even to the circles radiating from greatness, who, rarely sending designs to the Academy, still more rarely had them hung; who cultivated their own little stylistic vanities in their own remote hinterlands. Rarely do the names of these men appear on a printed page and then it is mostly in the 'tenders accepted' columns of the building papers, or in the advertisements of building sites ('apply to Mr —, architect'). Even when documentary attributions are forthcoming they are often unrealistic since there is no guarantee that the 'architect' was in fact the designer of the works which go under his name. The whole question is dark and prickly and it is already as hard to discover who really designed the Victorian villa as to name the masons and carpenters of our medieval churches; and this in spite of the fact that the sons and grandsons of many must still be living. Thus suddenly and effectively does time provide the antiquary with his employment.

But the analysis of the suburban villa is difficult for another reason. Its design did not derive directly from the work which was being done by the leaders of the profession. Only in the last two decades of the century is there an obvious and universal relationship between the work of known innovators and that of their unknown suburban colleagues. In the thirty years between 1850 and 1880 there was, as it were, a 'lower school' of designers which exercised considerable initiative of its own and, in fact, evolved what we think of as the Victorian 'vernacular,' a style which has remarkably little connection with the work of, say, Gilbert Scott, William Butterfield or G. E. Street. Any such connection would in any case be rather difficult, since these men were church builders, almost exclusively, and a small-house architect could not be expected to derive much inspiration from a Scott steeple, a Butterfield reredos or a Street font. The great figures did, of course, drop crumbs from time to time, in the shape of clergy houses and vicarages; and these were promptly gathered. But the 'lower school' was not dependent on such pickings. There were, here and there, certain architects, now almost forgotten, who had a strong desire to introduce a degree of artistic consequence into their rather humble employments. Who some of these architects were it will be my business to reveal in this article.

In the progress of the 'lower school' of Victorian designers there was no distinct break (as there was in the world of church building) between their work and that of the latest Georgians. They necessarily took over the traditional suburban house-plans – the 'double-fronted' and 'semi-detached' types – and attempted to endow them with 'character' rather than to replace them by something different. The Georgian tradition, undiluted, penetrates far into the Victorian age. It is still traceable in exceptionally thoughtless work of the 1880s and 1890s and was recognized, though not esteemed, as a norm till the end of the century. Professor Kerr, speaking[1] in 1857, said that the year 1842 marked the end of the period when architects were brought up exclusively to 'the classic business' while 1847 marked the change to eclecticism. This coincides accurately with one's observations and with the graph of house building in London. Almost pure Georgian design was practised well into the 1840s and as a preliminary to our enquiry into the more essentially Victorian phase we must look at a few examples of this legacy from a precedent epoch.

Two examples must suffice. Both consist of houses built on London suburban estates whose development was under the control of an architect of Georgian upbringing and sympathies. The first example is Nichols Square, off the Hackney Road. Nichols Square was planned and designed for J. B. Nichols, Esq., by the architect J. H. Taylor,[2] who exhibited a view of it at the RA in 1841. The houses were 'Tudor' of a type which might well have been built twenty years earlier in St John's Wood. Most were semi-detached, each pair presenting twin gables to the road.

The other example is provided by the Eton estate at Chalk Farm, where a number
201 of houses in Adelaide Road, Provost Road and Eton Villas are from designs approved by John Shaw,[3] surveyor to Eton College. These houses, built during the 1840s, are not Gothic, but Greco-Italian with projecting eaves; and in Provost Road the semi-detached pairs divide a single flattened gable between them. In Adelaide Road, the corner-houses, where cross-roads occur, are of a special design adapted to the more picturesque opportunities of their sites (a practice, incidentally, which continued throughout the century).

These examples characterize fairly enough the building boom of the 40s, which reached its peak in the years 1847–48. Most suburban houses of the decade adopt either the Gothic or the Classic mode and if there is any accentuation of character it is usually in the Italian direction. The Italian villa idea was not new but it was always possible to stress its quaintness in new ways and this was done by several architects of the 40s. The firm of Gough and Roumieu, for instance, invented an extravagant blend of Soanian abstraction and Italian vernacular which they employed at some houses in Tollington
204 Park[4] and again in their scheme for Manor Park, Streatham[5] which, ambitiously begun, never proceeded very far. Again in the years 1845–46 at St John's Wood Park, Harlesden and elsewhere,[6] Henry E. Kendall, junior, attempted to give some villa estates a flying start by composing a peculiar suburban style, an emasculate Italian with

203. Nos. 8 and 9 Gloucester Avenue, Regents Park, probably by H. Bassett, 1844 *204.* Houses in Tollington Park by Gough and Roumieu, 1840s

205. 'Sutton Lodge', Heathfield Terrace, Turnham Green, by Henry E. Kendall *206.* Nos. 21 and 22, The Park, Ealing, 1851, on a layout by Sydney Smirke

innumerable frills. One house in St John's Wood Park registers his style. Certain 203
houses in Regents Park Road[7] and Gloucester Crescent are akin to this style, while at the Twickenham end of Richmond Bridge was, till about 1960, a very quaint and self-conscious example – a diminutive Italian villa designed for a Dr Barry by an unknown architect.

In the 50s examples of the school could be multiplied indefinitely but I will note a
few manifestations only: the Park, Ealing, on a lay-out by Sydney Smirke, 1846: houses 206
dated 1851; Spring Grove, Isleworth[8] (J. Taylor, 1857 onwards – big double-fronted villas); Roupell Park[9] (Taylor again, 1858, as well as Banks and Barry); the Cedars estate, Putney[10] and Brockley Park estate[11] (both apparently by George Morgan 1865; only a few Italian houses were built). All these are as consciously Italian as anything built by Sir Charles Barry, and, indeed, rather less whimsical than many of the experiments of the 40s. They are among the last legitimate descendants of the Italian School, which, through the 60s and 70s, was progressively weakened by dilution and the contagion of French and other influences.

From about 1853, the great cry, in domestic architecture, was for *character*. There was a new crisis in the reaction from Georgian smoothness and it took the form not of a search for a 'new style' but of a desire to mix available styles in a way which should not only be propitious to the emergence of something really and truly new but thoroughly striking in itself. The crisis was certainly precipitated by the publication of *The Stones of Venice* (1851) with its rhetorical detachment from mere questions of style and grammar, and its passion for uncouth but expressive and 'characteristic' detail. The book set in a new light certain experiments of which nobody had taken very much notice – such things as James Wild's Christ Church, Streatham (1841) and his school in Shelton Street (1849), in both of which he had used nothing but brick but produced very decided character indeed. T. H. Wyatt had tried certain Romanesque experiments, slightly less original. And the alternating red and black bands of Butterfield's All Saints were already rising in Margaret Street. Character was the thing.[12]

Character, it was seen by the 'lower school,' could be distilled effectively from a blend of the styles – more so by this means than by stoic loyalty to any one, which was the policy of many men in the 'upper school.' The blending of styles and the abstraction from them of *character* appropriate to the 19th century was the course which the 'lower school' adopted with enthusiasm. They called their mixtures *eclectic*.

The suburban architecture resulting from this point of view is so complex that it is necessary to try to tabulate its sources. They were as follows:

1. *The Georgian Tradition*. This gave the siting and plan types, double-fronted and semi-detached; also the bay window and to some extent the materials. This was an undesired but inescapable source.

2. *The Italian Revival*, initiated by Barry, with its love of rich eaves-cornices and window dressings and its approach to medievalism through the use of round-headed windows, often in couples and informally distributed. There was an easy connexion between the less formal Renaissance types of design and some Italian Romanesque of the 12th century.

3. *The Gothic Revival*, especially in certain experimental manifestations like Wild's school in Shelton Street, Butterfield's All Saints, Margaret Street and Woodward's University Museum at Oxford.

4. *Bookish Influences* principally from Ruskin but also from Owen Jones, whose philosophy of ornament postulated 'general laws' and who asserted that 'no one (style) has more claim on our attention than another.' While Ruskin's influence was on the whole nostalgic, that of Owen Jones was in the direction of a conscious modernism. Street's *Brick and Marble in North Italy* was influential after its appearance in 1855, and Viollet-le-Duc's *Dictionnaire* (from 1854) exerted, in restricted circles, an influence which gradually circulated through the profession. A book which had a considerable influence in suburbia was Charles Parker's *Villa Rustica* of 1832, 1833 and 1841. The first two volumes show examples of villas actually seen in Italy. The third volume develops Parker's own highly mannered version of the Italian villa style.

5. *Contemporary French Architecture*. The least obvious but not least important source. French architects of the 1840s and 50s evolved some very infectious stylistic mixtures – fundamentally neo-grec, with an infusion of medievalism or something very near to it. They interested themselves in François 1er and Henri IV and re-adopted high slated roofs and turrets, features which found a ready response in England. Many architects visited France and the first edition of Victor Calliat's *Parallèle*[13] appeared in 1850; the book contained, among other things, a very original design by Viollet-le-Duc.

Such are the influences to be looked for in the eclectic work of what we have called the 'lower school.' They may seem to constitute a ridiculously pompous ancestry for so simple a thing as a suburban villa. But the fact is that the Victorian villa is far from simple – an amalgam of many traits produced by minds which have taken many impressions – very many more than they have been aware of.

And now, for some specimens of this eclecticism and its exponents. Let us turn first to the work of Charles Gray, who was born in 1828 and made a considerable name in certain circles before he was thirty. His sets of chambers in Covent Garden,

207. 'Egremont', No. 153 Tulse Hill, by Charles Gray, 1853. (Still exists but in a 'de-Victorianized' condition) *208.* Nos. 333–5 High Road, Wood Green, by Charles Gray, 1856

Buckingham Street and elsewhere were his most conspicuous works; but he also executed and exhibited suburban villas which, like the blocks of chambers, were designed in a manner entirely his own. Among the earliest and most interesting was a substantial, double-fronted house on Tulse Hill,[14] called (perhaps in allusion to the hero of Disraeli's *Sybil*) 'Egremont'. This was begun in 1853 when the architect was 207
twenty-five. Basically it was a double-fronted house of a kind which had been done in stucco with Grecian detail in the 20s and 30s and in cement with Italian detail in the 40s. In Gray's version some Italian characteristics remained: the first floor windows, for example, with their pilasters and archivolts, were very nearly orthodox. But everything else was changed. For the eaves-cornice, for instance, Gray substituted a corbel table consisting of a series of minute brick arches and deliberately colliding with the arches of the second floor windows. The porch faintly reflected Ruskin's illustrations to *The Stones of Venice*, the sturdy columns carrying free, naturalistic Corinthianesque caps. The dressings of the ground floor windows, however, with their strong 'surface' feeling, incised ornament and Greek acroters can only have been inspired by some specimens of the French neo-grec *cuisine*.

This house of Charles Gray's reflects very well the influences beginning to operate
in suburbia in 1853. His later houses included some in Wood Green,[15] cheaper and 208
therefore milder in their eclecticism. And he showed a villa at Highgate Rise, designed 'in his manner'[16] at the RA in 1859. Some others at Ealing belong to this year.

Gray was not exceptional in his desire to produce novelties, but he had a special *flair* for doing so and gained much attention from men of his own age and kind. Other suburban architects of the time in search of new mixtures were far less successful. Wehnert and Ashdown,[17] for instance, who were busy in many parts of the London sprawl, produced 'character' simply by coarsening and maltreating the Italian idea in order to make a great show with common bricks. Striking specimens of their work are

209. Maitland Park Villas, by Wehnert and Ashdown, 1855 (demolished) *210.* Nos. 82, 84 and 86 Highbury New Park, by Charles Hambridge, c.1857

209 a group of houses at Maitland Park, 1855, all in white brick.[18] Another suburban architect in search of 'character' was Charles Hambridge, whose work is to be found in Islington.[19] He had two styles at his command: an Italo–Greek style, strongly
210 reminiscent of contemporary German work, and a Romanesque style very close indeed
211 to that of Gray. The two can be seen next door to each other in Highbury New Park
212 (1857) where he designed and built a terrace, many houses and a very showy church. Taking much of the land himself he continued building for some years, enjoying both prosperity and the indulgence of a very eclectic taste. His use of encaustic tiles is ingenious and often delightful.

More interesting than Hambridge's work, however, is that of George Truefitt, the earliest known specimens of which belong to 1858. Truefitt was born in 1824 and at the age of fifteen was a pupil of the elder Cottingham. Then he passed through the offices of Sancton Wood and Eginton of Worcester and with the American Calvert Vaux, toured France and Germany making hundreds of sketches, some of which he published. His few large buildings are outside London and do not concern us here. His suburban work is to be seen chiefly in and around the Camden Road and especially on the adjacent Tufnell Park estate to which he was architect for over twenty years. His work here is important to our story.

Unlike his friend Charles Gray, Truefitt thought in Gothic. Also, unlike Gray, he did think. Gray got 'character' into his houses by the showy mixing of stylistic motifs; Truefitt by a certain bold appropriateness, corrected by genuine taste. He thought in Gothic, but discarded the ornamental appurtenances which had become the common signals of the style in its domestic applications – such things as Tudor labels, pinnacles, moulded chimney shafts and fretted barge-boards. His houses have a certain modest uncouthness, derived either from watching Mr Butterfield or from reading M. Viollet-le-Duc or, more probably, from both.

202 The little house – 'Worcester Lodge' – which Truefitt built for himself off the

Camden Road[20] in 1859 shows his characteristics early and well. The brick window arches are nearly flat, just the suspicion of a point at the centre saving them from Georgianism. The porch has a very flat segmental arch (out of one stone) and there is a corner window to the first floor drawing-room – no doubt a Venetian inspiration. There is no nonsense about stone mullions and quaint glazing: all the casements are filled with plate glass.

Truefitt's development may be traced through twenty years' work in certain villas in Camden Road[21] and in many others in Carleton Road, Tufnell Park.[22] The quality of these varies greatly; none advances far beyond the notable stylistic statement made in 1858. It was said ten years after that date that Mr Truefitt had been 'a not unimportant worker' towards a change of style in the London suburban house, and this cautious estimate[23] of his influence is probably rather less than the truth.

Charles Gray and George Truefitt especially were among the leading characters in the suburban architecture of the 1850s and early 60s. Neither of them, however, was big enough to inspire close imitation. In any case, the whole point of eclecticism was for each architect to compose his own amalgam to get 'character' in his own way. That is precisely what makes the study of the 'lower school' so baffling. While the personalities involved are undistinguished and largely unknown, their output as a whole defies general classification. Each man committed petty thefts from half-a-dozen different sources and disguised or failed to disguise them, in his own particular way. Nevertheless, there are three headings under which the whole suburban output can be studied. Briefly, they are these:

1. *Ornamental Brickwork.* The Elizabethan revival of the 1840s, the works of James Wild and a few others heralded the return to coloured bricks, but it was precipitated

211, 212. Nos. 45 and 47 Highbury Park by Charles Hambridge, c.1857

and further inspired by Butterfield's Margaret Street church and the books of Ruskin and Street. Polychrome brickwork lent itself easily and cheaply to striking effect. Nothing was simpler than to insert a few courses of red brick, and perhaps some yellow and blue, in a brown stock front. Only slightly less easy (since drawings had to be prepared in good time) was the composition of a rich eaves or verge cornice out of a few 'purpose mades' and an ingenious off-setting of common bats. Gray, Truefitt, Kendall and Hambridge all used polychromy in suburban houses of the 1850s and opened the door to the banquet of 'streaky-bacon'.

Polychromy was assisted by the introduction of Minton tiles in string courses and friezes. This practice derived some inspiration from Owen Jones and some, perhaps, from Butterfield's lavish employment of the material in his churches. Stone also was used in polychromy and subsequently the terracotta of Doulton, Blashfield and Cliff.

2. *Roof Treatment.* The late Georgian school gave its semidetached villas either steep 'Gothic' gables or flattened Italian gables with deep eaves. The new Gothic movement loved steepness but mixed its gables (sometimes crow-stepped) with hipped roofs and with gables hipped back before they reached the apex. Dormers rising flush from the wall-face were much liked and so were windows tucked close under the eaves.

Quite as irresistible as these Gothic variations was the French roof – the steep slated roof crowned by ironwork. This was imported first, perhaps, by Sir Charles Barry who crowned his design for Halifax Town Hall with such a roof (1859). Banks and Barry (i.e. the younger Charles Barry) domesticated the roof in an Alderman's villa[24] at Sydenham in 1862–3 and by that date or a little later it was universally popular. No difficulty was felt about combining it with notched-and-chamfered Gothic: indeed, the combination was enjoyed on many occasions.

3. *Window Openings.* These were, at once, a problem and an opportunity in the house of 'character.' The steeply pointed arch was obviously inconvenient in the domestic window, especially if it were to contain a sash. It was necessary to search for arches and lintels which, while flat or nearly so, were as far as possible removed from the detested slickness of the Georgian tradition. Wild had used stone lintels in the top storey of his St Martin's School. Truefitt took from Butterfield the nearly flat brick arch brought to a low point; he also used segmental arches and stone lintels with a shallow segment scooped out of the soffit. But what really conquered everything was
213 the *flat-sided arch*, a singularly meaningless mannerism which, nevertheless, gave exactly the 'character' that was required and was one of the most persistent mannerisms of the whole period.

As early as 1853, the flat-sided arch had begun to spread like a drug habit. J. S. Edmeston, in that year, spoke of it thus:[25] 'Some time back an architect dared to employ segmented arches with the springing line kept above the capital of the column and the archivolts returning down upon the abacus. Time was, when to have suggested anything so irregular would have been like luring a man to his certain destruction, and would have made him recoil with horror; but the combination was found not to be so very offensive, and straightway we find it repeated again and again in warehouses, public-houses, house-porches, etc., as something too delicious to be lost sight of.'

Now Edmeston was speaking of something which had emerged not from the

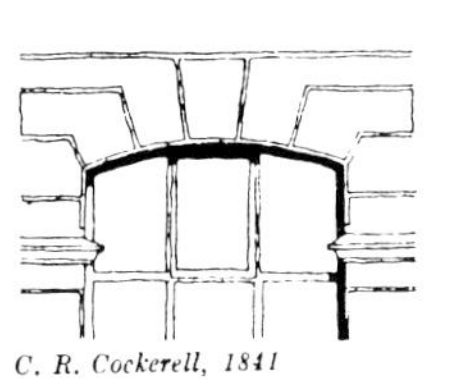
C. R. Cockerell, 1841

Sancton Wood, 1852

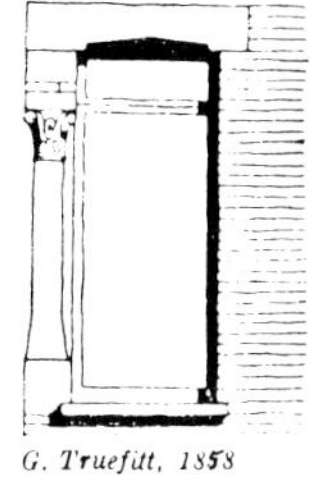
G. Truefitt, 1858

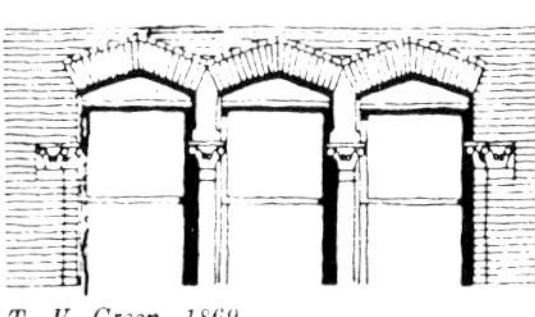
T. K. Green, 1869

213. Theme and variations. The flat-sided arch in the Victorian vernacular

Gothic but the Italian School. The architect who dared was none other than C. R. Cockerell who, in his Sun Insurance Office of 1841 had done very nearly what Edmeston describes. After a respectful interval, others had seized on this curious motif, adding the architrave.[26] By 1853, as Edmeston observed, it was ubiquitous. Why? That is, indeed, a deep question. The short answer is that this stilted, angular arch, rearing itself up abruptly from the capital had just exactly what people meant by 'character.' It distorted convention, crashed through the rules of taste, was 'self made'; it gave an impression of structural frankness, assigning to the ornamental attributes of architecture a subsidiary, merely pretty, rôle.

This so virile and striking mannerism was discovered to have a near counterpart in the medieval vocabulary. In certain varieties of Romanesque of the 12th century the lintel was used, with a bold chamfer, stopped at the junction with the jamb. Viollet-le-Duc had illustrated such things, both in his *Dictionnaire* and in a house he had built in Paris. This gave the impression of a stilt and the impression could easily be forced home by actually making the lintel descend a course or two below its soffit at either impost. This gave much the same illusion of solid, workmanlike building as the stilted segmental arch; and, indeed, the two could very easily be married. And married they were, in countless partnerships which if collected and tabulated would form a truly monstrous symposium. In one form or another, the stilted or flat-sided arch found its way into every region of Victorian building – only the higher reaches, where taste and scholarship reigned, being more or less exempt.

In suburbia, it flourished unchecked and in astonishing variety for more than thirty years. More than any other single mannerism, the flat-sided arch strikes the Victorian note – it is a true vernacular expression.

When we have generalized about these three subjects – ornamental brickwork, roof treatment and window openings – we have got about as far as generalization will take us. The variety in mid-Victorian suburban design is perfectly astonishing. If we try to envisage the work of the 1840s as a whole we must think of it somewhat in this way. The background is Italian – of the poorest sort; there is still much trite stucco-work with an increasing quantity of distorted and misplaced ornament and neglected proportion; the stucco is steadily giving place to brown or white brick. Against this dull and worsening background we find various things happening – the innovations of Gray, Truefitt and others, the spread of a taste for polychromy, the infiltration of second-hand Ruskinian and Streetian ideas and of Parisian innovations and the phenomenal recognition of the appropriateness of certain mannerisms – notably the flat-sided arch.

We can find during the 1860s in different parts of London examples of an incredible number of different styles. For instance, in Dulwich and Sydenham, a single firm of architects, Banks and Barry, was producing Italian, Tudor and Elizabethan houses all at the same time, while not far away John Norton was building English Gothic villas on the Crystal Palace estate. All this work, though it had its quirks and eccentricities, was untouched by the eclectic movement so forcibly advertised by Gray, in his Tulse Hill villa, a few years previously. In far-off Hampstead and on Hornsey Rise, Gothic villas of a peculiar notched-and-chamfered sort were going up: Theodore K. Green's houses in Fitzjohn's Avenue and Arkwright Road are the best examples. In 1868 J. S. Nightingale built his grotesque masterpiece, 'The Logs,' East Heath Road, influenced by Gray's work and coloured by French mannerism, while not far off Solomons and Jones showed themselves more positively Francophile in Caen Wood Towers. Further out, at Stonebridge Park, at Muswell Hill, Woodside Park and a dozen other nascent suburbs, different architects showed their different originalities. Between all these heterogeneous products there is a spiritual kinship, inescapable but extraordinarily hard to define: to call it a quest for 'character' is merely to provide a

214. Nos. 7 and 9 Avenue Road, Crouch Hill. Architect unknown

215. No. 37 Steele's Road, Haverstock Hill, by Batterbury and Huxley, 1870s
216. No. 38 Steele's Road, by T. Batterbury, 1873

name which still requires – and eludes – definition. What the mid-Victorians meant by 'character' may be apprehended equally by studying the anthropomorphic dogs of Landseer or by reading Samuel Smiles. The determination of common factors must be left to others.

The things which so delighted suburban architects of the 1860s flourished exuberantly all through the next decade, when some of the most bizarre eaves-cornices and flat-sided-arch combinations came into being. But from 1870, the year in which the bustle conquered the crinoline, a new spirit was abroad, and although it took some years to spread into the general suburban run of things, its wonderful applicability to the suburban scene was apparent at once. The 'Queen Anne Style,' for which the ground had been prepared by Thackeray's treatment of 18th-century themes, was born, as nearly as one can determine such events, in 1870; and it was born for a domestic, not a public or ecclesiastical career. The first thoroughbred example, J. J. Stevenson's own house in Bayswater Road, is a suburban house, though a large and exceptional one. Almost simultaneously, some artists' houses in Hampstead were built in the new style, the architects being Batterbury and Huxley. They were built in a then new street, off Haverstock Hill.

Steele's Road presents us with a most eloquent record of a moment of change in English taste. Ranged along the north side are eight detached houses, nearly all built for artists between 1870 and 1875. The artists were of the smaller sort who had become prosperous in the wonderful 1860s. At No. 39 there was G. G. Kilburne, painter and wood-engraver who sent such titles as 'Will he come?' 'Down!' and 'Too Late' to the Royal Academy; at No. 38, Edwin Hayes, RHA, whose 'Dutch Pinks Warping off *216*

217. Nos. 83–92, Third Avenue, Harrow Road, built by the Artizans', Labourers' and General Dwellings Company, 1881

Shore' embodied a first-hand knowledge of sailing; at No. 36, C. E. Johnson, whose
215 'The Swineherd' went to the Tate; at No. 35, J. D. (later Sir James) Linton who illustrated themes from Gil Blas and the life of Mary Stuart; and at No. 37, Francis Barnard, who illustrated for *Punch* and *Good Words*. There are one or two other houses as well. The earliest is No. 40 ('Downsbury'), a thoroughly crude, turreted, notch-and-chamfer Gothic house, very true to its date, 1873; the architect is unknown. Kilburne's house next door ('Hawkhurst House') shows Batterbury and Huxley in Gothic mood, with immense bargeboards, but big square sash windows and an obvious leaning to 'Queen Anne.' Then follows Hayes's 'Briscoe House,' again Batterbury and Huxley,[27] and this time quite definitely Queen Annish, with a hipped roof and moulded brickwork. Barnard's 'Warrington House' reverts to bargeboards, as does Johnson's[28] 'Morven House,' but Linton's[29] 'Ettrick House' is thoroughly 'Queen Anne.' The series is continued by No. 32 (Batterbury and Huxley) and No. 31, which is the house built for himself by the architect J. M. Brydon[30] in the fullest blooded 'Queen Anne,' with pilasters at the entrance and iron sunflowers sprouting from the dormers. Further east, for convenient comparison, is a row of houses in the regular Italian–eclectic idiom of the 1870s with straight-sided arched porches and coarse cement ornaments.

The Steele's Road houses show a particular juncture in taste very clearly. For further elucidation we have only to follow Batterbury and Huxley to Hampstead Hill Gardens, where they blossom into rose-red villas, all bedecked with the neatest rubbed-brick ornaments and reminiscent of the houses which occur in Kate Greenaway's drawings. No. 1, 'Studio House'[31] (1876) and No. 3 'Charlecote'[32] (for Charles Green, the *Graphic* artist, 1877) are the prettiest. They are rather trivial, these houses, lacking in control of proportions and spacing, but as straws in the wind of taste they have much significance.

These houses of Hampstead artists were, of course, ahead of their time and considered, when they were new, as something quite out of the ordinary. They are forerunners of the taste of the 80s and 90s when 'Queen Anne' ran on towards the age of Adam and innumerable fan-like ornaments and bayleaf swags began to grow in the groves of suburbia.

But now we must turn away from these artistic beginnings, sparse and special, and take a more general view of the situation in the 70s. During the two previous decades, we found our attention attracted all the time by fairly ample types of house, selling at £1,000 upwards – middle-class houses, built for families having at least three servants and a gardener. If we look for humbler types we do not so easily find them. We have to look towards the fringes of the built-up area – to districts in Kilburn or round the Portobello Road. Or we have to follow the dreary activities of the Land Societies. The artisan-class houses of this period are of no interest – the mere aftermath of expansions of the Bayswater type.

But quite suddenly, from 1877 to 1880, the whole picture changes. From a low trough the house-building graph soars up to a peak. And this peak represents the arrival of the small, lower-middle-class villa. In the decade 1877–87, London became ringed round with great blotches of this new villadom: street upon street, most of it lying at right angles to the main roads and consisting of houses either semi-detached or in rows so built as to give a semi-detached impression. Fulham, North Paddington, South Hampstead, parts of Highgate, and big areas east of the Lea Valley make the northern ring: Lewisham, Camberwell, Streatham and Putney contribute greatly to the southern.

The beginnings of this new wave of villa-building are to be found in that obscure and rather unattractive semi-philanthropic movement represented by the Land Societies. This is not the place to go into the history of the movement, which originated in the 40s and had a political complexion in so far as it represented an attempt on the part of political bodies to extend artisan suffrage by creating more householders in that class. But one scheme, closely related to the movement, is of special importance in London suburban housing. It is the *Artizans', Labourers' and General Dwellings Company, Ltd.*, founded in 1867 to enable working men to erect dwellings and become the owners of them.[33] The story of this enterprise, again, does not need to be told here, but its results constitute an important landmark in suburban development. Lord Shaftesbury laid the first stone of the estate at Lavender Hill in 1872 and part of it was opened in the presesnce of Disraeli, Lord Shaftesbury and others in 1874. In that year a second estate, adjoining the Harrow Road, was begun. *217*
Leases of the houses were sold on what is now called the hire-purchase system, at prices ranging from £150 to £310.

Now although the *Artizans', Labourers' and General Dwellings Company* was, in origin, philanthropic – crystallizing the concept of a 'Workman's village' which had floated for years in the Victorian mind – it was handled as a commercial speculation and the scheme was, in the long run, a pronounced success. It showed that there was a great market for small houses let on easy terms to the better-class artisan, the clerk, the foreman, the shop-assistant, people to whom the 60s had brought suddenly increased spending-power. This market was immediately exploited, and in 1880 the house-building graph soared to the highest point reached in the whole century.

The houses on the 'Shaftesbury Estate' as it was called, at Lavender Hill, were in close rows, but each house was expressed as a unit, with a rudimentary porch carrying the Company's monogram in its gable. The style was supposed to be 'domestic Gothic or Tudor,' but in fact the red-brick rows present the crudest possible blend of Romanesque with the Waterhouse brand of secular early Gothic. It is not so much the style, but the scale and arrangement of the rows which is reflected in all the remoter areas of suburbia.

Around 1880 certain types of villa sprang up everywhere as if by magic. Just how they emerged and who designed them it is impossible to say, for they belong to a level at which both the lowest type of self-styled 'architect' and many types of builder were functioning. The 'superior artisan,' a product of the 60s, was beginning to have his fling at the drawing board. In 1877, a weekly magazine, *The Illustrated Carpenter and*

218. No. 1 The Avenue, Bedford Park, by E. W. Godwin, 1876

219. Nos. 12 and 14 The Avenue, Bedford Park, by E. W. Godwin, 1876 *220.* Nos. 4 and 6 The Avenue, by Coe and Robinson, 1876.

Builder, Price 1d., was founded to serve his needs – both practical and æsthetic. Villa designs were published from time to time and the magazine served also as an exchange for small builders in search of designs and willing to pay a guinea or two for a set of plans and details.[34] The designs always derive from what architects had been doing in the 70s for the detached and semi-detached middle classes. They contain traces of Italian, of 'modern French' and of Gothic; the flat-sided arch enjoys an Indian Summer and the capitals, decked with ferns and roses, are descended from the carvings which O'Shea had executed on the museum at Oxford in the 50s. These villas, so familiar to all of us and so terrible in their familiarity, bring the ancient word 'Villa' down to a level inconceivable when Lord Burlington built the first and loveliest of English villas at Chiswick a century and a half before. At last this ancient, romantic word, Roman in ancestry, lordly in association, was brought down to the mud of Walham Green and trodden into the marshes of Leytonstone.

The early 80s saw the first great surge of villadom. There was another in the 90s and the waves followed each other during nearly forty years of the 20th century, each wave tinctured by the stylistic preferences exhibited in the previous decade's better class building. We have already seen, in the work of Batterbury and Huxley, what better class suburbia was producing in the 70s; but we have not yet looked closely at one particular centre of suburban building – a centre which was to prove as influential as any.

Jonathan Carr's Bedford Park project was to a certain extent inspired by the *Artizans' and General* estate at Lavender Hill. Carr designed to do for the middle classes what was being done there for the working classes. Norman Shaw was his architect, but the first villas to be built were by E. W. Godwin: some eighteen of them had been erected by the end of 1877. Godwin's villas at Bedford Park[35] struck a new note – new, *218*
at any rate, in suburbia. They were neither Italian nor Gothic nor eclectic nor Queen Anne; they owed acknowledgments to the tile-hung vernacular of the southern counties and were said to aim at obtaining effects 'by the use of good materials picturesquely handled.' The 'good materials' were red Suffolk bricks and Broseley

tiles; the 'picturesque' handling meant slight rearrangements of the standard plan and some ingenious play with gables, bays and dormers, giving the houses a more strictly three-dimensional character than was common.

219 Godwin's pairs of semi-detached houses at Bedford Park show twin gables to the
220 street, each gable tile-hung and projecting so as to make a lid to the bay-window running through the two lower storeys. A cheaper version of this theme was devised by Messrs Coe and Robinson,[36] whose houses alternate with Godwin's in The Avenue. Here the gables make a shallower V in the centre, while spreading further down on either side. The type is a very familiar one indeed and was to be multiplied thousands of times between Harrow and Woodford, Edgeware and Morden in the 1920s.

Richard Norman Shaw's own contributions to Bedford Park arrived almost at the same time as those of Godwin and Coe & Robinson, in the shape of semi-detached pairs with a continuous eaves and coved cornice towards the street and gables at the ends.[37] Very personal in design, as Shaw's works always are, and thoroughly artistic, they did not create a type so easily followed as the earlier villas. Shaw was followed at Bedford Park by Maurice B. Adams in whose work the Shaw idea is retained, though less well expressed. The whole estate has a very distinct character of its own and, at the time it was building, a character so pronouncedly different from what was happening elsewhere that it could not help becoming influential. This influence, however, took time to spread. The Bedford Park villas were too restrained and too little ornamented to be a sensational hit in the building world of the 80s. When in the years 1897–99, however, the house-building graph again soared to a sudden peak, the demure tile-hung gable and the dainty dormer were carried far and wide, superseding every vestige of the old styles – except, indeed, that extraordinarily persistent symbol of true Victorianism, the flat-sided arch.

Long before the end of the century, the degradation of the word 'villa' was complete; it had begun to signify contempt, as for something small, cheap, remote and ugly. 'Home' and 'cottage' were preferred as verbal symbols and the 'villa' relegated to a level of commonness from which it has never since ascended.

XIII · The British Contemporaries of Frank Lloyd Wright

221. Frank Lloyd Wright. Edward H. Cheney House, Oak Park, Chicago, 1904

222. Charles Rennie Mackintosh. Entrance to the Glasgow School of Art, 1897–99

THE TITLE of this essay carries certain implications, the most obvious of which is that Wright is seen in the character of the greatest innovator of the period in the United States and that it may be instructive to compare his performance with those of innovators in Britain through the same years. This is a perfectly legitimate approach and the natural one at the present time. The inevitable first move (in a paper as short as this) is to bring Charles Rennie Mackintosh on the scene as an innovator in many respects analogous to Wright – inevitable because, for thirty years now, the overwhelming incentive to the study of late 19th- and early 20th-century architecture has been pioneer-hunting, the extraction of the true genealogy of the Modern Movement. It is by virtue of hindsight that we award Mackintosh such a special place in the British architecture of his time, a place which his contemporaries did not award him. It is because we study him in relation to our own prepossessions that we exalt him above nearly all his fellows. I am not saying that this is wrong; but it is a limited and possibly even a temporary estimate; as historians we must try to see Mackintosh not only as a precursor and an important analogue to Wright but also as an integral part of the British architectural scene – if, indeed, he was an integral part of it. I think I can show that he was, and how he was, and I mean to devote this short paper mainly to indicating his relationship to his own and the previous generation – but chiefly his own, which is to say Wright's; for Wright was born in 1867 and Mackintosh in 1868.

First, let us get behind the barrier imposed by current attitudes and see how Mackintosh looked to an intelligent critic of 1924, the date of publication of Charles Marriott's *Modern English Architecture*. Marriott was art critic of *The Times* and his survey is tolerant and well-informed. The Glasgow School of Art is, however, mentioned only briefly, along with rather indifferent buildings by Worthington, Reilly and Blomfield, as a notable civic building 'in the provinces'; and Marriott's only further comment is as follows: the School of Art 'is important because of the great influence of Mr. Mackintosh's work on the Continent – in Germany, Holland and Sweden. It is hardly too much to say that the whole modernist movement in European architecture derives from him; and the Glasgow School of Art, as an early and successful attempt to get architecture out of building, making decorative features of structural forms, goes far to explain the reason why.'[1] That is all; Marriott then changes the subject.

I suppose only a *Times* art critic could be so devastatingly *fair*! But it is interesting how obviously little impact Mackintosh made on him; it is also interesting how what he calls 'the modernist movement' is to him something strictly 'continental,' like cafés and goatee beards, with no implications for Britain. But that is how it was. Marriott, whom I knew, accurately reflects, as I remember it, the pre-Corbusier, pre-Gropius British attitude to British architecture and Mackintosh's position within it. Insular? Well, perhaps a little.

But this insularity, which goes a long way back, had its importance, to the extent that without it we should have had no Mackintosh. Mackintosh, though he travelled, was as an architect a completely British product, as we shall see if we care to place him among a number of British architects – to say a 'group' would be misleading because there was no sense of combination or movement. All of these men recognized the same architectural ancestry and each was, in his own way, round about 1900, trying to be 'modern.' The principal names in this constellation (as we may call it) are as follows: Edgar Wood (b. 1860) and his partner, J. H. Sellers (b. 1861), A. Beresford Pite (b. 1861), C. R. Ashbee (b. 1863), Ernest Gimson (b. 1864), Baillie Scott (b. 1865), Charles Winmill (b. 1865), Dunbar Smith (b. 1866) and his partner Cecil Brewer (b. 1871), George Walton (b. 1867), Mackintosh himself, of course (b. 1868), and Charles Holden (b. 1875). This is a rather arbitrary list which could be expanded or contracted according to one's criteria of what was 'modern.' There was no sense of 'party' among these architects; none could be described as a leader. The elder architects they respected were Richard Norman Shaw and Philip Webb, both born in 1831 and thus a full generation older than the eldest star in my constellation. Nearer to them were C. H. Townsend (b. 1850), A. H. Mackmurdo (b. 1851) and C. F. Annesley Voysey and W. R. Lethaby (both born 1857). All of these younger men, except Townsend with his peculiar brand of Art Nouveau, were more or less dependent on Shaw and Webb; the one whose influence worked most strongly on our constellation was undoubtedly Voysey – not because he was a brilliant architect but precisely because he was not; Voysey's wilful, idiosyncratic, nursery simplicity was a much more effective touchstone, in the climate of 1900, than any amount of brilliance.

I am careful to establish the chronology of all these names because I am to talk about Frank Lloyd Wright's contemporaries, and it is as well to establish who were such and who were not. Thus Voysey and Lethaby were ten years older than Wright, Mackmurdo sixteen and Townsend seventeen years older. The constellation I have selected has a radius of eight years around Wright's birth-date, 1867. Mackintosh (b. 1868) is actually the nearest in time and for that reason, as well as for his obvious pre-eminence on the present-day historical map, it is convenient to consider him first. Let us look at his chief work, the Glasgow School of Art.[2]

The first portion was built from 1897 to 1899 when its architect was twenty-nine to thirty-one. It stands out in astonishing relief against the over-enriched and over-silhouetted Queenanities of its time – the renaissances of Colcutt, Aston Webb, Mountford, Caröe, Jackson and Ernest George. And yet the roots of the design are in the same soil. The lack of silhouette and of ornament is doubtless due to Voysey – the one influence which has always been accepted in relation to Mackintosh's early work. Howarth, in his book on Mackintosh,[3] illustrates a quaint little Voysey design for a studio which may well be relevant. But the sense of mass, the confident distribution, goes back to an older source, Norman Shaw. I cannot go into this relationship in detail but I will show you one Shaw building to which, consciously or unconsciously,
222 Mackintosh was indebted. The daring asymmetry of Mackintosh's entrance treatment
has often attracted comment. Now compare it with the entrance of Norman Shaw's
194 New Zealand Chambers, Leadenhall Street, London (1873: destroyed in the Second
World War).[4] Here is the same off-centre handling; and note also the association of this treatment with small-paned windows at the lower level only. If we accept this association as valid, we see at once how deeply rooted Mackintosh is in the very beginning of what got to be called (so oddly) the Queen Anne movement.

223 Now turn to the spectacular library wing added in the period 1907–9. This is more

223. Charles Rennie Mackintosh. Library wing of the Glasgow School of Art, 1907–9

challenging and seems, at first sight, inexplicable in familiar English or Scottish terms. These continuous bay-windows, of course, are part of the Shaw-Voysey inheritance, as we may see by glancing at Shaw's 180 Queen's Gate, London (1885),[5] at Voysey's houses in Hans Road (1891)[6] or at a dozen other cases of the same theme variously elongated and variously terminated below with moulded or unmoulded corbel-courses. But their elongation here is extravagant and emphasized by the grille-like metal windows. And there are other factors, factors wholly foreign either to Shaw or Voysey: a bizarre modelling, an irrational handling of architrave lines which, however remotely, recalls Michelangelo. These factors occur in none other of Mackintosh's designs, but as this part of the Glasgow School is the piece by which its architect is most frequently represented its interpretation is particularly worth while.

I think it may help if I switch now to the work of another architect in my
constellation, Charles Holden, of the firm of Percy Adams. Holden designed the
225 Central Reference Library at Bristol in 1904 or 1905 and, if we place this beside
Mackintosh's library wing, we see at once the kind of thing – if not positively *the* thing
– from which Mackintosh was abstracting many of his own forms. Note especially the
flattened, recessed gables and the vivid contrast in the two types of bay window: the
three cosy bays in the centre, the lordly vertical bay at either end. Holden's work here is
as easily related to Norman Shaw and Webb (with a strong infusion of Henry Wilson)
224 as Mackintosh's work to Holden's. The rear of the Bristol building, less style-
conscious than the front, is a strikingly direct statement for its time and analogous, up
to a point, with the rear of the Glasgow building.[7] But neither front nor back quite
solves the riddle of the Glasgow library wing.

Now take another work of Holden's, designed a year or so earlier than the Bristol Library, the extension to the Law Society's headquarters in Chancery Lane (1903).[8] Attached to a Neo-classical building of *c.*1830 this had perforce to be classical and here we have classical forms being handled by one who was, at the time (as Holden told me himself), chiefly an admirer and follower of Webb. The dentil cornice and the tiny pedimented windows are recognizably Webb but elsewhere, in the taut, sensitive profiles and in the strained proportions, there is an acute experience – direct or indirect – of Michelangelo. There is, I suspect, here again, an actual link with the modelling of the Glasgow work.

Michelangelesque or Cortonesque feeling comes and goes in the 'modernist' British architecture of the early 1900s. The year 1907, in which the library wing at Glasgow was begun, saw the completion in London of two buildings in which this

224. Charles Holden. Rear elevation of the Central Reference Library, Bristol, 1905–6

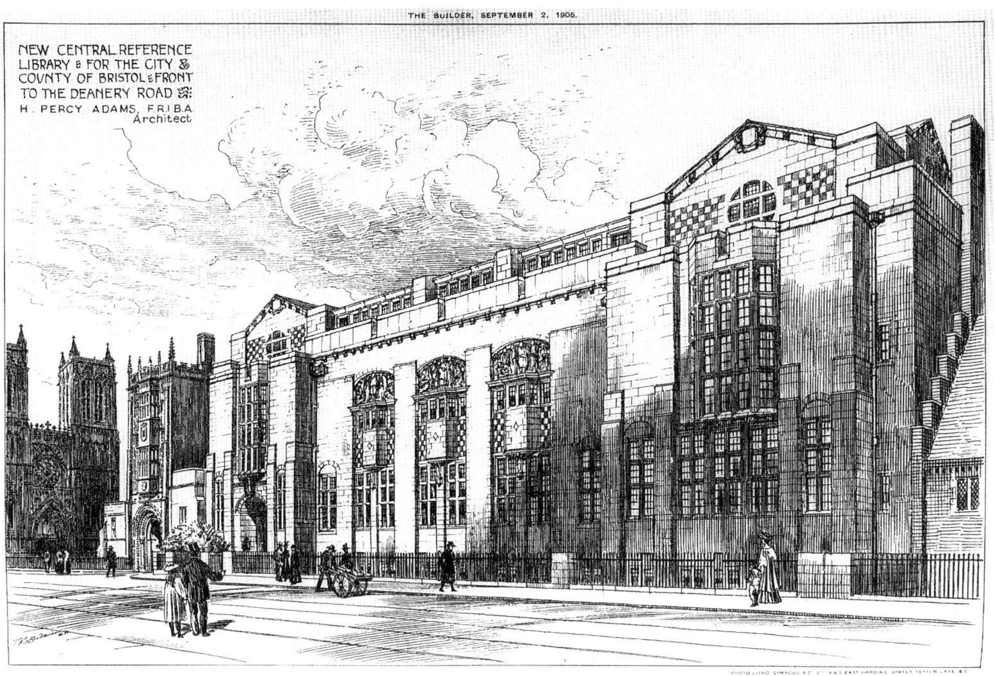

225. Charles Holden. Street elevation of the Central Reference Library, Bristol, 1905–6

inspiration led to results which were felt to coincide exactly with what 'modern' was thought to convey. Marriott, looking back from 1924, groups them specifically as such.[9] One of these buildings was by Holden, the other by an architect who is not one of my constellation and would have no business there, John James Joass.

Holden's 1905 building in the Strand for the British Medical Association (it is now *226* Zimbabwe House) is an almost grotesquely mannered work, a conscious challenge to conventional styles and with some vague feeling for the artistic movements of the time.[10] It is the nearest thing to English Futurist architecture. The latter aspect Holden underlined by employing young Jacob Epstein to carve nude figures of men and women between the second-storey windows; they were thought very shocking. The second work of 1907, Joass' building for the Royal Insurance Company in St James's *227* Street,[11] is entirely different but equally mannered – a brittle piece of T-square classicism resting on pairs of twin columns which look as if torn from the walls of the Laurentian Library. Up in the third storey are the Sistine *putti*, solidified by Bertram Mackennal, and lodged between the windows – much as the Epsteins are lodged by Holden.

It seems to me that these two buildings, taken together, show us what Mackintosh was up to in his library wing. He was merging the Shaw–Voysey inheritance with the kind of classicism with which Holden and Joass, in their very different ways, were experimenting in London, and then going on to caricature the whole thing with his gay and exquisite penmanship. I use 'caricature' in the sense of a witty definition of essentials: definition by omission and exaggeration. To be sure, Mackintosh's building has no nude sculptures and no putti – but the niches are there all ready to receive them in just the place where Holden and Joass would have put them. They are token niches; their function is understood – and dismissed. It is worth adding that Joass, born in the same year as Mackintosh, was a Glasgow man, learnt his classicism from the French trained Glasgow architect, John Burnet, and must in fact have been a fellow-pupil of Mackintosh's at the School of Art in its old premises. Where and how the necessary contacts took place, whether Mackintosh knew Holden or liked or disliked Joass I cannot tell you. I am only concerned here to demonstrate Mackintosh's work of 1907–9 as being inflected by the same cross-current of mannered modernity as some of the other architects of the time. Holden and Joass were the most conspicuous. There were others. In all, the test is a challenging rectangularity, more or less obscurely related to Michelangelo and the Baroque.

We must return to make a rather fuller assessment of the Glasgow School of Art. The plan is clean and neat but not specially remarkable except in so far as it is the horizontal trace of a three-dimensional conception which is remarkable. It is this spatial conception, rigorously pursued, which now appeals to us as so very important. It was lost on most of Mackintosh's contemporaries, whose sensibilities were trained to the material enclosure rather than the space enclosed, and many of whom found his gratuitous creation of planes by the manipulation of fencing and balustrading in metal or wood rather tiresome and affected. Voysey had played with metal and wood, too, but never for sheer formal effect. It is mostly from Voysey, I suppose, that Mackintosh gets the palisading idea for his library interior but he dramatizes it in a way that the modest puritanical Voysey would probably have detested. For Pevsner[12] on the other hand, this kind of spatial play places Mackintosh with the Guarinis and the Neumanns, and we see what he means. Moreover, it is in the library of the School of Art that we feel the closest affinity between Mackintosh and Frank Lloyd Wright. The rather theatric play of palisading reminds us of the furnished interior of the Robie house (1909); the rôle played by the geometrical light fittings is very much the rôle played by the not dissimilar fittings in the Unity Temple (1906). Is the affinity entirely accidental? I offer no comment, merely observing that already in 1902 the interior designs by Mackintosh for the *Haus eines Kunstfreundes* competition had been published by Kock of Darmstadt.[13] While the palisade theme certainly appears in Wright's furniture before that year, a room as a sort of space-cage of horizontals and verticals does not. Or (I put this to the Wright experts) does it? It is certainly a very close thing.

I have said nothing of the alleged 'Scotchness' of Mackintosh's work. The obvious case to examine is the house at Helensburgh built between 1902 and 1903.[14] Let us place this beside a house by Robert Lorimer (b. 1864), Mackintosh's Edinburgh contemporary, who really tried to be Scotch.[15] Of course there are Scottish bits and pieces about both houses – harled walls, battered chimneys and little round roofs. But they amount to little enough, even in Lorimer. The fact is that both houses belong to the same school of house design, the school in which the leading figure was M. H. Baillie Scott.[16] Scott was a master of the loose rambling plan – he liked to think of his houses as existing inside the *Dream of John Ball* where nobody dressed for dinner because informal dress was so much prettier. Between a Baillie Scott house and

226. Charles Holden. British Medical Association, London (now Zimbabwe House), 1906–7
227. J. J. Joass. Royal Insurance Company Building, London, 1906–7

Mackintosh's Helensburgh house the main difference is not that Mackintosh is more Scotch but that he has the sharper eye for formal relations, the crispness and bite of the fine graphic artist he was. And there perhaps is the really differentiating thing about Mackintosh: he approached architecture with the delicacy, the sense of mass, tone and distribution of a graphic artist – an Aubrey Beardsley whose genius ran happily and harmoniously into architecture. Apart from this his work is, as I hope I have shown, an integral part of the whole growth of architecture in Britain from Norman Shaw onwards. He is a completely insular product – a great provincial. Was not Wright also a great provincial?

The other members of my constellation I must dismiss quite rapidly. Some, like C. R. Ashbee[17] and Ernest Gimson,[18] are interesting less as architects than for developing in craftsmanship and manufacture the ideas of Morris and Webb. Edgar Wood[19] and Charles Winmill[20] are to be admired for bringing those ideas into the unpromising sphere of official local-authority architecture. Wood's schools at Middleton, Lancs (1910) and Winmill's Firestation at Hampstead for the LCC (1914) are beautiful demonstrations of how a knowledge of old vernacular building could make an acceptable functionalism in the early 20th century. Their strong sense of squareness – of mass – links them with Mackintosh, but it is about all that does. George Walton,[21] whose Glasgow career runs parallel with Mackintosh's, was an innovator in interior design whose architecture is experimental but somewhat uneven in quality. Beresford Pite[22] was a scholar-architect who brought Philip Webb and old Byzantium together in some buildings of much originality and power. There is no time to discuss these lesser figures and I will conclude with a few words about that interesting pair, Dunbar Smith and Cecil Brewer, whose first building is one which brings us very close to the central subject of our attention. In 1895 a limited competition was held for the Passmore-

Edwards Settlement (now the Mary Ward Settlement) in Tavistock Street, Bloomsbury, with Norman Shaw as assessor. Smith and Brewer won it with an ingenious plan and elevations relying mostly on Webb and Voysey.[23] But as erected the building was transformed in the most startling way. The hall component was turned right around and the street elevation became symmetrical with deep bands under the
228 eaves. Now these deep bands are thoroughly American and if we place the Mary Ward Settlement beside the Charnley House of 1891–92 it is difficult not to believe there is some connection. It cannot be proved. But Cecil Brewer did eventually go to North America in 1911 with a travelling bursary, so it may be that he always had a westward leaning. His great National Museum of Wales is American Neo-neo-classic, softened by his early contacts with the Webb school. The best-known work of the firm is Heal's store in Tottenham Court Road, completed in 1916.[24] Here there certainly is either American or German influence, but modified as all the buildings of these architects were by the persistent, gentle, always beneficent influence of Philip Webb.

I have given no more than a glimpse of Frank Lloyd Wright's British contemporaries, but I hope it has seemed a significant one. You may be curious to know what happened to my 'constellation' of pre-1914 British modernists. In 1914, the youngest of them (Holden) was thirty-nine, the oldest (Edgar Wood) fifty-four; too old for active service but not too old to give a lead in the post-war world of the 1920s. But this is precisely what none of them did. Only Holden became a successful major practitioner and his post-war works exhibit the merest flicker of his original talent. After 1918 it was Lutyens and Reginald Blomfield, Herbert Baker and Curtis Green, men quite as old or older than the constellation but (except for Lutyens) far less interesting, who carried everything before them. Lutyens, of course, outshone all and you may think it odd that I have said nothing about him. But I have been taking as my theme the innovators – the 'moderns.' Being 'modern' was something which Lutyens thought extremely silly. So the promise of pre-1914 British architecture quietly died, while a younger generation altogether began to discover Frank Lloyd Wright.

228. Dunbar Smith and Cecil Brewer. Mary Ward Settlement, London, 1895–96

XIV · Arches of Triumph: Sir Edwin Lutyens's Design for the Roman Catholic Cathedral, Liverpool

229. Lutyens's Liverpool Cathedral, a perspective by Cyril Farey looking towards the west front

230. The War Memorial Arch, New Delhi, designed by Lutyens in 1920

Far back from 1929, the year in which Sir Edwin Lutyens made his first sketches for Liverpool Cathedral, stand the triumphal arches of the Romans: the arches of Titus, Septimius Severus and Constantine in Rome, the arches at Ancona, Rimini, Pola, Orange and many more. The more accessible of these the masters of the Renaissance seized upon with delight and absorbed into their new classical language. Alberti looked at the arch at Rimini and applied its elements to the west front of the Tempio Malatestiano. At Mantua he did more. He took the triumphal arch inside the church and made it multiply, arch after arch, pier after pier, to make the deep chapels and to carry the vault of his nave. Here was the beginning of the classical church interior as we see it in St Peter's, Rome, and countless others in the western World. To say that the process was recapitulated by Lutyens in his designs for Liverpool would be somewhere near the truth. It would, perhaps, be nearer still to say that he re-invented it.

The Roman triumphal arch is a ceremonial object, the equivalent of a canopy. As the Romans left it to us it was braced and girded by an architectural order – nearly always Corinthian or Composite. But this is not of its essence, as French architects of the 17th and 18th centuries most inventively demonstrated. Blondel's Porte S. Denis and Chalgrin's Arc de l'Etoile have no order. They are hewn masses penetrated by arches and furnished with sculptural trophies, which, if stripped away, still leave the penetrated block with its symbolic force undiminished.

Whether or not by conscious act of adoption on his part, the theme of the triumphal arch is the key to Lutyens's great design: appropriately in a church which was to be dedicated to Christ the King. The arch of triumph was not a new theme for him. It had appeared in his work as early as 1911, with the Rand Regiments' memorial at Johannesburg, a relatively small monument which, with its pedimented arches and winged figures seems to celebrate the glamour of victory rather than to mourn the tragedy of war. After 1918 Lutyens memorials have more gravity. The giant War Memorial arch at New Delhi designed in 1920, imitates the Arc de l'Etoile but eclipses *230*
it in size and divests it of sculptural pomp: also it takes a step towards abstraction where, above the cornice, three masses of plain masonry graduate in an impressive harmonic series. About half the size of the New Delhi arch is the war memorial at Leicester, again deriving from the Arc de l'Etoile. But here there has been a slimming down and a cutting away so that the actual arch-forms leap out of the mass and the play with proportional relationships is more intense.

Then comes Thiepval, designed in 1922, the greatest of all Lutyens's memorials in *231*
size and the most liberated in form. For the first time he adopts the three-arch type, that of Septimius Severus and Constantine; a high centre arch between two lower arches but now, in addition, arches penetrating the sides. The Roman model is ruthlessly stripped, dissected and rebuilt, its massive shoulders cut away and their weight piled on top of the centre arch. Then, beneath the springing of this arch, the whole monument reproduces itself. It does so twice. Each of the lateral arches becomes the centre arch of a secondary monument, reproducing in its smaller arches the proportions of those of the first. The three monuments interlock with an appearance of innocent simplicity. In this interlocking the premises of the Liverpool design are, for the first time stated.

231. The Thiepval Arch, the memorial to the missing on the Somme, designed by Lutyens in 1922

229 The relevance of Thiepval to Liverpool is evident as soon as we look at the west front. [Here and elsewhere in this essay the points of the compass are used in their liturgical sense, the actual orientation of the cathedral being approximately north-south.] We see what appears to be a giant three-arch porch; and so it is. But when we look at the plan we discover it to be more than that. The piers which carry the three arches line up exactly with the piers which separate the nave from its four aisles. The cross-section shows that not only the piers but the arches which connect them across the nave and inner aisles exactly correspond with the arches of the west front. So the west front is no mere architectural frontispiece but the issue of a series of three 'tunnels' driving right through from the west end to the central space, then resuming and terminating in the sanctuary; 'tunnels', of course, in a diagrammatic sense, for the tunnel image is immediately shattered by the arches which penetrate its sides and which in common parlance, are the 'nave arcades'.

234 Each of these 'arcades' consists of two major arches, alternating with three minor arches. Either of the two major arches, with the two adjacent minor arches, gives us the 'triumphal' triad, so here we have a second exposition of the basic theme. In other words we have here two 'triumphal' series, set at right angles to each other – a west-east series and a north-south series. They have important differences and important similarities. The main difference is in the way they set out the theme. The west-east series consists of one major arch and four minor arches – a, a, A, a, a (of which only the

232. Plan of the Thiepval Arch   *233.* An early stage of the Liverpool Cathedral design showing the proposed west towers

three middle terms are articulated in the west porch). The north-south series consists of two major and three minor arches – b, B, b, B, b. An important similarity is that all the arches in both cases – A, B and a, b – are of precisely the same proportion: a ratio of 1 to 3. But the over-riding shared characteristic is that both series are in fact systems of 'tunnels'. What we have provisionally called 'nave arcades' are in fact systems of 'tunnels' driving north and south, right through to the outer walls. Again the 'tunnel' image dissolves when we realize that the sides of the major tunnels are necessarily penetrated by the advancing aisles, twice on the north and twice on the south. (The minor tunnels simply shoot through the piers, opening first into the inner, then into the outer aisles.)

It will be recognized that the interpenetration of the two 'triumphal' series is comparable to what happens at Thiepval, but infinitely more complicated because at Liverpool each of the two series has a different rhythm. Nevertheless, Lutyens has

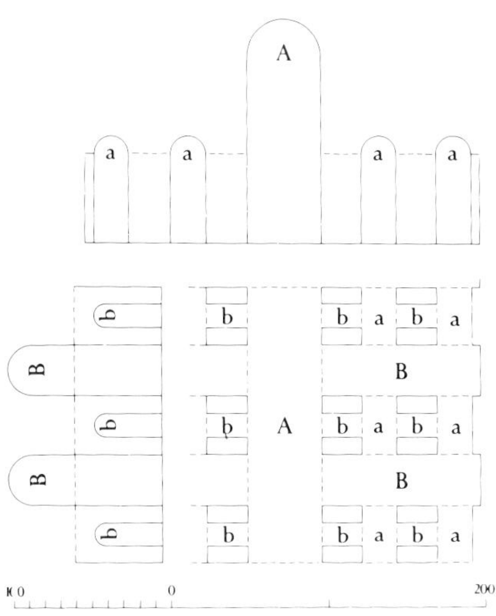

234. Diagram showing relative widths of nave and aisles in the 'Triumphal Arch' system, the proportions of the arches remaining constant

reconciled them with absolute precision, with the result that the whole mass of building constituting the nave and aisles is one indivisible arcuated system. In the north and south transepts the same thing happens but because they are shorter than the nave there is only one complete 'triumphal' triad. The sanctuary, again, is only one triad deep before the turn of the apse.

To set all this up in one's mind as a real-life experience is far from easy and it seems
235 that two pencil sketches by Walcot are the only guides to accurate comprehension. A vivid thumb-nail sketch by Lutyens himself does, however, enlighten us. In this sketch
236 we are looking at the north side of the nave, as if from a distance (and rather downhill!). We are at once struck by the shortness of the nave, compared with the sort of cathedral naves to which we are accustomed (a glance at the plan shows that, with the double aisles it is, in fact, broader than it is long). The sketch shows, on the left, the nave opening into the narthex and, on the right, into the domed central space. In the middle are the three piers carrying the two major arches, each pier penetrated by a minor arch. The sketch helps us to visualize the three-dimensionality of the system where, through the right-hand arch, we catch sight of one of the cross 'tunnels' disappearing northward and one of the two aisle 'tunnels' opening into it.

235. William Walcot. Unfinished perspective of the east end as it would have appeared from the central space. The screen-work which appears conspicuously in the drawing is supplementary to the main fabric as described in the text

236. A study by Lutyens for the north side of the nave, showing part of the central space

Lutyens's sketch helps us also to understand how the nave is covered. Transverse arches turn over from above the piers and between the arches are lunettes, each containing a vertical window-opening (Wren's device at St Paul's). What the sketch does not show is that the vaults between the main arches are crowned, in each bay, by a saucer dome (St Paul's again, with variations); an arrangement which is repeated on a smaller scale in the aisles.

We must try to imagine how this part of the cathedral would be lit. A main source of light would be the central space with its ring of windows in the inner dome. The narthex, designed on the same lines as the nave, would supply little. The aisle windows open once in each bay in the outer walls and twice into narrow areas hidden behind those walls. So there would perhaps be more light in the aisles than the nave. Certainly there would not be over-much illumination and what there was would come from small, bright inlets, high up in the structure. St Paul's Cathedral would by comparison, be radiant. Liverpool would be altogether more mysterious, more evocative than Wren's cathedral: atmospherically less Renaissance than Romanesque.

So much for the geometrical structure of the main body. Once the nature of the arcuated system is grasped it is as unforgettable as it is original. Subsidiary elements of the design now fall into place. Of these, the most important is the architectural 'order' which plays a vital part throughout the interior.

An order, expressed as pilasters or attached columns or both, was an essential attribute of a Roman arch and when Alberti brought the arch into his church at Mantua he made its Corinthian order the governing element of the design. So did Bramante at St Peter's. Lutyens does not do so. He had no lust for the 'colossal'. Although his order is, indeed, of commanding height (60 ft; 10 ft higher than Wren's Corinthian at St Paul's) it does not rise to the full height of the pier but falls 20 ft short of it. This gives the arches the curious effect of being 'stilted', which goes with Lutyens's expressed desire to bring something of the vertical urge of the medieval into his classical building.

Of the order itself something must be said. It contains all the conventional elements: pedestal, shaft with base and cap, architrave, frieze and cornice. In proportion it is close to Palladio's Ionic (nine diameters) and the entablature follows Palladio's Ionic profile almost exactly. The cap, however, with its ribs and flutings and unringing bells, is pure Lutyens – indeed, pure Delhi. The order appears most conspicuously where, in pilaster form, it frames the lesser arches in the piers. Here, and only here, is it allowed its full entablature. As the entablature moves round to the side of the piers it loses its cornice and the frieze is pulvinated. As it moves round again into the inner aisle the frieze also vanishes and only the architrave is left. It provides the imposts of the aisle arches. The frieze is restored between the arches, but the cornice is never seen again. This may seem like an arbitrary display of 'Mannerist' sleight-of-hand, but it makes sense. The order, as we have seen, declines to identify itself fully with the 'triumphal' series to which it adheres (the Bb series). But neither does it have any obvious relationship with the other series (the Aa series). There is a relationship, however, and the process just described defines it. The design is so contrived that the top of the architrave of the order is on the level from which the a arches spring. So the order is playing a devious game. In full dress it presents itself as part of the Bb series; but then it sidles round the corner, divests itself of cornice and frieze and hands over its architrave to the Aa series. This is the sole articulate communication between the two series until the grand emergence of their major arches in the central space, to which we shall come in a moment.

The order is the binding force of the interior. From the narthex to the eastern chapels it is always on the go: a compound rhythm pulsing through the whole body. Above the order is the twenty foot of vertical wall-space which 'stilts' the arches and invites an architectural arrangement for which there is no obvious precedent. Lutyens meets the situation with a syntactic improvisation in relief. On top of the order he mounts the legitimate supplement known as an 'attic'. On top of this he places a pedestal which, with equal legitimacy, supports the twenty-five foot high aedicule rising from the springing line of the arches. Attic and pedestal together fill the space amply and their tautological proximity (they are, after all, very nearly the same thing) is disposed of by the deep rectangular hollow which explodes in the attic and by the triangular play of a carved shield and two impanelled discs against the too insistent horizontals.

Wren's influence comes and goes. The modelling just described owes something to him and the columned and pedimented aedicules stand out like the upper windows (which are not really windows) in the exterior walls of St Paul's. The importance of these aedicules is a considerable matter, not only here but throughout the whole design, outside as well as in. They are never seen to contain figure sculpture and should perhaps be understood as symbols analogous to the triumphal arch, but of angelic delicacy. The aedicule has a Gothic potency and even in its Roman form may, in a proper context, speak with the accent of Chartres or Laon. In the Liverpool design it acquires this Gothic volatility. Swept up to the belfries and to the buttresses of the dome it becomes a triumphal sentry-box, as it were the lodging of a trumpeting angel.

It is now time to move into that square of building which contains the giant cylinder under the dome and the four tremendous piers which sustain its weight. Four arches open into this cylinder. These are the centre arches of the Aa series, seen first in the west, north and south fronts and which press through the cathedral to its central space where the opening from the nave is answered by the sanctuary arch on the east. Alternating with these arches are four semi-circular recesses or exedrae. These exedrae are on the model of the major arches of the nave bays (the Bb series) and so fine is the geometrical adjustment of the nave-and-aisles system that the diagonal axes of the exedrae fall exactly on the centre lines of the inner aisles of nave and transepts and the equivalent spaces in the sanctuary. Thus, in each exedra two arches penetrate the curved wall, one coming from the nave or sanctuary and the other from one of the transepts, and the openings are, by an adroit reduction of the aisle width, exact counterparts of the minor arches of the nave triad. Meanwhile, the outer aisles, likewise reduced, pass straight through, north, south, east and west, forming a kind of ambulatory around the square containing the domed space.

This perfectly harmonious conciliation of the nave and aisles with the central space can only have been reached by a fineness of adjustment extending to every part of the plan, no single piece being alterable without a vibration of change in all the others, and this is one of the marvels of the design. Dimensional interdependence of this complexity has rarely, if ever, been achieved in a cathedral design and certainly in no cathedral ever built.

The ordonnance of the nave sweeps round the walls of the central space and the incurving surfaces of the exedrae. The aedicules do not appear but their moulded profiles, with those of the attic-pedestal combination below and everything above up to the springing of the great arches traverse the entire circuit. Above this line the walls begin to curve inwards – an almost imperceptible curve introduced by Lutyens for a corrective purpose which need not concern us here.

The inner dome now begins to rise, at first with an inward-leaning wall pierced by twenty-four round-headed windows, recalling the similar lighting at Sta Sophia and S. Irene at Constantinople, then with a curve which would come to a point if it were not interrupted by a circular opening into the upper dome. The surface of the dome is un-enriched – an invitation and a challenge, no doubt, to the arts of the painter or mosaicist.

Thus far the dome, as seen from the cathedral floor. The greater part of it rises above. Lutyens accepted the tradition inherited from the Renaissance that a domed cathedral requires two domes – an inner shell to ceil the space below in due proportion and an outer shell to declare its rotund glory to the world. Lutyens followed Wren closely in the profile of his outer dome, the lantern surmounting it and the method of carrying the lantern on a cone concealed between inner and outer domes. But he departed from Wren in everything else. It was Wren's aim to poise the perfect model of a circular temple on the top of his cathedral – a model which would still be perfect if the cathedral body were displaced by a mound of earth. Lutyens saw things altogether differently. It was not, to him, a question of sustaining an aerial temple but of heaving up a domed mass out of, but still belonging to, the cathedral body; a mass with the power and security of a fortress. Wren hid the piers of his dome; they do not even emerge through the roof. Lutyens brings his piers into full view as a naked shelf and, not content with that, raises twin buttresses on each corner of the shelf going the full height of the drum, embracing it and glorifying its dominion over the body of the church.

238 This leads us to consider the exterior as a totality. In the main body, as in the dome, Lutyens strikes away from the great precedents. St Peter's and St Paul's both present us with two architectural performances, an interior act and an exterior act; significantly related, to be sure, but still distinct and separate. Lutyens presents us with *one*. The nearest historic precedent is Sta Sophia, whose exterior only makes sense as the 'inside-out' of the interior. This is true – but more subtly so – in the Liverpool designs, where the interior architecture is transmitted through the outer walls with eloquently selective emphasis. Identity of exterior and interior is most strongly expressed in the west and transept fronts where, as we have seen, the parallel 'tunnels' issue with thrilling effect. But the identity is continuous. All the off-sets which mark the springing-lines of the arches are marked outside as well as inside the walls. The aedicules outside are on the same level as those inside. Most important of all, there is no attempt to 'model' the exterior as if the architect hoped to engross and satisfy the eye without reference to the interior. Where windows come they are simple rectangular penetrations at points of interior necessity, not of exterior parade. The cathedral is one, whole, indivisible thing.

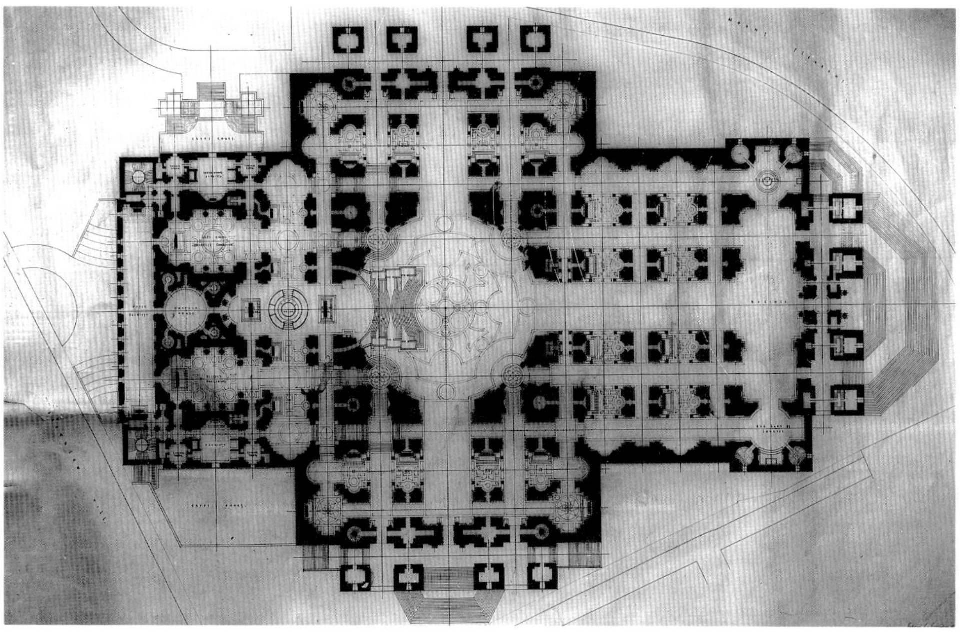

237. Plan of the Cathedral

238. Model of the Cathedral made by John B. Thorp and his son John Lesley Thorp

Not only in the walls but in the shelving and levelling of the volumes, the interior organization speaks. Westward of the dome, the high silhouette of narthex and nave, cut into simple gradations, ride magnificently above and behind the aisle walls. Eastward of the dome the massing terminates in the simple half-round of the apse and then descends to express the contents of the eastern limb, where changes in the plan initiate a new colloquy of forms.

The plan shows of what this eastern limb consists. There is the apse, with the *237*
circular grille of the organ well, and, next eastward, the circular chapter house, on either side of which are the Lady Chapel and the Chapel of the Blessed Sacrament, while to south and north are two sacristies and to the east a third sacristy with the library above. The two chapels, each about the size of one of Wren's larger City churches (St Mary-le-Bow, for instance), open off the sanctuary transept which is virtually a repetition of one of the crossing 'tunnels' of the nave. The floor is now ten feet above that of the nave, conducted to this new level by steps which first share most beautifully the circularity of two of the exedrae, and thence proceed in straight flights. The perpetually peregrine order at the new level necessarily loses its pedestal but

pursues its even course, now humbly bare-foot, round the sanctuary transept, into and out of the chapels. The chapels are brilliantly lit, with four glazed lunettes rising from their central spaces to the saucer domes; and over these domes rise octagon spirelets, very steep and sharp as a needle, movingly reminding us of the way Wren's St Martin, Ludgate, salutes the gravity of St Paul's.

A cathedral has by long tradition been expected to have western bell-towers. The Gothic cathedrals have them, St Paul's has them; Maderna even attempted, unsuccessfully, to raise two western campaniles at St Peter's. Lutyens always had such towers in mind for Liverpool and they appear in at least one of the early sketches, rising majestically behind the narthex. But the difficulty about these towers was to relate them to the dome. A merely pictorial relationship, as at St Paul's, could not be tolerated in the mathematical ambience of Liverpool. So the belfries were made to ride on the cross-axis of the cathedral, standing on the thickened walls behind the transept porches and inescapably related to the dome and its buttresses. Each tower rises, with its broad sides facing north and south, to something very like a triumphal arch, but one in which the secondary openings are set above, not below, the central arch, and these openings are not arches but aedicules: the same aedicules as those carried by the dome buttresses on precisely the same level. The purpose of the towers declares itself dramatically when we discover that every arch and every aedicule is filled with bells – the cathedral's voice.

Beneath the eastern limb of the cathedral is the crypt, that portion of the building which, begun to be built in 1933, was stopped by the Second World War; a melancholy fragment which serves, however, not only as a ratification of the scale and realism of the great design but as a reminder of one aspect of the architect's genius which neither drawings nor models can convey: his peculiar sympathy for and understanding of building materials. They are reflected here in the brickwork of the twin chapels, their vaults and arches turned with something more than Byzantine precision; and in the granite revetment of the exterior, where the challenge of the material brings out a savagely witty inventiveness.

The question whether a building can assume a place of authority in the world of architecture without actually being built is a curious one; but the answer is not in doubt. Bramante's design for St Peter's dome and Wren's great model for St Paul's still pull their weight in the history books and a whole treatise could be written on the influence of Bernini's rejected design for the Louvre. Lutyens's cathedral, no less than these, is a landmark in the architectural history of its time. It will survive as an architectural creation of the highest order, perhaps as the latest and supreme attempt to embrace Rome, Byzantium, the Romanesque and the Renaissance in one triumphal and triumphant synthesis.

XV · The Case for a Theory of 'Modern' Architecture

This was written in 1957 to be delivered as a lecture, and in this case, for reasons that I give in the Preface, I leave it unrevised in its original form. The only alteration I have made has been to put the word 'modern' in the title into quotation marks.

EVER SINCE THE MODERN MOVEMENT got on to its feet, questions have been asked about what it stands on. An association of some kind between what is vaguely called 'theory' and what is vaguely called 'modern architecture' continues, I believe, to be a topic frequently debated, and I am told that teachers in some of the schools feel a practical need for some sort of theoretical formula as a means of introducing students to the principles of modern design. Hence this paper, which offers nothing new but is simply an investigation – an attempt to discover whether there does exist any basis of principle applicable to modern architecture, different from the bases applicable to any other architecture or alternatively whether such a bases can be abstracted out of prevailing practice and ideas.

I should like to take this alternative first because it offers an obvious *prima facie* case. I think it is a bad case but it is necessary to put it up in order to put it down. Modern architecture exists to the extent that there are plenty of buildings which everyone in this room would immediately classify as products of the modern movement on the basis of certain recurrent formal arrangements and relationships. Embarrassed as we are by the use of such expressions as 'the modern style', 'manner' or 'idiom' there is positively no denying the consensus of characterization. Modern architecture is there all right. Furthermore, closely associated with this architecture is a number of ideas – ideas expressing modernity in one sense or another, nearly always either by analogy with the past or by analogy with some other activity than architecture. The architects who design the buildings tend to quote and promote these ideas and it would be very difficult to show that this complex of architecture and ideas is anything short of valid in relation to present-day conditions. There is indeed no other complex of forms and ideas which seriously rivals it. Now, in a situation like this, it may be argued, it should be possible to put together a theory of architecture without very much difficulty. It is simply a question of two rather prolonged exercises in analysis and synthesis. First, of assembling the ideas, examining their common trends of meaning and reaching a series of general concepts. Second, of abstracting formal characteristics from a select repertory of modern buildings, eliminating merely modish elements and providing a grammar of form. It would then only remain to illustrate how the forms embody the ideas. The whole exercise would, it may be supposed, add up to something like a Palladio of modern architecture, a pedagogical reference book not in any way restricting further development but consolidating the achievements of modern architecture, clarifying them and providing a departure platform for new experiments.

Such is the *prima facie* case for a specific theory of modern architecture. I have tried to make it sound plausible but of course it is hopelessly gimcrack. Only imagine for a moment the task of isolating characteristically modern forms from whole buildings. Only imagine the horror of stirring around in the rag-bag of aphorisms, platitudes and fancy jargon and trying to determine their common trend and resultant meaning. The imagination boggles, and when it does that it is a sure sign that something stupid is being attempted. So let us leave this whole enterprise and look for firmer ground on which to start our enquiry.

We had better consider first what is in our minds when we think about a 'theory' of architecture. The elementary meaning is a conspectus of knowledge in any particular field. A theory of architecture may be, like many of the treatises of the 18th century, purely encyclopaedic, without any explicit philosophical orientation at all. It may be, like Julien Guadet's famous work,[1] a series of discursive studies of types and elements, in lecture form, within a closed tradition whose validity is taken for granted. Or it may be of that curious kind represented by John Belcher's well-known book[2] of half a century ago in which a list of interesting words is compiled (scale, vitality, restraint, refinement, etc.) each providing the title for a short essay which gives it a glow of meaning, without ever reaching down to fundamental concepts at all.

But I suspect that what is in our minds when we talk about architectural theory now is something both less extensive and more profound than these – a statement of related ideas resting on a philosophical conception of the nature of architecture – in short, *principia*. Since Alberti wrote his *De Re Aedificatoria* in the middle of the 15th century there have been a certain number of statements of this kind, though not (when all derivatives are written off) quite as many as you might think and few, mercifully, as difficult to understand as Alberti. They are usually to be found lodged in some section of an encyclopaedic work (e.g. Alberti, Lib.ix) or forming introductions to a course of lectures (e.g. Durand) or, more rarely, as independent polemical essays (e.g. Laugier). It is worth emphasizing that to state the principles of architecture does not at any time take very many words. It is the demonstration by historical instance and the exposition of grammar which fills up the tomes. This evening my quest is for statements of root principle.

If we review the statements of principle which have attracted attention in the course of the last five hundred years we may be struck by the fact that they are much more easily related to each other than they are to the architecture prevailing at the time they were written; which suggests that just as architectural style has evolved from generation to generation, each changing the favoured accentuation of the last, so architectural thought has developed phase by phase with its own dialectic. There has been, in fact, an evolving process in theory just as there has been in style and the two processes have not made anything like the same pattern. Each has been and is in fact autonomous, to the extent that it would be possible to write a history of architectural theory without reference to a single actual building and even a history of architectural style without a single reference to architectural theory – though I am not suggesting that anybody should try.

The actual relationship of architectural theory to architectural production at any given time is problematic. It is perfectly possible for a new idea to be announced, cherished by one generation, turned upside down by the next and only in a third to be validated in architectural designs. Something of the sort happened with the 18th-century idea of rational architecture, to which I shall refer later on. On the other hand it is possible for architectural style to be revolutionized without so much as one corollary gesture on the plane of theory. Who has ever had a more powerful effect on architecture than Michelangelo? Yet his effect on the *theory* of architecture was nil. So we must bear in mind about theory that it is an historical process with a life of its own in its own medium of words and that there is no question either of principles being abstracted wholly from practice or of practice being necessarily a reflection of theory. This makes a pretty big hole in the proposition called 'A theory of modern architecture'. But it brings us nearer to a realistic view of what we are discussing.

In the present century a fairly large number of books – I make it about 120 – have been written about the nature and principles of architecture. Up to 1925 there was a modest issue of one book a year but in 1926 at least seven books (English, American and French) appeared, though oddly enough not one of these recognized that any fundamental changes were taking place in architectural thought. The general tendency before 1927 was to re-write the principles then stagnating in the Beaux-Arts tradition and to comment on them in essay style, but I do not know of a single book which investigated those principles historically or attempted to evaluate them philosophically (there is one outstanding exception which I will mention in a moment). After 1927 books stating the modern point of view began to appear. Between that year and the present there have been statements from Behrendt, Lurçat, Taut, Cheney, Platz, Hitchcock, Duncan, Gropius, Moholy-Nagy, Teague, Giedion, Fry, Saarinen and Zevi, to mention only some of those who have produced books; to collect the statements appearing in the form of papers, articles and catalogue introductions would be a mighty exercise in bibliography. The general character of all this writing is enthusiastic and propagandist. The authors tend to start with a belief in the new architecture and to write around their beliefs supporting them by picturesque and forceful analogies. Only rarely does one detect a realization that architectural thought is a continuing activity *sui generis* in which what is new must be distinguished by criticism of the past. But there are a few books of great penetration and to some of these we must now pay attention.

I suppose nobody will doubt that Le Corbusier's *Vers une Architecture*[3] has been the most consequential book on architecture written in this century. Published in 1923, it is still widely quoted and quite frequently read. It is not and does not claim to be a theory of architecture. It is a series of critical essays, reprinted in the order in which they first appeared in *L'Esprit Nouveau*, starting in October 1920. In the whole course of those essays nothing absolutely new is proposed in the way of architectural principle, but a great deal that had been forgotten is brought into the light of the present and exhibited with a quite uncommon flair for paradox. I think it would not be an unfair generalization to describe *Vers une Architecture* as a critique of the French rational tradition – a critique marking a new phase in that always vigorous and controversial zig-zag of thought. This French rational tradition is not, of course, the

Beaux-Arts tradition personified in Guadet, for which Le Corbusier expresses a good deal of contempt. It is, on the contrary, the tradition first of Jesuit intellectuals in the early 18th century, later of rebels and academy-haters, and indeed 'tradition', which suggests a handing-down of embalmed principle, is not at all the right word. It is an historical process advancing by a series of contradictions and reassessments, of which latter *Vers une Architecture* is the most recent. As I am going to suggest that this rational process is still a vital element in the contemporary theoretical situation perhaps I may briefly explain what I understand it to be.

It all hinges on the ancient body of Mediterranean beliefs, re-stated by Alberti;[4] and the hinge occurs in the age of Descartes. One could date its origin rather pedantically from Perrault's critique of Vitruvius.[5] It is picked up in the 18th century by the Abbé Laugier[6] whose two essays were the standard statements for half a century. But in 1802 Laugier was attacked as a muddler by Durand[7] who presented his students at the Polytechnique with an altogether tougher and more materialistic case. So far, the argument had proceeded against a background of belief in classical antiquity, but then, fifty years later, Viollet-le-Duc[8] took up a new position, still rationalist but transposing the background from classical to medieval antiquity and purporting to show that the 13th century was the sole repository of rationalist principle. Viollet-le-Duc was, directly or indirectly, the inspiration of many of the pioneers of the modern movement: Berlage, Horta and Perret among them.

This is, of course, a grotesque simplification, indicating only some of the more obvious peaks in a great range of argument. Many more names should go in, not all of them French: there is Cordemoy;[9] there is the mysterious Venetian rigourist Lodoli[10] whose influence is hard to estimate because he never wrote anything down; there is Frézier,[11] the engineer; there is half-French Pugin.[12] Again in rough caricature, one could sketch the process like this. Perrault said antiquity is the thing and look how rational; Lodoli seems to have said rationalism is the thing, down with antiquity; Laugier said up with *primitive* antiquity, only source of the rational; Durand said down with Laugier, rationalization means economics; Pugin said down with antiquity, up with Gothic and look how rational; Viollet-le-Duc said up with Gothic, prototype of the rational. Eventually a voice is heard saying down with all the styles and if it's rationalism you want, up with grain-elevators and look, how beautiful!

Well, now, in this process, which I take to be the main heritage of the modern theorist, there are certain essentials which hold their own throughout. At the bottom of it all is the axiom that architecture is an affair of simple geometric forms – regular solids[13] and their elementary divisions. This is inherited from Italian tradition and has a peculiar history of its own, passing from the quasi-medieval numerology of Alberti to the visual objectivity of the Cartesian world and on to the emphatic apprehensions of the revolutionary school of Boullée and Ledoux. In some form or another it is always there.

Then there is the rational issue whose course through the 18th and 19th centuries I have already sketched.

But there is also the question of antiquity and the measure of its authority and one very important thing about the whole rational process is that it tends to exclude antiquity as an *absolute* authority. However, antiquity was obstinately there all the time.

Only the theorists who never designed anything, like Lodoli and Laugier, could be really tough about antiquity. Those who designed had, in one way or another, to admit it for the important reason that the forms of classical antiquity or (in the 19th century) medieval antiquity, provided something which is essential to the creative designer – a bulwark of certainty, of unarguable authority on which his understanding leans while his conception of the building as a whole, as a *unity*, takes shape. The most interesting, indeed the dominating question, in a search for the modern *principia* is: where, if not in antique forms, or some equivalent substitute, is the source of unity?

Le Corbusier provides no answer to this in *Vers une Architecture*. There is no reason why he should. The book is really nothing but a lightly-etched reminder ('Trois rappels' is the title of the first chapter) of the main content of the rational process and it contains few ideas which could not be traced back into the line from Perrault to Viollet-le-Duc.

Le Corbusier's designs, let me say in parenthesis, are a different thing altogether. I have already said that architectural theory and architectural style are things apart – each with its own autonomous life and this is nowhere more obvious than in the case of the author of *Vers une Architecture*. His conception of theory is simply the solid intellectual platform, with foundations deep in the past, on which he stands to do something which has nothing to do with the past whatsoever. Le Corbusier has not *reasoned* himself into those architectural conceptions which have so profoundly influenced the expression of modern building. Nor is there any mystery about how they have come about, for it is by now an accepted fact of contemporary art-history that Le Corbusier's vision in the early days was that of the modern painters – the school of Picasso, Braque and Léger; that after they had discovered the power of converting the commonplace into pure conceptual painting, Le Corbusier discovered the power of composing the commonplaces and crude ingenuities of industrial building into equivalent architectural realities. But there is nothing in *Vers une Architecture* about that; and if the pictures of the author's own works were eliminated from the book it might easily be construed as foreshadowing some frozen Neo-classicism not far removed from that of Auguste Perret.

Obviously, the only thing about *Vers une Architecture* which helps us to envisage a case for a specifically new theory of architecture is the re-illumination of principles already established. If we were to argue from the example of Le Corbusier alone we might well conclude that the theoretical process stemming from antiquity was, in one form or another, the theory appropriate to the modern movement in architecture. That *may* indeed be the case. But we cannot leave the matter there for in another quarter altogether there have been theoretical inquiries of considerable importance and entirely different character. I am thinking of the sphere of thought represented by the Bauhaus.

Bauhaus thought has been pretty copiously manifested: in Gropius's own writings, in writings about Gropius and the Bauhaus and in the Bauhaus-bücher of the 1920s. But for anything like the systematic exposition of Bauhaus theory the most significant book is Moholy-Nagy's *The New Vision: from Material to Architecture*, based on lectures given at the Bauhaus in 1923–28. These lectures were given after *Vers une Architecture* had been published but they owe nothing to it, nor to the *Esprit Nouveau* circle from which it emerged. Moholy, of course, was a totally different kind of person from Le Corbusier – he represents in a fundamental sense that phenomenon of our time, the displaced person. Le Corbusier's Swiss background was happy and stable. Moholy's Hungarian background was far otherwise and when Le Corbusier was building a luxury villa on Lake Geneva, Moholy was pitched into a hideous and incomprehensible war without even the consolation of being on the winning side.[14] It is not surprising that whereas Le Corbusier turns naturally to a reassessment of the past, Moholy turns his back on it altogether. I do not know how conscious he was of turning his back on Le Corbusier but his book is in some respects a negation of *Vers une Architecture*. Admittedly he states what he calls the 'basic law' of design as the obligation 'to build up each piece of work solely from the elements which are required for its function',[15] a statement which is the genuine old-style rationalist article (it could well be a quotation from Laugier), but he then instantly declares that the basic law has limitations and he proceeds to search for an ultimate authority.

This ultimate authority is of course likely to be the source of unity of which I have already spoken. It is the *something* occupying the place which used to be filled by 'antiquity'. What is it? Moholy says it is 'biological'. The artist's freedom, he says, is 'in the last analysis determined biologically'. The words 'biological', 'biologically' crop up again and again throughout the book. 'Architecture', he says, 'will be understood . . . as a governable creation for mastery of life, as an organic component in living.' 'The standard for architects . . . will revolve around the general basis, that of the biologically evolved manner of living which man requires.' And, finally, 'architecture will be brought to its fullest realization only when the deepest knowledge of human life as a total phenomenon in the biological whole is available.'[16]

This preoccupation with biology and with the organic is obviously a very important issue in our investigation. The word 'organic' especially has had an almost magical significance for architectural writers ever since Louis Sullivan wrote of it as 'a word I love because I love the sense of life it stands for, the ten-fingered grasp of things it implies'.[17] That is not a very scientific statement but I have not yet found, among the many writings about organic architecture, any statement that is. Yet it is constantly used as an ultimate, as if organic values (whatever they may be) were absolute values.

Moholy's treatment of the biological idea is more interesting than most since he presses it harder and, in doing so, shows, in one direction, its perilous inefficiency. When he declares that the artist's freedom is 'in the last analysis determined biologically' he leads us surely to a determinism which begs the whole question. Moholy would like to construct a theory which is a perfect description of practice – which coincides with practice. He cuts himself off from inherited theory and postulates a new theory which would fit the biological (let us say psychophysical) needs of man like a glove. I suppose, if the most far-reaching implications of cybernetics were realized, if the artist's functions were at last to be explicable in mechanistic terms, some such theory might be arrived at. But that is such an awfully long way off that it is hardly worth considering in relation to the Modern Movement now in course of evolution; and in any case I doubt if anybody yet sees the determination of the artistic needs of society as even a remotely possible point on the scientific horizon. Notwithstanding the fine perceptions and immensely valuable practical suggestions contained in

Moholy's book, it seems to me that his insistence on the biological is a premature and purely verbal closure of the subject of modern architectural theory. It gives nothing to hold on to but this elusive myth of 'biological' finality.

Those who have written about 'organic' architecture have usually gone in a rather different direction from Moholy's. Frank Lloyd Wright's use of the expression 'organic architecture' is generally considered to be his own emotional tag for all fine, free and humane architecture but especially for that of Frank Lloyd Wright. Behrendt, Steinmetz, Saarinen and others have speculated on the 'organic' in desultory philosophizings. Bruno Zevi has investigated various recent uses of the word and in his book, *Towards an Organic Architecture*, devotes a whole chapter to 'the meaning and scope of the term organic in reference to architecture'. He does not discover any evidence of strikingly profound thought on the subject; not does he commit himself to any precise meaning. But he does write off various spurious or out-moded interpretations and, at the end of his study he does, in a single, rather casual remark, hit what I conceive to be the nail exactly on the head. He says that the organic conception of architecture is based 'on a social idea and not a figurative [I take it he means formal] idea'.[18] That rather wide interpretation would, I suspect, command almost universal agreement.

Zevi throws out this comment as if its truth was pretty obvious and I suppose it is, but I want to underline the proposition and see how it relates to the picture of the developing theoretical process which I have outlined. I suggested a few moments ago that although the rationalist writers of the 18th and 19th centuries tended to exclude antiquity as the ultimate authority, antiquity remained insistently there as the *source of unity*, the focus at which the architectural design was realized. Where, I asked, if not in antique forms, can the source of unity lie? Zevi's remark points to the answer. The source of unity in modern architecture is in the social sphere, in other words in the architect's programme.

From the antique (a world of form) to the programme (a local fragment of social pattern): this suggests a swing in the architect's psychological orientation almost too violent to be credible. Yet, in theory at least, it has come about; and how it has come about could very well be demonstrated historically. First the rationalist attack on the authority of the antique; then the displacement of the classical antique by the medieval; then the introduction into medievalist authority of purely social factors (Ruskin); then the evaluation of purely vernacular architectures because of their social realism (Morris); and finally the concentration of interest on the social factors themselves and the conception of the architect's programme as the source of unity – the source not precisely of forms but of adumbrations of forms of undeniable validity. The programme as the source of unity is, so far as I can see, the one new principle involved in modern architecture. It seems to be the principle which can be discerned through the cloud of half-truths, aperçus and analogies which is the theoretical effluent – not a very nice word, I'm afraid – of the Modern Movement.

Whether you accept this statement as a basic principle and a specifically modern principle depends upon a number of things. Mainly, there is the question, what a 'programme' is. A programme is a description of the spatial dimensions, spatial relationships and other physical conditions required for the convenient performance of specific functions. It is probably impossible to write out a satisfactory programme without a certain number of architectural relationships being suggested on the way and the character of these relationships may well be something different from the relationships in a predetermined stylistic discipline. The chief difference is that they involve a process in time. It is difficult to imagine any programme in which there is not some rhythmically repetitive pattern – whether it is a manufacturing process, the curriculum of a school, the domestic routine of a house, or simply the sense of repeated movement in a circulation system. Of course this pattern does not dictate a corresponding pattern in the architect's plan or anything crude like that but it does sanction relationships which are different from those sanctioned by the static, axially grouped dominants and subordinates of the classical tradition – different, but carrying an equivalent authority. The resultant unity can, I think, quite reasonably be described as a biological or organic unity, because it is the unity of a process. Moholy-Nagy[19] and after him Giedion[20] would see it as a space-time unity and you will recall Giedion's brilliant analogies between modern architecture and the concepts of modern physics on the one hand and the Picasso revolution in modern painting (involving the concept of simultaneity) on the other. Not that such analogies prove anything; and there is always the danger that they may seem to prove far too much; they are phantasms of the *Zeitgeist.* The actual reason why the principle embodied here is new is this. It is only in the past half-century or so that the programme has ceased to be evaluated merely *quantitatively* and has come to be evaluated *qualitatively*. This has to do with the fact that programmes have become more complex, more challenging and therefore more susceptible to qualitative generalization and evaluation. It has also to do with very much wider issues involved in the social revolutions and re-orientations of our time.

If we accept this principle – unity deriving from the programme – as truly a basic principle of modern architecture, how does it look when lined up with the inherited principles which we found that Le Corbusier had re-illuminated in *Vers une Architecture*? Here comes the crux of the whole matter. The conceptions which arise from a preoccupation with the programme have got, at some point, to crystallize into a final form and by the time the architect reaches that point he has to bring to his conception a weight of judgment, a sense of authority and conviction which clinches the whole design, causes the impending relationships to close into a visually comprehensible whole. He may have extracted from the programme a set of interdependent relationships adding up to a unity of the biological kind, but he still has to face up to the ordering of a vast number of variables, and how he does this is a question. There is no common theoretical agreement as to what happens or should happen at that point. There is a hiatus. One may even be justified in speaking of a 'missing architectural language'. Gropius[21] has stated the difficulty as the lack of an 'optical "key" . . . as an objective common denominator of design' – something which would provide 'the impersonal basis as a prerequisite for general understanding', which would serve 'as the controlling agent within the creative act'. That is a precise description of the functions served by antiquity in the classical centuries! The dilemma is really an enlargement of the flaw already apparent in mid-18th-century theory – the flaw that while antiquity was eliminated as an absolute, nothing was introduced which took its place as a universally accredited language of architectural form.

The flaw seems now to have widened into a veritable dilemma. Can it be resolved? Well, I can think of two possible approaches to its resolution. The first involves an extension of the rationalist principle into the sphere of engineering and the second involves a reconsideration of the geometrical basis and limitations of architecture.

Let us take the engineering question. The engineer is the heir to the basic tenet of the old rationalism – economy of means in construction. So long as traditional methods prevailed the architect could keep his eye on this ball, or at least persuade himself that he was doing so; but with the development of the science of the strength of materials and the application of mathematics to design he was rapidly overpassed by the engineer. The engineer ran away with the rationalist ball. It is no use pretending that we can lop off this issue as a stray limb of the rationalist process which has got outside the scope of architecture, because if we let the rationalist principle go modern theory collapses in a heap. No. It is necessary to declare that no theory of modern architecture can be logically complete which does not postulate the collaboration, immediate or remote, of architect and engineer; and here collaboration must stand for the design of components in factories as well as the personal achievements of a Nervi or a Candela.

But let us be clear about what the engineer's role really is and how different it is from that of the architect. For the architect, the source of unity for his design is, I have suggested, the programme. The engineer seeks unity in another way and another direction altogether. He seeks it within one component – even if it is a very complex component comprising the whole sectional trace of a large building. And it is a unity of interdependent calculable issues adding up to a total whose criterion is performance. His search for finality and the architect's are as wide apart as they can be. It would be altogether too facile to suggest that they are even complementary. Nevertheless, a whole view of architecture must necessarily extend to this latest metamorphosis of the rationalist process in the hands of the engineer.

The idea can be and sometimes is upheld that the engineer, as a result of his enforcement of the rationalist principle, invents forms and formal arrangements which the architect then absorbs into his vocabulary of expression and uses, sometimes in a strictly engineering way – and sometimes not.[22] This certainly happens. But the engineer is concerned strictly with components and although he may contribute significant inventions he cannot contribute a continuously related system of inventions – i.e. a language.

Thus the engineering issue does not wholly resolve the dilemma of modern architectural theory, and so we turn to the ancient axiom that architecture is fundamentally concerned with the regular solids and simple ratios. It is getting to have an old-fashioned look, this axiom, especially in an age which has discovered geometries other than Euclidean. Moholy-Nagy was eager to go behind the axiom to 'biological assumptions'. Mr Banham, in an article of 1955,[23] has offered us the attractive red-herring (I think it's a herring) of topology. In the field of practice, unfamiliar and complex forms are cropping up. Candela has built a concrete church in which all the surfaces are hyperbolic paraboloids. But surely the axiom stands as an over-all absolute necessity. Even if plans wriggle in the wildest of 'free' curves, even if engineering science introduces forms of great precision but visually unreadable complexity, we shall always seek to read through the complex to the simple, to seek the assurance of those simplicities which must be implied even when they are not stated. Very well. On this principle of geometrical absolutes it is possible to erect systems or disciplines to guide the architect towards that final ordering of form which he must achieve. Of these systems the most celebrated is Le Corbusier's *Modulor*. But the *Modulor*, like any other apparatus of the kind, is a system of control, not of expression (Le Corbusier says this as clearly as it could be said). It is not a language. And if I say that in my opinion the erection of proportional disciplines – purely intellectual contrivances – does bring the *principia* of modern theory into satisfactory relationship to each other and to actuality, it may well be objected that this theory excludes almost everything that has been most valued in the art of architecture as a means of expression in the past three thousand years. In answer to that, I have two things to say. The first is that if you accept the principle that the programme is the source of unity, the crucible of the architect's creative endeavour, you cannot postulate another principle, another crucible, at the other end of the designing process to satisfy the architect's craving for conspicuous self-expression. You cannot have it both ways. You certainly cannot have two sources of unity. Either the programme is or it is not the source. It is part of my case for a theory of modern architecture that it is the source. If you do not accept this case, I think you must consider whether, after all, architectural theory does not stand very much where it stood in 1920, or 1800, or even 1750, and whether the position of an architect who is concerned about expression or style is not that of a man feeling his way back to classicism or neo-classicism, or, to put the finest possible point on it, crypto-Neoclassicism.

The second thing that I would say is that it is quite possible that the missing language will remain missing, and that in fact the slightly uncomfortable feeling which some of us have that it ought to exist is nothing but the scar left in the mind by the violent swing which has taken place in the lifetime of one generation from an old order of principles to a new.

I have tried to demonstrate that in the light of all that has been written on architecture in the past thirty years a specifically modern theory of architecture does exist and that it exists not as an arbitrary invention of our time but as a new stage in the long evolution of theory since those forgotten men whom even Vitruvius knew as the Ancients. Modern theory is part of the history of ideas. It is, I believe, only as the history of ideas that it can be taught. The main thing is to get that history right and to get it clear.

Notes

Abbreviations used in the Notes

APSD	Architectural Publication Society Dictionary
AR	Architectural Review
AS	All Souls College, Oxford
BL	British Library
Cal SP	Calendar of State Papers
DNB	Dictionary of National Biography
DPR	District Probate Registry
HMC	Historic Manuscripts Commission
PRO	Public Record Office
RIBA	Royal Institute of British Architects
SM	Soane Museum
SP	State Papers

I · The Unromantic Castle

1 The main sources for the life of John Smedley are: J. Smedley, *Practical Hydropathy*, (10th ed., 1869); J. Buckley, *Matlock Bank . . . with a short sketch of J. Smedley*, etc. (1867); H. Steer, *The Smedleys of Matlock Bank*, (1897).
2 I am indebted to Miss Fern Millard for sending me illustrations and a description of Riber today as a 'Wild-Life Park'.

II · John Thorpe and the Thorpes of Kingscliffe

1 H. Walpole, *Anecdotes of Painting in England* (3rd ed., 1782). The note on Thorpe and his book is a Supplement, bound in at the end of Vol. 1.
2 Prospectus of Richardson's book (in the Soane Museum) quoting Dallaway.
3 I do not know who started this *canard*, but it had gained sufficient popularity for Campbell Dodgson to think it worth contradicting in his *DNB* article of 1898.
4 *The Builder* (1867), p. 206.
5 *RIBA Journal* (1 April 1911), p. 372 etc.
6 *Architecture of the Renaissance in England* (1894). In his later book, *Early Renaissance Architecture in England* (1901), Gotch was more cautious.
7 *RIBA Journal* (1894), p. 507.
8 *A History of Renaissance Architecture in England*, pp. 42–52.
9 *English Homes*, Period III, Vol, 1, pp. 183–185 and elsewhere. Tipping even considered Thorpe 'likely to have been the designer of Longleat'.
10 J. Bridges, *History of Northants* (1791), Vol. 2, p. 432
11 DPR Birmingham. Northants and Rutland Wills. Book Q. f. 48 (Cap. 104) Dated 23 July 1558; proved 26 October.
12 'Thomas Thorpe the eldest the 3rd daie of June anno domini 1596.'
13 BL Harl. 1184 f. 217b. BL Harl. 1094 f. 222b. BL Harl. 1553 ff. 191b, 88b.
14 I am indebted to Miss Joan Wake and the Northants Record Society for this information.
15 *Acts of the Privy Council 1619–21* (1930), pp. 101, 113 and 123. He and George Thorpe, his son, claimed the 'right of purlieu.' The Attorney-General accepted recognizances in £100 each from them and others for their attendance in Star Chamber.
16 DPR Peterborough. Archd. Court of Northampton. Lib. X, p. 261. Henry Thorpe provided for a copy of 'Mr. Perkens his Workes' (William Perkins, author of *Armilla Aurea*, 1590) to be chained in the parish church. He left to his son Thomas the 'seelinge' (i.e. panelling) in the parlour, 'all the cupples' (i.e. rooftrusses) and other carpentry work of his house. To another son he left his lease of Cliffe Mills.
17 See APS *Dict.*, s.v. Thorpe (. . .), not the article on John Thorpe. The Privy Council Registers are given as the source of this information, but the Register for the year 1607 does not exist. I have not yet ascertained the proper source, which is more likely to be in some City of London records.
18 PRO. SP (Dom) 15. Vol. 39, No. 83.
19 For information concerning Thomas Thorpe's connection with Blickling, I am particularly indebted to Mr James Lees-Milne, of the National Trust.
20 Cal. SP (Eliz.) Vol. 233, p. 679. Grant of lease to Robert Barnes and Tho. Thorpe of 2 messuages in Hanney, Lincs., 1590.
21 Kingscliffe Burial Register, 'Roger ye sonne of Henrie Thorpe gent,' 13 Jan. 1610–11. Previous entries have had no such qualification.
22 The first known reference with the style of gentleman is, however, the marriage licence of 1592.
23 The best descriptions of Kirby are in H. A. Tipping, *English Homes*, 1922, Period III. Vol. 1 and G. H. Chettle, *Kirby Hall* (Official Guide).
24 So described on the monument in Blatherwick Church erected by his grandson. The monument is very probably a work of Thomas Thorpe.
25 The most recent edition available in 1570 would be the quarto of 1566, containing Books 1–6, but the edition of 1559, comprising only 5 books, contains all the material relevant to Kirby.
26 Serlio (1559 ed.) Bk. 4, p. 72 *verso*.
27 *Ibid.* Bk. 3, p. 20.
28 *Ibid.* Bk. 4, p. 62.
29 *Ibid.* Bk. 4, p. 63.
30 Although Shute's book was printed by Thomas Marshe, the title-page bears the monogram of Cawood, another Elizabethan printer, who had previously used the same blocks in *Acts in the Parliament* (1555). See R. B. McKerrow, *Printers and Publishers Devices* (Bib. Soc., 1913), p. 47: *The First & Chief Groundes, etc.*, ed. in facsimile by Lawrence Weaver, 1912.
31 Hans Blum, *Quinque Columnarum exacta descriptio atque delinatio* (Zurich, 1550).

32 *English Homes*, Periods I & II, Vol. 2, pp. 133–4. J. A. Gotch, *Old Halls . . . of Northants* (1936), Pl. 65.
33 *English Homes*, Period III, Vol. 2, pp. 1–20. Gotch, *Old Halls, etc.*, Pl. 61.
34 J. A. Gotch, *Early Ren. Arch.* (1901), Pl. LVI, and *Old Halls, etc.*, Pl. 90.
35 *English Homes*, Period III, Vol. 2, pp. 21–30. Gotch, *Old Halls, etc.*, Pls. 39 & 41.
36 Gotch, *Early Ren. Arch.* (1901), pp. 17 & 18, Fig. 12.
37 *English Homes*, Period III, Vol. 1, p. 361. Also W. Douglas Simpson in *Archæological Journal*, Vol. 101 (1944), p. 119.
38 This was the date of the death of Sir Edward Griffin, the builder of the porch etc. at Dingley.
39 See E. St. J. Brooks, *Sir Christopher Hatton* (1946), p. 158.
40 *Country Life*, Vol. XXXII, p. 528.
41 Especially those shown in Walpole Soc. XL, pls. 115–6.
42 Will as quoted in note 16, p. 292.
43 Admon. Thomas Thorpe sen., late of Kingscliffe, 6 April 1626. DPR Peterborough. Northants Admons., 1595–1639, p. 163.
44 Admon. Thomas Thorpe, late of Kingscliffe, 8 January 1642. DPR Peterborough. Northants Admons. (1639–1684), p. 22.
45 We know that his father had no male issue when his grandfather made his will in July 1558. If Henry was born before the end of the year and three daughters within the next three years it would be possible for John to have been born in 1562. But he was the first child of a second marriage, so if we allow an extra year to cover the 'decent interval' we arrive at 1563. A later year is unlikely as it would make him less than twenty at his appointment in the Queen's Works.
46 Instances of children laying foundation stones are not infrequent. In 1577 the foundation stone of Parham House, Sussex, was laid by Thomas Palmer, the 2½-year-old grandson of the builder, Sir Thomas Parham (information communicated by the late W. H. Godfrey, quoting a privately published history of Parham). In 1627 John Evelyn, aged seven, laid one of the first stones of South Malling church, Sussex (*Diary*, ed. De Beer (1955), Vol. 2, p. 8). When the foundation of the Rathaus at Augsburg was laid, *c.*1615, the architect, Elias Holl, caused his small son to lay the second stone. He had himself, as a boy of three, been lowered into the foundations of the Maria Stern church by his father with a golden penny (H. Hieber, *Elias Holl* (Munich, 1923), pp. 25 and 10). I am indebted to the late Nikolaus Pevsner for this reference.
47 Among the Finch-Hatton MSS. at Lamport Hall (Northants Record Society) FH 272.
48 The year covered is 1584–5 N.S. Unfortunately, the accounts for the previous year are missing so we cannot be sure whether Thorpe obtained his office in 1583 or 1584. In the accounts for 1581 and 1582 there is no mention of Thorpe.
49 PRO. A.O.1. 2413 (Nos. 13–15), 2414 (Nos. 16–20), 2415 (Nos. 21–25), 2416 (Nos. 26–30), 2417 (Nos. 32–33). The accounts for 1602 and 1603 contain no references to Thorpe.
50 PRO. MP. f. 228. The date is that suggested by the editors of HMC (Vol. 234).
51 Assuming that this date, given on pp. 225–6 of the book, is the date of the drawing and not simply of the house.
52 BL Add. MSS. 18766 f. 16b.
53 J. Summerson, 'Three Elizabethan Architects' in *Bulletin of the John Rylands Library*, Vol. 40, No. 1. (1957), pp. 204–209. For the Banqueting House of 1581, see *The History of the King's Works* (ed. Colvin), Vol. 3, pp. 91–2.
54 Possibly the William Spicer of Nunney who made a contract with Sir J. Thynne in 1559, or else his son.
55 He died in 1615, when Inigo Jones succeeded him.
56 J. Summerson, *ut supra*, pp. 216–221.
57 J. Summerson, *Ibid*, pp. 204–209.
58 When Sir Edward Pytts built his house at Kyre, Worcs., begun 1588, he paid John Symons 20s. for a platt; later he obtained platts from several others including Robert Stickles (1613). *The Antiquary* (1890), where Pytts' account of the work is printed.
59 Stow, *Chron.*, p. 769.
60 Foster, *London Marriage Licences*, p. 1339.
61 As he states in his will.
62 She was baptized in St. Martin-in-the-Fields, 29 April 1575.
63 At Westminister Public Library, Buckingham Palace Road.
64 HMC Hatfield, Vol. X, p. 140.
65 'Mounsier Jammet in Paris his howse 1600,' Walpole Soc. XL, pl. 163.
66 PRO Pells Order Books, E 403. 2724, p. 79.
67 *Ibid.* p. 158.
68 References to Thorpe in the Pells Order Books are as follows: E 403, 2724, pp. 79, 158, 167; 2725, pp. 93, 111, 146; 2726, pp. 21, 41, 43, 123, 137, 161, 172, 204; 2727, pp. 23, 68, 133, 229; 2728, pp. 90, 200, 252, 254; 2729, p. 77; 2731, pp. 85, 126; 2732, p. 162; 2733, p. 96; 2734, p. 93; None in 2735 or 2736; beyond that number I have examined only 2740, 2745 and 2749, none of which contained Thorpe references.
69 BL Cotton. 1 August, i. 75.
70 Ref. previously given.
71 Possibly a Royal hunting lodge. See *VCH Northants*, Vol. 2, p. 579, where, however, a different site is suggested. I am told that there is a derelict farmhouse in the parish still known as Westhay Lodge. The OS shows it about a mile north of the village, west of the Stamford road.
72 Kingscliffe Burial Reg. 'John Ashley of Westy Lodge, Jan. 7, 1598.'
73 Visitation pedigree already quoted.
74 PRO. SP 14, Vol. 44, No. 48. Endorsed 'a certificat of ye repayre of Tho. Ashlyes lodge in Westhay 1609.'
75 See the exhaustive article, with many references, in DNB.
76 PRO. Patent Rolls, C. 66. 1902.
77 Cambridge Univ. Library. Ff. 4.30.
78 Cambridge Univ. Library M.m.iii.15.
79 PRO. Close Rolls. C. 54. 2053.
80 PRO. SC 11, Roll 626.
81 This was discovered by Mr Frederic Turner and communicated by him to the late Arthur T. Bolton, Curator of the Soane Museum. Unfortunately, Mr Turner did not give his sources.
82 *The Art of Drawing with the Pen and Limning in Water Colours, more exactly than heretofore taught, and enlarged; . . . published for the behoofe of all young gentlemen, by H. Peachum, Gent.* (London, 1606).
83 Article in DNB.
84 Az. a star or betw. three crescents ar.; for crest, a cock

gules, beaked, combed, legged and wattled or (Burke, *Gen. Arm.*).
85 For this information I am indebted to Mr Anthony Wagner, Richmond Herald.
86 Information by Mr Frederic Turner (see Note 81 above).
87 This document was acquired by the Soane Museum and is inserted in the Thorpe volume.
88 PRO. E 101, Bundle 435, No. 9.
89 The last entries in the Pells Order Books (E 403. 2733–4) are under the years 1613–15 and relate to the expenditure on repairs at Richmond Park.
90 *Acts of the Privy Council*, Jas. I, Vol. 3, pp. 14–15 and 36.
91 p. 18 in Thorpe's Book.
92 Will in PCC, Fines 108.
93 Cal. SP (Dom). Committee for Advance of Money, 1642–56, Part 1, p. 492.
94 *Ibid.*
95 These are the only grandchildren of Simon Greene mentioned in his will. Most of Thorpe's other children appear to be accounted for in the St Martin's Burial Registers, but as other Thorpes are found in the registers it is impossible to be sure of identifying them.
96 St Martin-in-the-Fields Burials '20 June 1646 Johes Tharp.' Tharp or Tharpe was the spelling adopted by the clerk for all Thorpe entries at this time.
97 *Registers of St Paul's, Covent Garden.* Vol. IV. Burials. Harl. Soc.
98 PRO. LR 2. Vol. 221 (Misc. vols. of surveys) pp. 120–122.
99 *The Surveyor's Dialogue* of John Norden (1607) gives a graphic account of the conditions prevailing.
100 John Summerson, *The Book of Architecture of John Thorpe in Sir John Soane's Museum*. Edited, with biographical and analytical studies. Walpole Society (1966), Vol. 40, pp. i–ix, 1–132; Pls. 1–123.
101 Walpole, Pl. 23a.
102 Walpole, Pl. 43.
103 Walpole, Pls. 120–21.
104 Walpole, Pl. 14.

III · Inigo Jones: Covent Garden and the Restoration of St Paul's Cathedral

1 Covent Garden has, nevertheless, been excellently described, since this essay was written, in the GLC, *Survey of London*, Vol. 36.
2 J. Summerson, *Georgian London* (revised ed., 1988), pp. 16–18.
3 'Russell, Francis, Fourth Earl of Bedford (1593–1641)' in *DNB*.
4 N. G. Brett-James, *The Growth of Stuart London* (1935), p. 161.
5 SP 16, Vol. 182, No. 34.
6 SP 16, Vol. 288, Nos. 43 and 51. In 1635 two sums of £1,000 were received by the Exchequer in confirmation of the Earl of Bedford's licence to build in Covent Garden.
7 Printed in R. Sanderson, *Foedera*, xviii (1726), 33 and R. R. Steele, *Tudor and Stuart Proclamations* (1910), No. 1420.
8 Printed in R. Sanderson, *op. cit.*, p. 97.
9 Pat. Rolls, C 66/2535.
10 *Diary of T. Burton* (ed. J. T. Rutt, 1828), ii. pp. 180–1, where a debate is recorded of 5 June 1657, on the Report of the Committee for the Bill against New Buildings. The (fifth) Earl of Bedford was liable to a heavy fine and had petitioned against it. Members moved for an abatement of his fine on the grounds that he had built and endowed a church and given money to the poor and to the minister. Captain Baynes said: 'I see no more equity for my Lord of Bedford than for others to be abated. If he built the church it did advance his houses' rents.' I am indebted to Professor Trevor-Roper for this reference.
11 'Livorno' in *Enciclopedia Italiana.*
12 P. Lavedan, *Histoire de L'Urbanisme* (1941), pp. 277–84.
13 Nevertheless, Covent Garden came to be seen in some quarters as a 'Place Royale'. In 1638, inhabitants of St Martin-in-the-Fields complained in a petition that there was no statue of brass of the king in the square. SP Charles I, Vol. 402, No. 75.
14 *I Quattro Libri* (1570), iv. pp. 88–89.
15 J. Stow, *A Survey of London*, ed. J. Strype (1720), vi. pp. 87–89.
16 Woburn Archives. *A Particular Account of the Earl of Bedfords Expence in Building Covent Garden Church*, 'begunne the 5th. of July 1631'.
17 H. Walpole, *Anecdotes of the Arts* (1782), ii. p. 274.
18 *Vitruvius on Architecture* (ed. and trans. F. Granger, 1931), i, pp. 239 and 241.
19 *Regole Generali* (Bk. iv of the *Architettura*), cap. 5.
20 *I Quattro Libri* (1570), i, cap. 14.
21 *Dell' Idea della Architettura* (1615), pt. ii, lib. 6, p. 55.
22 R. Com. Hist. Mon, *London*, Vol. 2 (West) p. 136, pl. 229.
23 An alternative attribution to Balthazar Gerbier, Buckingham's architect at York House, is suggested in J. Summerson, *Arch. in Brit. 1530–1830* (7th ed.), pp. 150–1, pl. 104.
24 Serlio, Book 4.
25 L. Hautecoeur, *Histoire de l'Architecture en France*, Vol. 1, (1943), p. 593. See also J. Summerson, *ut supra.*
26 Vitruvius, lib. 4, cap. 8.
27 *Quattro Libri*, Lib. 1, cap. 14, p. 16.
28 J. Webb, *The Most Notable Antiquity of Great Britain . . . Restored by Inigo Jones* (1655), pp. 1 and 44.
29 J. Webb, *A Vindication of Stone-Heng Restored* (1665; 2nd ed., 1725), p. 99. The accounts for the gallery are in E 351/3263.
30 Lib. vi, cap. 3.
31 As late as 1768 Milizia considered it *unica in Europa.*
32 In the library at Chatsworth. f. 192.
33 The MS. *Particular Account* (1631) in the Woburn Archives supplies the following facts about the building. The mason's work was by William Mason. The four columns at the east end cost £220 and a floor was provided 'to drawe out the Tracerie of one of the great collomes' (i.e. presumably the entasis. Webb comments on this in the *Vindication*, p. 45). Mason supplied pedestals for two crosses (probably for the pediments as shown in Hollar's view). Elizabeth Wandesteene supplied red and black Flanders tiles for the roof. The bricklayers were Thomas Scudamore and John Benson and the brickwork items mention both a vestry and a belfry. The joiner, Peter Penson, supplied false doors for the great doorway at the east end. Internally, there was marble paving in the chancel and Purbeck in the aisles. The pulpit and reader's pew had carving by Zachary Taylor, and the marble font was supplied by Andreas Carne and Thomas Miller. Goodrich and Pearce received £80 'for painting the

perspective groteske and other ornaments in the ceiling'. The total cost was £4,886. 5s. 8d. Further information about the church is given in B. Langley, *Ancient Masonry* (1736), i. pp. 218 and 225; Pls. xxvi, xxvii, and xliv. A plate (Pl. V*b*) shows the order and roof construction. The statement (p. 225) attributed to Sir James Thornhill that the church was built by (Nicholas) Stone is obviously wrong (probably Thornhill confused 'Mason' and 'Stone'). Harl. MS. 1831, f. 29, gives dimensions which show that the interior was originally designed to be 50 × 100 ft. In the same manuscript ff. 30, 31, and 33, are minor details concerning fittings.

34 Serlio, *Architettura* (1566), lib. ii, ff. 82–84, does not describe the order as Tuscan. Palladio, *I Quattro Libri*, lib. i, p. 21, gives a free treatment of it, without rustication, in his section on the Tuscan order. Jones uses this but restores the rustication.

35 In the Woburn Archives (Middx. Add.) is *A Booke of the perticular charge for the Portico Buildings on the North east parte of the Piazza* (MS.). These buildings occupied the site of the present Bedford Chambers. They comprised three houses, initially occupied (west to east) by 'Mr. Sidnam', 'Mr. Hubard', and Sir Edmund Verney. Extracts from Verney's lease (1634) are in *Archaeologia*, xxxv. p. 194. As in the case of the church, William Mason was the principal mason. John Taylor was the bricklayer, and Richard Vesey the carpenter. The name of 'Mr. Decause' (Isaac De Caux) occurs twice as having authorized variations in the mason's contract, which suggests that he was acting as the Earl of Bedford's executive architect. Above the stone arches the walls were of brick, stuccoed, and the eaves cornice of wood. The houses were entered from the 'piazza' through rusticated doorways fitted with double doors. At a higher level but still within the 'piazza' were 'clerestory' windows, presumably to light the entrance halls. Each house had a balustered staircase and the principal rooms were wainscoted. The cost of the three houses, including all trades, was £4,703. 16s. 5d.

36 Lib. vii, fol. 63.

37 L. Stone, 'Inigo Jones and the New Exchange', *Archaeol. Jnl.* cxiv (1959), 106–21.

38 F. 131 in 1566 ed. Serlio gives Raphael and Genga as authorities.

39 — Ralph, *A Critical Review of the Public Buildings . . . in and about London and Westminster* (1st ed., 1734; revised ed., here quoted, 1783), p. 78.

40 T. Malton, *A Picturesque Tour through . . . London* (1792–1801), p. 45. Malton's view (Pl. IV*a*) was published in March 1796 but purports to show it 'as it appeared about ten years ago', i.e. before Hardwick's restorations of 1788 and the fire of 1795.

41 I have found no expressions of strong admiration of Covent Garden church earlier than Colen Campbell's in *Vitruvius Britannicus*, ii. 1: 'the only piece the Moderns have yet produced, that can admit of a just Comparison with the Works of Antiquity, where a Majestick Simplicity commands the Approbation of the Judicious.' Strype, in his edition of Stow's *Survey* (1720) echoes this with 'the only View in imitation of the *Italians*, we have in or about *London*'. Ralph (1734) follows, as above. In 1735 Seymour, in his *Survey of London*, ii (bk. 4), 670, quotes an architect, probably Batty Langley, as admiring the church's 'solemn aspect' and 'simple Beauty . . . not to be paralleled by any that I know in and about London', while criticizing certain details. A wholly adverse opinion was that of Horace Walpole (*Anecdotes*, 1782) who could not only see no beauty in the arcades but confesses that 'the barn-roof over the portico of the church strikes my eyes with as little idea of dignity or beauty as it could do if it covered nothing but a barn'; he proceeds to the 'handsomest barn' story quoted earlier. Malton (1792) obviously echoes Ralph. E. W. Brayley in J. Britton and A. Pugin, *Public Buildings of London* (1825), i. pp. 108–17, gives a thoughtful and balanced estimate and is the first writer to point to the strictly Vitruvian character of the order. In Victorian times the church excited little interest though James Fergusson (*History of the Modern Styles*, 2nd ed., 1873, p. 289) considered that 'it would be extremely difficult, if possible, to quote another [church] in which so grand an effect is produced by such simple means'. Reginald Blomfield (*Renaissance Architecture in England*, 1897, i. p. 110) found the portico to be 'one of the most impressive façades in London' but failed to see why and called it 'Doric'. J. A. Gotch in his *Inigo Jones* (1928) took the view that nothing of Jones's work was left at Covent Garden and merely quoted Walpole's adverse opinion and the famous anecdote.

42 Shaftesbury (3rd Earl of), *A Letter Concerning the Art or Science of Design* (1712).

43 For Laugier's influence in England see J. Summerson, *Architecture in Britain 1530–1830* (4th ed., 1963), pp. 247 and 249.

44 L. Alberti, *Ten Books on Architecture* (trans. J. Leoni, 1726; reprint, 1955), vii, chap. 5. The first substantial changes in the fabric were made in a restoration of 1688 costing £11,000 (J. Britton, *Beauties of England and Wales*, x, pt. 4, p. 279). It was perhaps at this date that the Corinthian altar-piece was introduced of which there is a measured drawing in the RIBA. The bell-turret on the west gable (not shown by Hollar but prominent in the *Vit. Brit.* engraving and seen in most 18th-century views) may also have been set up at this time. In 1714 the parish spent £928 on a restoration (*Vestry Minutes*, vol. ii, in Westminster Pub. Lib.) but the work must have been clumsily done for in 1727, when Lord Burlington, 'out of regard to the memory of the celebrated Inigo Jones', restored it 'to its primitive form' at a cost of £300 or £400, it was said that 'it once cost the inhabitants about twice as much to spoil it' (*Weekly Jnl.*, 22 April 1727, quoted in J. P. Malcolm, *Londinium Redivivum*, 1807, iv. p. 219). The next restoration was in 1788, under Thomas Hardwick. He stripped the original stucco from the walls and substituted an ashlaring of Portland stone; removed the north and south porches; demolished the brick and stucco gateways to the church-yard and rebuilt them in stone, giving 'a more decided form' to the profiles (J. Britton and A. Pugin, *Public Buildings of London*, 1825, i. p. 113). Soon afterwards, in 1795, the church was reduced to a shell by a fire which started in the bell-turret. Engravings in the Crace Coll. (B.M.), pf. xviii, Nos. 72 and 73 show it during and after the fire. It was rebuilt by Hardwick, strictly adhering to the old forms. Between 1871 and 1872 there was a restoration by Butterfield when the north and south galleries were removed and the two small doorways in the portico stopped up (*The Builder*, 22 June 1872, p. 482). From 1887 to 1888 a more thorough restoration was undertaken by the Duke of Bedford, with Alfred J. Pilkington as architect. Hardwick's ashlaring (only 2½ in. to 3 in. thick) was stripped off and a red brick skin substituted (*Building News*, 17 February and 2 March 1888, pp. 270 and 344). It was perhaps at this time that the

arches in the north and south sides of the portico replaced the solid walls with their smaller arches.

45 The first part of the 'piazzas' to go was the southern half of the east side, burnt down in 1769, re-built without the arcades and rebuilt again in 1888. The northern half was pulled down in 1889. H. B. Wheatley, *London Past and Present* (1891), iii. p. 83. The eastern half of the north side was still standing in February 1930, the date of photographs in S. E. Rasmussen, *London, the Unique City* (1934; Eng. ed., 1937); the building had been much altered.

46 *The Builder*, 1877, p. 358. Ibid., 1878, p. 875. The builder was Cubitt but 'His Grace is busy himself over the scheme'.

47 I am indebted to Mr Gavin Stamp for drawing my attention to these, which he has published in *The Changing Metropolis*, 1984.

48 W. Dugdale, *History of St. Paul's Cathedral* (cont. H. Ellis; 1818), pp. 95 et seq. The history of the Elizabethan repairs is given in detail in the author's contribution to *The History of the King's Works* (ed. H. M. Colvin) Vol. iii, pp. 147–152.

49 In connexion with the New Exchange, built in 1608. L. Stone, *loc. cit.*

50 The drawing, identified a few years ago by Mr Colvin, is contained in a volume of miscellaneous engravings of St Paul's. I am grateful to the Provost and Fellows of the College for permission to reproduce the drawing here.

51 L. Stone, *ut supra.*

52 RIBA, Burl. Dev. Coll., I/2 (i).

53 W. Dugdale, *op. cit.*, p. 232. SP 16, Vol. 213, f. 28. The deputy was Edward Carter. 'Inigo Jones and St Paul's Cathedral', *London Topographical Record*, xviii (1942), pp. 41–43.

54 SP 16, Vol. 213 (Minutes of the Commissioners under the Commission of 5 January 1631).

55 *Ibid.* Also, Vol. 214, Nos. 43 and 45.

56 W. Dugdale, *op. cit.*, pp. 107–8.

57 SP 16, Vol. 259, No. 22.

58 SP 16, Vol. 257, No. 114; Vol. 259, No. 69; Vol. 266, No. 58.

59 SP 16, Vol. 275, No. 35; Vol. 283, No. 72; Vol. 324, No. 10; Vol. 339, No. 73; Vol. 357, No. 110; Vol. 381, No. 36; Vol. 383, No. 3.

60 SP 16, Vol. 277, No. 75; Vol. 294, No. 23; Vol. 312, No. 6.

61 SP 16, Vol. 276, Nos. 10 and 20; Vol. 314, Nos. 8 and 122; and many others.

62 SP 16, Vol. 301, No. 11; Vol. 368, No. 43.

63 St Paul's Cathedral Library, W.A. 1–15. W.A. 12 (1639–40) is missing but is to be found in Lambeth Palace Library (F.P. 321). The accounts are from April 1633 to September 1641 and are signed by Inigo Jones, Michael Grigg (as paymaster), and Edward Carter (as Jones's 'substitute'). John Webb was clerk engrosser throughout.

64 'Carving of the Foliage for the windows' in August 1633 (W.A. 1).

65 W. Dugdale, *op. cit.*, p. 104. The new tower was to be 'in proportion to the church with a spire of stone suitable thereto.'

66 M. Whinney, 'Some Church Designs by John Webb', *Jnl. of the Warburg and Courtauld Institutes*, vi (1943), Pl. 39.

67 'A piece of architectural juggling in almost impossible circumstances', *Architecture in Britain 1530–1830* (4th ed., 1963), p. 76.

68 W. Kent, *Designs of Inigo Jones* (1727), ii, Pl. 50. Flitcroft's drawing is in the library at Chatsworth.

69 In Hollar's views they look like balls but pineapples are specified in the accounts (W.A. 13).

70 *I Quattro Libri*, lib. iv. cap. 7.

71 R. T. Gunther, *The Architecture of Sir Robert Pratt* (1928), pp. 197–8.

72 J. S. Ackerman, *The Architecture of Michelangelo* (1961), Pl. 46*a*.

73 Jones had already improvised on the theme of triglyphs and metopes in the Doric entablature of the screen in the Somerset House chapel (I. Ware, *Designs of Inigo Jones*, 1735, Pl. 30), where scrolls take the place of triglyphs while the intervals are filled with foliage and a mask. This in turn seems to relate to a note by Inigo in his Palladio (lib. iv, p. 15) referring to one of Lord Arundel's marbles which had scrolls ('cartottzi') instead of triglyphs and gorgon's heads in the metopes – 'a rare invention and to bee imitated'. The note is dated 27 July 1633. A model of the St Paul's cornice was made in January, 1636 (W.A. 5).

74 R. T. Gunther, *loc. cit.*

75 W. Dugdale, *op. cit.*, p. 106.

76 SP 16, Vol. 271, No. 88.

77 Accounts, W.A. 3.

78 *I Quattro Libri*, lib. iv, cap. 10 (1 Tempii del Sole, e della Luna)."

79 *Ibid.*, cap. 9.

80 Hollar's etchings, made for Dugdale, *op. cit.* and a sketch, perhaps by T. Wyck in the Bodleian (Gough, xx, 2B; repr. *Wren Soc.*, xiv, Pl. 52) are the only contemporary records. The source of information for Flitcroft's drawing, engraved for Kent, is unknown but its accuracy is to a considerable extent confirmed by the building accounts.

81 In January 1636, Andreas Carne (who supplied the Font at Covent Garden) modelled a lion's head in clay, cast it in plaster and turned out six papier-mâché heads for a model cornice made by the carpenters. (Accounts, W.A. 5). In June 1638, Enoch Wyatt was making models 'serveinge generally for the whole worke as of Cherubino heades, the Lyons Heades and drops and for the parooles' (? parells or window dressings) (W.A. 9).

82 Zachary Taylor carved some of the enrichments and Thomas Decritz painted black on gold lettering in the frieze in October 1639. The model was taken down in December (Lambeth Palace Library, F.P. 321).

83 J. Webb, *A Vindication* (2nd ed. 1725), p. 48.

84 *Ibid.*, pp. 44 and 226.

85 *Ibid.*, p. 27.

86 Dugdale, *op. cit.*, p. 115.

87 *Wren Soc.*, i, Pl. 26.

IV · Christopher Wren: Why Architecture?

1 J. S. Wren, *Parentalia* (1750), pp. 184–5.

2 G. Vasari, *Lives of the . . . Painters etc.*, tra. Mrs J. Foster (1904), Vol. 1, p. 421.

3 *Ibid.*, p. 413

4 T. Birch, *The History of the Royal Society* (1756), Vol. 1, p. 230.

5 Wren to Sancroft, 7 May 1666, *Wren Soc.*, xiii, p. 44.

V · The Penultimate Design for St Paul's Cathedral

1 The attitudes of various writers to the Warrant design

are summarized in Viktor Fürst: *The Architecture of Sir Christopher Wren* (1956), p. 41.
2 G. Webb: *Wren* (1937), p. 86. Webb goes on to suggest that 'the choir plan of the warrant design is the one on which work was immediately begun and is that of the present St Paul's'. This is going too far in view of the fact that none of the dimensions of the Warrant design is of the executed structure.
3 The warrant with the designs attached to it is at All Souls and is reproduced in *Wren Soc.*, I, Pls. 9–13.
4 *Wren Soc.*, XVI, pp. 7 and 8.
5 S. Wren: *Parentalia* (1750), p. 283.
6 I should like to express my gratitude to the Warden and Fellows for their generosity in the matter. The drawing is the result of collaboration between Mrs Ison as executant, Mr Walter Ison and myself. Mr Ison's criticism and advice have been most valuable throughout the preparation of the drawing and of this article.
7 *Wren Soc.*, I, Pl. 23. The small reproduction, however, is inadequate for study as much depends on pencil lines which are barely perceptible in the original. They have been slightly strengthened in the reproduction here.
8 The section through the pediment of the window produces a chaotic result if followed literally in elevation. This probably represents a hesitation by Wren as to the right projection of this feature. In Mrs Ison's drawing the greater projection of two alternatives has been taken as involving the minimum departure from the original in other respects.
9 The dimensioning of St Paul's is best studied in the working-drawings reproduced in *Wren Soc.* where figured dimensions are given, if rather sparsely. There are no figures on A.S., ii, 34 and dimensions have had to be scaled.
10 The first occurrence of unequal openings into the central space of a basilican plan for St Paul's is probably in the drawing A.S., ii, 42 (*Wren Soc.*, I, Pl. 26). This plan stands out from all the others by reason of its unusual outline. E. Sekler: *Wren and his Place in European Architecture* (1956), p. 121, has even suggested that it might derive from Sta Maria, Loreto. The real controlling factor here, however, is the orientation. The plan is an attempt to design a new cathedral on the same axis as the old and to preserve Inigo Jones's west portico. Site considerations restricted the overall nave-aisles width to 112 ft (Warrant design 120 ft). To obtain the desired 40 ft width of nave the aisles had to be narrow so that unequal openings to the central space were inevitable. Wren must have studied here the workability of unequal openings before transferring the idea, for other reasons, to his revision of the Warrant design.
11 See diagrams in J. Summerson: *Sir Christopher Wren* (1953), for the changes in dimensions. The aisle walls change from 10 ft to 12 ft 4 in. in thickness and the aisle loses a foot. The introduction of flying-buttresses, transferring weight to the aisle walls, would explain this and the Penultimate design certainly had flying-buttresses under the aisle roofs. They are shown in St P. 133A.k
12 A. T. Bolton in *Wren Soc.*, XVI, pp. xi–xii. The Pre-fire design also shows diagonal lighting to the central space but by far less satisfactory means.
13 *Wren Soc.*, II, Pl. 22.
14 The pencillings are of decorative import and seem to suggest moulded panels and leafy pendants much as in the Warrant design but without figures.
15 In fact, the domes of the Warrant design and of A.S., ii, 17 are not hemispheres, as will be seen at once by comparing ills 53 and 62 with the corresponding diagrams in ill. 59. Above the crowns of the arches the dome is part of a convex cone – *i.e.* a figure produced by rotating a segment of a circle. Below the crowns of the arches Wren must have considered it as hemispherical for the intersections of the cone with the rising octagon would give ellipses, whereas the arches are shown as semicircular. It is, of course, only in the spandrels that the hemispherical surface would be realized and the transition from this to the conical surface would scarcely be perceptible to the naked eye even if it were not 'lost' in the carved ornament shown in the Warrant design.
16 *Wren Soc.*, II, Pl. 22.
17 The main reason is as follows. There is a large and highly finished drawing (A.S., ii, 29; *Wren Soc.* I, Pl. 19) of the south elevation of the cathedral showing a dome based on Mansart's first design for the Invalides, and west towers based on Bramante's Tempietto. Everything below dome level is as executed, with one important exception – there is no rustication. Considering that all sculpture is minutely shown the omission of the rustication must surely mean that it was not intended when the drawing was made. Now the contracts with Marshall and Strong for the lower part of the choir, dated 17 August 1675, refer to 'Six Courses of Plinth & Rustick Ashler'; the decision to rusticate had been taken. One may add that certain detail drawings leading directly to A.S., ii, 29 but with minor variations (St P., i, 27 and 28) are without rustication. A small area of rustication on St P., i, 28 seems to have been sketched in experimentally. It seems, therefore, almost certain that the drawing A.S., ii, 29 was made before August 1675 and therefore that every part of the design of the cathedral except the dome and west towers was complete before the building was begun.
18 Wage book for October 1685 to 30 September 1686. *Wren Soc.*, XIV, 3 *et seq.*
19 Two drawings which must belong to lost variant versions of the Penultimate design indicate the existence of concealed flying-buttresses. The most explicit is St P., ii, p. 133 (*Wren Soc.*, III, Pl. 11), which is a section through the clerestory wall, aisle roof and balustrade (the elevation of a transept portico reproduced as if part of the drawing has nothing to do with it). The other drawing is St P., i, p. 64 (*Wren Soc.*, XIII, Pl. 9), a section through the lower part of a transept showing the curve of a flying-buttress, slightly sketched.
20 The drawing A.S., ii, p. 29 (*Wren Soc.*, I, Pl. 19) dealt with in note 17 above, is almost certainly the first complete representation of the totality of the cathedral as we know it. Subsequent revisions of the dome and west towers were of course numerous, but that is another story.
21 A. Blunt: *Art and Architecture in France 1500–1700* (1953), pp. 149–50. Y. Christ: *Eglises Parisiennes* (1947).
22 *Wren Soc.*, I, Pl. 16, 17 and 18. By 8 February 1673 Wren seems to have had the elements of the Great Model in mind (*The Diary of* R. *Hooke*, ed. H. W. Robinson and W. Adams (1935), p. 27) and the Greek Cross design can therefore with reasonable safety be referred to the previous year.
23 *Wren Soc.*, I, Pl. 21
24 *Wren Soc.*, XIII, Pl. 2 (top right)
25 *Wren Soc.*, I, Pl. 14 and 21.

VI · The Classical Country House in 18th-Century England

1 I leave this statement, made in 1959, as it stands. It is happily no longer true and in the now enormous bibliography of the English country house there are books which go a long way to correct the imbalance noted here. I would mention in particular Mark Girouard's *Life in the English Country House* (1978). Chapters 1, 6, 7 and 8 in his book amplify and strikingly illuminate the social significance of the country house in the 18th century.
2 An index of 'Country Homes and Houses' illustrated at various times in *Country Life* is published annually.
3 Tipping, H. A., *English Homes*. Periods I–VI (1 or 2 Vols. each, 9 Vols. in all). Published in the 1920s and now out of print. In part superseded by C. Hussey, *English Country Houses* (hereafter cited as *E.C.H.*), 3 Vols.: *Early Georgian* (1955), *Mid-Georgian* (1956) and *Late Georgian* (1958).
4 For the purpose of this essay a list was made from H. M. Colvin, *Biographical Dictionary of English Architects, 1660–1840* (1st ed. 1954), of all country houses whose commencement dated between 1700 and 1800. To this was added a number of houses mentioned in county histories, books of views, etc., which have not been attributed to an architect.
5 R. T. Gunther, *The Architecture of Sir Robert Pratt* (1928).
6 H. A. Tipping, *English Homes*, Per. IV. Vol. i, p. 205.
7 Representative examples are: Melton Constable, Norfolk, 1664–70; Combe Abbey, War., 1680–91; Uppark, Sussex, 1686.
8 J. Summerson, *Architecture in Britain, 1530–1830* (7th ed., 1983), p. 170.
9 M. D. Whinney, 'William Talman', *Jnl. of Warburg and Courtauld Institutes* (1955), xviii, 1–2.
10 F. Thompson, *A History of Chatsworth* (1949).
11 *Wren Soc.*, Vol. vi, pp. 83 and 85 and Pl. 21.
12 A house for Henry Guy at Tring, of which *Wren Soc.*, Vol. xii, Pl. 2 may be the plan (see Vol. xix, p. 152). Fawley Court, Henley-on-Thames, and Winslow Hall, Bucks. (Vol. xvii, pp. 51–75), have been attributed to Wren, but in neither case is the evidence satisfactory.
13 D. Green, *Blenheim* (1951).
14 J. Kip and L. Knyff, *Britannia Illustrata*. A French edition entitled *Nouveau Théâtre de la Grande Bretagne* appeared in 1708, a new English edition in 1709, an English second volume in 1715 and a new French edition in 3 vols. in the period 1714–16.
15 *The Complete Works of Sir John Vanbrugh*, Vol. iv: the letters (ed. G. Webb), p. 25.
16 In or after 1718, as Sir Richard Child is described in the reprint as Lord Castlemaine, which he became in that year.
17 *Country Life* (22 April 1916).
18 *Ibid.*, 25 May 1918.
19 *Ibid.*, 15 June 1918.
20 The Courtyard front of Buckingham House is well known from many sources but I have found no representation of the garden front. The courtyard front had four pilasters in the centre and two at the ends. Most imitations of Buckingham House have only four pilasters in all, two marking the centre break and two at the ends. Does this arrangement follow the garden front?
21 *Country Life* (1 and 8 July 1949).
22 *Ibid.*, 16 May 1914.
23 B. Little, *The Life and Work of James Gibbs* (1955).
24 *Vit. Brit.*, i (1715), p. 4.
25 *Ibid.*, p. 5.
26 *Ibid.*, p. 4.
27 Jones was referred to as 'the English Vitruvius' as early as 1662, by W. Charleton in his *Chorea Gigantum*. J. A. Gotch, *Inigo Jones*, 1928, p. 22.
28 *Vit. Brit.*, i (1715), p. 2.
29 *Ibid.*, p. 5.
30 H. M. Colvin, *Biog. Dict. Brit. Architects*, p. 452.
31 ? 1680–1750, youngest son of Sir Josiah Child, chairman of the E.L.C. He succeeded his brother in 1704. He was a Tory till 1715, when he adhered to the Whigs. He became Viscount Castlemaine in 1718 and Earl Tylney in 1731 (*G.E.C.*).
32 *The Survey of London*, xiii, p. 167.
33 *The Particulars . . . of the Estates of . . . Directors of the South Sea Company* (1721), p. 43.
34 *Victoria County History: Essex*, Vol. iv (1956), p. 30.
35 C. Hussey, *E.C.H.: Early Georgian*, (1955), p. 66.
36 *Vit. Brit.*, iv (1767), pp. 58–64.
37 C. H. C. and M. I. Baker, *Life of James Brydges* (1949), p. 116.
38 C. Hussey, *E.C.H.: Early Georgian*, p. 66.
39 *Country Life* (21 Aug. 1946); E. Newton, *The House of Lyme* (1917).
40 *Vit. Brit.*, i, p. 5.
41 *Vit. Brit.*, iii, Pl. 40.
42 P. Morant, *The History . . . of Essex* (1768), p. 31.
43 Wilton may have suggested the fenestration and the rusticated base seems to have been studied from the Queen's House, Greenwich.
44 *Vit. Brit.*, i, p. 5.
45 C. Hussey, *E.C.H.: Early Georgian* (1955), pp. 147–54. The engraved view by Schwertfegger reproduced here (Figure 74) is from the 1770 ed. of W. Kent, *Designs of Inigo Jones*.
46 As given on the engraving of 1734 (Hussey, *E.C.H.: Early Georgian*, p. 147).
47 C. Hussey, *ibid.*, pp. 187–94.
48 Hussey (*ibid.*, p. 154) points out that Davenport, Salop., 1726, is an earlier example of this plan. He gives reasons for believing that Burlington may have made suggestions for Nostell.
49 W. Ison, *The Georgian Buildings of Bath* (1948), pp. 135–43.
50 J. Wood, *Essay Towards a Description of Bath* (1749), p. 432.
51 C. Hussey, *E.C.H.: Mid-Georgian* (1956), pp. 51–69.
52 See p. 113.
53 C. Hussey, *E.C.H.: Early Georgian*, pp. 81–6; I. Ware, *Plans, Elevations and Sections of Houghton* (1735).
54 *Vit. Brit.*, ii, Pls. 83–4.
55 *Wren Soc.*, xii, p. 17 and Pl. 14.
56 *Vit. Brit.*, ii, Pls. 59 and 60.
57 J. H. Plumb, *Sir Robert Walpole: The Making of a Statesman* (1956), p. 23.
58 *Vit. Brit.*, i. Pls. 86–7.
59 The Houghton window-dressings are the subject of a plate at the end of C. Campbell, *Andrea Palladio's Five Orders* (1729).
60 J. Gibbs, *A Book of Architecture* (1728), Pl. 56, 'for a Gentleman in Wiltshire'.
61 *Country Life*, 19 and 26 March 1948.
62 *Ibid.*, 10 April 1915.

63 C. Hussey, *E.C.H.: Early Georgian*, pp. 195–9.
64 D. Stroud, *Capability Brown* (1950), pp. 92–3.
65 C. Hussey, *E.C.H.: Early Georgian*, pp. 131–46; M. Brettingham, *The Plans . . . of Holkham* (1761); *Vit. Brit.*, v (1771), Pls. 64–9.
66 R. Wittkower, 'Lord Burlington and William Kent', *Archaeolog. Jnl.*, Vol. cii (1947).
67 See below, p. 109.
68 *I Quattro Libri* (1570), lib. 2, p. 66.
69 C. Hussey, *E.C.H.: Mid-Georgian*, pp. 70–8; *Vit. Brit.*, iv (1767), Pls. 45, 51; J. Paine, *Plans of Noblemen's and Gentlemen's Houses*, ii (1783), Pls. 42–52.
70 J. Paine, *Plans etc.*, ii, Pl. 50.
71 A. Graves, *The Society of Artists* (1907), p. 186.
72 A plan on these lines occurs among some sketches by James Adam in the Clerk of Pennycuik collection (photostats in Soane Museum) dated 1753–5.
73 *Country Life*, 29 August and 5 September 1925.
74 For Adam's handling of the orders see J. Summerson, *Architecture in Britain: 1530–1830* (3rd ed. 1958), pp. 250–1.
75 A. T. Bolton, *The Architecture of* R. *and* J. *Adam* (1922), i, p. 37.
76 See note 121.
77 G. Richardson, *New Vit. Brit.*, (1802), i, Pls. 19–21.
78 H. Colvin, *Biog. Dict.* As Porden was born *c.* 1755, he would probably have been in the office during the erection of Heaton.
79 The date is from Colvin. I know of no description of this house.
80 For example: Baron Hill, Beaumaris (1776–9); Hurstmonceaux Pl., Sussex (*c.* 1777); Bowden House, Wilts. (1796).
81 *Country Life* (25 May 1929). Model and drawings in the Soane Museum.
82 Compare Tyringham (Figure 97).
83 J. Paine, *Plans, Elevations, etc.*, i, Pls. 1–29.
84 *Country Life* (3 and 10 January 1914).
85 R. Morris, *Rural Architecture* (1750), preface.
86 J. Crunden, *Convenient and Ornamental Architecture* (1767).
87 T. Rawlins, *Familiar Architecture; consisting of Original Designs for Gentlemen and Tradesmen* (1768).
88 Jose MacPacke [James Peacock], *Oikidia, or Nut-shells . . . Small Villas* (1785), p. 4.
89 C. Middleton, *Picturesque and Architectural Views* (1793), p. 9.
90 J. Malton, *A Collection of Designs for Rural Retreats* (1802), pp. 7–8.
91 *Vit. Brit.*, iii (*c.* 1724), p. 8. The reference is to the view of the Thames 'and the adjacent villas' from the tower of Claremont.
92 W. Kent, *The Designs of Inigo Jones* (1727), i, Table of Plates.
93 J. Gibbs, *Book of Architecture* (1728), Pl. 56. 'A draught made for a gentleman in Wiltshire'.
94 See p. 105.
95 H. Walpole, *Letters* (ed. Toynbee, 1903), iii, p. 119. Of Mereworth, Walpole says, 'Though it has cost an hundred thousand pounds, it is still only a fine villa'.
96 T. Rawlins (of Norwich), *Familiar Architecture* (1768), *passim.*
97 J. Lewis, *Original Designs* (1780), p. 4.
98 C. Middleton, *Picturesque and Architectural Views*, p. 9.
99 C. Hussey, *E.C.H.: Early Georgian* (1955), p. 58.
100 C. Hussey, *E.C.H.: Mid-Georgian* (1956), p. 234; *Vit. Brit.*, iii, Pls. 41–3.
101 *Vit. Brit.*, iii, Pl. 46.
102 *The Survey of London*, Vol. xiii, chap. 11.
103 *Country Life* (25 March 1916); H. M. Colvin, *Biog. Dict.*, p. 414; M.P.G. Draper and W.A. Eden, *Marble Hill House*, 1970.
104 *Vit. Brit.*, iii, Pl. 93.
105 R. Morris, *Essay in Defence, etc.* (1728), chap. xi and Pl. opp. p. 84.
106 *Vit. Brit.*, iv, Pls. 1–4.
107 *Country Life* (9 and 16 February 1916); R. Wittkower, 'Lord Burlington and William Kent' in *Archaeolog. Jnl.*, Vol. 102 (1947); J. Charlton, *A History and Description of Chiswick House and Gardens* (HMSO, 1958).
108 J. Gibbs, *Book of Architecture* (1728), Pl. 55; Colvin, *op. cit.*, p. 344.
109 *Country Life* (17 and 24 March 1944).
110 C. Hussey, *E.C.H.: Early Georgian*, p. 127.
111 No description of this house has been published. I am much indebted to Mr Jasper More for supplying me with a photograph and particulars.
112 W. Ison, *The Georgian Buildings of Bristol* (1952), pp. 177–81; I. Ware, *A Complete Body of Architecture* (1756), Pl. 40.
113 I. Ware, *op. cit.*, Pls. 54 and 55 ('a house built for Alexander Johnston, Esq., in Scotland'); and Pls. 56 and 57 ('a building designed for James Murray, Esq., of Broughton at Kellie').
114 *Country Life* (4 June 1910); aquatint by T. Malton in his collection of views of Taylor's works.
115 Data from Colvin, *op. cit.*; aquatint as above.
116 These bays were a popular feature in English design till well into the 19th century. In early examples they may be regarded as parts of octagons, protruding from the house, and thus as strictly formal elements in a formal plan. Mr John Harris has drawn my attention to a villa plan in the Ashmolean Museum, Oxford (Gibbs drawings, ii, p. 28), with four of these bays, probably in the hand of John Talman and therefore earlier than 1726. But the plan seems to me to be derivative in character and I suspect a Burlingtonian original. In executed works an early example is at Saltram, Devon, *c.* 1745, almost certainly by Ware (C. Hussey, *E.C.H.: Mid-Georgian*, p. 125). The popularity of 'Octangular bow windows' is noted by J. Crunden in *Convenient and Ornamental Architecture* (1767); a house built with them, he says, 'makes a great figure in the eyes of country people, and renders, as they think, the house very chearful'.
117 *Country Life* (29 June 1944); *Vit. Brit.*, iv (1767), Pl. 74.
118 A close imitation in brick and stone is Bedfont Lodge, Bedfont, Mx., built for George Engelheart, miniature painter to George III, in 1783. A design 'in the style of' Asgill House, is in R. Elsam's *An Essay on Rural Architecture* (1803), Pl. 6.
119 *Country Life* (28 April and 5 May 1923). The house has since been demolished.
120 *Vit. Brit.*, iv., Pls. 8–10, without architect's name. Colvin, *op. cit.*, p. 866, quotes W. H. Leeds as an authority for the attribution.
121 I. Ware, *A Complete Body of Architecture* (1756), Pls. 52 and 53. *Vit. Brit.*, v (1771), Pl. 46. The inclusion of a plate in the latter work, in spite of earlier publication, seems to confirm the importance attached to Wrotham at the time.
122 C. Hussey, *E.C.H.: Early Georgian*, p. 204.

123 *Vit. Brit.*, v, Pls. 36–7.
124 *Ibid.*, iv (1767), Pls. 11–13.
125 A. Oswald, *Country Houses of Dorset* (1935), p. 93; *Vit. Brit.*, v, Pls. 61–3.
126 *Vit. Brit.*, iv (1767), Pls. 11–17.
127 C. Hussey, *E.C.H.: Mid-Georgian*, p. 111.
128 *Country Life* (30 July and 6 August 1938).
129 N. Pevsner, *Hertfordshire* (1953), p. 101.
130 *Vit. Brit.*, v, 11–13.
131 A. Rowan, *Designs for Castles and Country Villas by Robert and James Adam*, 1985.
132 C. Hussey, *E.C.H.: Mid-Georgian*, p. 135.
133 *Ibid.*, p. 184.
134 J. Soane, *Plans, Elevations and Sections* (1788), Pls. 18–22.
135 The designs of Tyringham were not published by Soane till 1832. *Country Life* (25 May and 1 June 1929).
136 G. Richardson, *New Vit. Brit.*, Pl. 10.
137 The use of the word 'tribune' for a small central lobby or hall uniting the back and front parts of a house goes back to an ideal plan dedicated by Colen Campbell to Lord Halifax (*Vit. Brit.*, i, Pl. 28).
138 J. Lewis, *Original Designs* (2nd ed., 1797), Pls. 3–8.
139 J. Summerson, *The Life and Work of John Nash* (1980).

VII · Sir John Soane and the Furniture of Death

1 (J. Soane), *Memoirs of the Professional Life of an Architect* (1835), pp. 13–14. A. T. Bolton, *The Portrait of Sir John Soane*, p. 4.
2 Plates xxxviii and xxxix. Preliminary sketches for the design are in the Soane album labelled 'Original Sketches' (Soane case C). Among finished drawings in the museum there are only plans (xlv, 1(16)).
3 J. Harris, *Sir William Chambers* (1970), pp. 24–25; Pls. 4, 6, 7, Fig. 1.
4 Soane drawings, xiv, 1 (19).
5 Probably No. 98, Picture Room Recess, Soane Museum.
6 Soane drawings, lxiii, 6.
7 This type of ceiling had been anticipated by George Dance II at Cranbury Park, Hants. D. Stroud, *George Dance* (1971), Pls. 24 and 25, where a derivative from Pietro Santo Bartoli, *Gli Antichi Sepolchri* (1699 and 1768) is suggested.
8 That the design of this gateway specially intrigued Soane is shown by the number of variations in Soane drawings, xxxii, 1.
9 J. Soane, *Sketches in Architecture* (1793), Pls. 2–10.
10 Engravings of wall decorations at the Villa Negroni. A set of eight hangs in the Breakfast Room at the Soane Museum, but all have been trimmed for framing. The Museum has untrimmed proofs of Nos. 1, 2, 4 and 8 (two of each). Nos. 1 and 2 are signed by Angelo Campanella after R. Mengs; Nos. 4 and 8 by the same after A. Maron. They are dated between 1778 and 1786.
11 Marked sale catalogues are in the Soane Museum Library.
12 A. T. Bolton, *The Works of Sir John Soane* (1924), p. xxx. J. Wilton-Ely, 'The Architectural Models of Sir John Soane', *Architectural History*, xii (1969), p. 37.
13 Soane drawings, lxiii, 6 (23–48). J. Wilton-Ely, *op. cit.*, p. 37, fig. 18c (the caption is misplaced).
14 The main sources for the history of the Dulwich art gallery and mausoleum are: *Memoirs of the late Noel Desenfans Esq containing also, a plan for preserving the portraits of Distinguished Characters etc.* (1810); E. Cook, *Catalogue of the Pictures in the Gallery of Alleyn's College . . . Dulwich* (1914); articles on N. Desenfans and F. Bourgeois in DNB.
15 PRO, PROB 11/1465.
16 *Ibid.*
17 Soane drawings, xlvii, 3. Bolton, *Works, ut supra*, p. 21.
18 Soane drawings, lxvii, 6 (15).
19 Desenfans's will, *ut supra.*
20 Cook, *Catalogue, ut supra.*
21 PRO, PROB 11/1559.
22 The design passed through many stages as is shown in Soane drawings xv, 1 and 2 and lxv, 4 and 5.
23 Sir J. Soane, *Lectures on Architecture*, ed. A. T. Bolton (1929), p. 126.
24 Soane drawings, xxxii, 2A.
25 Soane drawings, xxxii, 3 (48).
26 Bolton, *Portrait, ut supra*, pp. 179–180.
27 Soane drawings, lxiii, 6 (5–9). The monument and its iron enclosure were restored in 1925 by a group of architects led by Maurice B. Adams and W. R. Lethaby. The ironwork has mostly vanished, presumably taken for 'salvage' in the Second World War, but a fragment remains. A drawing by Raffles Davison of the monument as restored is in *The Builder*, 1926, p. 686.
28 Soane drawings, lxiii, 7 (2).
29 B. de Montfaucon, *L'Antiquité Expliquée*, V, pt. 1, Pl. 122.
30 Soane drawings, lxiii, 7 (26).
31 Soane drawings, xlv, 4.
32 Bolton, *Portrait, ut supra*, pp. 218–219. The quotation which follows is from Vergil, *Aeneid*, vi, II. 885–688
33 *A Summary of the Minutes of the Commissioners for the National Debt* (HMSO, 1961), M 172–173.
34 Soane drawings, xlviii, 1. J. Wilton-Ely, *op. cit.*, pp. 26–29, Figs. 17a, b, c, and d, 18a and b and 21d (caption misplaced).
35 S. Mayer, *The Great Belzoni* (1959). Bolton, *Portrait, Sir John Soane*, 1927.
36 J. Summerson, 'Gandy and the Tomb of Merlin', AR, April 1941.

VIII · The Evolution of Soane's Bank Stock Office

1 H. R. Steel and F. R. Yerbury, *The Old Bank of England, London* (1930), Pls. lxiii, lxiv and lxvi (photographs) and folding plate (measured drawing of longitudinal sections). Sets of Yerbury's photographs are in the Soane Museum and the National Monuments Record.
2 Records by Soane of Taylor's halls, showing the mode of construction, are in SM, Drawer 1, Set 2, Nos. 11, 12 and 13. The vertical timbers supporting the roof appear to have been fixed in iron 'shoes' with a vertical member transferring the weight to the column below. The specimen in the museum (Inventory M2 and M3) consists of an entablature and capital removed from Taylor's 4 p.c. Office on its demolition in 1815.
3 SM Pf. 3/3, 4, 5, 12, 37, 49.
4 The idea of new orders, based on forms derived from Nature had, however, been propagated by the Abbé Laugier in his *Observations sur l'Architecture*, 1765, Part vi. The idea of a central column supporting a radial vault

may conceivably have been suggested to Dance by medieval chapter-houses (Westminster Abbey, Lincoln, Salisbury).

5 The only dated drawings after Chawner's survey of November 1791 are those dated 1 March and 10 March 1792, from both of which it is obvious that the design was still fluid. However the Journal and the Day Book of the Soane office show that Soane's pupils, Thomas Chawner and Frederick Meyer, had been engaged on drawings of the Bank Stock Office and that Soane had already submitted two sets of plans. On 21 and 22 November 1791 Chawner was 'drawing sections' and on 23 November, Chawner and Meyer were 'drawing section and plan of alterations'. On the following day 'Mr. Soane took with him No. 4 sketches of designs for Bank Stock Office, viz. 1 plan, 1 plan showing the skylights, 1 longitudinal section and 1 latitudinal section'. On 1 December the Journal records that Soane was 'at the Bank with plans and sections for alterations to Bank Stock Off.'. On 2 December Meyer was copying plans and sections and on 3 December Chawner and Meyer were 'drawing sections' while Chawner was 'drawing a perspective'. On 6 December 'Mr. Soane took No. 7 drawings of Bank Stock Office to the Bank', viz. 1 perspective view, 1 longitudinal and 2 latitudinal sections, 2 plans and 1 'plan and section as it now is'. He also delivered a Report. On 7, 13 and 15 December both Meyer and Chawner were engaged on perspective views. No further drawings are recorded until 25 February 1792 when Chawner was making a 'rough drawing' and Meyer a section which engaged him again on 27 and 29. No drawings by pupils or clerks are recorded in March, the month when the design must have been finalized. The explanation for this is probably that the final working drawings were made in Soane's office at the Bank of England and not at his house in Welbeck Street. The draughtsmen employed at the Bank in 1792 were William Lodder and Charles Ebdon and to them must probably be ascribed the highly finished set of sections and plans at various levels (Pf. 3/12, 33, 37, 48 and Dr. 1, set 4, No. 6) as well as the drawing for an under-floor heating scheme (Pf. 3/34–36) and a number of large-scale details of very high quality, many of which are not as executed (Pf. 3/39–47). In the Soane Museum is a wooden model (cf. Fig. 1), referred to in Soane's office Day Book 1782–93, Saturday 23 February 1793: 'The Bank about Model of the Stock Office 6 days Parkin'.

6 'Original Sketches' (Soane cpd., shelf c (1)), Nos. 170, 173, 174, 176 and 177.

7 D. Stroud, *George Dance* (1791), p. 94; Pls. 2 and 25.

8 *Ibid.*, pp. 113–15, 118; Pls. 36, 39a.

9 R. Wood and J. Dawkins, *Ruins of Palmyra* (1753). The references, keyed to letters on the drawing, are noted as 'C. Pal. pl. 51 and pl. 23' (floriated panels) and 'E. Pal. pl. 15 fret and pl. 19 fret'. Another reference reads 'B. The Temple of the Winds with Variations' but the relevance of this is obscure.

10 In France the use of fire-clay cones for vaults had already been recommended by the Comte d'Espie, *Manière de rendre toutes sortes d'édifices incombustibles ou traité de la construction des voûtes faites avec des briques et du plâtre* (Paris, 1754), a book noted by Laugier in the second edition of his *Essai*; see R. D. Middleton, *Warburg Journal*, XXVI (1963), 102.

11 This is not, strictly speaking, a Byzantine building, having been rebuilt by the Crusaders in the 12th century. It may be described as Sicilian Romanesque on a Byzantine plan.

12 Soane had a coloured drawing made for his own lectures, 1809 onwards, based on Lebrun. SM Dr.26, Set 8. Soane exhibited the drawing as showing 'the degraded state of the arts' at the period.

IX · Charting the Victorian Building World

1 The 'Building *World*' as used here is not to be confused with the 'Building *Industry*' whose components can be precisely defined in terms of organized labour.

2 The copy in the RIBA library is handsomely bound in gilt-embossed cloth.

3 H. Hobhouse, *Thomas Cubitt, Masterbuilder* (1956), pp. 442 and 454.

4 *Ibid.*, App. 5, pp. 490–1.

5 *The Builder* (1868), p. 201.

6 John Richards, *Treatise on the Construction and Operation of Wood-working Machines* (1872); *On the Arrangement, Care and Operation of Wood-working Machines* (1873).

7 M. H. Port (ed.), *The Houses of Parliament*, pp. 120, 215, 217, 284–5.

8 *The Builder* (1860), p. 553.

9 *The Builder* (1878), p. 865.

10 Hobhouse, *op. cit.* pp. 310 et. seq. *The Builder* (1852), p. 285.

11 *Bricks and Brickmaking: An Historical, Technical and Descriptive Sketch* (a pamphlet issued by Wood and Ivery of the Albion Blue Brick and Tile Works, N. Bromwich). Reviewed in *The Builder* (1878), p. 863.

12 *The Builder* (1867), p. 6.

13 *Building News* (1869), pp. 136, 141. J. Simmons, *St Pancras Station* (1968), p. 63.

14 Hobhouse, *op. cit.*, pp. 308–9. For hollow bricks in general see S. B. Hamilton, 'The History of Hollow Bricks', *Trans. British Ceramic Soc.*, (February 1959).

15 *Building News* (1866), pp. 254–5.

16 *The Builder* (1870), pp. 485–7.

17 *The Builder* (1868), p. 354; (1871), p. 419; (1873), p. 199 for an account of Wellington Mills, Lambeth, which Parr and Strong apparently undertook as architects.

18 *The Builder* (1864), p. 727 gives the upper part of the Gloucester Road houses, with details of the tiles. For 'The Logs' see *The Builder* (1868), pp. 876–7.

19 *The Builder* (1862), pp. 904–5, 925–7; *APSD.*, *s.v.* Taylor, John. Another invention of Taylor's was a combination of concrete and facing bricks. It was executed at Hersham Lodge, Walton, Surrey. *The Builder* (1868), pp. 658–9.

20 Port, *op. cit.*, Pl. VII.

21 M. D. Wyatt, *Specimens of Geometrical Mosaic Manufacture by Maw and Co.* (1857).

22 See illustration of Simpson and Sons' 'Art-tile Chimney-piece' at the International Exhibition, 1871, designed by H. W. Lonsdale. *The Builder* (1871), p. 346.

23 *Building News* (1859), p. 196.

24 *The Builder* (1863), p. 899.

25 *The Builder* (1868), pp. 523–5, 530–1. At the architect, Charles Barry Jr's request, the material was tested at Kirkcaldy's testing works in Southwark Street.

26 *The Builder* (1870), pp. 467–69.

27 *Survey of London*, Vol. 38, p. 189.

28 *Ibid.*, p. 210.

29 Article on Sir H. Doulton in DNB. *The Royal Doulton*

Potteries: a Brief Summary of the Rise and Expansion during six Reigns. (N.D.; *c.* 1925).
30 Cf. Doulton's whole-page advertisements in *The Builder* (1871), p. 55 and elsewhere.
31 *Survey of London*, Vol. 38, p. 107.
32 *APSD, s.v.* 'Cement'. Also, paper by J. B. White in *Civil Engineers Journal*, 1882.
33 *The Builder* (1844), p. 285.
34 See the correspondence on the nature of cements, started by James Pulham in *The Builder* (1845), p. 160 and continuing on pp. 160, 275, 293.
35 *The Builder* (1871), p. 315.
36 *The Builder* (1871), p. 405.
37 *APSD, s.v.* Paving.
38 *The Builder* (1843), pp. 431, 450. In 1857 Arrowsmith introduced their patent Solid Swiss Parquetrie 'which is gradually becoming known in England and promises to supply a want'.
39 Arrowsmiths advertised occasionally in *The Builder* (e.g. 1871, p. 96).
40 Wyman's *Architect's, Engineer's etc. Directory* (1868).
41 J. Gloag and D. Bridgwater, *History of Cast Iron in Architecture* (1948).
42 W. Fairbairn, *On the Application of Cast and Wrought Iron to Building Purposes* (1854), pp. 82, 83. Figs. 35, 36 and 37.
43 *The Builder* (1866), pp. 147–8. Article based on experiments at Kirkaldy's testing works.
44 Advertisement preceding title-page in W. and T. Phillips, *Architectural Iron Construction*, Pl. 1, 'Beams and Girders', (1870).
45 *APSD* (Papworth's grangerized copy in the Soane Museum), *s.v.*, 'Iron'.
46 Port, *op. cit.*, pp. 101, 217.
47 Macfarlane's richly illustrated catalogue (5th ed., 1862), a copy of which is in the British Library, contains designs for the following: pipes, gutters, roof plates, terminals (finials, crosses etc.), railings, panels (ventilators, gratings and floor plates), columns (pilasters, brackets and spandrels), sign letters, desks etc., standards, lamps, drinking fountains, ablutionary appliances, urinals, water-closets, ordure closets, ash bins and plumbers castings.
48 *The Builder* (1871), pp. 244–5.
49 *The Builder* (1865), p. 29.
50 *APSD, s.v.* 'Floor (Fireproof)'; also 'Fox and Barrett's fireproof construction'.
51 Crook, *op. cit.*, p. 143.
52 *The Builder* (1858), pp. 289–90.
53 *The Builder* (1871), pp. 80–81.
54 Trevor I. Williams, *A History of the British Gas Industry* (1981), p. 33.
55 *APSD, s.v.* 'Sunlight or Sunburners'.
56 William G. Kirkcaldy, *Illustrations of David Kirkcaldy's System of Mechanical Testing.* Pivately printed, 1891. B.L. 8765. g. 21.
57 *The Builder* (1872), p. 24.

X · The London Building World of the 1860s

1 *Illustrated London News* (1860), I, p. 229.
2 GLC Record Office, County Hall: MBW 1,772, 1,773, 1,774. The peak year was 1868, when fees were received in respect of 8,863 new buildings.
3 T. C. Barker and M. Robbins, *A History of London Transport*, I (the 19th century), 1963.
4 *Accounts and Papers, 1863*, LIII, pt. 1, p. 391.
5 *Ibid.*, p. 394.
6 *Accounts and Papers, 1873*, LXXI, pt. i, p. xl.
7 The practice of publishing tenders started in *The Builder* in 1845, with the object of exposing careless or dishonest estimating by builders leading to wild variations in prices. The lists were sent in by architects and were perhaps solicited, though there was also the incentive of self-advertisement.
8 *The Builder*, (1860), p. 109.
9 R. W. Postgate, *The Builder's History* (1923), p. 197.
10 *Report of the Royal Commission on Trade Unions*, 1867, P.P. 1867, XXXII, p. 105.
11 *The Builder*, contains periodical reports on the Builders' Benevolent Institution. See especially 1861, p. 740, for report of annual dinner at which the Lord Mayor, William Cubitt, presided.
12 *Building News*, (1866), p. 87, mentions the small builder, employing not more than six men, 'whose largest jobs are only shop-fronts'. The census returns for 1851 show that at that date more builders employed ten men than any other number. *Accounts and Papers, 1852–3*, LXXXVIII, pt. 1, p. 28.
13 H. Hobhouse, *Thomas Cubitt, Masterbuilder* (1971), Chap. 2. E. W. Cooney, 'The Origins of the Victorian Master Builders', *Economic History Review*, ser. 2, VIII (1955–6), pp. 167–76.
14 See the account of the London building industry in F. H. W. Sheppard, *London 1808–70: The Infernal Wen* (1971), pp. 95–101.
15 Hobhouse, *op. cit.*, p. 102.
16 Four or five hundred men digging foundations at the Foreign Office were 'discharged gradually as the work goes on'. *Report . . . Trades Unions, ut supra*, p. 107.
17 *The Builder* (1851), p. 734. The strike was for a short Saturday. Myers met five or six hundred of the men in discussion.
18 *Ibid.*, (1876), p. 211. This figure was stated in the account of a visit by the Architectural Association to the works in Gray's Inn Road.
19 Public Record Office, 1861 census returns, RG9/126, f. 62.
20 *The Builder*, (1870), p. 831.
21 *Ibid.* (1856), p. 31.
22 *Ibid.* (1865), p. 32.
23 The quotations are from the obituary notice of William Higgs, *The Builder*, (1883), I, p. 93.
24 Postgate, *op. cit.*, p. 171.
25 Public Record Office, 1861 census returns, RG9/362, f. 17.
26 B. Ferrey, *Recollections of A.N.W. Pugin* (1861), pp. 185–6.
27 Will, Probate Registry, Somerset House. Among Myers's effects were 'a dining-room table designed by me', an ebony and painted cabinet representing the life of St Joseph, a portrait of himself and three other paintings, a drawing by him of the reredos as restored at Beverley Minster, the original drawing by Haag of the Medieval Court at the 1851 Exhibition, and various books, prints, drawings and manuscripts. Owen Jones's *Grammar of Ornament* and Myers's watch were itemized among bequests to the eldest son. Myers lived at 143 Clapham Road but the house has been demolished.
28 *Illustrated London News* (10 May 1862), p. 481. *The Times*, 6 December 1895, p. 6, quoting *Sussex Daily News. Ibid.* (8 March 1902), p. 9.

29 R. K. Middlemas, *The Master Builders* (1963), pp. 126–7.
30 *Ibid.*, pp. 130, 136.
31 Wills of Charles and Thomas Lucas, Probate Registry, Somerset House.
32 D. Braithwaite, *Building in the Blood: the Story of Dove Brothers of Islington* (1981).
33 Will of Benjamin Dixon Dove, Probate Registry, Somerset House.
34 *The Builder*, (1873) p. 651.
35 *Report . . . Trades Unions, ut supra*, p. 107.
36 *The Builder* (1857), p. 224.
37 *The Times* (9 October 1884), p. 5, col. 6.
38 *The Builder* (1883), I, p. 93.
39 *Ibid.* (1868), p. 201.
40 Hobhouse, *op. cit.*, Appendix 5, pp. 490–1.
41 Greater London Council, *Survey of London* (ed. F. H. W. Sheppard), XXXVII.
42 *Victorian Suburb: a Study of the Growth of Camberwell* (1961); 'The Speculative Builders and Developers of Victorian London', *Victorian Studies*, XI, supplement (1968).
43 *The Builder* (1874), p. 530.
44 There is no history of the RIBA. *The Growth and Work of the RIBA* (ed. J. A. Gotch, 1934) contains a historical sketch by the editor and other papers. See also C. L. Eastlake, 'An Historical Sketch of the Institute', *Trans. RIBA*, 1875–6, pp. 258 *et seq.*
45 J. Summerson, *The Architectural Association, 1847–1947* (1947).
46 B. Kaye, *The Development of the Architectural Profession in Britain* (1960).
47 Sir Gilbert Scott's account of his fellow pupils in Edmeston's office, which he entered in 1827, is relevant. G. G. Scott, *Personal and Professional Recollections* (1879), pp. 57, 67.
48 A typical case is described in a letter to *The Builder* (1858), pp. 214–15, of a youth who, being articled for five years at a premium of nearly £320, found himself 'placed exactly on a footing with salaried clerks and messengers'. On remonstrating, he was told that this treatment was 'customary in the profession'.
49 H. Lovegrove, *Some Account of the District Surveyors' Association of London* (Beckenham, 1915). C. C. Knowles and P. H. Pitt. *The History of Building Regulation in London 1189–1972* (1972).
50 Obituary notice, *The Builder* (1887), II, p. 798.
51 Seventeen warehouses by him occur in *The Builder*'s lists of tenders between 1860 and 1868. Obituary notice, *The Builder* (1877), p. 328.
52 Obituary notice, *The Builder* (1901), II, p. 468.
53 Obituary notice, *The Builder* (1900), I, p. 406.
54 *The Builder* (1861), p. 130.
55 Article in *The Dictionary of National Biography*.
56 Article in *The Dictionary of National Biography*.
57 Article in *The Dictionary of National Biography*.
58 For a good account of the administration of the Office of Works see article in *The Builder* (1877), pp. 897 *et seq.*
59 *The Builder* (1868), p. 827.

XI · The Victorian Rebuilding of the City of London, 1840–1870

1 For a good brief account of the London money market at this period, see F. H. W. Shephard, *London 1808–70: The Infernal Wen* (1971). For architecture, the only modern work is Henry-Russell Hitchcock, *Early Victorian Architecture in Britain* (New Haven, 1954), which, however, only deals with the years before 1851. The main sources are the periodicals of the time, especially *The Builder* and *Building News*, in which the more significant buildings are illustrated and described. In addition, *The Builder* contains valuable editorial reviews of city architecture of which the following are the most important: *The Builder*, 16 (1858), pp. 717–18, 842–43, 862–64; 22 (1864), pp. 678–80, 713–15, 769–70; 24 (1866), pp. 641–43, 677–79, 792–94.
2 *The Builder*, 22 (1864), p. 748.
3 *The Builder*, 24 (1866), p. 641.
4 B. Kaye, *The Development of the Architectural Profession in Britain: A Sociological Study* (1960), pp. 109–12.
5 H. E. Raynes, *A History of British Insurance* (1948).
6 The building is demolished, but the sculpture, in Coade's patent stone, is preserved at the Horniman Museum, London.
7 H. M. Colvin, *A Biographical Dictionary of English Architects, 1660–1840* (1954).
8 *The Builder*, 22 (1864), p. 713.
9 *Civil Engineer and Architect's Journal*, I (1837), p. 29.
10 A. E. Richardson, *Monumental Classic Architecture in Great Britain and Ireland during the Eighteenth and Nineteenth Centuries* (1914), p. 92.
11 W. Schooling, *Alliance Assurance 1824–1924* (1924).
12 D. Watkin, *The Life and Work of C. R. Cockerell* (1974), pp. 225–29; P. G. M. Dickson, *The Sun Insurance Office 1710–1960* (1960).
13 Raynes, *op. cit.*
14 *London and Its Vicinity Exhibited in 1851* (1851), pp. 240–42, gives a list of companies with dates of foundation.
15 *The Builder*, I (1843), p. 470.
16 *Companion to the Almanac*, (1849), p. 237. This book is usually bound together with the *British Almanac* but paged separately.
17 *The Builder*, 15 (1857), p. 22.
18 It stood on the curved angle of Cannon Street and Budge Row. Very small photographs in *The Builder*, 78 (1900), pp. 214–15.
19 *The Builder*, 10 (1852), p. 582; *Civil Engineer and Architects' Journal*, 16 (1852), 8. Cost £8,000.
20 *The Builder*, 17 (1859), pp. 392–93. Reliefs in spandrels represented history, industry, mercy, peace, plenty, sculpture, painting, faith, temperance, music, and poetry.
21 *The Builder*, 15 (1857), p. 319.
22 *Building News*, 13 (1866), pp. 25–27; *Illustrated London News*, 47 (1865), p. 604.
23 B. E. Supple, *The Royal Exchange Assurance: A History of British Insurance, 1720–1970* (Cambridge, 1970), p. 182.
24 *The Builder*, 15 (1857), pp. 118–19.
25 *Companion to the Almanac* (1859), p. 257; (1860), p. 250.
26 *The Builder*, 18 (1860), pp. 640–41.
27 *Building News*, 4 (1858), p. 723; 12 (1865), p. 447.
28 *The Builder*, 23 (1865), pp. 502–3. Cost: about £16,000.
29 *The Builder*, 21 (1863), pp. 11–13. Cost: about £13,000.
30 T. E. G. Gregory, *The Westminster Bank through a Century* (1936), i, p. 288. *Companion to the Almanac* (1839), pp. 236, 238. Watkin, *Life and Work of C. R. Cockerell*, pp. 221–25.
31 *Companion to the Almanac* (1858), p. 246.
32 A. L. G. Mackay, *The Australian Banking and Credit System* (1931), p. 4.

33 *The Builder*, 13 (1855), p. 79.
34 *Companion to the Almanac* (1857), p. 243.
35 *The Builder*, 16 (1858), pp. 863–64. Lowest tender was £4,666 (*The Builder*, 14 (1856), p. 392). W. Laxton, *Examples of Building Construction*, Vol. for 1857–56, Pls. 13, 14, 19–22.
36 *The Builder*, 18 (1860), p. 804. Contract price, £14,830 *The Builder*, 20 (1862), 604–5.
37 *The Builder*, 22 (1864), p. 758–59.
38 *Building News*, 12 (1865), pp. 608–9, 613.
39 *The Builder*, 23 (1864), pp. 607, 609.
40 *The Builder*, 23 (1865), pp. 329, 834–35, 901–3, 909. Sculpture includes groups representing Manchester, England, Wales, and London; single figures representing Birmingham, Newcastle-under-Lyme, and Dover; and panels representing arts, commerce, science, manufactures, agriculture, and navigation.
41 *The Builder*, 29 (1871), pp. 646–47.
42 *The Builder*, 31 (1873), pp. 906–7.
43 *The Builder*, 35 (1877), pp. 882–86.
44 W. T. C. King, *History of the London Discount Market*, (1936), pp. 196, 217 *et seq.*
45 *The Builder*, 24 (1866), pp. 678–79, 792. *Building News*, 15 (1868), pp. 11, 29, 147.
46 E. I'Anson, 'Some Notices of Office Buildings in the City of London', *Transactions of the RIBA*, 15 (1864–65), pp. 25–36.
47 *Companion to the Almanac* (1846), p. 235.
48 *Building News*, 3 (1857), pp. 1125, 1127.
49 *The Builder*, 18, (1860), p. 291.
50 *The Builder*, 17 (1859), p. 322.
51 *The Builder*, 29 (1871), pp. 187, 189.
52 *Building News*, 14 (1867), pp. 142, 145.
53 *The Builder*, 22 (1864), 273. *Building News*, 11 (1864), 134–35.
54 *Building News*, 13 (1866), pp. 595, 661, 678, 695.
55 *The Builder*, 22 (1864), pp. 769–70.
56 *The Builder*, 24 (1866), pp. 466–67.
57 *The Builder*, 28 (1870), pp. 227, 230.
58 *The Builder*, 19 (1861), pp. 124–25.
59 *The Builder*, 29 (1871), pp. 506–7. *Building News*, 25 (1873), pp. 8, 17.
60 *The Builder*, 31 (1873), p. 379.
61 *Ibid.*, pp. 358, 606–7.
62 *Ibid.*, p. 632.
63 *Companion to the Almanac*, (1854), p. 257; *Illustrated London News*, 26 (1854), p. 269.
64 *The Builder*, 16 (1858), p. 717. *Building News*, 3 (1857), p. 261.
65 *The Builder*, 22 (1864), pp. 62–63.
66 *The Builder*, 17 (1859), p. 632.
67 *The Builder*, 22 (1864), p. 362.
68 *The Builder*, 24 (1866), pp. 850–51.
69 *The Builder*, 26 (1868), pp. 747–49.

XII · The London Suburban Villa, 1850–1880

1 At the AA. Reported in *The Builder* (1857), p. 575.
2 He died in 1865. APS *Dictionary*.
3 Son of the architect of St Dunstan's in the West; he died in 1870.
4 S. Lewis, *The History and Topography of Islington.*
5 *The Builder* (1849), p. 163, and RA Catalogue, 1849.
6 Prospectus maps with highly imaginative perspective sketches are in the RIBA Library. Another estate by Kendall was at Twickenham, where he designed the grotesque Tudor villa on the site of Pope's villa. A characteristic and amusing villa by him is 'Sutton Lodge', Heathfield Terrace, Turnham Green. (Pl. 205).
7 Apparently by H. Bassett, 1844. See RA Catalogue for that year.
8 APSD, under *Taylor, J.*
9 *Building News* (1858), p. 752.
10 *The Builder* (1856), pp. 645 and 668.
11 *The Builder* (1856), p. 512.
12 'Let us glory in all styles; character is the thing,' said Alfred Bailey in a paper at the Architectural Association. *The Builder* (1853), p. 713.
13 *Parallèle des Maisons de Paris construites depuis 1830 jusqu'à nos jours.* (1st ed. 1850; 2nd ed. 1857). In effect, a continuation of Krafft. The copy in the AA Library belonged to Charles Hadfield.
14 For Mr R. Griffith, whose monogram was displayed on the pilasters of the porch. Tenders in *The Builder* (1853), p. 444. A view of the house was exhibited at the Architectural Exhibition, 1856. *The Builder* (1856), p. 70. Although still standing, the house (No. 153 Tulse Hill) having been wrecked by bombing, was stripped of its ornaments in 1947 and is now unrecognizable.
15 Nos. 311 and 313 and Nos. 333 and 335 ('Alma Villas') High Road. They were for sale at £550 each. *The Builder* (1856), p. 70.
16 *The Builder* (1859), p. 322. I cannot trace this villa.
17 See APSD under both names.
18 *The Builder* (1853), p. 429; *Building News* (1857), p. 1202.
19 *Building News* (1857), pp. 108, 383 and 857.
20 It is No. 1 Middleton Grove (formerly Road), Islington, N7, and is part of a group of houses, all by Truefitt. *Villa and Cottage Architecture* (1868), Pls. LV and LVI.
21 Nos. 326–342 (even).
22 The whole road has Truefitt character, but it looks as if, in some cases, a builder had a pretty free hand. Moreover, three other architects, Ledbury, Cowell and Dennison, contributed houses to the estate.
23 *Villa and Cottage Architecture*, pp. 31–32.
24 'Fairwood', No. 104 Sydenham Hill, an Elizabethan style house. Derelict in 1947. See *Village and Cottage Architecture*, Pl. LXIII to LXV.
25 Presidential address at the AA 7 October 1853, reported in *The Builder* (1853).
26 Perhaps Sancton Wood, in Nos. 42–44 Gresham Street, City, 1852, was the first to do this.
27 *The Builder* (1873), p. 376. Cost £1,700.
28 *The Builder* (1875), p. 517. Cost £2,293.
29 *The Builder* (1874), p. 404. Cost £2,000.
30 *Building News* (1875), p. 80.
31 *The Builder* (1875), p. 742.
32 *The Builder* (1877), p. 464.
33 *The Builder* (1872), p. 623 and *The Builder* (1874), p. 636. E. Hodder, *The Life and Work of the Seventh Earl of Shaftesbury* (1886), Vol. 3, p. 360.
34 In the *Notes and Queries* column for 1882, for example, 'Spread Eagle' wrote: 'Will some kind reader furnish me with a design for three villas in a row, the cost of the three not to exceed £850. Please state terms for details etc.' G. M. Jay promptly furnished a design, which was reproduced, though it is not recorded whether 'Spread Eagle' applied for and paid for the 'details'.
35 *Building News* (1876), p. 622; *Building News* (1877), p. 36.

36 *Building News* (1877), p. 192.
37 *Building News* (1877).

XIII · The British Contemporaries of Frank Lloyd Wright

1 Charles Marriott, *Modern English Architecture* (London, 1924), p. 129.
2 T. Howarth, *Charles Rennie Mackintosh and the Modern Movement* (London, 1952).
3 *Ibid.*, p. 247.
4 R. Blomfield, *Richard Norman Shaw* (London, 1940), p. 49.
5 *Ibid.*, p. 46 and Fig. 47.
6 N. Pevsner, *Pioneers of the Modern Movement*, (London and New York, 1936), p. 151, Pl. 48.
7 The two illustrations of the Bristol Library reproduced here (Pls. XXIII, 4, 5) are from *The Builder*, 2 September 1905. They would certainly be known to Mackintosh. Photographs of the completed building were published in the *Architectural Review*, XXIV (1908), pp. 239–47.
8 Illustrated with perspective by Raffles Davison, plan and description, in *The Builder*, 15 May 1903; with photographs in *Architectural Review*, XIX (1906), pp. 120–27.
9 Marriott, *op. cit.*, p. 124.
10 The illustration reproduced here is from *Academy Architecture*, II (1908), p. 29. See also *The Builder*, 8 December 1906.
11 The illustration reproduced here is from *Academy Architecture*, II (1908), p. 22. See also *Architectural Review*, XXV (1909), p. 47.
12 Pevsner, *op. cit.*, p. 160.
13 Howarth, *op. cit.*, p. 157.
14 *Ibid.*, pp. 94–107.
15 C. Hussey, *The Work of Sir Robert Lorimer* (London, 1931). For a design by Lorimer strictly comparable to the Helensburgh house see *The British Home of To-day* (ed. W. Shaw Sparrow; London, 1904), p. B58.
16 M. H. B. Scott, *Houses and Gardens* (London, 1906).
17 Pevsner, *op. cit.*, (references as indexed).
18 *Ernest Gimson, His Life and Work* (London, 1924).
19 J. H. G. Archer, 'Edgar Wood', *Journal of the Royal Institute of British Architects*, LXII (1954–55), pp. 50–53.
20 J. Winmill, *Charles Canning Winmill* (London, 1946).
21 N. Pevsner, 'George Walton, His Life and Work', *Journal of the Royal Institute of British Architects*, XLVI, (1939), p. 537. (Reprinted in *Studies in Art, Architecture and Design*, II, London, 1968).
22 H. S. Goodhart-Rendel, 'The Work of Beresford Pite and Halsey Ricardo', *Journal of the Royal Institute of British Architects*, XLIII (1936), p. 117.
23 *Building News* (9 August 1895), p. 189 and inset plate.
24 Both works are illustrated in Marriott, *op. cit.*, pp. 88, 152.

XV · The Case for a Theory of 'Modern' Architecture

1 J. Guadet, *Elements et Théorie de l'Architecture* (5th ed., 1909).
2 J. Belcher, *Essentials in Architecture* (1907).
3 Le Corbusier, *Vers une Architecture* (1st ed., 1923). Trans. as *Towards a New Architecture* (1927 and 1946).
4 The *De Re Aedificatoria* was written about 1450. The standard English translation is that of G. Leoni (1726 and 1739); it is available in a reprint (ed. J. Rykwert, 1955).
5 C. Perrault, *Les Dix Livres d'Architecture de Vitruve* (1673), Bk. V, cap. i (note 1) and Bk. VI, cap. v (note 8). These references are quoted by F. Algarotti, *Saggio sopre l'Architettura* (Vol. 3 in the *Opere*, 1791) as predictions of the rationalist attitude.
6 M. A. Laugier, *Essai sur l'Architecture* (1753) and *Observations sur l'Architecture* (1765).
7 J. N. L. Durand, *Précis des Leçons d'architecture données a l'école Polytechnique* (1802).
8 E. Viollet-le-Duc, *Entretiens sur l'Architecture* (1863–72).
9 De Cordemoy, *Nouveau Traité de Toute l'Architecture* (1714).
10 For Lodoli see E. Kaufmann, *Architecture in the Age of Reason* (1955), pp. 95–9 and J. Rykwert, *The First Moderns* (1980).
11 Frézier, *Dissertation sur les Ordres d'Architecture* (1738).
12 *The True Principles of Pointed or Christian Architecture* (1841) is a plea for Gothic as a rational style.
13 Dr J. Bronowski warns me that 'regular solids' in a strict sense includes figures never regarded as basic to architecture and excludes others which are. Time forbids reconsideration but, with this warning, my meaning will not, I think, be misunderstood.
14 For biographies of Le Corbusier and Moholy-Nagy, see M. Gauthier, *Le Corbusier, ou l'Architecture au Service de l'homme* (1944) and S. Moholy-Nagy, *Moholy-Nagy: experiment in totality*, (1950).
15 *The New Vision*, p. 54.
16 *Ibid.*, pp. 159–60.
17 *Kindergarten Chats* (1947). Elsewhere (p. 47) Sullivan uses 'organic' to mean that 'the part must have the same quality as the whole', an idea which goes back to Alberti.
18 B. Zevi, *Towards an Organic Architecture* (1950), p. 76.
19 *The New Vision*, p. 163.
20 *Space, Time and Architecture* (3rd ed., 1954), p. 432.
21 *Scope of Total Architecture* (1956), p. 49.
22 For a discussion of this point by an engineer, see Ove Arup, 'Modern Architecture: the Structural Fallacy', in *The Listener*, 7 July 1955.
23 'The New Brutalism', in *Architectural Review*, December 1955.

Sources of essays and of illustrations

Photo W.H. Allen/courtesy of Salmon Speed Architects: **146**; Photo Architectural Press: **100, 110, 111, 112**; Photo Annan: **223**; Commonwealth War Graves Commission: **231**; Copyright *Country Life*: **21, 69, 84, 87, 88**; Photo Keith Gibson: **222**; Reconstruction drawing by Leonora Ison: **55**; Photos A.F. Kersting: **86, 137, 230**; Photo Emily Lane: **145**; Copyright the Roman Catholic Archdiocese of Liverpool Trustees Incorporated: **229**; The British Architectural Library, RIBA: **31, 40, 49, 119, 180, 233, 235, 236, 237, 238**; British Museum, Department of Prints and Drawings: **24, 25** (Crace Collection xviii, 67), **26** (Crace Collection xviii, 62), **29** (Crace Collection xviii, 51), **32** (Crace Collection xviii, 66), **34** (Crace Collection xviii, 73); Greater London Photo Library: **190, 192**; Guildhall Library: **155**; National Portrait Gallery: **50**; The Dean and Chapter of St Paul's Cathedral: **57** (St P. i, 14), **58** (St P. i, 67); Courtesy of the Trustees of Sir John Soane's Museum: **97, 99, 105, 107, 108, 109, 115, 117, 118, 121** (Dr, ii, set 4), **122, 125** (Pf. 3/1), **126** (Pf. 3/18), **127** (OS 170), **128** (OS 175), **129** (OS 171), **130** (Pf. 3/15), **131** (Pf. 3/16), **132** (Pf. 3/19), **133** (Pf. 3/26), **134** (Pf. 3/22) / photo Conway Library, Courtauld Institute of Art: **5** (T 95), **18** (T 49), **19** (T 50), **20** (T 22), **23** (T 34) / photo Architectural Press: **101, 102, 104, 106, 114, 116** / photo Sydney Newbery/Architectural Press: **120**; Tate Gallery Archive, John Piper: **1** (83.6.6), **2** (159.2.6), **3** (82.3.4), **4** (81.2.1); Department of Prints and Drawings, Victoria and Albert Museum: **65**; Photo Royal Commission on the Historical Monuments of England: **6, 7, 9, 11, 13, 14, 15, 17, 68, 76, 96, 143, 177, 184, 188, 195**; The Warden and Fellows of All Souls College, Oxford: **53** (A.S. ii, 34), **54** (A.S. ii, 14), **60** (A.S. ii, 31), **61** (A.S. ii, 25), **62** (A.S. ii, 17), **63** (A.S., ii, 32), **77** (i, 84); The Bodleian Library: **48** (Gough XX, 2B); The Provost and Fellows of Worcester College, Oxford: **39, 41**; Sir John Summerson: **202, 203, 204, 205, 206, 208, 209, 210, 211, 212, 214, 215, 216, 217, 218, 219, 220**; Photo Timothy Summerson: **138**; Photo Eileen Tweedy: **201**; Photo F.R. Yerbury/ copyright The Bank of England: **123**.

Reproduced from books:

Academy Architecture 1908: **226** (ii, p. 29), **227** (ii, p. 22); Arthur Ashpitel, *Treatise on Architecture* 1867: **150** (p. 259); Daniele Barbaro, *Vitruvius* 1556: **27**; Thomas Birch, *A History of the Royal Society of London for Improving of Natural Knowledge* 1756, volume I: **52**; *The Builder* 1843: **174** (p. 470), 1848: **175** (p. 258), 1857: **176** (p. 319), 1859: **197** (p.632), 1860: **163** (p. 819), 1861: **162** (p. 807), **193** (p. 125), 1862: **183** (p. 605), 1863: **165** (p. 533) **166** (p. 371), 1864: **182** (p. 759), 1865: **156** (p. 677), 1866: **164** (p. 957), **199** (p. 851) 1868: **140** (p. 354), **198** (p. 749), 1870: **158** (p. 146), **159** (p. 11), **167** (p. 467), 1871: **144** (p.55), **147** (p. 96), **148** (p. 406), **187** (p. 647), 1873: **194** (p. 607), 1874: **186** (p. 884), 1905: **224** (p. 254), **225** (p. 254); *Building News* 1857: **169, 191** (p. 1125), 1858: **178** (p. 273), 1860: **157** (p. 733); Colen Campbell, *Vitruvius Britannicus* 1715–25: Volume I, 1715 – **67, 70, 71, 72**. Volume II, 1717 – **30, 78**, Volume III, 1725 – **73, 79, 93**, Volume IV, 1767 – **82, 94**, Volume V, 1771 – **81, 91, 92**; Samuel Clegg, *Practical Treatise on the Manufacture and Distribution of Coal-Gas* 1866: **153** (p. 351); William Dugdale, *The History of St. Paul's Cathedral* 1658: **43** p. 163, **44** p. 162, **45** p. 126–7, **46** p. 114; Henry Fox and G. Barrett, *Construction of Public Buildings and Private Dwelling Houses on a Fireproof Principle Without Increase of Cost* 1849: **152**; Roderick Gradidge, *Edwin Lutyens: Architect Laureate* 1981: **232**; Henry- Russell Hitchcock, *In the Nature of Materials: The Buildings of Frank Lloyd Wright* 1942: **221**; Hermione Hobhouse, *Thomas Cubitt, Master Builder* 1971: **141**; *The Illustrated London News* 1863: **154** (Vol. XLIII, p. 493), 1866: **161** (vol. XLIX, ii. p. 341), 1868: **196** (vol. II, p. 105), 1869: **160** (Vol. LIV, p. 317); William Kent, *Designs of Inigo Jones* 1727: **42**, 1770: **74**; Batty Langley, *Ancient Masonry* 1736: **28**; Corneille Lebrun, *Voyage au Levant* 1714: **135**; James Lewis, *Original Designs in Architecture* 1780–97: **98**; David Loggan, *Oxonia Illustrata* 1675: **51**; Walter Macfarlane, catalogue of Walter Macfarlane and Co. 1870: **151**; Thomas Malton, *The Works of Robert Taylor*: **90**; Thomas Malton, *Picturesque Tour through . . . London* 1796: **33**; Bernard de Montfaucon, *L'Antiquité Expliquée* 1719 Volume V: **113** (part I, plate 22); Robert Morris, *Essay in Defence of Ancient Architecture* 1728: **64**; James Paine, *Plans, Elevations and Sections of Noblemen and Gentlemen's Houses*, vol. II, 1783: **83**; Andrea Palladio, *I Quattri Libri* 1570: **22, 47**; Henry Peacham, *Graphice* 1612: **16**; W.T. Phillips, *Architectural Iron Construction* 1870: **149**; John Richards, *Treatise on the construction and operation of Wood-working Machines* 1872: **139** (plate 69); William Schooling, *Alliance Insurance* 1924: **173**; Sebastiano Serlio, *Architettura*: Book III, 1540 **8**, Book IV, 1566 **10, 37** (fig. 131), Book VII, 1584 – **36** (fig. 63); John Shute, *The First and Chief Groundes of Architecture* 1563: **12**; *Stationers Almanack* 1838: **168**; Isaac Ware, *Complete Body of Architecture* 1756: **95b**.

The following photographs from books are reproduced by courtesy of the Trustees of Sir John Soane's Museum: **33, 46, 74, 78, 79, 81, 82, 83, 90, 91, 92, 98, 135**; The British Architectural Library, RIBA, London: **149, 150, 159**.

The essays in this book originally appeared in the following publications:

I The Unromantic Castle: *Architectural Review*, February 1940

II John Thorpe: *Architectural Review*, November 1949

III Inigo Jones: Master Mind Lecture, British Academy, *Proceedings of the British Academy*, Vol 50, 1964

IV Christopher Wren: *Notes and Records of the Royal Society*, Vol 15, July 1960

V The Penultimate Design for St Paul's: *Burlington Magazine*, Vol CIII, March 1961

VI The Classical Country House: *Royal Society of Arts Journal*, Vol CVII, July 1959

VII Sir John Soane and the Furniture of Death: *Architectural Review*, March 1978

VIII The Evolution of Soane's Bank Stock Office: *Architectural History* (Journal of the Society of Architectural Historians of Great Britain), Vol 27, 1984

IX Charting the Victorian Building World: Lecture delivered at the South Bank Polytechnic, London, September 1976 (previously unpublished)

X The London Building World of the 1860s: Walter Neurath Memorial Lecture, delivered at London University, March 1973; published same year by Thames and Hudson

XI The Victorian Rebuilding of the City of London: Russell Van Nest Black Memorial Lecture, delivered at Cornell University, May 1974

XII The London Suburban Villa: *Architectural Review*, August 1948

XIII The British Contemporaries of Frank Lloyd Wright: *Acts of the Twentieth International Congress of the History of Art*, New York, 1963

XIV Arches of Triumph: Catalogue of the Lutyens Exhibition, Hayward Gallery, London, 1981

XV The Case for a Theory of 'Modern' Architecture: *Royal Institute of British Architects Journal*, June 1957

Index

Figures in italic refer to illustrations.